The Kaiser's Chemists

The Kaiser's Chemists

Science and Modernization
in Imperial Germany

Jeffrey Allan Johnson

The University of North Carolina Press

Chapel Hill and London

94 93 92 91 90   5 4 3 2 1

Library of Congress Cataloging-in-Publication Data

Johnson, Jeffrey Allan.
   The Kaiser's chemists : science and modernization in imperial
Germany / by Jeffrey Allan Johnson.
      p.   cm.
   Includes bibliographical references.
   ISBN 0-8078-1902-6 (alk. paper)
   1. Kaiser Wilhelm Institut für Chemie—History.   2. Science and
state—Germany—History—20th century.   3. Chemistry—Germany—
History—20th century.   I. Title.
QD18.G3J64   1990
540'.943—dc20   89-70576
                                                              CIP

Contents

9
Military Strength and Science Come Together:

Illustrations

Tables

Preface

Writing a book can be many things, not all of them pleasant, but one of the pleasantest tasks must be the writing of a preface thanking those who have helped bring the book to fruition. This book evolved from a dissertation completed in 1979 under Arno J. Mayer in the Department of History at Princeton University. I would like to begin by thanking him for challenging me to develop the material in the dissertation into a real case study of science in German modernization. That was the idea with which I began the research for the dissertation, but it was really not until after rethinking the completed dissertation that I convinced myself that this model of modernization actually makes sense. I hope that the following arguments will convince my readers as well. Others whose suggestions or critiques have substantially contributed to this book in various ways include the other members of my dissertation committee, Charles C. Gillispie, John Servos, David Abraham, and Arnold Thackray; Mark Adams; Bernhard vom Brocke; Lothar Burchardt; David Cahan; Elisabeth Crawford; Gerald Feldman; John Heilbron; Konrad Jarausch; Robert Kohler; Peter Lundgreen; Charles McClelland; Larry Owens; Manfred Rasch; R. Steven Turner; and Jürgen Wilhelm. I am, of course, solely responsible for whatever errors remain.

I received support to complete the research for this book from the German Academic Exchange Service, the Research Foundation of the State University of New York, and the International Research and Exchanges Board (IREX) in cooperation with the government of the German Democratic Republic and with funds provided by the National Endowment for the Humanities and the United States Information Agency. None of these organizations is responsible for the views expressed here. I am grateful to the staffs of the many libraries and archives listed in my bibliography, as well as the following not listed, for their generous assistance in providing me access to sources and furnishing me with copies of documents or illustrative materials: Bayerische Staatsbibliothek, Chemische Gesellschaft der DDR, Deutsches Museum, University of Düsseldorf, University of Pennsylvania (E. F. Smith Collection), SUNY-Binghamton, Case Western Reserve University, and Villanova University. I am particularly grateful to the managements of the BASF, Bayer, Th. Goldschmidt, Hoechst, Krupp, and Siemens corporations, as well as the Max-Planck-Gesellschaft, for opening their collections to scholarly research.

Additional help came from Günther Beer, Alan Beyerchen, Eric Elliott, Menso Folkerts, Walter Greiling, Axel von Harnack, Karl Heinig, Friedrich Herneck, Christa Kirsten, Alfred Neubauer, Patricia Rife, Alan Rocke, Walter Ruske, Dieter Schmidt-Ott, Ivo Schneider, Jeffrey Sturchio, Klaus Sühnel, and Günther Wendel. An early version of the book manuscript was typed by the Manuscript Center of SUNY-Binghamton. Special thanks to those, too numerous to mention, whose friendship and hospitality so enriched my research trips.

The editorial staff of the University of North Carolina Press has been extremely helpful, particularly Lewis Bateman, the executive editor, who has been both encouraging and patient in awaiting my drafts. Ron Maner and Margaret Morse have been very helpful in preparing the manuscript for publication. I have also benefited from the encouragement and patience of many others, not least of whom are the long-suffering members of my family. Without their support I could not have completed this book. I therefore dedicate it to them and to all those whose dreams and actions let me hope that sanity and peace may yet triumph in our crazy world.

A Note on Names: During the period covered in this book, several individuals' names changed. In the text I have generally referred to them by the name they used at the time under discussion. For instance, Friedrich Schmidt did not become Friedrich Schmidt-Ott until about 1917; therefore, he is called by the former name in the text, although his papers and writings are listed under the latter in the bibliography. Other changes generally involved the addition of "von" to a name when the person was ennobled, as was Adolf Harnack in 1912. I have not always included the "von" when using the last name alone, however, and I have sometimes used a shorter form for such lengthy names as Krupp von Bohlen und Halbach, which here appears as Krupp von Bohlen.

The Kaiser's Chemists

I

The True Land of Unlimited Possibilities: International Competition, German Modernization, and the Dynamism of Science

We [Germans] do not possess, as do America and Russia, almost all the raw materials that we refine. Germany's greatest riches are undoubtedly the intelligence and industriousness of its population, and with this we must reckon.
—Karl Goldschmidt, manufacturer, 1904

Chemistry and with it all natural science is the true land of unlimited possibilities.
—Emil Fischer, organic chemist, 1911

The Problem

In 1911 Emil Fischer, Germany's leading organic chemist, addressed the inaugural meeting of the Kaiser Wilhelm Society for the Advancement of the Sciences, an organization composed mainly of businessmen who had provided substantial sums for the founding of new research laboratories. In a speech entitled "Recent Successes and Problems of Chemistry," he asserted that "chemistry and with it all natural science is the true land of unlimited possibilities."[1] Fischer backed these words by myriad examples of new scientific perceptions in all fields, but above all of chemical research being translated into practical uses. In particular, Germany could now replace expensive, naturally occurring substances, formerly imported from abroad, with synthetics and artificially produced substitutes based on cheaper, domestically available substances. His speech that day, with the Kaiser himself present in the audience, climaxed more than half a decade of effort directed toward getting the Imperial German government to recognize the economic and political value of chemistry by providing financial support for a new chemical research institution. Fischer's friend Carl Duisberg, one of the directors of the Bayer dye corporation, was "extraordinarily pleased"; at last the "highest authorities" had a "clear and comprehensible" picture of "the significance of our science and industry."[2]

And yet Fischer, Duisberg, and their allies among the most prominent German chemists and chemical industry had failed, and were to continue to fail, to win the Imperial government's support. The Imperial bureaucracy had rejected their proposal for an Imperial Institute for Chemistry, both in its original form in 1905–6 as well as the version that emerged from the Imperial Chemical Institute Association they founded in 1908. Instead, their efforts had culminated in the establishment of the Kaiser Wilhelm Society, which was in 1912 to open its first two research institutes, one for chemistry and one for physical chemistry.[3] Unlike the planned Imperial Institute, however, these institutes were funded almost wholly by private contributions, albeit orchestrated by the Prusso-German bureaucracy under the "protection" of Wilhelm II. One year later the society opened a third major institute for experimental therapy, including a section headed by a biochemist. Then on July 27, 1914, it opened an institute for coal research, directed by yet another chemist. In this case the director had been hand-picked by Emil Fischer, who was by this time the most influential scientist in the society. On the following day, the First World War broke out. Within a few months all four of these institutes had been integrated into the German war effort. They conducted research both in the area of weapons such as poison gas and in strategic resources, especially synthetics to replace naturally produced goods cut off by the British blockade.

How does one evaluate these events and the negative attitude of the Imperial government in view of the significance claimed for chemistry by scientists like Fischer and eventually demonstrated during the First World War? Several related issues need to be raised in this connection. First, one must establish a historical frame of reference within which to place the various arguments for and against an Imperial Chemical Institute. There is, as yet, no generally accepted historical model of the origins of modern scientific institutions or of the interaction between changes in science and changes in modern society as a whole.[4] What is required is an approach that will look at the modification of institutions that results from the emergence of modern science in two senses: the changing relationship between science and its social context on the one hand, and the changing character of scientific theory and practice on the other. This chapter is intended to provide a suitable perspective for viewing both aspects of the changes that affected the development of academic and industrial chemical research institutions in Imperial Germany. The two chapters that follow examine in detail how these changes brought Emil Fischer and his colleagues to advocate an Imperial Chemical Institute, why they proposed the plan they did, and where they sought their initial support.

Second, one must understand the forces that brought about successive transformations in the original plan, ultimately leading the chemists into an alliance with the Kaiser Wilhelm Society and producing the Kaiser Wilhelm Institutes. These changes present a case study in the pattern of institutional innovation during the final prewar decade of Imperial Germany, which will be examined in the fourth through seventh chapters from the perspective of German "conservative modernization" as defined in the first chapter.

Third, one must consider how well the institutes in their final form achieved the original scientific and social goals of Fischer and his allies. None of the previous historical studies of the Kaiser Wilhelm Society as an institution has closely examined what the institutes meant for the development of scientific research in Germany. Through a detailed examination of the single discipline of chemistry, a more precise assessment can be made. The eighth chapter addresses this issue in connection with the general institutional problems of chemistry in Imperial Germany discussed in the earlier chapters.

Finally, one must consider the degree of continuity between the events that preceded the outbreak of war and those that followed. The problem of continuity between the peacetime and wartime policies of the German government, and ultimately between the policies and institutions of Imperial Germany and those of the Third Reich, is one that goes back at least two decades, to the controversy over Fritz Fischer's *Griff nach der Weltmacht*.[5] Under the influence of Fischer, Hans-Ulrich Wehler, and their supporters, the pendulum of German historiography swung during the seventies from an excessive emphasis on discontinuity to an equally excessive emphasis on the fundamental continuities from 1871 to 1933, or even 1848 to 1945.[6] It is well, however, to examine the problem of continuity in a different context, that of the continuity between the peacetime and wartime development of scientific institutions. The tendency among scientists who participated in the war was to emphasize the discontinuities—the breaking off of normal research projects under the new pressures of war.[7] Yet was it only a coincidence that the scientists who were most closely involved in the effort to create the institutes also provided the most influential participants in the chemists' war? Although wartime scientific service for their emperor may be said to have defined the group I shall call the "Kaiser's chemists," it was their previous peacetime struggles to get increased support for science under the circumstances of Imperial Germany that set them in place and shaped their thinking. The Kaiser's chemists and their institutes may thus serve as models of the institutional and intellectual continuities between peace and war that have been ever more sharply delineated in twentieth-century science, above all in those nations giving highest priority to military strength. The concluding chapter addresses these issues, which also underlie much of the discussion in the earlier parts of the book.

Between Two Competitions: The Institutional Dilemma of Modern Science

Within what historical framework, then, can the emergence of a plan for an Imperial Chemical Institute best be understood? The point here is to provide general motivations for institutional innovation in science, and to connect this to a larger pattern of institutional change during the late nineteenth and early twentieth centuries. From this perspective it will be possible to clarify the commonly assumed, but still vaguely understood, role of science in "modernization." One of the most historically sophisticated case studies of modernization describes it as "the process by which societies have been and are being transformed under the impact of the scientific and technological revolution," whose central phenomenon is defined as "an increase in the ratio of inanimate to animate sources of power to and past a point of no return as far as the accompanying social patterns are concerned." In regard to science, the authors postulate that "widespread belief in rational inquiry is a primary characteristic of modernity, and the advancement of knowledge and its dissemination through education are essential in the process of modernization." Finally, they list "the scientific revolution of the sixteenth and seventeenth centuries" first among "the immediate antecedents of the process of modernization in Western Europe."[8] Thus science appears to be a prime mover; but what moves science?

According to one Western sociological perspective, "traditional" societies could not provide a continuously increasing flow of natural knowledge, and their technology could rarely use that knowledge without destroying the basis for further scientific innovation. Innovations that did occur were quickly integrated into religious or magical systems of belief, which tended to dogmatize the innovation and conceal its actual origin. This promoted social stability and discouraged further tinkering or questioning, but it could also lead to cultural stagnation.[9] Modern societies have been able to solve these problems; thus science's modernity may spring from the same source as its dynamism. Isaac Newton came close to a modern view of the prospects for science with his well-known image of himself as a child playing beside the vast ocean of undiscovered truth, but that also implied that science might eventually navigate to its farthest shores. Since the advent of a Darwinian evolutionary consciousness, however, science has come to look more like an open-ended quest.[10] That was one of the ideas captured in Emil Fischer's vision of "unlimited possibilities." What then is the source of this dynamism, especially in regard to institutions?

In part it has to do with the modern world's ability to break down the barriers between rational and practical knowledge, as suggested in Francis Bacon's aphorism, "knowledge is power," which became a popular slogan in later centuries among boosters of science-based industry.[11] Marxists too, whether orthodox or revisionist, have tended to focus on the symbiotic relationship between science and first commercial capitalism, then monopolistic industry or "organized capitalism." Capitalism harnessed science as a "productive force" or served as a "stimulus to scientific progress," creating new scientific institutions to serve the needs of industrial development.[12] While there is certainly much truth in this picture, the analysis still does not get at the sources of dynamism within science itself.

Alan Beyerchen's recent study of the "stimulation of excellence in Wilhelmian science" provides a more penetrating view of institutional dynamism in Imperial Germany. "If competitiveness at the forefront of science and technology is one of the hallmarks of modernity," he begins, "then Germany at the opening of the twentieth century was one of the most modern countries in the world." He finds the source of this competitiveness not in "any one institution or even set of institutions," but rather in the "complex dynamic arrangement" of interacting and innovating institutions, which blurred the distinctions between "pure science, applied science, and technology" and which were fostered by modern-minded scientists, businessmen, and government officials. One of the key elements in the German "arrangement" was a very effective institutionalization of "the dynamic interaction between applied science and pure science in the form of a dual legitimation of basic research—'applied science' when directed and 'pure science' when undirected." In other words, the methods could be the same in each case, and only the motivations would differ. Bypassing "institutions moving too slowly for the times," chiefly the universities, the Germans were able to create institutions like the Kaiser Wilhelm Society in which this kind of research could go forward in close connection with actual or potential technological applications, yet without impairing the quality of the science. Quite the contrary: the connection itself improved the science.[13]

Beyerchen's focus on the new institutions for "basic research" highlights a central, but still problematic, aspect of the changing relationship between science and technology during this period. The origins of the Kaiser Wilhelm Institutes for chemistry can be discerned in this light, but it also suggests the need to focus more sharply on the character of the new institutions, their relationship to the older parts of the German scientific system, and their impact on scientific research. For while the new institutions certainly helped to "stimulate excellence" in Imperial Germany, the very complexity and dynamism of their interactions brought to the forefront new social problems that were henceforth to characterize the enterprise of modern science. This book examines these problems. It is perhaps best to begin, however, with another aspect highlighted in Beyerchen's analysis: the essential role played by the "competitiveness" that the new institutions so clearly manifested and that is also an inherent element in the dynamism of modern science.

One way to examine the connection between competition and institutional innovations is to recall that science has both a national and an international character. Adolf von Harnack, first president of the Kaiser Wilhelm Society, pointed out during the 1920s that "education is national, but scholarship is international. What does this imply? Two things: first, that we are in a constant competition with other civilized peoples; second, that we must exchange our scholarship with theirs." This required, among other things, "getting insight into the methods and way of working of other [nations' scholars]."[14] From Harnack's dual perspective it is clear that scientists, caught between the national institutions that gave them material support and the international disciplinary group that set their intellectual standards, could become a means of bringing innovative ideas and institutional forms across national boundaries. Thus, international scientific competition, like political, economic, and other forms of competition, could promote modernization in individual nations and induce in them the periods of exponential growth that some quantitative studies have shown to be a regular feature in the history of science.[15] Of course, one might ask, competition for what? A scientist would probably answer that the goal is to win respect and authority among one's scientific peers by being the first to give them acceptable answers to as many "interesting" questions as possible—interesting to them, of course, not necessarily to anyone else.[16]

It appears that by the end of the nineteenth century, internationality was most pronounced in the mathematical and experimental sciences such as physics, where the basic intellectual content and methodology did not significantly differ from one Western nation to another. Physics, and probably chemistry and mathematics as well, had truly become international enterprises.[17]

The international character of these sciences stemmed partly from a long-standing European tradition of the supranational republic of letters and science. Late-nineteenth-century intellectual and organizational developments placed this tradition on a new footing by making the physical and mathematical sciences international in structure as well as in spirit. Vestiges of Latin and Greek, the old international scholarly languages, remained in scientific nomenclature, whose real basis by the turn of the century was a new international language of discourse based on shared principles of mathematics and mechanism. International unity within each discipline was reinforced by the establishment of formal networks—international congresses, associations, and standing committees to set standards or fix nomenclature, and international journals and scholarly exchanges to disseminate the latest results of research—as well as informal connections between scholars in various countries pursuing similar interests.[18]

If it is accepted that these international patterns characterize "mature scientific communities" in the sense defined by Thomas Kuhn, then they would also have achieved an "unparalleled insulation . . . from the demands of the laity," so that the criteria for the acceptability of scientific work could to some extent override personal, national, and other kinds of prejudices.[19] Indeed, Kuhn's argument suggests that the peculiar dynamism of science depends on this insulation, which under ideal circumstances would make it not only possible but necessary for a conservative German chemist to recognize the relevant scientific work of a French socialist, and vice versa. In nineteenth-century terms, this implies that "pure science" was the most international and thus the most dynamic kind of science.

But scientific internationalism was shaped and limited by the political realities of the nineteenth century. "Science did not escape the rise of nationalism but adapted to it."[20] International scientific competition developed within the framework of competing national units. Moreover, in most Western countries scientists were based primarily in educational institutions and were thereby subject to those institutions' specific conditions and constraints. National differences thus existed in scientific style, disciplinary emphasis, and career patterns. Nor were ostensibly international institutions, like the Nobel awards, immune to national biases.[21]

The realities of international competition in modern science forced scientists continually to monitor the institutional as well as the intellectual development of their principal foreign competitors, and to respond to especially stimulating innovations by adapting them in their own settings. Normally one would expect innovations to be transmitted primarily from the leading or "central" scientific nation, where the growth of science seemed to be strongest, to nations on the "periphery." Nevertheless at critical times of unusual fluidity and rapid change in science, such as at the beginning of the twentieth century, competition became especially intense on all sides. At such times the leaders, after a long period of success, would fear incipient stagnation or decline from the obsolescence of their own institutions, while innovations abroad might threaten to shift the center elsewhere. A complete analysis would bring out the pattern of almost simultaneous, reciprocal exchange of innovations among scientists in several competing nations, whereby a significant idea in one was quickly copied or modified in others, leading to further responses in the first, and so on. An added complication in the process arose from what has been called "cultural imperialism," as leading nations that were also imperialist powers, like Germany, sought to impose their scientific institutions on "peripheral peoples." Each nation's responses would differ, of course, according to the compromises required by the social conditions peculiar to scientific institutions in each.[22]

In trying to effect changes in national institutions, scientists could find their normally desirable autonomy and insulation working to their disadvantage if they could not easily demonstrate that the scientific results they expected had intrinsic worth to society as a whole.[23] The problem presented to scientists like Emil Fischer was thus to find points in common with laymen in the political, economic, and eventually also the military elites, in order to obtain support for the innovations they wanted. It is not surprising, therefore, that public discussions of the international state of science tended to focus upon the most obvious national indicators: first on indicators of prestige, such as the number of "discoveries" and "breakthroughs" made or Nobel Prizes won by scientists of a particular nation, then on indicators of social support, such as new laboratories built or large philanthropic foundations created, and ultimately on examples of the technological results attributable to scientific research.[24] These indicators, together with slogans like "knowledge is power" or "standstill is retreat," lent themselves to nationalistic interpretations in the popular press or in memoranda to government officials and potential patrons. Yet it would be wrong to dismiss such publicly expressed and often exaggerated concerns of scientists about international competition as mere rhetoric. They appear instead to be an essential element in the dynamism of modern science. By focusing attention on international competition in laymen's terms, scientists could more easily achieve the domestic institutional reforms that they deemed necessary to improve their competitive position in their own terms. The process was related to a broader pattern of institutional modernization, whereby the perception of a "foreign threat" or domestic "backwardness," often demonstrated by defeat in war, has been used to justify domestic reforms.

The foregoing suggests two potentially contradictory elements in the dynamism of modern science. One might be called the "pure" competition, within the international scientific community as such, which is conducted according to its own rules. "One of the strongest, if still unwritten," of these rules, says Kuhn, "is the prohibition of appeals to heads of state or to the populace at large in matters scientific."[25] Yet in the second, more "practical" source of science's dynamism, the competition to develop national scientific institutions, precisely such appeals have proved to be obligatory. They have tended to hinge on questions of prestige and power, rather than on the solutions to the knowledge-puzzles that make other benefits possible. Those who provide support for scientific institutions on the basis of practical arguments will naturally expect results, which they may try to ensure in various ways; but their goals will not necessarily match those of the scientists themselves. Thus modern science faces a Faustian dilemma that some scientists have sought to resolve through institutions for "basic research." Although the phrase gained currency in the wake of the Second World War, the idea was already implicit in the German planning for the Kaiser Wilhelm Institutes. Such institutions seem to offer a means of pursuing the practical side of "unlimited possibilities" or "endless frontiers" while preserving at least some of the values of "pure science" such as freedom of inquiry.[26] Whether they have actually resolved the dilemma is another question, but they are a logical outcome of the institutional dynamism of modern science.

The development of modern science can thus be seen as a special case of the modernization of society as a whole, involving similar but distinctive processes of international competition and domestic reform in a struggle to find the best institutional settings for producing knowledge and for transforming that knowledge into power. Looked at in these terms, it should be possible to write an international history of the institutional development of science in the modern world. The present work is aimed at the more modest goal of elucidating the situation in one country—Germany—and in one discipline—chemistry. That country exemplifies a leading scientific nation caught in a period of rapid change, its scientists facing the unenviable task of criticizing many of the institutional patterns that had contributed to their own previous scientific success. Chemistry was, of course, one of the most successful disciplines in Germany at the turn of the century and thus faced precisely this problem, but it also exemplifies the Faustian dilemma of modern science. A discipline with obvious applications could offer ready arguments for lay support, yet obtaining such support entailed sacrificing a measure of scientific autonomy in the new Kaiser Wilhelm Institutes. Because the institutes reflected a compromise, it would have been surprising if there had been no resistance to their establishment; as it happened, of course, the chemists got more than they expected. This too is revealing of the pattern of modernization in Imperial Germany. That pattern needs some clarification, before the changes in chemistry can be examined in more detail.

Scientific Institutions and the Dilemma of German Modernization

Consider three possible patterns of modernization: a conservative pattern, in which existing forms are shielded from the impact of innovation, which develops new forms unconnected to the old; an integrative pattern, in which innovations affect older institutional forms and are themselves modified by them; and a revolutionary pattern, in which innovations destroy and replace older forms. Conservative modernization amounts essentially to a "quarantine on modernity" for an indefinite period, but it presents a dilemma. Can any society survive and flourish while divided against itself? If not, how and to what degree can the new be eventually integrated with the old, without destroying the old order?

In the early nineteenth century, a predominantly conservative pattern of change was set in the leading German states, especially Prussia, in the wake of the Napoleonic conquests and the British industrial revolution. To meet these foreign threats, it was necessary to accept change in some areas while limiting its effects in others, necessarily producing a combination of modern and unmodern elements that were kept in balance, insofar as possible, by guidance from a conservative bureaucracy.[27] The conservative pattern was confirmed after German unification, especially in the wake of the economic recession that began in the mid-1870s. In particular, the government provided special favors for and subsidies to the Junker landowners east of the Elbe River, who became the backbone of the conservative parties and the dominant members of the Prusso-German administrative and military hierarchies. Thus an economy emerged in which the most sophisticated technologies and giant corporations flourished in some branches while handicrafts and labor-intensive agriculture were preserved elsewhere.[28]

Even in the earlier part of the nineteenth century there had been many anomalies in the conservative pattern of segregating old and new institutions; by the end of the century, the quarantine on modernity was becoming increasingly difficult to maintain. While the East-Elbian agrarian sector struggled under the weight of an obsolescent Junker lifestyle, industry transformed the western German cities and Berlin. The newly wealthy urban elites pressed for a greater share of social status and political power, and their burgeoning factories fed a growing internationalist social-democratic movement committed to overturning the old order. Although such fundamental social changes were largely beyond bureaucratic control, some enterprising Prusso-German bureaucrats saw them as an opportunity to weld together a more powerful nation by fostering more integration between old and new institutions and groups: "modernizing" Junker agriculture by promoting technological improvements and industry in the East, "feudalizing" the business elites by granting them titles and permitting intermarriage with the old aristocracy, and "nationalizing" the Social Democrats by making workers dependent on social welfare legislation, by promoting nationalism in the schools, and by trying to maneuver the leaders in the Reichstag into supporting the regime on issues like defense.

Yet the trend to greater modernization and integration met with strong resistance throughout the still-conservative social order. In the expanding Prussian Army and the Imperial Navy, for example, the administrative elites sought to uphold their static social and institutional priorities in the face of dynamic technical and military priorities.[29]

A perfect symbol of this era was the man who presided over it, Kaiser Wilhelm II, who combined in his own personality some of the modern attitudes of his ill-fated father Friedrich III, together with the "feudalistic romanticism" of his great-uncle, Friedrich Wilhelm IV. He extended the hand of friendship to industrial leaders, even some Jews, while finding his closest friends among anti-Semitic aristocrats and among a narrow circle of military aides. Outwardly giving scant respect to the few constitutional limitations on his rule, he detested parliamentary politics and believed in his own divinely ordained infallibility. He had a gifted but impulsive mind, quick to learn, yet susceptible to flattery; moreover, he had an underlying sense of insecurity deriving from an unhappy childhood and in part magnified by the deformity of his left arm. Wilhelm concealed these inner weaknesses with a cult of power. Whether it be the traditional power of the Prussian military or the new power of modern technology, as long as it magnified himself, he loved to associate himself with its trappings.[30] Moreover, he sought new ways to maximize the power of Imperial Germany—and by extension, his own—by harnessing technological power to the pursuit of military power. A Prussian Army supplied with the most sophisticated artillery from the house of Krupp and an Imperial Navy equipped with the most up-to-date battleships, both unquestioningly loyal to himself and to the old social order, epitomized the kind of integrative modernization Wilhelm wanted.[31]

With these policies and the underlying social changes that motivated them, Imperial German institutions around the turn of the century came to resemble "present-day Victorian houses with modern electrical kitchens but insufficient bathrooms and leaky pipes hidden decorously behind newly plastered walls."[32] The image would be even more exact if one imagined such a house newly enlarged by adding several rooms, some wholly contemporary, others using materials and technologies of recent date, yet designed so that the external appearance imitated Victorian design even when that worked against the most efficient operation of the newer technologies. Although the social structure of Imperial Germany was extended and modified in various ways to accommodate innovations, the fundamental outlines of the conservative pattern remained intact. Changes occurred, but they still tended to be channeled away from existing institutions and into new ones; it was in these that the integration of old and new forms was most conspicuous.

How did these trends affect scientific institutions? Among the conserva-

Illus. 1-1. Kaiser Wilhelm II in a characteristically bellicose pose, around 1908 (Bildarchiv Preussischer Kulturbesitz)

tive forces in Wilhelm's Germany were the state university professors, who had largely abandoned the radicalism of 1848 in return for a privileged position that allowed them to "enjoy the economic status of leaders, . . . spared financial worry, in fact all thought of money."[33] Drawing their ideology of scholarly "purity" not from modern science but from classical neohumanism, a largely self-perpetuating caste of academic "mandarins" had insulated themselves, with the blessing of the state governments, from the supposedly corrupting materialistic influence of the business and industrial bourgeoisie. Insofar as the universities served a practical role, it was mainly to train young men for the traditional professions, the higher bureaucracy, and teaching in classical secondary schools. Other vocations that could be learned in the philosophical faculties, like pharmacy and dentistry, were commonly denigrated as "bread studies," and their professors often held a secondary status.[34] Attitudes toward the "purity" of scholarship thus not only reflected cultural snobbishness but could even be tinged with Victorian sexual moralism, as when Adolf Harnack, by profession a theologian, spoke of the "state and academy" bringing capital together with scholarship "in a *clean* bed. Of our state one can truly say that in regard to scholarship it is *clean.*"[35] Science could flourish in this environment because as long as the academic scientists were good teachers and avoided radical politics, the educational bureaucrats were willing to let them pursue their own priorities in research. Until late in the nineteenth century the German academic system, decentralized among several competing state educational bureaucracies, had been especially responsive to institutional innovations in many fields of science.[36]

Rather than expanding the functions of the universities to deal with the problem of industrialization, the state bureaucracies had created a succession of new, more or less separate colleges of technology, which also meant creating a "new middle class" of engineers, technical bureaucrats, and industrial researchers to guide the modernization of the German economy. Initially these institutions were viewed as centers for systematizing and transferring existing technological knowledge, not for research that might invent new technologies or discover scientific principles of technological value. At first the vested interests of the universities and their academic elites were left uninfringed, along with their characteristic forms of authority and status and their ideology of autonomy and "pure science." Thus the new institutions not only had a lower academic status than the universities, but their professors were also not as independent as their university colleagues. Similar colleges existed for agricultural purposes, but in the case of Prussia they came under the separate purview of the Ministry of Agriculture.[37]

A third category of scientific institutions that had developed by the turn of the century was a network of official agencies and institutes whose purposes were to provide technical assistance to various branches of the economy and to assist the bureaucracy in its regulatory functions, a role sanctioned by century-old traditions of police power. In view of their functional similarities to the colleges of technology and agriculture, it is not surprising that some agencies were established in connection with them and served as additional centers for specialized training. The College of Technology in Berlin had, for example, a Mechanical and Technical Testing Institute that was set up in the 1870s to test the products of the iron and steel industry, while the College of Agriculture had institutes for testing and improving the products of the sugar and alcohol industries.[38]

Most scientific and technical agencies were on the state level; Imperial institutions only emerged gradually, because the federal constitution of the Reich allocated scientific functions in principle to the states. Nevertheless, although the smaller states and the Prussian conservatives tended to resist efforts to expand the prerogatives of the Imperial bureaucracy, the Reich did acquire such national agencies as a patent office, a health office, and a bureau of weights and measures, in all of which science played a supporting but subsidiary role. In 1887, the founding of the Imperial Institute for Physics and Technology raised the broader possibility of a national institution in which scientific research would play a central role. Werner Siemens, founder of the Siemens electrical manufacturing concern and an inventor as well as a scientific researcher in his own right, had proposed that the institute should "carry science into technology. The whole thing would be scientific, with one section performing new scientific research and the other making technical use of existing scientific knowledge."[39] Siemens's idea that pure science could go "hand in hand" with its application to technology, and moreover that the Imperial government had an obligation to foster this interaction, clashed with conservative views and met with understandable resistance in the Reichstag. A move to eliminate funding for the scientific section was only narrowly averted, especially by the lobbying of then Crown Prince Friedrich, apparently one of the few high-ranking Prussian aristocrats sympathetic to Siemens's ideas. The complete institute was saved only through emphasizing the economic benefits that scientific research might secure, as well as the threat of foreign competition in science-based industry. Only the Social Democrats had sufficient faith in science to support "the advancement of pure science for its own sake,"[40] perhaps because of their fundamental principles as advocates of Marxian "scientific socialism."

As it happened, despite its excellent equipment and many first-rate academic physicists who eventually produced experimental research with considerable theoretical significance, the Imperial Institute never really became the broad-ranging, national research institution envisioned by

Siemens. Instead its primary value, from an official perspective, lay in its work on establishing physical standards; even Siemens had stressed this, pointing out the importance of forestalling French ambitions to dominate international electrical standardization.[41] Nevertheless the Imperial Ministry of the Interior had been brought into the business of supporting an institution that had conducted academic-style research in the physical sciences, and the precedent was set for later proposals along these lines.

Although the budgets and operations of existing official institutions expanded between 1887 and 1905, no new Imperial scientific institutes were established, partly because of financial constraints. Under a revenue-sharing program enacted in 1879 in conjunction with Bismarck's introduction of a protective tariff system, the state governments were entitled to distributions of surplus income, if any, from the Imperial budget. On the other hand, they had to provide "matricular contributions" to that budget, so that any enlargement of Imperial functions came in part at the direct cost of the state budgets. As long as there was a surplus, of course, the conservatives and the smaller states had little cause for complaint; but after 1890 there ceased to be a surplus, and with the increasing costs of the military and the social welfare program, the Imperial budget was placed under increasingly severe constraints. This gave added force to the stubborn defense of "states' rights" by the smaller states, particularly Bavaria, and helped in 1897–99 to defeat a proposal for an Imperial Materials Testing Institute, which would have taken over the staff and functions of the similar Prussian institute in Berlin.[42]

Research was slow to be developed within the colleges of technology and government agencies. What must also be recalled, however, is that the "research imperative" within the universities was hardly more than a generation or two older. The internal structure of the universities reflects the late and incomplete integration of their research function. In Berlin, for example, after 1810 the new university had competed with the older academy of sciences, which retained its ostensible claim to being an elite research institution even while most of the real research effort was effectively transferred to the university. Late in the century almost all of the academicians were full professors, who alone officially belonged to the university faculties; but only some of the professors, mostly in the philosophical faculty, were also academicians.[43] Formally the faculties were only indirectly involved in research through their control over academic promotion, doctorates, and the *Habilitation* or lecturing privilege, which initially were not always based upon contributions to scholarship.[44] The principal responsibility of the faculties was always teaching, yet that meant only the medieval method of lecturing. The faculties had no control over laboratory teaching in the university institutes, which grew up as appendages of individual professors to whom the government directly provided special facilities, assistants, and financial support. It was of course in the institutes that, ultimately, scientific research and training for doctorates became concentrated.[45] The force advancing such scientific research was supposed to be a competition to discover new knowledge, not economic benefits. The essentially new idea of bureaucratic support for systematic research in the universities could thus be justified by the time-honored courtly tradition of patronage for the arts and sciences.

How did Wilhelm II's accession to power in 1888 affect Prusso-German scientific institutions? The young Kaiser began his reign with not entirely pleasant memories of his experiences in the German educational system, and he was ready to sponsor academic reforms that might promote greater national unity, strength, and resistance to the socialist movement. On the one hand, he insisted on purging the universities of those few scholars who had dared to become active socialists, like the Berlin University physics lecturer Leo Arons;[46] on the other, he fostered scholars whose ideology of pure scholarship did not preclude mobilizing their intellectual resources for the Fatherland. One of his favorites was Adolf Harnack, who was to become the first president of the Kaiser Wilhelm Society. Harnack's "concern was to work toward permeating the traditional, conservative basis of the Prusso-German polity and Church with modern ideas. That could then lead to an unprecedented increase in the vitality of the German organism. . . . It was a question of working from liberal perspectives toward the reconciliation of opposites."[47]

Although the "reconciliation of opposites" was never fully achieved, and although "liberal perspectives" were scarcely to be found in the Prusso-German bureaucracy of that era, Wilhelm and his ministers did respond to advocates of institutional modernization in science and technology by measures that both enhanced the status of science-based technology in academic institutions and promoted its integration with agriculture and other conservative institutions, including the military. One of the first events of his reign was the establishment of a Central Testing Station for Explosives (later called the Military Testing Office) under the Prussian War Ministry.[48] The Kaiser also "protected" the colleges of technology, and in 1899 Wilhelm celebrated the centennial year of higher technical education in Berlin with full military pageantry. He also took advantage of the occasion to disregard the objections of university scholars by granting the colleges the right to award doctoral degrees, the symbol of their hard-won ability to perform systematic, creative research. It was also he who "modernized" the Berlin Academy of Sciences by insisting that at least one technologist be found who could display scientific achievements that would qualify for membership. He somewhat reluctantly agreed to grant equal matriculation rights at the universities, in principle at least, to graduates of nonclassical secondary schools (in practice, equal access to training in theology was denied, and in other key disciplines like law and medicine, it was long delayed). Moreover, efforts were made on the Prussian and Imperial levels to encourage the modernization of the agrarian East. In the years after 1897 the Prussian government built two additional colleges of technology in the Eastern cities of Danzig and Breslau, as well as establishing additional research institutions for agriculture and agriculture-related industries in Berlin and in the city of Bromberg in Posen, the poorest of the Eastern provinces. At a time of growing enrollments, significantly more official money went to cover new science and medical students in the Eastern universities than those in the West and even in Berlin, which were nevertheless more attractive to students.[49]

The first new Imperial institute since 1887 was created in Berlin in 1905; it was the Imperial Biological Institute for Agriculture and Forestry (a testing installation to study plant disease) formerly a section of the Imperial Health Office. Vocal support for the establishment of the original installation within the Health Office in 1898 had come from a coalition of the Imperial party (the more modern-minded "free" conservative faction, many of whose leaders had interests in Silesian industry as well as agriculture), various liberal groups, and Social Democrats. These supporters emphasized the importance of applying science to "transform our entire agriculture," in the words of a socialist, and enhance Germany's economic independence. They also looked to the United States as well as the earlier Imperial Physical and Technical Institute for models. As with the earlier institute, the responsible minister in the Imperial Office of the Interior was not particularly enthusiastic about the project, while the silence of the German Conservatives and Catholic Center party leaders bespoke their lack of enthusiasm for developing Imperial institutions—even those that might be in their own interest. Yet unlike the Physical Institute, the new installation was relatively cheap; the first appropriation was only 30,000 marks.[50]

An enormously influential bureaucrat who helped to carry out, if not necessarily to originate, Prussia's scientific and technical policies under Wilhelm II was Friedrich Althoff, director of academic affairs in the Prussian Ministry of Education until 1907. Althoff responded to fiscal constraints by enforcing the utmost stringency in the budgets of academic institutions, and by concentrating resources for specific fields at designated provincial universities, like Göttingen for scientific research. In essence he was moving Prussia toward a more centralized, less internally competitive academic system, while focusing more attention on Germany's international academic position.[51]

It should be noted that by the turn of the century, although Germany's chief political rivals remained Britain and France, with Russia looming in the East, the greatest economic and technological challenge was emerging from the United States of America. The American economy had grown as quickly as the German during the late nineteenth century, and it was better endowed with land and natural resources. Thus the president of the Massachusetts Institute of Technology was probably right when he declared in 1903 that the "Germans need fear in the industrial world neither the Englishman nor the Frenchman, only the American."[52] In the scientific world, Americans also gave the Germans cause for concern by transferring large portions of their wealth to scientific institutions.

If exponential increases in support are essential to scientific growth, the Americans were creating the basis for faster growth than the Germans during the decade and a half after 1895. In 1910–11 the Prussian Ministry of Education deemed twelve American public and private universities worthy of comparison with the twenty-one of the German system. They found that whereas the average annual budget of a German university was 1.67 million marks, each American school was already spending an average sum equivalent to 5.80 million marks annually. A glance backward would have revealed that American expenditures per university had quadrupled since the mid-nineties, twice the rate of increase in Germany. Worse, American expenditures per student had nearly doubled, while the Germans were barely keeping ahead of their enrollments.[53] Thus American academic salaries, still considered relatively low at the turn of the century, were becoming "comfortable" by the time of the First World War. Although direct comparisons are complicated by the emphasis in American universities on more general education of younger students, during this period the top American universities were also developing strong graduate programs that emphasized research in the German style.[54] Thus the American academic system was fast gaining the ability to challenge the Germans; much of its new-found wealth came from private contributions.[55] Perhaps more important was that the Americans demonstrated that scientific work could be promoted within both public and private institutions.

Up to the turn of the century, however, relatively little money from American private endowments was going to scientific research, as opposed to higher education in general. Then came the establishment in 1901–2 of the Rockefeller Institute for Medical Research of New York and the Carnegie Institution of Washington. Each of the two philanthropic endowments had some ten million dollars in capital during its early years, producing a combined annual interest on the same order as the total budget of one of Germany's largest universities, and each organization sought to foster research alone, often in projects on a grand scale. While Rockefeller concentrated his resources in the biomedical fields, Carnegie provided for grants to "exceptional" researchers "in every department of study" throughout the country. As Carnegie put it, he intended his endowment to "secure" American "leadership in the domain of discovery and the utilization of new forces for the benefit of man."[56]

At the same time, the Americans were also promoting scientific work within public institutions, and they were "catching up" with German developments in some respects by creating bureaucratic scientific regulatory institutions like the National Bureau of Standards. Founded in 1901 and modeled in part on the German Imperial Physical and Technical Institute, it had broader functions, including a section for chemistry. The bureau's relatively modest initial appropriation of $250,000 was equivalent to about 1 million marks, more than twice what its German model would receive as late as 1907. In the meantime the bureau's budget continued to increase, reaching $700,000 (2.9 million marks) by 1914.[57]

The trans-Atlantic reverberations of these developments can be felt in statements like the 1902 presidential address of Sir James Dewar to the British Association for the Advancement of Science. As chief scientist at the Royal Institution, he noted with some awe that the interest from Carnegie's endowment for one year exceeded all that had been spent by his institution in the previous hundred. Research was becoming so expensive that without endowments on Carnegie's level, "the outlook for disinterested research is rather dark"; yet carelessly administered endowments "might obviously tend to impair" science's traditional motivating force, research "for its own sake." A few years later, in a speech designed to generate financial support for scholarship from German industry, Hermann Schumacher, professor of economics at Bonn University, praised "the carriers of the idea of centralization in economic life—men like Rockefeller and Carnegie—who have also become the carriers of the idea of centralization in science. Although today . . . the scientific staffs [of the new American institutions] often fail to match their prodigious endowments, there is an undeniable danger that in the future the situation may change to our disadvantage."[58] In essence, the Americans had taken a dramatic leap forward in supporting scientific research, accelerating the process of exponential growth and challenging their foreign competitors to respond.

How were Germans to meet the challenge? Schumacher's group expressed a widespread hope that, in the spirit of integrative modernization, Germany should create "modern" institutions that would bring together "two mostly isolated, opposing parties," scientists and industrial leaders, and in the process open new sources of private support for science.[59] In turn scientific research would strengthen German industrial technology. Althoff also realized the need for significant increases in funding for science; if funds could not be extracted from the Prussian budget, they could perhaps be made up from the Imperial budget or from American-style private donations to scientific institutions, even though such approaches ran generally contrary to German bureaucratic traditions. Perhaps the most important precedent for either had been the Imperial Physical and Technical Institute, established with the help of Werner Siemens's gift of some half a million marks' worth of "real estate or capital."[60] Thus it was natural for Althoff to encourage modernizing chemists to propose the creation of an Imperial Chemical Institute that might be partly funded by contributions from private industry.

Could "pure" scientific research coexist successfully with "materialism" in the form of industrial subsidies and interests? Could a dynamic technology be fostered by university-trained scientists? By the turn of the century, one German academic discipline best exemplified the possibilities for an apparently successful resolution of this dilemma. "In chemistry, science and industry are symbiotically related." So, in 1913, wrote Professor Otto N. Witt, director of the Institute for Technical Chemistry at the Berlin College of Technology. Science, he went on, is motivated by "ideal values," industry by "material values," yet the two are everywhere related and provide mutual reinforcement.[61] The world dominance achieved by the turn of the century by both German industrial and academic chemists, at least in the areas related to organic chemistry, suggested that one could indeed have the best of both worlds.

Chemistry also offered a possible model for resolving the larger dilemma of German modernization: How could Germany, with its limited resources, its continuing predominance of traditional forms, and its late entry on the world stage as a unified nation and imperialist power, possibly match its older, long-established competitors among the great powers? Even so young a nation as the United States offered a seemingly more dynamic social order combined with vast and immeasurably rich agricultural land and mineral deposits. These advantages had led a recent visitor, the German businessman Ludwig Max Goldberger, to dub America the "land of unlimited possibilities"; it would be Germany's main future competitor.[62] Germany's land and resources, while rich, were hardly unlimited; the world map offered few other opportunities not blotched with the colors of foreign empires. As a chemical manufacturer acknowledged, "We [Germans] do not possess, as do America and Russia, almost all the raw materials that we refine." How then could one overcome these limits? The manufacturer continued, "Germany's greatest riches are undoubtedly the intelligence and industriousness of its population, and with this we must reckon."[63]

Chemical science and technology graphically demonstrated how "intelligence and industriousness" could make up for shortages in other resources. In 1906, answering critics who had asserted that the chemical industry was bound for stagnation, the general secretary of the Chemical Industry Association borrowed Goldberger's image to proclaim chemicals the "industry of unlimited possibilities," citing the "endless perspectives" being opened by current scientific research into the creation of synthetic substitutes for previously imported raw materials like silk, rubber, nitrates, and ultimately even food proteins.[64] Five years later came Emil Fischer's address to the inaugural meeting of the Kaiser Wilhelm Society with his similar reference to "the true land of unlimited possibilities," based on similar prospects, even more grandly portrayed, of industrial fruits from scientific research in chemistry; Goldberger sat in the audience as one of the society's founding members.[65] To call chemistry the "true land of unlimited possibilities" was to say that the conquests of science and technology were not simply as good as imperial conquests, however, but better; for unlike natural resources, the capacities of human "intelligence and industriousness" might truly be unlimited. That vision appears to be an essential element of the modern outlook that Fischer and many of his fellow chemists shared. As patriotic Germans, moreover, they shared a satisfaction in knowing that their discipline and its industrial manifestations were adding to Germany's world prestige and economic strength.

Both on the level of science and technology as well as on the level of national strength, of course, these visions represented ideals that many, perhaps most, of the social elites in Imperial Germany did not share or shared only in part, if at all. Given the foregoing discussion of the problems of institutional change in science as well as in German society, one would not expect an easy move from these visions to real institutions requiring expensive resources that would have to be taken away from competing priorities. In the process one would expect to see all the dynamics of modernization in action, as the proponents of change learned how to juxtapose appeals for internal reforms with warnings of external threats, how to identify their own priorities with those of the society as a whole, and eventually how to adjust their own plans in order to gain the greatest possible support for them while achieving some degree of integration into existing academic institutions. In so doing, the Kaiser's chemists also shaped themselves, beginning with the decision by Emil Fischer and his associates to enter the thicket of institutional reform in Imperial Germany. Why they chose to do so is discussed in the next chapter.

2

We Must Do More for Inorganic and General Chemistry: The Making of Three Institutional Reformers

We must do more for inorganic and general chemistry again, if we are not to be put to shame by other countries.... To gain more experience in this area, I am spending all my free time in the Imperial Physical and Technical Institute.
—Emil Fischer to his mentor, Adolf von Baeyer, 1898

But chemistry cannot wait.... Hence there remains no other possible choice than to free ourselves from the all too slowly moving process of development of those [academic] institutions, and to take the initiative in creating new functional forms to meet the needs of chemical science and technology.
—Wilhelm Ostwald, December 1906

What made institutional reformers of Emil Fischer, Wilhelm Ostwald, and Walther Nernst? Probably no single factor can account for their willingness to propose and work toward an Imperial Chemical Institute. Nevertheless, the combined effect on each of them of several related factors brought the three men together in 1905. First, each of the three chemists felt special responsibilities and opportunities to act as disciplinary leaders and organizers. A significant element of their leadership had been directed toward creating professional and institutional links between academic and industrial—or "pure" and "applied"—chemistry; such links were to be an essential aspect of their proposal. Second, all three had experienced frustrations—and Fischer and Ostwald, occasionally debilitating stress—from trying to balance the demands of research and teaching within German chemical institutions. This was related in turn to their growing realization that changes in the world of academic and industrial chemistry from at least the mid-1890s onward would necessitate greater institutional emphasis on specialties previously neglected in Germany, particularly inorganic, physical, and analytic chemistry. It was their conclusion that the German academic system would not accommodate all these needs within existing institutions that led most immediately to the proposal for an Imperial Chemical Institute which, it can be argued, epitomized their idea of a modern research institution.

Fischer, Ostwald, and Nernst as "Modern" Leaders of Chemistry in Germany

Consider first the status of the three chemists as disciplinary leaders. In a period in which modernization involved the cultivation of relationships between science and industry, with chemistry in the forefront, they could be considered among the leading academic modernizers. Beyond this, they were trying to promote theoretical and institutional reforms that would permit chemistry to continue to flourish as a creative scientific discipline amidst the stresses of tremendous growth brought on in large part by the fruitful interaction of academic and industrial chemistry in Imperial Germany.

Emil Fischer's scientific work was on the frontier between classical organic chemistry and biology. By 1905 he deserved the title of the world's foremost living organic chemist, having become, in 1902, the first of his kind to win a Nobel Prize. His younger colleague Richard Willstätter recalled him and their common mentor Adolf von Baeyer as the "leaders and classic figures of the era of analysis and synthesis in organic chemistry."[1] His work had led him from the relatively simple, aromatic compounds emphasized by academic and industrial organic chemists during his younger years in the 1870s and 1880s, to a systematic effort to synthesize groups of the principal chemicals related to living substances and thus to apply the methods of classical organic chemistry to biology. He began during the late 1880s and into the 1890s with the sugars, followed by the purines and after the turn of the century by a dramatic, albeit ultimately unsuccessful, foray into protein chemistry, where most industrial applications of chemical synthesis still lay far in the future. His earlier successes nevertheless carried him to the highest institutional levels of chemistry in Imperial Germany.[2]

In 1892, his fortieth year, Fischer had succeeded August Wilhelm von Hofmann as principal *Ordinarius* professor of chemistry at the University of Berlin, one of the largest and most prestigious of the Prussian universities; he became a member of the Berlin Academy of Sciences and was director of the First Chemical Institute at the University of Berlin. That institute had served as the offices for the German Chemical Society (*Deutsche Chemische Gesellschaft*), founded in 1867 and presided over by Hofmann for more than half the years until his death. Although Fischer did not emulate Hofmann's domination of the presidency, he did acquire much of Hofmann's professional influence while taking up the advisory

Illus. 2-1. Emil Fischer in his laboratory, 1905 (Max-Planck-Gesellschaft Photo Archive)

role that the Prussian government expected of a professor in Berlin, in addition to teaching and research. Fischer was well suited to the role of an *Ordinarius* in Berlin; his distinguished appearance, serious manner, and "autocratic nature" made him an ideal symbol of scientific authority, whose criticism younger colleagues could ill afford to risk.[3]

When Fischer took office in Berlin, there were considerable institutional and social differences between "pure" and "applied" chemists, as with most other branches of physical science and technology. In chemistry the institutional distinction between "pure" and "applied" chemistry had served during the late eighteenth and early nineteenth centuries to foster the establishment of the former branch as an independent discipline in the philosophical faculties of the German universities.[4] The "applied" branches, like pharmaceutical and agricultural chemistry, insofar as they were established in the philosophical faculties, were usually degraded to the secondary status of "bread studies" and allocated to lower-ranking professors with limited facilities. "Applied" chemistry was even segregated into separate but unequal professorships and laboratories in the chemistry departments of the colleges of technology, whose "pure" chemists also had clearly superior facilities. Not until the 1890s did the departments begin to reorganize their principal chairs according to specialization, chiefly "organic" and "inorganic chemistry," each encompassing both the pure and applied aspects of its specialty.[5]

Fischer's field, organic chemistry, had helped to lower the barriers between pure and applied chemistry by a remarkably fruitful cooperation between the German academic and industrial chemists who built the industry of coal-tar products, first mainly dyes, then related chemicals such as drugs. In large part as a result of this multilayered cooperation, Germany had by the early 1880s gained world leadership in most areas of pure and applied organic chemistry. The German successes partly derived from the nature of organic chemistry itself, whose problems "had significance for teaching, research, and industry alike."[6] This happy combination made it possible for university chemists to retain the external appearance of teaching and completing pure research, the results of which could nevertheless often readily be developed by their former students and other business contacts into industrial products. By the end of the 1880s, the dye industry's demand for new products had reached the point that academic research was insufficient, and they had begun to develop their own facilities for large-scale, systematic research and development, staffing them with degreed chemists and in several cases hiring former professors as laboratory directors. By this time, aside from several smaller competitors, five principal research-intensive German dye firms had established themselves: the BASF, Bayer, Hoechst, Cassella, and Agfa.[7]

Although under Hofmann's leadership the German Chemical Society had helped to shape the Imperial Patent Law of 1876–77, which helped to promote industrial research, and although Hofmann's own scientific research had contributed decisively to the development of the coal-tar dye industry, Hofmann had insisted on keeping formal barriers between science and industry. The Chemical Industry Association of Germany (*Verein zur Wahrung der Interessen der chemischen Industrie Deutschlands*) had thus been established in 1877 as a separate organization to promote the predominantly economic goals of the factory owners and directors, while the German Chemical Society remained dominated by academic chemists who kept its main activities "in the area of pure science."[8] A decade later, the Association of German Chemists (*Verein Deutscher Chemiker*, until 1896 called *Deutsche Gesellschaft für angewandte Chemie*, or "German Society for Applied Chemistry") had been founded to disseminate innovations in chemical technology and promote the interests of the now rapidly growing group of employed industrial chemists, who had little voice in either of the older organizations. Taking the more modern approach of combining scientific with economic and political concerns, the new group grew rapidly, while the German Chemical Society immediately lost members and was not to regain the level it had had in 1887 until the 1900s.[9]

Under Fischer's leadership a series of significant changes began in the organization of the German Chemical Society. It assumed new literary tasks, taking control of the main German chemical abstracts publication as well as of the Beilstein compendium of organic-chemical literature. Using appeals for contributions from the entire professional community of German academic and industrial chemists, the society also raised funds to begin construction of the Hofmann-Haus, its first separate headquarters, which opened in Berlin in 1900. Because contributions alone did not suffice, a Hofmann-Haus Company was formed to assume responsibility for the building and land; the society was principal investor, its funds matched by those of a group of forty-two other investors. This enterprise revealed in a more than symbolic way the growing dependence of the pure scientists upon industrial capital.[10]

Fischer's social background enhanced his relations with many of the leading businessmen in the chemical industry. His father had been a prosperous merchant and manufacturer in the Rhenish town of Euskirchen. Fischer's personal ties to former students and colleagues who had gone into industry reinforced patent and consulting ties that linked him profitably to several leading firms. During the 1880s he himself could have become director of research for the BASF at a salary of 100,000 marks, an unheard-of sum for an academic. While he had refused the position to maintain his scientific freedom, and while the bulk of his later research did not have direct practical applications, Fischer was nevertheless always aware of potential profits from his research. At times only the thinnest of lines—such as the degree of generality that Fischer perceived in his scientific results—separated the publishable from the patentable,[11] so that the distinction between "pure" and "applied" chemistry became arbitrary. Socially and intellectually, Fischer thus stood far closer to industry than most German professors. In the sense that modernization fosters manifold interactions between science and industry, he was a decidedly "modern" scientist.

Fischer accordingly took decidedly "modern" positions in support of reforms like granting university status to the colleges of technology and giving graduates of modern secondary schools the same rights to matriculate at universities as their classically trained brethren; he had nothing but scorn for his more tradition-minded colleagues' "stubborn refusal to abandon antiquated views and practices."[12] At the same time, Fischer had begun to see the increasingly powerful chemical industry as a useful ally in prodding the bureaucracy toward change that would benefit academic chemistry. His business friends had responded to his call of distress in 1896, using the influence of the Chemical Industry Association to help persuade the Prussian government to grant Fischer the expensive new institute that it had promised him in 1892, but had so far withheld purportedly for fiscal reasons.[13] During the controversies of the 1890s over the establishment of a national examination for chemistry students, Fischer's moderating influence had helped to effect a compromise among the interests of chemists in the universities, the colleges of technology, and industry. This compromise may well have paved the way for a more far-reaching agreement, whereby the colleges gained their right to grant degrees and titles.[14]

Fischer was thus overall an advocate of institutional reforms that would foster the relationship between industrial and academic chemistry in many ways. He was also willing to foster closer relationships between organic chemistry, his own special field, and other subdisciplines of chemistry. This meant, in particular, dealing with the physical chemists. While Fischer and most of his fellow German chemists were staking out the border area between chemistry and biology, a much smaller but perhaps more ambitious (and certainly more vocal) group explored the boundary between chemistry and physics. Their organizational leader was Wilhelm Ostwald. Whereas Fischer rose within the chemical establishment in the German universities to become an archetypal insider in his profession and in the German academic system (insofar as that was possible for a chemist at the time), Ostwald, who was almost the same age, seemed to delight in being an outsider, a critic of the establishment, and a gadfly.

Ostwald literally was an outsider, being originally a Baltic German from the Russian Empire. Almost from the very beginning of his career he had been a determined critic of the conventions of organic chemistry, and his

Illus. 2-2. Wilhelm Ostwald, drawn by Klamroth, probably during the early 1900s (Photo by Photographische Gesellschaft in Berlin, obtained courtesy of E. F. Smith Collection, Van Pelt Library, University of Pennsylvania)

criticism sharpened as he grew older. His seemingly boundless ambition, energy, and ability to inspire his followers, plus an extraordinary facility at writing and an above-average share of organizational talent, more than made up for occasional shortcomings in the intellectual depth of his research. Probably his most significant accomplishment was in creating the institutional and disciplinary basis for a new approach to physical chemistry pioneered by himself, Jacobus van't Hoff of the Netherlands, and Svante Arrhenius of Sweden during the 1880s.[15]

Under Ostwald's leadership, physical chemists gained a sense of community and apartness from the organic chemists who dominated the German Chemical Society. Part of this separate identity had to do with the vigor with which Ostwald preached the gospel of the new theories, so that he was able to attract intensely loyal followers. He had begun by advocating the existence of ionic as well as molecular solutions; in the nineties he was doubting the existence of atoms. Ostwald disdained structural chemistry and its syntheses. Later he was proud to recall that "it was not infrequently claimed that I was no chemist, because I never produced a new substance."[16] Ostwald made it his goal to reform chemistry by making it more quantitative and susceptible to abstract mathematical theorizing, like physics, while moving it away from the organic chemists' emphasis on synthesis. Instead, he and his associates set out to develop precise theories of chemical behavior, especially in solutions. Ostwald propagated his and his associates' ideas in innumerable books as well as in the *Zeitschrift für physikalische Chemie*, which he had begun editing in 1886 with nominal help from van't Hoff. It turned out that the precise theories they sought were hard to come by except in extremely dilute solutions. That led van't Hoff to comment wryly in 1890 that "whereas the chemico-chemists always find in industry a beautiful field of gold-laden soil, the physicochemists stand somewhat farther off, especially those who seek only the greatest dilution, for in general there is little to make with very watery solutions."[17] The physical chemists around Ostwald thus appeared to be accusing their colleagues of insufficient purity as well as insufficient precision. Within a few years, however, as the pace of modernization in Germany quickened and the pattern became more integrative, they too would find themselves moving closer to industry.

From 1887 until 1905 Ostwald's institutional base was at Leipzig, one of the few universities to have two full professors of chemistry. For the first decade his "second institute" was virtually the only independent center in Germany for university teaching and research in physical chemistry of the new type (there were a few others of an older variety, best represented until 1889 by Robert Wilhelm Bunsen at Heidelberg). By the mid-nineties other institutes and laboratories had begun to appear, however, as the "take-off" of the electrochemical industry (a branch of heavy inorganic chemical manufacturing) offered possibilities for an academic-industrial symbiosis that might rival the organic chemists'. Significant support for the new field came from at least one established leader of the organic dye industry, Henry Böttinger of Bayer, who was counting on eventual profits from physical chemistry.[18]

Seeking a disciplinary forum separate from the existing "pure" and "applied" organizations dominated by often hostile organic chemists, in 1894 the physical chemists and electrochemists had established the German Electrochemical Society (*Deutsche Elektrochemische Gesellschaft*) under Ostwald's leadership. His inaugural address had acknowledged the need to emulate the organic chemists by promoting systematic industrial research in electrochemistry that would be "a direct continuation" of academic research. "That is the secret of the success of the German chemical industry: it has realized that science is also the best practice."[19] Like its larger counterparts in both pure and applied chemistry, the new organization served to promote technological advances through cooperation between academic and industrial chemists, and it became a focus for the disciplinary organizing of physical chemists, so that its meetings saw intense discussions of theoretical as well as technological issues. Thus, in line with other trends at the turn of the century, this organization was bridging the gap between "pure" and "applied."

Ostwald himself saw his main task as an organizer of physical chemistry and a teacher of future academic chemists; but he also trained a large number of analytic chemists for industrial careers. Many new analytic techniques and devices came out of his institute, and he published the first text to place analytic chemistry on a coherent theoretical basis in the new physical chemistry.[20] By the turn of the century, after the Saxon government provided him with a new Institute for Physical Chemistry, he was also exploring the field of catalysis, which offered potential industrial benefits in the form of techniques that could solve the "problem of time" by speeding up reactions and improving efficiency.[21] The development of the refrigeration and gas industries also opened new opportunities for physical chemists. In view of the changing situation, in 1902 the Electrochemical Society adopted Ostwald's suggestion to take a broader name, the German Bunsen Society for Applied Physical Chemistry (*Deutsche Bunsen-Gesellschaft für angewandte physikalische Chemie*).[22]

Despite continuing scientific differences with many academic organic chemists, in 1897–98 Ostwald found a common ground with them in organizing the Association of Laboratory Directors, of which he became the first secretary. In 1899 and 1900 he even held office in the German Chemical Society as one of the vice presidents, along with Fischer, among others. His opposition to an official licensing examination for chemists had, however, outraged at least one of the businessmen proposing it,

Böttinger of Bayer, his former ally as vice president of the German Electro-chemical Society.[23] Their deepening animosity exemplified the difficulties that Ostwald, unlike Fischer, repeatedly encountered when moving from rhetoric to actual dealings with business.

By 1905, in any case, Ostwald had lost much of his old enthusiasm for teaching and even for research, apparently feeling that he no longer had the energy to hold his position as leader in his own discipline, which was growing and changing rapidly.[24] His most likely successor as preeminent leader of the physical chemists in Germany was Walther Nernst. De-scended from a respectable East-Elbian Prussian family (his father was a judge in the civil service), Nernst had studied physics and taken his degree at Würzburg in 1887 under Emil Fischer's friend and colleague Friedrich Kohlrausch. Nernst had then gone to Leipzig, where he fell under Ostwald's spell and became his assistant for physical chemistry, after which he had gone on to Göttingen during the 1890s to establish Prussia's first university institute for physical chemistry and electrochem-istry. That had come with the help of Böttinger and the individual en-dorsements of Ostwald as well as Fischer. In his address at the opening of this institute in 1896, Nernst had thus emphasized not only the ideal goals of physical chemistry as a general scientific discipline, but also the eco-nomic motives for its establishment and nominal emphasis on electro-chemistry. Around the turn of the century he joined Felix Klein's new Göttinger Association for the Promotion of Applied Physics and Mathe-matics, whose key industrial benefactor and organizer was none other than Henry Böttinger. The organization cooperated with the Prussian government to endow a series of academic institutes of applied science and technology at Göttingen.[25] Thus Nernst was familiar with the idea that businessmen, academics, and government could join forces to pro-mote scientific research.

Throughout his career Nernst proved to be as adept as Fischer in balanc-ing his principal theoretical interests with practical and technical applica-tions. He was an active leader of the Electrochemical Society, whose jour-nal he helped edit during 1896–99, and he made significant contributions to the understanding of electrolytic technology and the design of batteries as well as to analytic instrumentation and techniques. Most notably he sold his "Nernst Lamp" to the AEG (Allgemeine Elektrizitäts-Gesell-schaft) electrical corporation during the late 1890s for a million marks. Nernst's success in dealing with industry may explain why his students gave him the unofficial title "Commercial Councilor,"[26] which in its official version was awarded by the German bureaucracy to prominent business-men; on the other hand, it is likely that the title was not used wholly in praise, and that they only used it behind his back.

Nevertheless, Nernst's own rhetoric suggested that beneath his admira-

Illus. 2-3. Walther Nernst at his desk, 1906 (Bildarchiv Preussischer Kulturbesitz)

tion for and willingness to participate in the industrial-scientific symbiosis of chemistry lay a lingering sense of doubt about the "materialism" it entailed, as contrasted to the spiritual heights of physics.[27] Moreover, both he and Ostwald had aligned themselves in 1899 with more conservative scholars who opposed allowing the colleges of technology to grant doctorates.[28] Insecure in their institutional positions in the universities, the physical chemists evidently (and rightly) feared competition from newer laboratories that were more open to industry and might draw off resources that might otherwise go to themselves.

All the same Nernst, who drove his own automobile to Berlin when he moved his family there in 1905, could rightly be called a "modern professor,"[29] not simply for being at home with technological innovation, but also for his sophisticated "pure" theoretical and experimental work on the frontier between physics and chemistry. More than a decade younger than either Fischer or Ostwald, his prestige was still much less than theirs in 1905 (he had held no offices in the German Chemical Society), but while Ostwald was on the verge of retirement from scientific work, Nernst was on the eve of his most far-reaching accomplishment, the development of a "heat theorem" that came to be accepted as the Third Law of Thermodynamics.[30] Like Ostwald, Nernst had tremendous vigor, ego, and ambition, plus a quick and fertile mind. His mathematical ability and his grasp of theoretical ideas were probably better that Ostwald's, but he was also less critical of the prevailing views in general and organic chemistry as well as somewhat more effective at dealing with businessmen. During the 1890s, as Ostwald had attacked "scientific materialism" in the form of the atomic theory, Nernst accepted the latter's practical usefulness in his text on theoretical chemistry "from the perspective of Avogadro's Rule and thermodynamics."[31] This less extreme outlook, as well as Nernst's evident creativity, helps to account for Fischer's willingness to support Nernst's candidacy for the second *Ordinariat* in chemistry at Berlin, whose institute would henceforth be specifically devoted to physical chemistry. As Ostwald prepared to take up other interests, Nernst thus seemed poised to assume much broader influence among his chemical colleagues, and he too, like Ostwald, wanted to promote physical chemistry through institutional innovation.

Thus in the summer of 1905 Fischer, Ostwald, and Nernst represented an emerging modern chemistry not only in their advocacy of close relations between academic and industrial chemistry, but also in their work on the physical and biological ends of chemistry's disciplinary spectrum, site of some of the most extensive scientific changes of the twentieth century. One might therefore ask how they perceived these changes and Germany's role in making them, as well as why they came to the conclusion that Germany's existing research institutions were inadequate and a new one was needed. That is the subject of the next section.

Threats to German Dominance? Chemistry in Transition, 1905

"Chemistry has changed," Adolf von Baeyer wistfully remarked in 1905, just before his seventieth birthday and in the year he won the Nobel Prize for his achievements in synthetic organic chemistry. Yet he added, "I would not study organic chemistry again."[32] It was surely not that organic chemistry was no longer growing, as can be seen from the numbers of known structural formulas of organic compounds. These had increased from about 20,000 in 1883 to about 74,000 in 1899, and by 1910 would double again,[33] largely as a result of work by people trained in the laboratories of Baeyer, Emil Fischer, and their former students. Perhaps it was that very growth that troubled Baeyer, a master of simple, patient, test-tube chemistry who, despite his large institute, had made use of relatively few research assistants and students in his own work.

Changes in Organic Chemistry

Emil Fischer had not only helped to pioneer the use of more expensive, complex apparatus to deal with the increasingly complex biological compounds that he was investigating, he had taken a different, more "modern" approach to organizing research as well. As he said in his own Nobel lecture in 1902, "mass production methods which dominate modern economic life have also penetrated experimental science. . . . Consequently the progress of science today is not so much determined by brilliant achievements of individual workers, but rather by the planned collaboration of many observers."[34] The larger the organization, unfortunately, the fewer the opportunities for individual advancement and recognition, or even intellectual independence. Although already widespread among many disciplines, this problem had become especially pronounced in organic chemistry, with institutes and laboratories much larger and the proportion of *Ordinarius* professors and directors at the top much smaller than in most other disciplines.[35]

The same was true in the chemical industry, as the emergence of a few giant concerns and an apparent diminution of innovation presented the prospect to young chemistry students that they would become little more than anonymous cogs in a giant industrial machine. The dye corporations had achieved a long-sought goal at the turn of the century, when several new processes were introduced for synthesizing indigo, until then the king of vegetable dyes and the last major dye export of the British.[36] The advent of synthetic indigo opened the way to reducing competition and cutting the costs of research in many other dyes, the returns on which were far less than now promised by indigo. Merger talks began in 1903 and took their most ambitious form when Carl Duisberg, who had recently entered the directorate of Bayer, returned from his own trip to Goldberger's "land of unlimited possibilities." He exuded enthusiasm for an American-style chemical trust that could encompass the entire dye and pharmaceuticals industry and even produce its own raw materials and intermediates, so as to become independent of the Ruhr coal producers. Instead of a single, immensely powerful chemical trust, however, three new groupings had emerged by 1905 from the talks within the coal-tar chemical industry: the "Triple Alliance," a profit-sharing "I.G." (*Interessengemeinschaft*) or "community of interests" among the BASF, Bayer, and the smaller Agfa firm in Berlin; the "Dual Alliance," an exchange of stock between Hoechst and Cassella in Frankfurt, later expanded by the acquisition of the Kalle dye works; and the "Pharma I.G.," a grouping of

Illus. 2-4. Carl Duisberg, director of Bayer and chairman of the Association of German Chemists, around 1908 (Courtesy of the Bayer Archive)

several smaller pharmaceuticals manufacturers. Within the larger, oligopolistic concerns production was allocated and research shared on the basis of rational cooperation. Duisberg was not content to rest with this partial success, however. As he told Emil Fischer in November 1904, the Triple Alliance would inaugurate a "new epoch in the dye industry."

Eventually all of the German firms would be forced into Duisberg's trust, which would seal "the world domination of the German chemical industry for the coming decades."[37]

Not all shared Duisberg's enthusiasm. Merger movements, as in the electrical industry, were generally considered to result from the manipulations of the great banks; while this might not be true in the case of the chemical industry, the public could easily perceive the mergers of 1904–5 as a symptom of crisis in the industry,[38] or at least a harbinger of inefficiency. Critics argued that the dye corporations had reached the natural limits of their development, that significant new products no longer lay just beyond the horizon. The general secretary of the Chemical Industry Association acknowledged the criticism in 1906, noting that the research staffs of the dye companies, "which once were active in expanding the borders of the field, are now used more for internal consolidation and for the improvement of what is already known."[39] Duisberg's trust proposal of 1903 had in fact placed the "scientific laboratories with their numerous first-class chemists" and the large-scale industrial testing facilities of the dye factories high on the list of expenses to be reduced through merger.[40]

No wonder, then, that by July 1905 Emil Fischer was hearing people say chemistry was no longer a worthwhile career, and he was worried that insufficient social status for German chemists was scaring away talented young men. Accordingly he wrote to encourage E. Merck and Carl Duisberg, the leaders of the Association of German Chemists, in their efforts to promote professionalization.[41] Precisely at this time, Fischer was also beginning to discuss with Ostwald and Nernst a proposal for an elaborate new research institution, one of whose effects might be an elevation in the status of the chemical profession in Imperial Germany and an improvement in the public's evaluation of career opportunities in chemical research. That in turn could bring more talented people into his laboratory. He could also have counted on support from Duisberg's new concern for any project that would promote centralization and transfer some of the long-term costs of chemical research to the government, while offering a measure of control to the dominant industrial groups.

Changes outside Organic Chemistry

Such calculations, while certainly likely to appeal to Emil Fischer, were unlikely alone to have given him common ground with Nernst and Ostwald. Their common concern was that the tremendous growth of organic chemistry and its institutions for the mass production of new compounds had left few resources remaining in the general chemical institutes for other fields such as inorganic, physical, and analytic chemistry, which Germans did not dominate as they did organic chemistry. Since the mid-1890s foreign scientists had achieved impressive results in these fields. In particular, by applying precise analytic methods to atmospheric nitrogen gas, the British scientists Lord Rayleigh and William Ramsay discovered the element argon, one of a new group of rare gases; the Swiss chemist Alfred Werner set forth the theory of coordination chemistry to explain the structure of complex inorganic compounds; while in France, Henri Moissan invented the electric arc furnace, which he subsequently used to decompose fluorides of carbon; and following Henri Becquerel's discovery of radioactivity in uranium, Marie and Pierre Curie laboriously extracted and purified from uranium ore two new radioactive elements, polonium and radium.[42] All of these scientists eventually won Nobel Prizes for their work.

Ramsay especially impressed Fischer, who became his friend. During this period Fischer also befriended Jacobus H. van't Hoff, the Dutch chemist who had provided part of the theoretical framework for stereochemistry and subsequently contributed several seminal innovations in physical chemistry, bringing him the first Nobel Prize in Chemistry in 1901. After van't Hoff declined an offer to succeed August Kundt as professor of physics in 1894, Fischer had helped to arrange for him a less pressured position as member of the Academy of Sciences and honorary full professor at the university. In Berlin, van't Hoff spoke out for the institutional advancement of inorganic and physical chemistry, pointing out the possible benefits for organic and biochemistry; for example, in 1898 he suggested that equilibrium theory might be applied to Fischer's special interest, the synthesis of the proteins.[43]

Thus as early as 1896 Fischer's allies in industry had used the slogan "standstill means retreat" to highlight presumed dangers from foreign competition as they pressured the Prussian government to approve Fischer's new institute in Berlin. This was not simply rhetoric; by mid-1898 Fischer was privately telling Baeyer, "We must do more for inorganic and general chemistry again, if we are not to be put to shame by other countries." He had therefore designed his new institute to undertake research in areas outside classical organic chemistry. That had required a "truly large sum" for apparatus and furnishings (more than half a million marks, exceeding the total cost of almost any other university institute but only about one-third of the total for this one). Thus, besides the now-conventional private laboratories for the director and his leading subordinates, Fischer incorporated a wide variety of special-purpose laboratory rooms into the design of his institute, equipping it "with all the means of the modern era," not only on the biological frontier, but also on the physical and inorganic side. He intended it to be the model for a new generation of university laboratories, which could provide autonomy to specialists in several subdisciplines while building "bridges from the center to the peripheral parts of the discipline" and carrying over "new general methods to the problems of the special branches." During its construction Fischer even set aside organic chemistry for awhile in order to learn "physical technique" in such areas as electrochemistry and thermochemistry. For this purpose he carried out some joint experiments in the Imperial Physical and Technical Institute with its president, his old friend Friedrich Kohlrausch.[44]

Fischer's concern about Germany's relative weakness in inorganic and physical chemistry was certainly justified from an economic perspective. During the late 1890s the German chemical industry was only able to keep pace with its competitors in these areas, not dominate them as in organic chemistry. Although the availability of domestic sources of lignite provided relatively cheap energy that allowed the German electrochemical industry to compete with foreign nations with bountiful coal or hydroelectric power (Great Britain, France, the United States), the chief issue in the industry during this period was not the development of new processes or products, as in organic chemistry, but the design of more efficient equipment.[45] That required chemists with physical and engineering insight, not just the qualitative, preparative skills that most students learned in the big organic laboratories of the universities. On the other hand, Nernst argued in 1899 that Germany could not dominate the world in electrotechnology because the colleges of technology, where engineering was mostly taught, were unable to pursue innovative research as the universities did.[46]

Concern about Germany's competitive situation seems to have manifested itself among at least part of the Prusso-German bureaucracy on the occasion of German participation in the St. Louis Exposition of 1904. The Prussian Education Ministry chose a representative of physical chemistry, not organic, to prepare the chemical part of the German exhibition there. The young chemist chosen, Fritz Haber, was then an *Extraordinarius* professor at Karlsruhe College of Technology and already well versed in American affairs.[47] Although he was a relative newcomer to physical chemistry and largely self-trained, his reputation was growing; in 1902 the Bunsen Society had sent him to the United States on a fact-finding tour, which resulted in an "acclaimed" report on chemical education and the electrochemical industry. While pointing out a number of weaknesses in the American system, including its continuing dependence upon German science and industry in organic chemistry, his report also provided evidence of the Americans' vast potential and rapidly growing independence from German developments in inorganic and physical chemistry. He argued that German chemists, on the other hand, suffered from a lack of attention to these fields in their chemical education, which thereby limited Germany's participation in the development of modern chemistry as a whole.[48] Nernst and Ostwald, as established leaders of physical chemistry, were well aware of potential American competition; both men had several American students, and both seem to have visited the United States during the St. Louis Exposition (and at other times) to become more familiar with the situation there. Although the Americans had not yet won a Nobel Prize and their articles were relatively rarely cited by German authors, Germans nevertheless had reason to be uneasy about the future.[49]

Germany's growing dependence on imports of certain key inorganic resources also became a matter of concern to many chemists in Germany around the turn of the century. In 1900, as Anglo-German antagonism increased during the Boer War, Ostwald had suddenly realized that a defeat at sea would cut off German imports of nitrates, needed to supplement domestic sources like coking by-products for making fertilizers and explosives. After an unsuccessful attempt to apply his understanding of catalysis to develop and sell to the dye corporations a technique for synthesizing ammonia from electrolytic hydrogen and atmospheric nitrogen, Ostwald had been engaged in a related business venture, developing a method for oxidizing ammonia to produce nitrates. In 1905 Ostwald contracted with Griesheim-Elektron, the leading German electrochemical firm, as scientific consultant in this area. In 1906 Griesheim-Elektron was also to sign a similar consulting agreement with Walther Nernst, whose investigation of the nitrate problem arose out of the thermodynamic studies that also led to his heat theorem.[50] By 1905 Haber, the newcomer, had also begun working on a technical study of gas reactions, which by 1908 was to culminate in the first commercially practicable ammonia synthesis. During this period other chemists and firms produced several competing processes for synthesizing nitrogen-containing compounds. Even the BASF and its "Triple Alliance" became involved in this field, a sign of the dye corporations' growing diversification and interest in physical chemistry—it was becoming increasingly clear that many of their "unlimited possibilities" lay outside their traditional strengths in organic chemistry.[51]

Physical chemistry was even beginning to look useful to the dye corporations in their traditional areas of interest. As the production of dyes and related compounds became increasingly complex and diversified, there was a growing need for efficient, qualitative analysis of dye compounds; classical organic chemistry was not especially suitable for meeting this need, but physical chemistry could help. Although Nernst and Ostwald were both interested in applying physical chemistry to analytic chemistry, they were perhaps too busy to work in this area, while the dye companies were wary of committing resources to research that would not result in proprietary products. The first major publication to attack this problem had just appeared in 1904, however; its author was an American.[52]

Thus by 1905 Fischer, Ostwald, and Nernst wished to improve Germany's competitive position in science and industry, particularly by promoting research in increasingly significant areas outside classical organic chemistry, and they could expect that German industry would also support efforts to improve facilities for academic-style research in these areas. But what form should these improvements take?

Limitations to Institutional Reform in the German Academic System

In essence, one might improve the existing academic research facilities in three ways: by expanding the facilities of existing general chemical institutes to accommodate a greater range of diverse subdisciplines, by building a series of independent "special institutes" or specialized laboratories to accommodate these subdisciplines of chemistry within existing teaching institutions or academies, and lastly by building completely new research institutions outside the existing academic system but connected to it in some way. All would require more money, though the first was probably cheaper than the second; the third approach would vary in cost according to its details, but it would have the signal advantage of requiring the least significant changes within existing institutions.

Fischer had initially been inclined toward the first choice, not only because it offered economies of scale that would make it cheaper, but also because it did not require the agreement of the philosophical faculties to the creation of several new, specialized full professorships. Influential full professors already argued that there were too many specialists in the upper ranks for the universities to properly carry out their educational function.[53]

Yet to continue the old pattern of having a single general institute encompassing all aspects of chemistry raised the difficult question of how such an institute could be financed and administered. Between 1892 and 1910, chemical institute budgets failed to rise in the same proportion as overall university spending in the smaller states and in Prussia (except Berlin). Even in Berlin, where the budget of Fischer's new institute was the largest in the country, official support for chemistry did not rise in proportion to increases in enrollments, so that by the turn of the century the demands of teaching must have absorbed abnormally large amounts of resources, leaving proportionally less for research.[54] Overworked and underbudgeted, the chemistry professors had no choice but to use their fee income and their industrial connections to subsidize their institutes, even though the latter might have made them increasingly unpopular among their colleagues in the philosophical faculties.

In regard to administration, the situation in the general institutes was also less than satisfactory. Around the turn of the century, Prussia had established section heads in most of its larger institutes, including Fischer's. He argued that these subordinates should be kept free to do independent research but that teaching in the institute should be centrally directed.[55] Yet he was unprepared to subordinate classical organic chemists in general institutes to physical chemists who were not "real chemists," at least not at universities where only one "pure" chemical institute existed.[56] In practice that meant physical chemists could become directors of larger institutes only at a few major universities like Berlin and Leipzig.

Moreover, Fischer found his approach almost unworkable even in his own new institute in Berlin. Granting autonomy in research to subordinates was easy to say but harder to do when it came down to questions about who would have the well-trained and dedicated assistant who was always hard to find, the equipment that was in short supply, and the research funds that were limited. His section heads were not really free to carry out systematic research programs on their own. Fischer soon realized that they preferred to leave his institute, no matter how well equipped, to take positions that would confer intellectual independence (even at a college of technology). In any case, the senior physical chemists at Berlin feared competition from Fischer's institute and extracted from him a promise not to appoint a section head in their field.[57] The pressures of his biologically oriented research also kept him from pursuing the research he had undertaken with Kohlrausch on the physical side of the discipline. He had no facilities at all for research in radioactivity, so when young Otto Hahn arrived in 1906 with a recommendation from Ramsay, Fischer had to accommodate him in a small woodworking shop.[58] Such were the limits of Fischer's dream that his "model institute" could adequately support fields outside his own organic chemistry!

Even in his own field, Fischer's energies did not suffice to maintain a full teaching load, administer a big institute, and pursue intensive research. Within three years after the institute's opening, at a time when enrollments of chemistry students had peaked everywhere in Germany, Fischer had a serious breakdown from "overwork." He took about a year (1903–4) to recover, while systematically divesting himself of various routine examining and lecturing responsibilities in order to minimize distractions from his protein research, which in the best of circumstances he expected to take at least ten to fifteen years to complete. Fischer's inheritance of two-thirds of a million marks from his father, who died around this time, and his six-figure income from investments and patents made it easier to forego course fees.[59] When Fischer reduced his work load, however, his subordinates had to assume extra burdens, which further interfered with their ability to do research and thus further reduced his institute's effectiveness as a center for general chemistry.

Precisely at this moment, however, the Prussian government was beginning to restrict the fee incomes of "academic big industrialists" like Fischer and other chemistry professors directing the largest general institutes. After 1897, new professors whose incomes from fees exceeded certain limits had to give up half of the excess to the government; professorial resistance forced the government to exempt incumbents, but Fischer was still obliged to subsidize his new institute with twenty percent of his annual laboratory course fees. Such changes reduced but did not eliminate the inequities in professorial incomes; indeed they may even have increased the established professors' resistance to the creation of new chairs and special institutes, which could further reduce their incomes.[60]

What then of the second approach, the creation of many independent, specialized institutes and laboratories? The departmental structure of the colleges of technology, their long-standing limits on course fees paid to individuals, and their formal purpose of serving industrial development, made them more inclined toward formal specialization than were the universities. By 1905 there were separate laboratories for electrochemistry or physical chemistry at six out of ten colleges of technology (all but one of the rest taught it in conjunction with some other field), but there were institutes of the same type at only five out of twenty-one universities. Such specialized laboratories and institutes were small and not very well supported, however; the average budget of the college laboratories in 1903 was little more than half that of the university institutes, while the budgets of university institutes directed by specialists in nonorganic fields were far lower during this period than those directed by organic chemists.[61]

Specialized research might, however, be more easily promoted in those universities which were connected to academies, presuming that the academies themselves could be revived as research institutions in themselves. Aside from Fischer's ability to obtain political support among his friends in business, one reason why his ministry was willing to provide him with such an elaborate institute was the special status of Berlin, which was not only the capital but also the home of one of the few German academies of sciences. Before the creation of the first large chemical institute at the University of Berlin during the mid-nineteenth century, the Prussian capital (like Munich) had had an "academic" chemical laboratory solely devoted to research. Subsequently, however, it had become part of the new teaching institute and ceased (again like the Munich laboratory) to have an independent status as a research institution; its director was a full professor first, with all the duties that entailed, and an academician second.[62]

Although Emil Fischer had designed the facilities of his new institute to take into account the academy's formal rights to a quarter of the land and building, he claimed those rights for his own use and did not accommodate Jacobus H. van't Hoff, an academician without an institute.[63] Because van't Hoff was only an honorary full professor at the university, his salary was small (on the *Extraordinarius* level), and while it entailed only a small amount of teaching and minimal participation in faculty affairs, it also provided a correspondingly small income from course fees. Van't Hoff thus held what came to be called a "research professorship"; the only difficulty was that it offered almost no official support for research. His geochemical experiments on the Stassfurt salt beds, by attracting private support from a leader of the German Potash Syndicate, helped to make up for the lack of official support.[64]

At the turn of the century, while the Prussian government was limiting the fee incomes of its full professors, a few reformers were encouraging it to provide more funds for academic researchers. At Berlin, the leading humanistic supporters of the latter idea included old Theodor Mommsen, who died in 1903, and Adolf Harnack, whom Mommsen had welcomed into the academy in 1890 with prophetic words: "like big government and big industry, so has big scholarship [or big science]—performed by many but led by one—become a necessary element of our developing civilization. . . . Big science, like big industry, needs operating capital."[65]

In 1898 Harnack proposed that the Prussian government forestall further specialization in university professorships by establishing a "career for pure scholarly researchers" in the form of subordinate research positions for the Prussian academies.[66] By being restricted mainly to research, the new positions would not threaten the full professors' incomes from course fees; Germany's capacity for scholarly research could thereby continue to expand without threatening vested interests in the universities.

The Prussian government did create a few such positions within the humanistic class of the Berlin Academy on the occasion of its bicentennial in 1900, leading the scientific class to request additional support for itself as well.[67] In 1899–1900, and again in 1903, Fischer had therefore written to Althoff on behalf of that section to request a laboratory for precision work in chemistry, in order to accommodate van't Hoff and to work on the measurement of atomic weights, which was the area in which Fischer felt his new institute to be most deficient. Again Fischer cited the threat of foreign competition.[68]

During this period the value of an academic research laboratory for precision analysis in chemistry became even more evident as the Berlin Academy provided some financial support for the massive third edition of a reference work on the major physical and chemical constants. The work had been undertaken by Fischer's colleague, Hans H. Landolt, the director of the Second Chemical Institute at Berlin, and by a physicist collaborator, with the help of some fifty assistants and contributors. The Physical and

Technical Institute had provided some research facilities, but there was no equivalent laboratory on the chemical side. Landolt, moreover, could not complete the work; ailing, he decided to retire.[69]

Althoff had in fact promised a laboratory, but could not provide it, due to lack of money and the unsuitability of the Berlin Academy's new building.[70] Plans to establish a third full professorship in chemistry, which might have lightened the load on Fischer and his colleague, had not worked out either. Then the question arose of a successor to Landolt. In hopes of obtaining a first-rate physical chemist, offers were made in 1904 to Arrhenius and even to Ostwald (apparently van't Hoff did not want the position). Finally, the choice fell on Walther Nernst.

Walther Nernst's Institute for Physical Chemistry and Electrochemistry in Göttingen had apparently been the first Prussian special institute officially restricted to "advanced" chemistry students.[71] That gave it an emphasis on research in keeping with Göttingen's status as the only other Prussian university with an academy of sciences. In 1903 a second special institute opened at Göttingen, for inorganic chemistry. Gustav Tammann, its first director, had also been trained in physical chemistry. Both Nernst and Tammann, although full professors and regular members of the faculty, had minimal routine or introductory teaching responsibilities and could be considered "research professors." Unfortunately, their laboratories had modest physical plants and very small budgets, and their directors' small teaching loads gave them relatively small supplementary incomes from fees as well. Nernst had to pay from his own pocket to expand his institute; fortunately, his income from the sale of the "Nernst lamp" provided him with the necessary funds.[72]

Thus Nernst came to Berlin already familiar with the advantages and limitations of state-supported academic research laboratories. The institute he took over from Landolt was to be converted into a specialized institute for physical chemistry, but it was not to be an academic laboratory in the strict sense. Nor did Nernst intend to follow Landolt's program of measuring chemical constants in general; he would have enough to do just developing his heat theorem and related research. Thus the need remained for the academic research laboratory that Fischer had proposed earlier.

The situation became more complicated in January 1905, when Wilhelm Ostwald decided to retire from his Leipzig post; he wrote Fischer and Althoff to ask for a van't Hoff-style research position with the academy.[73] Apparently after hearing from the Berliners that an institute would be unavailable, Ostwald explained that he would not require an institute because he did not want to teach physical chemistry but to pursue his philosophical interests.[74] (Though he did not mention it, Ostwald surely also wanted to be in Berlin in order to be closer to where his process for converting ammonia to nitric acid was to be tested.) Complicated as Ostwald's reasoning leading to his retirement clearly was, a key factor bringing him to the critical point had been his complaints about the burdens of teaching, which had been more difficult for him since his own breakdown during the mid-nineties. For several years, it appears, he had been looking for a good opportunity to leave his institute. In 1904, like Fischer a year earlier, he demanded exemption from lecturing; unlike Fischer, however, Ostwald found his request voted down by the humanist majority in his faculty; this insult precipitated his decision to resign.[75]

Ostwald would not change his decision, even after receiving an invitation to be Germany's first exchange professor at Harvard in the fall semester of 1905–6. Ostwald himself, along with Harnack and other German academic modernizers, had advocated the establishment of the exchange during his visit to the United States in 1904. Althoff had secured official support for the idea, in part hoping to popularize in German academic circles the American idea of private support for research.[76] The man Fischer wanted to invite from Harvard in return was also a physical chemist, Theodore W. Richards, who had worked in Ostwald's and Nernst's laboratories during the 1890s and had even been offered the research professorship in inorganic chemistry at Göttingen in 1901. While rejecting it, no doubt because the Prussian government funded the position so poorly, Richards found the idea attractive. He proposed it to the new Carnegie Institution (which chose to emphasize research grants instead) and was able to establish something like an academic research professorship for himself at Harvard. There he was winning international acclaim (and eventually the first American Nobel Prize in chemistry) for his time-consuming, precise determinations of atomic weights, based on his theoretical understanding of physical chemistry and using methods that Fischer wanted his own students to learn. Although Harvard sent a theologian for the first exchange, Fischer did persuade the Prussian government to send one of his own assistants to Harvard to study for a term under Richards; the following year did bring Richards to Berlin.[77]

Thus the coinciding retirements of Landolt and Ostwald, together with the advent of the German-American exchange professorship, brought Ostwald, Nernst, and Fischer together in 1905 in Berlin and focused their attention on the international status of chemistry in Germany and on the limitations of existing academic institutions for upholding that status in certain fields, particularly precision analytic research in connection with physical and inorganic chemistry. Fischer's own experience was proof of the inability of a large general institute, however sympathetic its director, to promote all areas of chemistry equally; with organic chemists in control, and most of the students bound for jobs in the organic chemicals industry, the other subdisciplines simply could not compete effectively for scarce resources.

The second alternative of putting physical and inorganic chemists into special institutes and academic research professorships was not working very well either, as Ostwald and Nernst could attest, because the official support available for such positions was too small to provide the facilities and large incomes that made the established full professorships and large general institutes so attractive to organic chemists. Nor did the faculties look kindly upon the creation of new specialized full professorships and the division of institutes, which of course would mean reducing incomes from course fees. One could of course leave the promotion of inorganic and physical chemistry to the colleges of technology, which were more open to formal specialization; but most university chemists, including Ostwald and Nernst, had scant respect for their capacity to promote research.[78] Given their differing perspectives, Fischer, Ostwald, and Nernst logically sought common ground in a third alternative, proposing a new research institution that would suffer neither from the financial limitations and conservatism of the universities, nor from the inferior reputation of the colleges of technology. An Imperial Chemical Institute would fit these criteria; it could also be seen as a response to an American initiative, the newly created National Bureau of Standards, which had improved on the German Imperial Physical and Chemical Institute by including a division for chemistry.[79]

Before considering their proposal in detail, I would like briefly to reconsider the situation just discussed in light of the arguments about modernization and institutional change in science set forth in the first chapter. I have argued that the impulse to change in scientific institutions arises out of international competition, just as do other impulses toward modernization. Without his perception that momentous changes had begun in physical and inorganic chemistry, and that many of these changes were occurring abroad, Fischer certainly would not have been concerned about promoting these fields in Germany. He had no such sense that German predominance in his own field was in danger from abroad, but by the 1890s he had already come to realize the political value of "foreign threats" in obtaining funds from his government for more research facilities. By 1905, Ostwald and Nernst were also well aware of and interested in developments abroad, particularly in the United States, and were willing to promote exchanges with the scientists of that country to help advance their own subdiscipline, physical chemistry. All three were also advocates of closer relations between scientific research and industry, which is a hallmark of modernity.

It can be argued as well that all three men were modernizers in a strictly scientific sense. The research they performed and promoted was crucial in advancing a new type of modern science that differed from the classical chemistry of the nineteenth century. I am here using the term "modern" in a sense analogous to its use in physics, in which the transition from classical Newtonian approaches to the modern physics of relativity and quantum mechanics began roughly between the 1890s and the First World War. Ostwald's advocacy of physical chemistry helped to make possible the relationships between these two disciplines, which were to modernize chemistry in turn by introducing these new approaches, and Nernst's research further advanced the process of integration. On the biological side, the transition from classical to modern in chemistry is less clearly defined and probably far more protracted. Yet the understanding of the chemical structure of life is certainly at the heart of modern biology, in the form of molecular biology; and that understanding was one of Fischer's long-term goals.

Finally, one should note that as modernizers, the three chemists were conservative in the time-honored pattern of Prussian bureaucratic reforms; i.e., they ultimately chose a pathway to institutional reform that would create something new without, they hoped, having to change existing institutional patterns or greatly infringe upon vested interests, including their own. Ostwald most clearly expressed their position when he argued later that one could not establish research institutes within the universities because any "attempt to establish an individual in a special position" would meet all-out resistance from other professors. The discipline of chemistry alone could not change the entire academic corporate structure, yet it was the chemists' misfortune to suffer the "problems connected with the fusion of teaching and research . . . first and most intensely." With the enormous industrial demand for trained chemists, academic laboratory directors were under so much pressure from teaching that they could "no longer carry the full burden of their profession." Outsiders, even professors in other sciences, could not appreciate how far chemistry was in advance of the other fields in this respect. "*But chemistry cannot wait* until the same situation has arisen in other sciences, bringing the majority of professors to recognize the new requirements." National prosperity could not wait either. "Hence there remains no other possible choice" than to free chemical research from the "all too slowly functioning process of development" associated with academic institutions; the chemists themselves must create "new functional forms" to serve their science and industry. The particular form Ostwald and his allies had in mind was, of course, an Imperial Chemical Institute.[80]

3

The Reich Must Join In with Us:
The Plan for an Imperial
Chemical Institute

One dare not ignore the recent, energetic efforts that have been made abroad to catch up with us, especially in the United States of America. . . . What Werner von Siemens said of physics twenty-two years ago, when he advocated founding the Imperial Physical and Technical Institute, is equally true . . . of academic chemistry today. In the future chemistry too must have research institutes which are freed from instructional duties and are so richly equipped that they can also undertake costly experimentation.
—Emil Fischer, February 1906

The Reich must join in with us. . . . We do not just want to ask, however; rather we also have, I believe, a right to demand.
—Carl Duisberg, February 1906

The Proposal

For more than a decade the Imperial Physical and Technical Institute has not only demonstrated its right to exist, it has exerted an unexpectedly far-reaching, even authoritative influence on various branches of physics and has played a decisive role in a great many questions of electrotechnology and physical technology in general. Its industrial significance is revealed in the fact that facilities modeled on the German Imperial Institute have recently appeared in England and North America.

The wish has often been expressed for an institution that would similarly promote chemistry, the sister science of physics. In view of chemistry's multifaceted and direct significance for practical life, one could even say that physics took precedence in this respect through an historical accident.[1]

So began the confidential "Preliminary Draft of a Memorandum on the Establishment of an Imperial Chemical Institute," which some forty academic and industrial chemists received in September 1905. Its signatories were of course Emil Fischer, Wilhelm Ostwald, and Walther Nernst. The previous chapter has discussed the "historical accidents" that brought them together at this particular time, inclined them to support reforms in the German academic system that would benefit chemical research, and led them to propose a new institution rather than trying to change or enlarge those supported by the state governments. Why an Imperial Institute, however? What goals did they expect to achieve, and in what kind of research organization? What in the current state of Imperial politics might have led them to hope for success, and how did they expect to mobilize the necessary political forces?

The most important criterion for success in persuading the Imperial government was a sound Imperial budget, preferably a surplus. That had certainly not been the case in 1900, when Nernst's younger colleague Emil Bose had proposed an Imperial Chemical and Technical Institute. Thus although Fischer had endorsed the idea to Althoff, and the physical chemists in the Bunsen Society had discussed it, no one had taken action.[2] Bose's proposal could not draw attention from the debates over tariff policies, the brief but sharp recession of 1900–1901, the Boer War, and the naval building program. Because of the latter, together with increases in the army budget, the Imperial government was already encountering chronic deficits. By 1905 the situation had considerably changed. Although mainly designed to benefit agriculture and heavy industry, a series of new trade treaties coming into effect as a result of the protective tariffs passed in 1902 promised to generate sufficient new revenues to overcome the government's deficit and permit it to undertake new projects. At the same time, the international situation appeared to justify leveling off German armaments spending. Russia's defeat and internal upheavals had greatly weakened Imperial Germany's greatest potential military opponent in the East, while a German diplomatic victory against the French over Morocco had seemed to end the threat of an Anglo-French alliance in the West (not until the Algeciras conference of 1906 did the threat revive).[3]

The second most important criterion for success in Imperial politics was the support of powerful interests. Between 1900 and 1902 the chemical industry had been too weak and disunited to have much impact on Imperial trade policy, and too distracted to concern itself with an Imperial Institute. As noted in the previous chapter, the subsequent wave of cartellization and mergers had produced a smaller, more powerful group of leaders who were seething over the second-class status to which the Imperial government had relegated them in trade policy, and they were in a mood to demand some kind of compensation.[4] But would they unite behind an Imperial Institute?

The year 1905 also seemed opportune because various changes in Imperial scientific institutions provided a natural break in continuity. In 1905, for instance, the biological branch of the Imperial Health Office became an independent Imperial Biological Institute. There was also a new president in the Physical and Technical Institute, Emil Warburg, who was on good terms with Fischer, to whom he partly owed the professorship for physics he had held at Berlin. Warburg's son Otto was also about to complete a doctoral degree working with peptides under Fischer, who started him on an academic career in biochemistry.[5] Warburg was thus not likely to resist a proposal by Fischer for an independent Imperial Chemical Institute, as he might have by demanding its incorporation into his own institution as an expanded chemical section.[6]

Any of the three scientists might have taken the initiative in 1905. In fact Ostwald was the first of the three to prepare a memorandum on the subject. The others discussed it and agreed to prepare a joint proposal. For some reason, however, the form of Ostwald's paper did not appeal to them. Instead Nernst substituted his own version and sent copies to Fischer and Ostwald for corrections and additions. By September, with Ostwald on his way to the United States, the others were ready to offer his "preliminary memorandum" for discussion by German chemists and businessmen.[7] What goals did it set forth, and what organization did it outline for their attainment?

The existing Physical and Technical Institute offered an attractive model in many respects, combining pure and applied research, academic and industrial influences that ideally achieved a fruitful balance while avoiding the drawbacks associated with academy or university and tapping the Imperial government's now larger sources of income.[8] Thus the three chemists in part proposed a straightforward, chemical analogue to the Physical and Technical Institute. The new institution, like its model, was to be located in or near Berlin, and it was to be administered by a president and curatorium, or administrative council. As the older institute specialized in physical measurement, the basis of experimental physics, the Imperial Chemical Institute would be a center for "analytic chemistry in the widest sense," the basic discipline for chemical research and the field requiring "a greater amount of funds and time" than normally available in academic laboratories. As the Physical Institute's technical section specialized in instrumentation and standardization, the Chemical Institute would improve the analytical methods in greatest demand and would promote precision in chemical measurement, in part by testing and certifying reagents or standard solutions. As its model had become a national authority in questions regarding physical units, the Chemical Institute too would become a "supreme court" for nonroutine questions of chemical analysis requiring scientific arbitration (e.g., between consuming and producing industries where the price and quality of a commodity depended upon its chemical composition, and where each side produced an analytical method giving a different result). Finally, as the older institute had played a role in determining international units, the Chemical Institute too could attain prestige in areas like the determination of atomic weights, "the fundamental constants of every analysis," which German chemists had recently rather neglected.[9]

But there were some significant departures from the physical model in the memorandum. It did not suggest calling the institution "Chemical and Technical" or advocate dividing it into two distinct "scientific" and "technical" sections, which might have implied some disunity of interest between academic and industrial chemistry. Instead the memorandum referred to the proposed facility simply as a "Chemical" Institute and suggested several specialized sections, each for a separate subfield.[10] Even so, the memorandum distinguished between "scientific" and "technical" goals, both however featuring physical chemistry.

Besides the systematic redetermination of the atomic weights and the improvement of analytic techniques, the new institute's scientific tasks were to include the determination of "reliable physical constants for well-defined chemical substances," thus benefiting analytical handbooks such as *Landolt-Börnstein*, shedding additional light on the periodic table of the elements, and facilitating work with the "commonly used" (i.e., chiefly industrial) organic compounds.[11] The memorandum listed many different technical tasks of possible interest to the German government or to industry. In general the institute would seek to separate systematic errors involved in a specific analytical procedure from circumstantial errors introduced by individual experimenters.[12] Moreover, it was to have a "strongly educational impact" on academic and industrial chemists alike by exemplifying the best methods of precision research and calculation in analytic chemistry. If successful, the institution would thereby fulfill Ostwald's and Nernst's long-standing goal of making chemists more "scientific," that is, more mathematically minded.[13]

Who was to head such an institution? The memorandum made no suggestions. Ultimately the three men were able to agree upon Ernst Beckmann, Ostwald's colleague and professor of applied chemistry at Leipzig. He was one of the few chemists of his day who had worked closely with both a classical organic chemist (Johannes Wislicenus) and a physical chemist (Ostwald), so that he could be acceptable to both opposing schools. In fact, with Fischer's approval Althoff had offered him a position in Berlin in 1903 as a full professor of technical chemistry in charge of the new university Institute for Pharmaceutical Chemistry, but the Saxon government successfully countered that with the renovation of Beckmann's institute in Leipzig. Beckmann had a respectable experimental record, especially in developing methods for measuring physical constants of chemical substances, and he was experienced in administering a large organization. Nevertheless he hardly enjoyed the prestige Hermann von Helmholtz had had as first president of the Imperial Physical and Technical Institute, so the proponents did not choose to bring out his name in the early stages.[14]

The concluding section of the memorandum, containing "ideal" arguments for the Imperial Institute, echoed Werner Siemens's criticisms of inefficiency in the academic research organization; but the tone was comparatively muted except for its patriotic references to the need for increasing national scientific prestige and commercial profits and thus to maintain Imperial Germany "at the head of all peoples." German chemical research could only remain above all others in the international competition, however, if the Imperial government would "provide sufficient funds." When Werner Siemens had made a similar plea two decades earlier, he had backed it with his own land and funds.[15] The three academics who signed the preliminary memorandum could not do that, so they directed their memorandum initially not to the government, but to a select group of academic and industrial chemists. These might form the nucleus of a politically forceful alliance that could also generate capital donations on the order of Siemens's 1884 grant that had led to the Imperial Physical and Technical Institute.

The Chemical Industry Association liked to use the slogan, "In Unity is Strength."[16] The Imperial Institute's proponents sought their allies among the strongest, most unified branches of industry and schools of academic chemistry; above all they sought allies who in themselves reflected the academic-industrial symbiosis. One of the first people with whom they conferred was Otto N. Witt, former editor of *Die Chemische Industrie*, president of the International Chemical Congress at Berlin in 1903, professor at the Berlin College of Technology, and director of the college's newly completed Institute for Technical Chemistry. Witt's roots were in organic chemistry, but his interests had lately shifted to problems related to electrochemistry and physical chemistry, like the development of synthetic nitrates to replace the dwindling supplies of natural nitrates imported from South America. With Witt's help, the proponents prepared a list of about forty men, representing the elite of industrial and academic chemistry, whom they invited to discuss the memorandum in Berlin in October 1905.[17]

Besides Fischer, the dominant school of organic chemistry was to be represented by Fischer's mentor Adolf von Baeyer of Munich, Otto Wallach of Göttingen, and Carl Liebermann of the Berlin College of Technology. These three shared not only the common characteristic of being organic chemists, but also the rather uncommon one of being academics of Jewish descent with connections to the elite of assimilated and con-

Table 3-1. Membership of the Select Committee for the Founding of an Imperial Chemical Institute, 1905–1908

Member[a]	Position,[b] Institution/Agency/Branch	Contribution?[c]
Academics		
Max Delbrück (I,A)	Prof. & Dir., Institute for Commercial Fermentation, Berlin Agricultural College	Yes
Emil Fischer (P,A)	Prof. & Dir., Chemical Institute, Berlin University	Yes
Walther Nernst (P,A)	Prof. & Dir., Physical-Chemical Institute, Berlin University	Yes
Wilhelm Ostwald (P)	Prof. & Dir. (retired), Physical-Chemical Institute, Leipzig University	No
Otto N. Witt (I,A)	Prof. & Dir., Institute for Technical Chemistry, Berlin Technical College	No
Government Officials		
Hugo Thiel	Dir., Department of Domains, Prussian Agricultural Ministry	[d]
Friedrich Althoff	Dir., Department of Academic Affairs, Prussian Education Ministry	[e]
Adolf Martens	Dir., Prussian Materials Testing Office	[f]
Ernst Hagen	Dir., Technical Section, Imperial Physical and Technical Institute	[g]
Industrial Members		
Henry T. von Böttinger (I)	Triple Alliance (Bayer), Dir., Organic products	Yes
Carl Duisberg (I,A)	Triple Alliance (Bayer), Dir., Organic products	Yes
	Association of German Chemists, Chairman (1907-12), Professional association of industrial chemists	Yes
Heinrich (von) Brunck (I,A)[h]	Triple Alliance (BASF), Dir., Organic and inorganic products	Yes
Franz Oppenheim (I,A)	Triple Alliance (Agfa), Dir., Organic products	Yes
E. A. Merck (I,A)	Pharma I.G. (E. Merck), Dir., Organic products	Yes
	Association of German Chemists, Chairman (to 1907), Professional association of industrial chemists	Yes
Julius F. Holtz (I,A)	Chemical Industry Association, Chairman, Trade association representing major concerns	Yes
Emil Ehrensberger (I)	Krupp, Metals, Dir., armaments	Yes

Table 3-1. Continued

Member[a]	Position,[b] Institution/Agency/Branch	Contri-bution?[c]
Heinrich Heraeus (I,A)	W. D. Heraeus, Dir., Metals	Yes
Wilhelm von Siemens	Siemens, Dir., Electrical manufacturing	Yes[i]
Carl von Linde	Linde, Dir., Refrigeration, industrial gases	No

Sources: Printed minutes of the Select and General Committees for the Founding of an Imperial Chemical Institute, 1905–1908, in VCR-1, nos. 22–25. For industrial contributions, see table 5-1.
[a]I = invited to October 1905 meeting; A = attended meeting; P = proponent of meeting.
[b]Prof. = prófessor; Dir. = director.
[c]Contribution by the individual or organization to the Imperial Chemical Institute.
[d]Site (Dahlem).
[e]University professorship.
[f]Actively opposed.
[g]Did not oppose.
[h]Ennobled during 1905–8.
[i]Through Carl Harries.

verted Berlin Jewry, including (in Wallach's case) Franz Oppenheim, senior director of Agfa since Carl A. von Martius's recent retirement.[18] Besides the organic chemists, three chemists were invited from the side of inorganic or physical chemistry, led by Jacobus H. van't Hoff, then serving as president of the German Chemical Society (see tables 3-1 and 3-2).

Technical chemists or chemists from colleges of technology appeared on the list of invitees in somewhat disproportionately large numbers; the most significant were men with political connections like Carl Engler of the Karlsruhe College of Technology, member of the supervisory board of the BASF and a National-Liberal deputy to the Reichstag from Baden.[19] Another was Max Delbrück, professor and director of the large Institute for Commercial Fermentation at the Berlin Agricultural College. Of all those invited, he had the closest ties to the powerful agrarian elites east of the Elbe. His prominent family also included a brother, Hans Delbrück, professor of history at the University of Berlin and an influential "mandarin intellectual," as well as a cousin, Clemens Delbrück, a rising member of the Prusso-German bureaucracy.[20]

The business contingent was led by Julius Holtz, a retired director of the Schering drug firm who had long been full-time chairman of the Chemical Industry Association. The largest group of invitations went to the leading producers of coal-tar dyes and pharmaceuticals and to others like E. A. Merck, then chairman of the Association of German Chemists and direc-

Table 3-2. Membership of the Chief (General) Committee for the Founding of an Imperial Chemical Institute, 1905–1908[a]

Member[b]	Position,[c] Institution/Agency/Branch	Contri- bution?[d]
Membership Accepted		
Academics		
Adolf von Baeyer (I)	Prof. & Dir., Chemical Institute, Munich University	No
Ernst Beckmann (I,A)	Prof. & Dir., Institute for Applied Chemistry, Leipzig University	Yes
Heinrich Beckurts	Prof., Braunschweig College of Technology	No
Eduard Buchner	Assoc. Prof., Berlin University	No
Hans Bunte (I)	Prof., Inorganic chemistry, Karlsruhe College of Technology	No
Otto Dieffenbach	Prof., Darmstadt College of Technology	No
Carl Engler (I,A)	Prof., Organic chemistry, Karlsruhe College of Technology	No
Adolf Frank	Prof., Berlin College of Technology	No
Walther Hempel (I,A)	Prof., Inorganic chemistry, Dresden College of Technology	No
Alexander Herzfeld	Prof. & Dir., Institute for the Sugar Industry, Berlin Agricultural College	No
J. H. van't Hoff (I,A)	Honorary Prof., Berlin University, Academy	No
Paul Jacobson (I,A)	Assoc. Prof., Berlin University General Secretary, German Chemical Society	No Yes
Ludwig Knorr	Prof. & Dir., Chemical Institute, Jena University	Yes
Hans Landolt (I,A)	Prof. & Dir. (retired), Second Chemical Institute, Berlin University	No
Carl Liebermann (I,A)	Prof., Organic chemistry, Berlin College of Technology	Yes
Richard Meyer	Prof., Braunschweig College of Technology	No
Adolf Miethe (I,A)	Prof., Photochemistry, Berlin College of Technology	No
Ernst Schmidt (I)	Prof. & Dir., Institute for Pharmaceutical Chemistry, Marburg University	No
Adolf Slaby	Prof., Electrotechnology, Berlin College of Technology	No

Table 3-2. Continued

Member[b]	Position,[c] Institution/Agency/Branch	Contribution?[d]
Gustav Tammann (I,A)	Prof. & Dir., Institute for Inorganic Chemistry, Göttingen University	No
Otto Wallach (I)	Prof. & Dir., Institute for (Organic) Chemistry, Göttingen University	No
Hermann Wichelhaus (I,A)	Assoc. Prof. & Dir., Institute for Technology, Berlin University	Yes
Government Officials		
Karl von Buchka (I,A)	Dir., Food Testing Laboratory, Imperial Treasury Office	No
Emil Heyn	Dir., Chemical Testing Section, Prussian Materials Testing Office	No[e]
A. Heinecke (I,A)	Dir., Prussian Royal Porcellain Manufacture	No
(Friedrich?) von Hollmann	Admiral, Imperial Navy	No
Ferdinand Kurlbaum (I,A)	Scientific Member, Imperial Physical and Technical Institute	[f]
? Stoehr	Councillor, Imperial Admiralty	No
Emil Warburg (I,A)	President, Imperial Physical and Technical Institute	[g]
Industrial Members		
Mainly Organic Products		
Gustav Aufschläger	Nobel Dynamite Trust, Dir., Explosives	Yes
A. Bannow (I,A)	Schering-Kahlbaum (C.A.F. Kahlbaum), Dir., Fine chemicals	Yes
Gustav von Brüning (I)	Hoechst-Cassella, Dir., Organic products (some inorganic)	Yes[h]
Heinrich Caro (I)	Triple Alliance (BASF), member, supervisory board, Organic and inorganic products	Yes
Carl Duisberg (I,A) (1907-Select Committee)	Triple Alliance (Bayer), Dir., Organic products	Yes
Leo Gans (I)	Hoechst-Cassella Chairman, supervisory board, Organic products	No[i]
Wilhelm Haarmann (I,A)	Haarmann & Reimer, Dir., Organic products	Yes
Gustav Kraemer (I)	AG für Theer-und Erdöl-industrie, Dir., Organic products, oil	Yes

Table 3-2. Continued

Member[b]	Position,[c] Institution/Agency/Branch	Contribution?[d]
Carl A. von Martius (I,A)	Triple Alliance (Agfa), retired Dir., Organic products	No[j] Yes[k]
Fritz Roessler (I)	Degussa, Dir., Cyanide Processes, Organic products	Yes
Wilhelm Will (I,A)	Center for Scientific and Technical Investigation, Dir., Explosives	No

Mainly Inorganic Products, Miscellaneous

Eduard Arnhold	Private holdings, Upper Silesia and Berlin, owner, Banking and heavy industry	No
Fürst Henckel von Donnersmarck	Upper Silesian Pig Iron Syndicate; private holdings, owner, Heavy industry	No
Adolf Frank, Dieffenbach	German Acetylene Association, Industrial gases	No
Heinrich Fresenius	Fresenius Analytic Laboratory, Wiesbaden, Dir., Commercial chemical analyses	No
Fritz Friedländer	Oberschlesische Kokswerke (also Schering-Kahlbaum), owner, Heavy industry and chemicals	Yes
Krey	Riebecksche Fabriken, Dir., Lignite	No
Bernhard Lepsius, Ignatz Stroof (I)	Griesheim-Elektron, Dirs., Electrochemicals and organic products	Yes
Peters	Association of German Engineers, Managing Dir., Machine industry	No
Heinrich Precht (I)	Potash Syndicate (Neu-Stassfurt), Dir., Heavy chemicals	No[l]
Otto Schott	Schott & Gen., Dir., Technical glass	Yes
Emil Schrödter	Association of German Iron Technologists, Chairman, Heavy industry	No
K. Wessel	Deutsche Solvay-Werke [?], Dir., Heavy chemicals	Yes

Product Unidentified

Bergmann	? (Tegel), ?	?
H. Fritzsche	? (Leipzig), ?	?
Emil Müller	? (Berlin), ?	?
M. Schlumberger	? (Mülhausen, Alsace), ?	?

Table 3-2. Continued

Member[b]	Position,[c] Institution/Agency/Branch	Contri-bution?[d]
Membership Declined		
Government Officials		
Theodor Lewald	Councillor, Department of Scientific Affairs, Imperial Office of the Interior	No
Max Richter	Undersecretary of State, Prussian Commerce Ministry	No
Industrial Officials		
von Boch	? (Metlach), ?	?
Rudolf Dyckerhoff	Dyckerhoff & Söhne, Dir., Portland cement	No
von Oechelhäuser	? (Dessau), ?	?

Sources: Same as table 3-1.
[a]See also those listed in table 3-1.
[b]I = invited to October 1905 meeting; A = attended meeting.
[c]Prof. = full professor; Assoc. Prof. = associate professor; Dir. = director.
[d]Contribution by the individual or organization to the Imperial Chemical Institute.
[e]Actively opposed.
[f]Did not oppose.
[g]Did not oppose.
[h]For Hoechst only.
[i](Cassella) Actively opposed.
[j]Individually actively opposed.
[k]Firm.
[l]One other firm in Syndicate did contribute small amount.

tor of the Merck Co., Darmstadt, the leading member of the newly organized Pharma I.G. The Merck family tradition of academic-industrial cooperation went back to collaboration with Justus Liebig in the early
nineteenth century.[21]

The balance of the contingent invited from industrial chemistry were
men representing the dominant company or concern in various strategic
branches of organic and inorganic products such as petroleum, potash,
electrochemicals, explosives, and armaments. Even with the omission of
the soda and sugar industries, the list of invitees probably included most
of the chemical industry's "big firms," defined by the Association of Ger-

man Chemists as companies employing at least twenty academically trained chemists; as late as 1910 there were only eighteen such firms.[22]

Despite including Emil Warburg as well as Karl von Buchka, an old colleague of Nernst's from Göttingen now representing the Imperial Treasury Office as head of its foodstuffs testing laboratory, the proponents made no effort to involve a representative of the all-important Imperial Office of the Interior, which oversaw Warburg's Institute; nor any Prussian official (like Friedrich Althoff) who might also be interested. As to the heads of the Imperial Health Office and the Prussian Materials Testing Office, both of whom administered chemical research and testing, Fischer intended to disarm their potential opposition by approaching each individually.[23]

The final selection by Fischer and his colleagues unquestionably represented strength in the chemical community. Did it represent unity as well? The response to the invitations gave some hint of how the discussions would go (see tables 3-1 and 3-2). The academic chemists rallied well behind the plan. Holtz and Merck came, representing the big associations of industrial and technical chemists. But only a few of the non-Berliners and the inorganic chemicals manufacturers took time to participate, thus depriving the meeting of several industrial branches that might have been expected to be especially interested in the industrial side of physical chemistry. Even several of the major dye manufacturers stayed away, although Carl Duisberg of Bayer sent a strongly worded letter supporting the plan.[24]

On the morning of October 14, 1905, in the Hofmann-Haus of the German Chemical Society in Berlin, twenty-six men met with Fischer and Nernst to talk over the Imperial Institute. Wilhelm Ostwald, meanwhile, had left for an exchange professorship in the United States. The group unanimously endorsed the plan in principle and then approved the Physical and Technical Institute's model of leadership by president and a curatorium to be drawn from the "widest" possible circle of interested parties. As the preliminary memorandum had suggested, it also departed from the model by proposing an organization based on subfields rather than divided between a "scientific" and a "technical" section, despite objections from the physicists present, who along with Max Delbrück feared that in the new arrangement the institute's scientists might find their freedom to conduct research infringed upon by the demands and restrictions of routine testing. Nevertheless the chemists present pointed out that for specific problems it would be impractical to attempt a strict separation between "scientific" and "technical" aspects.[25] This "modern" point of view was decisive.

After Professor Carl Engler of Karlsruhe warned against offending the political sensibilities of the smaller states through a centralizing mentality that assumed Berlin would be an ideal location for the institute, the group unanimously decided to keep the question open. The issue of centralization arose again when Carl Alexander von Martius, who had already objected to the proposed institute, outlined his own plan for a scientific and technical agency within the Office of the Interior.[26] Martius placed a very low priority on the actual construction of a central laboratory. The work, he argued, should be decentralized; only planning should be concentrated. Martius's proposal received some support, notably from Witt, but in general Fischer and his allies stressed the need for an actual laboratory that was neither to compete with nor plan the work of others. Speaking for the Treasury Office, however, Karl von Buchka endorsed Martius's warning that an Imperial Institute would have virtually no chance to be funded in the near future. Lacking decisive counterarguments, Fischer and his friends concentrated instead on the steps to be taken to exert pressure on the state and Imperial governments. It was agreed to announce the project at a public meeting and to approach appropriate ministries and the leaders of all parties in the Reichstag including the Social Democrats, who could generally be counted on to support scientific research.[27]

Fischer now asked, "Would industry be prepared if necessary to make sacrifices for the realization of the plan?" Although there was a precedent for this idea in Werner Siemens's contributions to the Physical and Technical Institute, the preliminary memorandum had not even mentioned it, and Fischer kept his phrasing tentative. The three representatives of the Triple Alliance dye group each supposed that industry would indeed be ready to provide "considerable funds," but a debate began over the form of such subsidies.[28] Whereas Duisberg joined Oppenheim in warning that corporations could provide isolated capital contributions but not regular, long-term subsidies to the budget, Max Delbrück argued to the contrary that the latter was a more practicable approach. The debate tapered off without resolution. It was not to be resolved for several years.

Fischer concluded the meeting by having the assembly constitute itself "chief committee with the right of cooptation."[29] (Gradually the Chief Committee was to become more commonly known as the "General Committee," as it will be called here; see table 3-2 for members.) A "select committee" was also elected to undertake the active development of the plan. The Select Committee consisted of five professors, including the three original proponents, as university chemists, plus Witt and Delbrück to represent the colleges of technology and of agriculture, and seven prominent factory directors or owners (see table 3-1), including Emil Ehrensberger of the Krupp concern, to represent heavy industry.

But the plan's prospects for solid industrial and political support were still unclear. Martius had voiced doubts that many others might share; and although Delbrück and Ehrensberger represented the nucleus of a wider alliance with the economic pillars of the German political system, the big landowners and heavy industry, Delbrück too had expressed doubts, and Ehrensberger had not even appeared.

The Attempt to Forge a Broad Coalition, October 1905–February 1906

There was much to do before the plan could be fully publicized. Nernst undertook most of the paperwork and coordinated the distribution of printed matter, while Fischer approached some of the key officials who had to be persuaded. Early in November he discussed the project with Hugo Thiel, a director in the Prussian Ministry of Agriculture, and with Friedrich Althoff in the Prussian Ministry of Education. Thiel was chairman of the commission for subdividing the royal domain of Dahlem, outside Berlin, and Althoff was trying to develop a research complex there; thus several scientific institutions were already in or near Dahlem, including the Imperial Biological Institute.[30] Thiel and Althoff joined the Select Committee.

Nernst's chief problem was to revise the memorandum in accordance with the majority views expressed at the October meeting. Besides facing the worrisome question of cost by estimating the institute's initial construction and furnishings at 1.6 million marks, or about what Fischer's institute in Berlin had cost, Nernst tried to broaden the institute's appeal by adding to the section on technical tasks. From a political perspective, the most significant task was the testing of agricultural products, including alcoholic beverages and fertilizers. Nernst sent copies of the revised memorandum to the members of the Select and General committees for further distribution. Other copies went to thirty-three professional and trade associations in chemistry, heavy industry, and agriculture.[31]

Most of the political contacts planned in October had been made by the time the Select Committee met on January 15. Its major decision, taken unanimously after long debate, was to propose that the institute be located in Berlin after all. Fischer had apparently obtained decisive support from Emil Ehrensberger, the Krupp director, who was Fischer's former student and owed his start in industry to Fischer's recommendation.[32] Once agreement was achieved in the Select Committee, the General Committee was never given a chance to discuss the issue. Fischer also took steps to ensure that the institute and especially its location would not be announced in the *Zeitschrift für angewandte Chemie* before the February assembly.[33]

At the Select Committee meeting or soon thereafter, Fischer and Nernst began to sense that there was widespread suspicion of the Imperial Physical and Technical Institute in industrial circles. Fischer then discussed the problem with Friedrich Althoff and with Althoff's confidant, Professor Wilhelm Lexis, a Göttingen economist interested in the development of German educational and scientific institutions. Althoff persuaded Lexis to help revise the memorandum on the Imperial Chemical Institute by adding two new introductory sections. One stressed the value of the Physical and Technical Institute, another the economic significance of chemical research and the threat of "increasingly sharp foreign competition." Now that France, America, and England had acquired chemical laboratories equal to the Germans', Germany must improve its own facilities, particularly by adding an Imperial Chemical Institute, to maintain its lead.[34] The confident tone of Nernst's original draft was gone for good.

This new draft came in mid-February, too late to influence the responses of many organizations. Of over thirty groups asked for their opinion, twenty-eight eventually took some position that has been recorded. While nearly all expressed sympathy, few offered to cooperate in any specific way. Although the professional organizations of chemists and most of the groups representing chemical manufacturers were understandably favorable, the groups representing chemical importers and wholesalers as well as manufacturing industries peripherally related to chemistry were somewhat negative. In all, thirteen different groups used some negative or at least noncommittal language, many either doubting the project's necessity or wishing to eliminate portions of the plan.[35]

Yet many agricultural groups expressed interest, as did the German Agricultural Society, representing the technically oriented *Rittergutsbesitzer* (owners of knightly estates), and the fertilizer and alcohol associations, whose industries involved chemical processes. To attract the alcohol industry Fischer and Nernst had included Max Delbrück on the Select Committee and specified his Institute for Commercial Fermentation among those to be represented in the Imperial Institute's curatorium.[36] Several other groups now asked for similar representation, modifications of the program, or at least some guarantee that the new institution would not duplicate the work of existing public or private testing and research facilities. The sugar manufacturers' group in fact rejected the project outright on the grounds that their industry already had a central laboratory, yet at first they were balanced by the sugar technicians' association, who called the project an "urgent necessity."[37] Overall, the agricultural interests might support the plan, but only for a high price.

Although several Prussian officials had joined the Select Committee, Theodor Lewald of the Imperial Office of the Interior and Undersecretary of State Max Richter of the Prussian Commerce Ministry declined to join even the General Committee. Lewald's refusal was an especially bad sign, because his official responsibilities included the scientific institutions of the Imperial government. The Select Committee did bring into the General Committee some representatives of the technologically progressive Imperial Navy, as well as Prof. Adolf Slaby, the Kaiser's favorite technologist.[38]

By the time of the public assembly the total in the General Committee had reached a respectable sixty-nine, approaching double the number of October. Its imposing array of academics and industrial members, with a sprinkling of government officials (see table 3-2), served a chiefly decorative function. Not it, but the Select Committee, undersigned the invitations to the February assembly, at which Fischer and his friends hoped to impress the Imperial government with the unity and determination of the chemical profession.[39]

The Trumpet Blast of German Chemistry

On February 21, 120 men gathered in the great hall of the University of Berlin. Emil Fischer welcomed them in the name of the committee for the Imperial Chemical Institute. In his opening remarks, Fischer pointed out above all that scientific training and research had helped the modern German chemical industry to become virtually independent of foreign imports. Recently, however, the great foundations of North America had made rich donations to research and teaching; the same was not true in Germany, whose chemists lacked time and money for nonroutine work even in the best-supported institutes. The state governments lacked the funds to "close the gap" by setting up academic research laboratories. Besides, the "spirit of our time" did not favor "the establishment of such pure academic institutes," lacking the stimulation either of students on the one side, or of applied chemistry on the other. Thus: "What Werner von Siemens said of physics twenty-two years ago, when he advocated founding the Imperial Physical and Technical Institute, is equally true . . . of academic chemistry today. In the future chemistry too must have research institutes which are freed from instructional duties and are so richly equipped that they can also undertake costly experimentation." If Imperial money was available for Imperial institutes for health, physics, and biology, as well as oceanic research or expeditions to the South Pole, why not for the equally valid and valuable science of chemistry?[40]

The following discussion of the plan was dominated by two long, rambling speeches, by Ostwald on the academic arguments for an institute and by Duisberg on the industrial arguments. Together they effectively absorbed over half the time available for debate.[41] Both men stressed the theme that research in schools and factories, however exemplary, could not fully accomplish certain important scientific tasks. Academic institutions could not effectively carry on research that had ceased to be appropriate for doctoral training, or that, like Fischer's projected protein synthesis, was too mechanical, tedious, and boring to attract bright young academic researchers. The dye factories could not do this work either, because they had created their large research staffs primarily to extract profits from "grazed-over" areas, still offering potentially profitable applications but unable to hold scientific interest.[42] No factory would undertake work that might benefit its competitors or chemistry in general—"there we draw the line." Hence, for general research that was unsuitable for academic institutions or the existing technical testing laboratories of the state governments, the industry needed an "impartial" center in which paid specialists could undertake large-scale research "factory-style —if I may so express it," Duisberg added. Or as Ostwald joked, one could "put discoveries and inventions on order, just as one might order a couple of beers"; in each case, the "only question" was when, not if, they would come.[43]

Both speeches concluded by calling on the Imperial government to give science enough funds to ward off the threat of foreign economic competition, especially from North America. Ostwald called the U.S. National Bureau of Standards "an Imperial Chemical Institute, already fully operational."[44] "Standstill is retreat," cried Duisberg, adding ominously that the amounts being spent on chemistry in the United States were on a scale "perhaps never to be available to us." The chemical industry had so far received very little from the Imperial government in return for its benefits to the German people; hence "the Reich must join in with us. . . . We do not just want to ask, however; rather we also have, I believe, a right to demand."[45]

The remainder of the discussion did not quite recapture the spirit of Duisberg's ringing challenge. The assembly did approve Fischer's initial resolution endorsing the institute in principle, along with the recommendation that it be located in Berlin. At the insistence of Adolf Martens and Emil Heyn, representing the Prussian Materials Testing Office, the assembly also agreed to ask the Select Committee to strike from the memorandum any reference to the Imperial Institute's acting as a "supreme court" of chemistry or to its performing technical work in areas already included among their agency's responsibilities.[46] Following this compromise, however, the assembly rejected a motion by one of Martius's allies to amend the institute plan by including a department for commercial and technical questions.[47]

Fischer now broached the crucial question: "costs and collection of the same." Speaking on behalf of the industrial interests, Oppenheim offered a "handsome christening gift" to the new institute, but he refused to say how much, meanwhile repeating Duisberg's demand that the bulk of the capital and operating funds come from the government, in order to compensate the industry for "the extraordinary damage done to the chemical industry by the trade treaties which go into effect in a few days."[48]

Althoff had urged Fischer to keep the official cost estimates low and to use industrial subsidies to cover any excesses, but despite Fischer's efforts to set this tone, Oppenheim moved the discussion in exactly the opposite direction. Just as Holtz of the Chemical Industry Association had moved to vote on a resolution by Oppenheim calling for a minimum cost estimate of two to three million marks, much higher than Nernst's memorandum had suggested, Fischer broke in with a reminder: "We are only estimating the costs approximately. There is no question of coercing the Reich. After all, we come only as petitioners."[49] He thus got the assembly to let the Select Committee work out a compromise version of the estimates.

Nearly three hours had passed, making an end to the discussion long overdue. After receiving approval for the Select Committee to petition Chancellor Bülow and follow up with delegations to the chancellor and to the secretaries of the Interior and the Treasury, Fischer urged his audience to take up the cause with the Reichstag and, "to a certain degree," the public.[50] With this plea ringing in their ears, the assembled dignitaries went on their way. Fischer and his friends had what passed for the general consent of the German chemical profession, both academic and industrial.

Across the channel, British scientists were impressed. A few weeks after the meeting, the *Danziger Zeitung* published some of their reactions under the title, "The Trumpet Blast of German Chemistry." The phrase stemmed from Henry Roscoe, an old chemist whom the paper labeled the best of the English. In an open letter to the British science journal *Nature*, Roscoe had asserted that industrial chemistry in England was sluggish because it lacked the capital support available in Germany. The Germans' Imperial Chemical Institute plan was a "trumpet blast" challenging their foreign competitors, especially the Americans—who were moving in the same direction of greater support for scientific research of fundamental value to industry. The British, on the other hand, seemed content to let themselves fall ever further behind.[51] Roscoe could hardly have anticipated how indifferent the German political and economic elites would be to their chemists' call.

The Institute Proposal as Modernization

Reviewing the proposal for an Imperial Chemical Institute, one may be impressed by its overall modernity. In it, political, economic, and scientific considerations overlapped and reinforced one another.

The new proposal was in some ways a model of what the academic proponents would have liked to see introduced throughout the German academic system, bridging over institutional gaps between divided subdisciplines and promoting the status of chemistry as a discipline and research as a career. The specifically scientific goals of the proposal were also recognizably modern, including not only increased sophistication and precision in chemical analysis but the promotion of physical and mathematical methods in chemistry. Ostwald and Duisberg had expressed another aspect of the emerging modern style in science by referring to the routinization of research, which offered the possibility of planned, profitable investment in science. Even the proposed organization of the institute testified to the more modern outlook of the chemists, who were unwilling to distinguish as the physicists had between "pure" and "applied" or "technical" research; conditions in chemistry enabled its practitioners to transcend some of the self-righteousness and status prejudices inherent in the nineteenth-century usage of these words.

The plan's most enthusiastic supporter in industry was Carl Duisberg, one of the most "modern" of the corporate directors in the values he placed on industrial research and large-scale, centralized organizations. Duisberg too had been recently frustrated by the incomplete achievement of his proposed chemical trust, and for him too the centralization implicit in the plan was a natural extension of his ambitions and provided an indirect path toward the broader goal of reorganizing the chemical industry. Thus he, as well as the academic chemists, was following the pattern of Prusso-German modernization.

The political form of the proposed institution, as an Imperial rather than a Prussian agency, continued a trend toward national institutions that would integrate science, industry, and politics—thus following the path marked out by Werner von Siemens with the Imperial Physical and Technical Institute. The chemists' approach might be considered even more modern than Siemens's; for whereas his proposal had emerged from confidential discussions held under the aegis of the Prussian bureaucracy with almost no participation by the interested professional and technical organizations, the academic chemists planned on an Imperial institution almost from the beginning, and they attempted to establish a broad consensus among the professional and industrial elites, as well as some key bureaucrats such as Althoff, before formally petitioning the government. Even so, with Althoff involved, the Prussian bureaucracy was playing its time-honored role in shaping the course of institutional modernization. Althoff was a modernizer almost in spite of himself, for in essence his desire to centralize scientific institutions and their financial support stemmed from fiscal considerations: he could not obtain sufficient funds to support research laboratories from the Prussian government, so he was willing to try to shift the burden to the Reich.

It is worth noting that the preliminary memorandum, directed toward a small group of insiders, made little use of the classic modernizer's tactic of appealing to an external threat. Certainly Fischer was no stranger to this tactic, but it is likely that he hesitated to use it to persuade the leaders of the dye industry, who well knew Germany's strength in this branch and would hardly have reacted favorably to a message of fear. Only the revised version—tailored to Althoff's specifications to appeal to the Imperial bureaucracy—trumpeted the danger of economic and scientific competition from abroad. The main speakers at the public meeting echoed the same theme, with special reference to the United States with its new federal scientific institutions and private endowments for research. Although the American "threat" hardly appeared anything but peaceful, the focus on it added a new dimension to the general feeling of encirclement that increasingly oppressed the Germans in view of the intensifying European military and diplomatic polarization. With Russia temporarily neutralized, the German chemists were asking the government to redirect its resources to meet the new threat from the West.

Nevertheless, such rhetoric could not persuade everyone, and the proposal encountered growing opposition to its substance and its implications. Thus the next chapter will examine the other side.

4

Must There Be a "President" for Every Science?: Sources of Opposition to the Plan

---

It would certainly very much enhance the position of the Dual Alliance if we could take the leadership in this matter away from Duisberg.
—Leo Gans to the directors of Hoechst, November 1906

Must there be a "president" for every science in the German Empire?
—Adolf Martens, Director, Prussian Materials Testing Office, to Prussian Minister of Education, December 1906

The Sources of Opposition in Industry, Agriculture, and Science

To be approved by the Imperial German government, the project for an Imperial Chemical Institute had to obtain support not only from within the chemical industry, but also from heavy industry and agriculture, the most influential branches of the German economy. It also had to adapt to the priorities of the Prusso-German bureaucracy itself. Unfortunately the project quickly encountered opposition in the chemical industry and other branches, as well as hostility from some bureaucrats and even a few scientists. The sources of opposition to the plan can be understood better by looking at them within the context of German social, economic, and political institutions.

Opposition to the plan arose from two major sources, one related to perceived shortcomings in the existing Imperial Physical and Technical Institute on which the Imperial Chemical Institute was to be modeled, the other related to the new institute's expected role in the German political economy. The Imperial Physical Institute had in fact faced occasional public and political hostility in the past. Its scientists were repeatedly obliged to defend their institute against the ever-present threat of budgetary emasculation. Moreover, the gift of land in the value of half a million marks, with which Werner von Siemens had in 1884 ensured that the proposal for an Imperial Institute would be accepted by the Imperial bureaucracy, had been called a "Trojan horse."[1] There was even some justification for this, in that between 1887 and 1905 the operating budget had quadrupled to more than 400,000 marks—exceeding the combined official budgets of the institutes for physics at all twenty-one German universities as late as 1910.[2] The rapid rise in the institute's cost, combined with the chronic Imperial budget deficit that set in after 1890, helps to explain the government's reluctance to establish other Imperial institutes before 1905. Besides the expense, however, other problems had exacerbated hostility to the Imperial Physical and Technical Institute.

By early 1906 Fischer knew that businessmen held many objections to the Physical Institute and, potentially, to a chemical sister institution. Among them were the inadequacy of its ties to industry, the slowness of its operation, its overly "bureaucratic" organization, and the insufficiency of its benefits to industry generally, considering its cost. Yet to scientists its salaries, except for the president's, were too low to hold the best younger men.[3]

Consider first the Imperial Physical and Technical Institute's industrial ties and technological benefits. Because Werner von Siemens had played a key role in getting the Imperial government to establish the institute, one might easily gain the misleading impression that he had created it primarily to serve the Siemens electrical manufacturing firm. Yet Siemens had sought to foster in it scientific research as well as technological development. By 1906 technical work consumed the bulk of its resources, particularly for the development, testing, calibration, and standardization of instruments such as thermometers, as well as for the establishment of standard units of measurement for electricity, heat, light, and other physical phenomena used in utilities and other technical processes. While certainly helpful to branches of the economy such as the gas-lighting and electrical industries, the manufacturers of thermometers in the glass industry, and the manufacturers of scientific apparatus in the platinum industry, these services perhaps did not loom large in the minds of many other businessmen.[4] Or if they did, they may have evoked more jealousy than praise. Some industries had clearly benefited more than others, and although its board and presidents had tried scrupulously to uphold impartiality, a new institution might yet become an extension of some other concern's industrial laboratories. Finally, even while the institute was creating industrial benefits, its relations with industry and even the Siemens concern were also marred by conflicts over divergences between scientific and industrial interests. After 1905 Warburg was able to develop friendlier relations with industry than his predecessor had had, but only by devoting more time and resources to technological as opposed to scientific interests.[5]

The complaints about the Imperial Physical and Technical Institute's slowness of operation and excessively "bureaucratic" organization were also no doubt corroborated from an industrial point of view. Without the profit motive to justify its work, the institution could not be directly influenced by industrial concerns and interests. The businessmen could approve the general direction of research and testing through the curatorium, or governing board, but they could not regulate the day-to-day conduct of experimental activity. Senior, permanent officials of the institute were primarily responsible to the director of its technical section and to its president, who also directed the scientific section, but they were also employees of the Imperial Office of the Interior, which was ultimately responsible for the institute. Friedrich Kohlrausch, the president from 1894 to 1905, treated these officials according to bureaucratic guidelines.[6] They could thus work regular hours, without the ties of loyalty and enthusiasm that bound students and assistants to their professors in academic institutions, or the fear for their jobs that motivated employees in private industry.

Thus, as late as 1905 the Imperial Physical and Technical Institute could not be used as an unambiguous demonstration to German businessmen that the Imperial government should promote scientific research with the expectation of reaping major economic benefits. The proposed chemical sister-institution faced further obstacles arising from the dramatic changes within the chemical industry during the years just before the proposal was announced in 1905. The rapid growth of the Bayer company, and of Carl Duisberg within it, had evidently produced resentment among a few competitors, who could have read his memorandum of 1903 on the formation of a giant chemical trust as a plan for Bayer to take control of the industry.[7] To them, Duisberg's support for the proposed Imperial Institute was only to give Bayer a dominant influence on its curatorium and get the principal benefits from its research. Two "grand old men" of the industry, Carl Alexander von Martius and Leo Gans, certainly betrayed personal antagonism as well as economic competitiveness.

Martius had been one of A. W. von Hofmann's assistants in London and Berlin. He had been one of the young chemists who organized the German Chemical Society in 1867 and urged Hofmann to take its leadership. Although son of a titled Bavarian scholar, Martius himself chose to pursue an industrial career. He had founded and led Agfa, the largest dye corporation in Berlin, until he retired at the turn of the century. Martius had also presided over the constituent assembly of the Chemical Industry Association in 1877 and became a fixture on its board of directors for the next quarter-century. In order to promote industrial influence upon the policies of the Imperial bureaucracy, he had helped organize and lead the Industrialists' League, a decentralized band of many different, relatively uninfluential branches of industry, and in 1897 the "Center for the Preparation of the Trade Treaties," joined by most of the export-oriented industrial interest organizations in opposition to protectionist heavy industry and agriculture.[8]

Martius had long hoped to establish an Imperial agency with industrial representatives, to regulate questions such as occupational safety and health, pollution, tariffs and taxes, etc. In 1892 the Chemical Industry Association had therefore discussed with the Association of German Engineers the possibility of unifying the various Imperial scientific and technical institutions, including the Imperial Physical and Technical Institute, to form a single Imperial Commercial and Technical Authority. When the engineers limited their goal to research, the two associations could not agree.[9] "The thought of making the Physical and Technical Institute the starting-point and center for the Reich's actions in the technical area foundered on the strictly scientific character of this institution," wrote Martius in describing the creation of Siemens and Helmholtz, "which was little open to the needs of commercial life."[10] In 1901–2 he tried to revive the idea of a Commercial and Technical Authority through joint action with the Industrialists' League. The new proposal was almost ready in 1905, when Martius was evidently outraged to discover that Emil Fischer and his allies were working on a project that seemed destined to re-create in chemistry the "strictly scientific" Imperial Institute of Siemens and Helmholtz. Martius clearly resented the fact that Fischer and the other proponents had not consulted him before drawing up their plans. Social considerations may also have deepened his resentment. Proud of being the first businessman in the chemical industry to be ennobled, of having earned for himself a "von" like his father's, he could look down on upstarts like Duisberg and Fischer.[11] All of these reasons probably played a role in making Martius the earliest and one of the most determined opponents of the new proposal. His prestige in the chemical industry and his "personal relationship" to the Imperial Office of the Treasury also made him one of its most dangerous foes.[12]

Martius had argued strongly against the Institute in October 1905, after which he skipped the February meeting, then published a general attack on the plan in the journal of the Chemical Industry Association. In that attack he argued with a series of double-edged claims. The institute was not needed to perform the tasks proposed for it, but it could not perform them in any case. It would be biased in favor of its industrial contributors, but it would get no contributions in any case. And so on. The institution he proposed instead, a commercial and technical authority, would not do research on its own, but rather set tasks and provide funds to other existing agencies.[13]

Another chemical journal reviewed his article and mentioned rumors "that unanimity on the necessity of an Imperial Chemical Institute was not obtained, and impressive voices against the project are now emerging."[14] Unable to silence these "voices," Fischer and his friends replied to them. Fischer addressed the Berlin Association for the Advancement of Industry, heading off any attempt by Martius to win over this group, while Ostwald, in the absence of a writer in "technical circles," published his own reply to Martius.[15] Both Fischer and Ostwald spoke of giving chemistry the same rights that had been given physics in its Imperial Institute, and they also played on the prestige of their own industrial supporters to justify their claims about the Imperial Institute's value to industry. They noted, for example, that Martius saw no need for a control station to test the purity of chemical preparations, yet impure chemicals were a source of many errors and nine-tenths of the extra work in precise research. Despite Martius's predictions, no representative of a preparation factory had criticized this aspect of the plan. Neither scientist doubted that significant financial support would also be forthcoming from both industry and government.[16]

For the time being, Martius made no further public opposition, but another industrial opponent soon came forward. Leo Gans had promised his full cooperation and support in the fall of 1905, but in November 1906 he decided to make the Imperial Institute project a battleground between the Hoechst-Cassella "Dual Alliance" and Duisberg's Triple Alliance. Gans, like Martius, was a survivor of the generation that had founded the leading dye companies back in the sixties and seventies. Gans had remained in active control until the consolidation of 1904, when Cassella had narrowly avoided a disaster instigated by Duisberg. Gans's firm had been the one large dye company omitted by Duisberg from his trust proposal of 1903, ostensibly because Cassella was the only one still a private partnership. The prospect of competitive isolation had quickly induced Cassella's owners to issue stock, which they exchanged with Hoechst. Gans had then withdrawn to the council of supervisors, evidently nursing a bitter grudge against Duisberg. The Imperial Institute project offered a good opportunity for revenge. Thus in trying unsuccessfully to persuade his partners in Hoechst to withhold their support, Gans told them that "it would certainly very much enhance the position of the Dual Alliance if we could take the leadership in this matter away from Duisburg [sic]."[17]

In Die chemische Industrie, Gans thus attacked the proposed institute by stressing the dangers of bureaucracy and the need to maintain the time-honored German system of decentralization. Going even farther than Martius had, Gans proposed a Carnegie-style national endowment for research grants to needy chemists.[18] He thought this plan could attract the "great majority" of academic chemists; he even claimed in private that

Fischer himself would support Gans's idea rather than the "Ostwaldian fantasies."[19]

Gans's article brought a rebuttal from Ostwald, who for the first time attempted to justify centralization and to reassure businessmen that the Imperial Institute would be responsive to industrial needs. The academic proponents of the institute plan had not included technical goals merely to sweeten the pill for industrial investors, he insisted; "*precisely in the interest of pure science, permanent involvement with applications was to be aimed at from the beginning.*"[20] Gans remained unconvinced, of course.

More criticism of the planned institute came from the side of agriculture, or rather, from Max Delbrück and Albert Stutzer, two academic scientists with close ties to agrarian business interests. Delbrück's Institute for Commercial Fermentation in Berlin was supported by the alcohol industry, and Stutzer, a full professor of agricultural chemistry at Königsberg, had previously been a private analytic chemist for agriculture.[21]

Stutzer objected to the institute's proposed function as a supreme court of analysis; "a supreme, bureaucratically organized Imperial Institute" should not "be regarded as infallible in this regard." Instead he defended "extensive decentralization" in the system of judgmental analyses; each branch of industry should determine its own needs. Stutzer conditionally accepted the rest of the plan, "even though the progressive centralization of the scientific institutes in Prussia has already led to great abuses," namely the neglect of the provincial facilities.[22] This was perhaps a reference to the many big technical institutes in the Berlin Agricultural College.

Delbrück, a beneficiary of the "centralization" of scientific institutions in Berlin, could scarcely object to the proposal on those grounds, but he too professed to be worried by the threat of bureaucratic "ossification." At the annual convention of the Association of German Chemists in June 1906, he also suggested that "commercial policy" might necessarily limit "academic freedom" in an Imperial Institute. Yet he added that all these issues could be resolved, above all through "the living, compelling cooperation" of the chemical industry, represented in an influential, not "merely decorative" curatorium. The association applauded an informal resolution to this effect.[23]

As noted earlier, the proposal had initially met with a positive reception from the Association of German Sugar Technicians. They soon came into line with the Association of the German Sugar Industry, however, announcing that "we want no new schoolmasters and no new authorities."[24]

With those exceptions, the agricultural organizations that the chemists contacted had seemed enthusiastic about the plan. Their endorsements perhaps reflected a long tradition of German agricultural chemistry, going back to the mid-nineteenth century. Yet almost none of these expressions of support later materialized in the form of monetary contributions or active political engagement. The plan's advantages to agriculture were vaguely defined, while Stutzer's criticisms of centralization probably spoke not only for East-Elbian provincial academics, but for Junker land-owners as well. As noted in Chapter 1, the Prussian government had already begun to respond to their interests by strengthening the academic and research facilities in the Eastern provinces. The creation of the Imperial Biological Institute in 1905 was thus followed by the Kaiser Wilhelm Institute for Agriculture in Posen a year later. These, added to the existing network of specialized institutes and agricultural testing stations, may have satisfied even the most enterprising, science-oriented landowner. Equally important, the chemical industry had fought the agrarian interests over the Imperial government's new trade policies; by openly expressing their hostility to these policies while advocating the Imperial Institute, businessmen like Duisberg could easily have alienated potential agrarian supporters.

A similar gulf of hostility stretched between the chemical industry and heavy industry, primarily meaning the coal and steel producers, who with the big landowners represented the dominant and most politically conservative branches of the German economy. There was more than a little ill-feeling between the free-trade, export-oriented directors who led the Chemical Industry Association and the protectionists who led the Central Association of German Industrialists (Centralverband deutscher Industriellen), the organization of coal and steel as well as textiles. A brief interlude of harmony between the two organizations in the eighties had ended when the Chemical Industry Association withdrew from the Central Association over differences in trade policy and probably also industrial relations, in which the chemical industry had to be more conciliatory because of its dependence upon highly skilled labor.[25] Above all, the coal-tar chemical industry and the coal industry had opposing economic interests as consumers and producers. After the turn of the century, the Rhenish-Westphalian Coal Syndicate's price increases had exerted pressure on the chemical industry, leading the three biggest dye firms to consider jointly operating a coal mine in 1904; in 1907 Duisberg's "Triple Alliance" finally did so.[26]

The mutual hostility was such that when Emil Fischer sought support for his proposal from Hugo Stinnes, one of the leaders of the Ruhr coal industry, he learned that Stinnes's presence on the Select Committee for the Imperial Chemical Institute might offend some of the "older gentlemen" in the chemical industry.[27] Further inquiries with the Ruhr coal magnates led nowhere. As with the agrarians, there was little reason to expect them to support an enterprise they did not control, and they could hardly expect to be offered much control over an Imperial Chemical Institute in Berlin. On the other hand, neither Fischer's group nor the Imperial bureaucracy were prepared to locate an institute in a city like Essen. Only the personal obligation felt by Fischer's former student, Emil Ehrensberger, gave the chemists a sympathetic ear in the Ruhr, and even Ehrensberger had originally opposed the idea of an Imperial Chemical Institute.[28]

There was little initial opposition to the Imperial Institute proposal from academic scientists, aside from Delbrück and Stutzer. As Fischer noted in June 1906, "not one single scholar" had supported the arguments of Carl von Martius.[29] Yet the problem of inadequate salaries for the permanent officials of the Imperial Physical and Technical Institute, which Fischer had recognized as a source of criticism from academic scientists, was both serious and growing. Even senior scientific members with long tenures were leaving for other positions that offered either better incomes or more academic freedom.[30] As a centralized, hierarchical institution, it resembled the large university chemical institutes; most of the income and academic independence went to the one man at the top. Not surprisingly, the leading academic chemists, themselves beneficiaries of this system, remained generally silent on this point. Nevertheless two analytic chemists, Emil Heyn and Gustav Keppeler, did attack the project on other grounds, connected to intradisciplinary politics within chemistry and to the question of centralizing German scientific institutions.

Emil Heyn, head of the section for chemical analysis at the Prussian Materials Testing Office, collaborated with the director of that office, Adolf Martens, to produce two memoranda containing a scathing diatribe against the "alleged" scientific reformers behind the Imperial Institute. Invoking the shade of the late Clemens Winkler (1838–1904), an analytic chemist of the old school, they attacked the "representatives of the so-called 'physical-chemical' tendency" with its "questionable theories," who now sought to distort the "free" struggle of scientific opinions by buttressing their own side with "material and 'official' predominance." This diatribe against the physical chemists did bring out some basic truths in the situation. The Imperial Institute's proponents did seek academic reform, including greater emphasis for certain fields, and the Imperial Institute was a very indirect way to achieve it. "The memorandum's cry of distress over the lack of funds for individual academic laboratories ought logically to have been transferred into an energetic protest against those who withhold these funds," went Heyn and Martens's critique.[31]

Furthermore, both Ostwald and Nernst really must have seemed like upstarts to many of the older analytic chemists, who resented their insistence that chemical analysis should be more firmly based upon the theories and methods of physical chemistry. According to the memorandum on the Imperial Chemical Institute, "questions about the precision of the analytical methods proposed by various researchers [for determining atomic weights] have as yet been given practically no scientific treatment.

Despite the many determinations in the literature, it is generally impossible with them to distinguish the personal error of the experimenter from the systematic error of the method. The latter error, which alone must be known to evaluate the method, cannot be clearly established. . . . Only thorough scientific investigations"—possible only in an Imperial Institute, not in existing analytical laboratories whose heads were overburdened with routine work—"can achieve the goal of freeing any particular case of analysis from the arbitrariness which still necessarily besets so many analytical procedures."[32]

These contentions sparked the opposition of Gustav Keppeler, business manager of the Association of German Chemists and lecturer for chemistry at Darmstadt Technical College. In January 1907, with Gans present to encourage him, he presented a scathing report to the Association's Frankfurt local group. He denied the basic premise of the Imperial Institute project, that "teaching activity would preclude research at the same institution," and he attacked the applicability of its historical precedent. The Imperial Physical and Technical Institute might have been necessary during the eighties, when the newly founded electrotechnical laboratories at the colleges of technology had been unable to master the research problems arising from industry and the university physics institutes were "too remote from such tasks." The need for an Imperial Institute in physics was no longer so acute, however, and the situation was even less compelling in chemistry, with its academic-industrial ties and massive applied research facilities. "Rather let us further perfect the system which has arisen from the needs of the industries themselves."[33]

Keppeler did not deny that academic chemists currently neglected analytic chemistry, but he doubted that the institute would improve the situation. Like Heyn, he attributed the lack of academic analytic chemists to the field's lack of status in the universities. Keppeler correctly pointed out that, as compared to institute directors, the analytic section heads had far more routine teaching, less assistance, and fewer advanced students. An Imperial Institute would only further devastate the field of analytic chemistry by luring teachers away from the universities. Thus like Heyn he concluded that the solution was to funnel more support to analytic chemistry within existing academic institutions, and like Gans he argued for an Imperial research fund, not an Imperial Institute. His arguments were so reasonable that Carl Duisberg, as chairman of the Association of German Chemists, had to be dissuaded from suppressing Keppeler's report.[34]

What substantial arguments did the proponents of the Imperial Chemical Institute have in favor of centralization? Neither Fischer nor Ostwald ever raised or refuted Martius's accusation that the Imperial Institute plan was an attempt to end the time-honored German system of decentralized scientific facilities. Obviously, it was. "I would be the last to support centralization, if there were an alternative," Ostwald proclaimed. "But my honest and not easily won conviction is that in this case there is no other way." Only a central laboratory could concentrate energy on large-scale problems, only a research center could develop a tradition and a fund of "collective experience." A grants program, on the other hand, possessed the disadvantages to be seen in the recently established Carnegie Institution of the United States. Admittedly that institution had achieved much good, notably by supporting the atomic-weight determinations carried out by T. W. Richards at Harvard. Besides this there was much which to Ostwald looked good only on paper. Moreover, Carnegie grantees had often found their regular institutional support cut back, negating the benefit of the grants. Consequently the president of the Carnegie Institution had supposedly complained to Ostwald that the grants system produced relatively meager results at disproportionately high administrative costs. A program that had begun amid universal acclaim would now have to be "abandoned or at least severely curtailed" in favor of a larger, more centralized project.[35] Ostwald's assertion was correct. From 1904 to 1908 the Carnegie Institution did reduce its expenditures for smaller grants by more than two-thirds while increasing expenditures for a few "large projects" ninefold.[36]

Fischer similarly attacked Martius's proposed agency. Although it would at least distribute Imperial funds around the country, he implied that the ultimate effect would be insignificant compared with what an Imperial Institute would do to "maintain and raise the scientific prestige of German chemistry." Elaborating on his financial arguments, set forth in February, against academic research laboratories on the state level, Fischer argued that only a government with a tax base the size of Prussia's or the Reich's could hope to compete with the financial strength of the U.S. government and the conspicuous spending of the wealthiest American philanthropists.[37] The financial issue was clearly decisive, particularly because the Prussian government was not even prepared to support academic decentralization within its own system. The opponents of the Imperial Chemical Institute thus missed the point with their defense of decentralization and their observations that the best way to improve the state of analytic chemistry would have been simply to provide more money to existing academic institutions. With his fiscally dictated policy of concentrating resources for particular fields at particular institutions, Friedrich Althoff was deliberately undermining decentralization.[38] A centralized Imperial Chemical Institute, whose proponents promised to resolve all the presumed problems of analytic chemistry without requiring any more money for existing academic institutions, fitted perfectly into Althoff's policy. It is therefore time to take a closer look at the situation within the Imperial and state bureaucracies.

The Sources of Opposition within the Bureaucracy

Why should the Prusso-German bureaucracy have opposed the creation of a new bureaucratic institution? Certain agencies feared that a new institution would infringe on their responsibilities and draw off resources that might otherwise have gone to them; underlying and intensifying this fear was the fiscal and social conservatism of the financial authorities, both on the Imperial and on the state level. To them, moreover, an Imperial Chemical Institute represented a priority low enough to be safely ignored, particularly when its natural constituency, the chemical industry, was still relatively weak and internally divided.

The bureaucrat most fearful of an Imperial Chemical Institute was Adolf Martens, director of the Prussian Royal Materials Testing Office. A few years earlier, his agency had almost become an Imperial Institute for Mechanical Technology, but the smaller state governments had opposed it on behalf of their own agencies until the Imperial government's growing budget deficit finally killed the plan. Only then, in 1903, did the Prussian government give Martens's agency a stately, well-equipped new building.[39] Now Martens had no desire to see the president of another Imperial Institute assuming the role he himself had once coveted in vain. Although he was an engineer and not a chemist, he could not accept the idea that such an institution would be a "supreme court" of chemical analysis, and he thus worked against it with all the force he could muster.[40]

As early as October 1905, after receiving a copy of the memorandum proposing the Imperial Chemical Institute, Martens wrote to Fischer pointing out all the areas among its technical goals that already belonged to the Materials Testing Office's authorized field of activity.[41] Further encouraged by an early letter of support that Emil Ehrensberger wrote before Fischer was able to persuade him otherwise, Martens and Emil Heyn, head of his chemical testing section, undertook detailed criticisms of the project.[42] Besides the diatribe against physical chemistry discussed earlier, and the above-mentioned statement that a new institute would only duplicate existing government facilities, especially Martens's own, their critiques also pinpointed the Imperial Institute's sociopolitical function. "Must there be a 'president' for every science in the German Empire? . . . Should the development of German chemical research really depend upon whether it proceeds from a First-class or Fourth-class Councillor?"[43] Thus Martens attacked the efforts by the proponents to enhance the status of chemistry by enhancing the titles of its leading practitioners.

Martens wrote to his superiors in the Prussian Ministry of Education, which funded his agency, and to Ehrensberger as well as several other potential allies in business and government, including Brunck of the BASF. He received some sympathetic replies; but Brunck was irritated, while Ehrensberger, now under Emil Fischer's influence, merely secured for Martens a seat on the Select Committee.[44] At the public assembly in February 1906, Martens and Heyn were able to get Fischer and Nernst to limit the proposed functions of the Imperial Institute and to dispense with the idea of a chemical "supreme court," though the institute might still make judgmental analyses in areas where it had "earned an authoritative position."[45]

Despite the protests of Martens, it was unlikely that the Prussian Ministry of Education would oppose the proposal for an Imperial Chemical Institute. Friedrich Althoff's interest ensured at least some official support. Althoff saw the Imperial Chemical Institute as, first, an addition to the "scientific colony" that he had been trying to develop since the nineties in the Prussian crown lands of Dahlem, an area a short distance southwest of Berlin. This was a far cheaper way to expand the city's scientific institutions than buying land in the capital itself. Thus the Royal Botanical Garden had been located there, followed by the Imperial Biological Institute and the university's new Institute for Pharmaceutical Chemistry. The new laboratories of Martens's Materials Testing Office were not far away.[46] A second reason for Althoff to favor an Imperial Institute was of course that it promoted his policy of scientific concentration while avoiding the pressure on his own budget, which would have arisen had the proposal taken the form of a state-supported academic research laboratory. This point of view was also likely to commend the proposal to the Prussian finance minister, Baron Georg von Rheinbaben, who was a friend of Henry Böttinger, the commercial director of the Bayer dye firm. Böttinger accompanied Fischer and Nernst to their first audience with Rheinbaben in September 1906.[47]

The same financial reasoning that conditioned the Prussian bureaucracy's support implied the Imperial government's hostility to the proposal. Since 1903 the Imperial Treasury Office under Baron Hermann von Stengel had been wrestling unsuccessfully with the problem of the chronic Imperial deficit. Although the proponents of the Imperial Institute had hoped to share in the income from new tariffs, the return to protectionism under Bülow since 1902 had not solved the government's financial problems, in large part because it had not been designed to do so. Instead it had had a primarily political purpose, as part of the *Sammlungspolitik* that Bülow and the late Prussian Finance Minister Miquel had devised to reinforce the allegiance of the titans of agriculture, heavy industry, and the Catholic Center party. In conjunction with this policy, Bülow had, with the Kaiser's encouragement, arranged for considerable increases in military and naval spending in support of a more vigorous approach to overseas imperialism, designed to elevate the government's prestige and thus to weaken its domestic critics at both ends of the political spectrum: the patriotic left-liberals who otherwise might ally with the Social Democrats in support of internal reforms, and the radical nationalists on the right who attacked the government for weakness in foreign policy. In the process, however, it further aggravated the Imperial deficit, which in 1904 amounted to 24 million marks out of a budget of 36.3 billion marks.[48] While a deficit of less than one-tenth of one percent may seem innocuous enough by the standards of the 1980s, at the beginning of the century it was unacceptable. Without considerable improvement in the government's income, it would be scarcely possible to get the bureaucracy's approval for potentially expensive new projects that fell outside the principal priorities of the Imperial budget, i.e., expenditures for armaments and imperialism. These categories alone accounted for nine-tenths of the Imperial government's expenditures from the turn of the century to 1913.[49]

Could not the proposal have been included within this category of expenditures for "defense," though? Could not the military authorities suspect the strategic value that chemistry would have during a major war, just as chemists like Ostwald had already suspected when attempting to synthesize nitrates? Perhaps—but by emphasizing analytical rather than synthetic chemistry, the proposal focused attention on the goals least likely to be of military value. Even had the chemists tried to feature synthetics, the Prussian military authorities might have ignored them. It had taken these chemically unsophisticated officers a long time to be convinced that pure synthetic indigo, the German chemical industry's greatest triumph, actually contained the same coloring substance as natural indigo, a more expensive import of irregular quality. Emil Fischer joked that the synthetic color was "too beautiful" for the Prussian Army because it failed to match their standard uniform. It was not until 1902, five years after the BASF initially marketed indigo, that the Prussian general staff finally authorized its military use.[50]

The proponents of the institute may nevertheless have tried to interest the military by involving several representatives of the explosives and armaments industry. These included Ostwald's friend Wilhelm Will, director of the explosives industry's research center in Neu-Babelsberg, near Berlin, as well as of one chemical section of the official Military Testing Office in Jungfernheide, and of course Emil Ehrensberger. At Krupp, Ehrensberger directed an elaborate new scientific and technical testing facility, whose purpose was to develop new steel alloys for armor plate and weaponry.[51]

Despite the participation of some Imperial Naval officials, however, the Prussian Army's higher authorities were conspicuous by their absence from the General Committee. In view of the extreme status-consciousness of Prussian officers, they might well have been expected to leave matters like chemical science and technology to lower-level officials like Will.

There is no evidence that the proponents of the institute even attempted to contact the Prussian War Ministry or the Kaiser's Military Cabinet. Even had the social barriers not existed, these agencies would hardly have welcomed overtures from the chemists. For Graf Schlieffen, retiring chief of the Prussian General Staff, had just prepared his military "testament," detailing his plan for a lightning victory in the West. His premise—surely reinforced by the specter of the Russian collapse and revolution of 1905, and by the Kaiser's nervousness about domestic socialist opposition to a war—was "that a modern war must not be long drawn out because it ruins the highly developed industrial economy of the participants." Since Schlieffen's original plans did not even take the problem of a British naval blockade into consideration, despite requiring that German forces over-run neutral Dutch and Belgian territory,[52] it is hardly surprising that the high command would have shown little interest in a proposal for a chemical research laboratory project whose principal military function would have been to offset the effects of a long, ruinous, modern war. Despite protests by German naval leaders of the economic dangers posed by the Schlieffen plan, the military leadership apparently did little to mitigate these dangers before 1911.[53]

Thus in 1905–6 little support was to be expected from the military bureaucracy for an Imperial Chemical Institute. Nor did the budget situation improve as much as its proponents had hoped. During this period Stengel attempted to carry through a "finance reform" designed to open new sources of income for the Imperial government and to put the government's finances on a sound basis. He did succeed in winning approval for the largest increase in taxes since 1879, but the "reform" as such was largely ineffective. After a single year's surplus in 1905, largely resulting from the initial impact of the tariff increase, there were repeated budget deficits increasing from 45.5 million marks in 1906 to 238.2 million marks in 1908, by which time an economic recession had further compounded the problem.[54] Under these circumstances the proponents of the Imperial Chemical Institute could hardly persuade the government to accept it.

One might wonder why the effect of the chemical industry on the Imperial balance of trade did not produce a greater political-economic impact on the government, since after all the development of synthetics was steadily reducing Germany's chronic trade deficit. Nevertheless, in 1900 the chemical industry's overall contribution to that end was still much less than either the ferric metals or the machine industry's. Despite the rapid growth of chemical exports, the positive trade balance of this industry would remain lower than either of the others as late as 1913 (see table 4-1).

From the government's perspective, moreover, the dye industry up to 1907 remained a peripheral branch of the German economy in terms of its

Table 4-1. Share of Selected Branches in German Foreign Trade, 1900–1913 (in millions of marks)

Year	Branch	Imports	Exports	Trade Balance
1900	Iron and steel	120	480	+ 360
	Nonelectrical machinery	80	200	+ 120
	Chemicals	260	340	+ 80
	All foreign trade	5,840	4,560	− 1,280
1913	Iron and steel	100	1,340	+ 1,240
	Nonelectrical machinery	80	680	+ 600
	Chemicals	440	1,000	+ 560
	All foreign trade	11,120	10,180	− 940

Changes, 1900–1913	Absolute	%	Absolute	%	Absolute	%
Iron and steel	− 20	(− 17)	+ 860	(+ 179)	+ 880	(+ 244)
Nonelectrical machinery	No change		+ 480	(+ 240)	+ 480	(+ 400)
Chemicals	+ 180	(+ 69)	+ 660	(+ 194)	+ 480	(+ 600)
All foreign trade	+ 5,280	(+ 90)	+ 5,620	(+ 123)	+ 340	(+ 27)

Source: L. F. Haber, *Chemical Industry, 1900–1913*, p. 109; figures converted into marks, not adjusted for inflation (approximately 10 percent during this period).

share in total employment. Even considering the unquestionable dynamism of the dye firms, the chemical industry as a whole accounted for less than 1 percent of the German labor force, an insignificant proportion compared with either agriculture or heavy industry, which were by far the dominant branches of the German economy. Even if the figures in the chemical industry were enlarged by adding the employees of the German Potash Syndicate, most of whom were included in the mining group, the chemical industry would be far from dominating the employment patterns in Imperial Germany. Moreover, the chemical industry as a whole, whose employment had increased by about half again since 1895, was not even growing faster than the equally innovative machine industry, which had nearly doubled its labor force during the same period (see table 4-2). Yet the machine industry's attempt to obtain an Imperial Institute for itself had already failed.

Of course, one could account for the slow growth of the labor force in the technologically intensive chemical industry by pointing to its disproportionate increases in productivity. It has been estimated that at the turn of the century the chemical industry's total domestic production was about one billion marks, or about 3 percent of the German net national product

Table 4-2. Employment Trends in Agriculture, Heavy Industry, Machines, and Chemicals, 1895–1907 (in hundreds of thousands of persons, with percentage of total employment in parentheses; bottom line shows percentage change in employment, 1895–1907)

Year	Total Economy	Agriculture	Heavy Industry[a]	Machines	Chemicals
1895	240.5 (100)	102.4 (43)	17.3 (7)	5.8 (2)	1.15 (.5)
1907	280.8 (100)	98.8 (35)	23.9 (9)	11.2 (4)	1.72 (.6)
Change	+ 40.3 (+ 17)	− 3.6 (− 4)	+ 6.6 (+ 38)	+ 5.4 (+ 93)	+ .57 (+ 49)

Sources: Imperial Occupational Census Data for 1895 and 1907, industrial figures summarized in *Statistik des Deutschen Reichs*, 221:62; corrected agricultural figures in Tipton, *Regional Variations*, pp. 82, 152–62.
[a]Sum of census categories III (mining, etc.), IV (industry of stones and earths), and V (metalworking).

of more than 32 billion marks. That was six times its share in the labor force. In contrast, the labor-intensive, technologically backward agricultural sector, with some 40 percent of the labor force, produced only about one-quarter of the net national product.[55] That logic would suggest, however, that the chemical industry had no need for assistance from the government, certainly not in regard to scientific research.

That also appears to have been the line taken by the most determined opponent of the proposed Imperial Institute, Martius, whose personal connection in the Imperial Treasury Office evidently guaranteed him a friendly hearing there. Indeed Martius might reasonably have expected that his own idea for a commercial and technical authority, with its emphasis on regulation rather than research, would have better fitted the established pattern of scientific agencies in Imperial Germany.[56] Instead the Imperial bureaucracy took the division within the chemical industry, and the absence of strong support by either heavy industry or the major agrarian interests, as a signal for inaction on either proposal. Thus, rather than rejecting outright the proposed Imperial Institute, which had been endorsed by some of the leading scientists and businessmen in the nation, the Imperial government presented the proponents with a series of delays and increasing financial demands.

Before Martius had published his first attack, Chancellor Bernhard von Bülow had invited Fischer to an audience that produced no definite results.[57] After the formal petitions were submitted to the chancellor and to Secretaries Arthur von Posadowsky-Wehner of the Interior Office and Hermann von Stengel of the Treasury Office, Fischer complained to Althoff that Bülow's illness prevented him from taking positive action.[58]

After seeing Posadowsky's subordinate, Theodor Lewald, at the end of June, Fischer decided not to seek formal audiences with either Posadowsky or Stengel until fall.[59]

Lewald, whose administrative responsibilities included chairing the curatorium of the Imperial Physical and Technical Institute, had told Fischer that before the Imperial government could consider subsidizing the annual budget of an Imperial Chemical Institute, industry must demonstrate its interest in the plan by providing both the site and all of the initial capital costs, i.e., 1.6 million marks as estimated in the memorandum.[60] Well before the economic recession of 1907–8 had placed its budget under severe pressure, the government supplemented this demand through a new policy for salaries in the Imperial Institute. In view of the criticisms made of the low salaries in the Physical and Technical Institute, the government expected the chemists to ask for a higher salary level, not just for the president but for his section heads, whose positions were to be competitive with those of full professors, perhaps even those of first-rate industrial chemists. That would certainly make the Imperial Institute the nation's and probably the world's most prestigious scientific research institution. Unfortunately, the government was not prepared to offer salaries that its own administrative bureaucrats did not receive. As Posadowsky told the Reichstag in the spring of 1907, "Prominent chemists receive salaries in industry that you would never approve and we cannot, with regard to the other official categories." Posadowsky's solution was to have a staff composed of very few permanent bureaucrats.[61] Instead, most researchers would work at the institute for a limited time to accomplish set tasks. Their salaries would come not from the government but from an industrial endowment fund to be collected in addition to the building fund. Donors would be guaranteed some influence on the institute through the curatorium's power to administer the endowment fund; and groups like the supporters of Max Delbrück's Institute for Commercial Fermentation, whose "statutes" precluded their making capital contributions, could also take part by providing long-term, annual subsidies for "particular research areas."[62] Thus, including the salaries fund, which was to total 2 million marks, a total of 3.6 million marks had to come from private sources.

Here was the Imperial government's reply to Carl Duisberg's "demand" of February 1906.[63] If the chemical industry really wanted an Imperial Chemical Institute, if it really believed that there must be a "president of chemistry" in Germany, then it must be prepared to pay virtually the entire cost of building and maintaining the institution. Fischer and his friends had hardly expected to have to appeal to the chemical industry for more than about half a million marks, the same value as the land Werner von Siemens had once donated to establish the Imperial Physical and

Technical Institute; but the Imperial government had learned its lesson from that; with chemistry there would be no Trojan horse. In one sense the demands were not unreasonable. With Althoff's support the land could be had from the Prussian government, and Ostwald himself had suggested the idea of a fluctuating staff to avoid bureaucratic ossification.[64] But who would donate several million marks for an institution that the Imperial government had not even conditionally accepted?

The fund-raising efforts in the chemical industry and the organization to which they led, the Imperial Chemical Institute Association, are described in the next chapter. Before examining them, I will consider briefly, in conclusion, the significance of the industrial, bureaucratic, and scientific opposition to the proposed Imperial Chemical Institute.

First, the fact that no full professors of chemistry opposed this plan is significant. As an Imperial institution, and one with no connection to teaching or to existing academic institutions, it did not threaten any of their interests and might even offer them a position free from the high enrollments that then overwhelmed them all. One of them might also become a new "president of German chemistry." The full professors who did criticize the plan, Stutzer and Delbrück, each spoke in part as representatives of related disciplines that could not expect direct benefits, in part as representatives of East-Elbian agrarian interests. These took a dim view of the creation of new Imperial institutions in any case, but an especially dim view of institutions that might be controlled by people like the leaders of the chemical industry, some of whom were liberals and others Jews—albeit rather moderate in the first case and usually converts in the second. Delbrück took credit for the Office of the Interior's decision in 1907 to increase its demands for industrial contributions, which suggests the degree of influence which the agricultural interest groups had on the Imperial bureaucracy.[65] The new plan seems designed to force the chemical industry to offer a share in control to the agricultural-industrial interest groups, and to those in heavy industry as well, if either were interested.

Because similar conservatism marked heavy industry as compared to the chemical industry, however, it is not surprising that the leaders of heavy industry showed no more enthusiasm for the project than did the agrarians. Instead, both heavy industry and agriculture displayed a kind of provincialism, demanding that any new scientific research institution be created in their own region and placed under their own control.

The attitude of Heyn and Keppeler, the two analytic chemists, also reflects disciplinary as well as institutional conservatism. In their case, however, the demand that more support be channeled to existing institutions hits at a central problem with the entire enterprise. If it were really to "reform" German academic institutions, it must approach those institutions directly. Nevertheless, Fischer and his friends evidently realized that a direct approach to university reform would be extremely costly and difficult, besides alienating many of their potential allies among the full professors.

Besides, a direct effort to effect reforms in or supply more funds to existing academic institutions would not necessarily have accomplished Nernst and Ostwald's goal of promoting physical chemistry through analytic chemistry. Nor would it have definitely avoided the opposition from Martius and Gans within the chemical industry. These opponents may have argued in favor of the decentralization of research and so on, but they opposed the project more for political and economic than scientific considerations.

The attitudes of the various members of the bureaucracy in opposition were comparatively straightforward. Martens did not want any more institutional competition, while the Imperial government did not want to spend money for purposes that did not obviously fall among its major political priorities. Although the chemists made at least a muted appeal to the military authorities, they were still far from identifying the needs of their science with national defense or imperialism, and in any case the Prussian general staff was thinking along completely different strategic lines.

The chemists' ideal, which had also been Werner von Siemens's ideal, was a central, Imperial institution pursuing scientific research in areas that promised to produce results of general value to industry. Their assumption, which to some extent was also Friedrich Althoff's assumption, was that competition among different firms and branches of industry and among the different constituent states of the German Empire should be disregarded in the face of international economic and scientific competition. Those views made them modernizers. Their opponents, very different in position and political ideology, were united by a commitment to the German tradition of decentralization, whose alleged obsolescence they refused to concede.

5

How and Where Are We Going to Collect Such Great Sums?: The Imperial Institute Association as Investment in Research

How and where are we going to collect such great sums? A great deal of water is going to run down the Spree before the requisite donors have gathered in sufficient numbers.
—Carl Duisberg, March 1907

Standstill means retreat. . . . In the peaceful competition of nations, Germany can conquer only in the sign of scientific and industrial progress. . . . With the great sums that must be raised to provide armaments for a possible war, one ought not to shrink from small expenditures on facilities for a peaceful contest.
—Ernst Beckmann, *On the Establishment of an Imperial Chemical Institute*, 1908

Potential Motivations for Private Supporters of the Imperial Institute: Investment vs. Philanthropy

As Emil Fischer later acknowledged, the opposition of Carl von Martius and his allies had shattered any hopes for a major government subsidy to the Imperial Institute.[1] The rhetoric of professional prestige, national interest, and academic reform alone could not unite the German chemical community; a scientific program promising something to everyone, but most of all to the physical chemists, could not help but raise a multisided opposition. Against that, Fischer would have needed a powerful and influential ally like Werner von Siemens, who had forced the Imperial Physical and Technical Institute past its bureaucratic obstacles.[2] How, and how effectively, Fischer and his friends sought support in the absence of a Siemens offers an illuminating perspective on Imperial Germany's social priorities regarding science, and thus on the modernity of the German social structure.

The Imperial bureaucracy had demanded that the Imperial Chemical Institute project be financed largely through private means, but it had not created any financial incentives like tax deductions for charitable or philanthropic contributions. It even maintained a disincentive, a tax of five percent on gifts even to private, nonprofit organizations.[3] What then was the likelihood of obtaining funds from industrial or philanthropic sources, and what would be the effect of relying on one or the other? Granting the complexity of any donor's motives, one might still expect corporate support to be justified by eventual profits. Profits there might be, even if one accepted Duisberg's argument that improvements in quantitative precision and in generally applicable analytic methods might not reward an individual firm with patentable innovations. The rewards could be indirect, as this type of research made economic sense for the entire industry.

Even so, were the leaders of the chemical industry willing to pay for an Imperial Institute? The existing plan did not establish a definite relationship between financial support, administrative and scientific control, and the apportionment of industrially beneficial results. In an industry still disorganized, heterogeneous, and competitive, how many firms would risk investing large sums in so vague an enterprise without a guarantee of some return, especially since the big dye concerns, and Duisberg's Triple Alliance in particular, seemed likely to control it and thus reap the lion's share of the benefits? There was also the question of business conditions. The high profits of the 1905–6 boom period, enlarged by brisk sales of strategic chemicals during the Russo-Japanese War, made it an ideal time for the institute's proponents to ask for industrial support; but generosity among the businessmen could vanish with the first cloud on the economic horizon, like the financial panic of 1907. That ushered in a recession that was brief but sharply felt in the chemical industry.[4] Finally, Duisberg and the other leaders of the Triple Alliance had demanded that the taxpayers shoulder most of the expense and risk of the undertaking while leaving as much as possible of the control and benefits to industry.[5]

In the emerging contest of wills between bureaucracy and industry, as well as between contending industrial factions, the chief loser would be the Imperial Institute and its academic proponents. But perhaps the deficits could be made up from philanthropy, which is not to be confused with pure generosity. In his "Gospel of Wealth," Andrew Carnegie preached philanthropy as a way to defeat socialism and "bind together the rich and poor in harmonious relationship." Yet his priorities included contributions to academic institutions, which might bind together rich businessmen and "poor" scholars, of course, but provide only indirect benefits to the truly poor.[6] In this case a likelier effect of philanthropy would be social status.

One of Carnegie's contemporaries, Thorstein Veblen, included a brief reference to "pure" patronage in his Theory of the Leisure Class, a devastating analysis of the atavistic "pecuniary culture" of the American business elite. Veblen portrayed the chief beneficiaries of industrialization paradoxically flaunting preindustrial symbols of status like "conspicuous consumption" and "conspicuous leisure." Traditional "higher" or "pure" academic institutions evoked a particularly grand aura of conspicuous leisure that the wealthy could promote and vicariously share through patronage, which in turn exemplified a form of conspicuous consumption dictated perhaps by little or no expectation of practical economic gain.[7]

Questionable as these characterizations may be in the American case, they apply particularly well to Imperial Germany, in which industrialization had not overthrown the preindustrial social structure. Veblen's German contemporaries Werner Sombart and Max Weber accused the German industrial and business elite of failing to achieve bourgeois class solidarity and of wanting only to be absorbed into the aristocracy, the easiest path to individual political power and social status.[8] From the 1890s on, it was understood in Berlin that suitable acceptance of aristocratic values, including the exercise of patronage, would be fittingly rewarded by status in the form of official honors and titles.[9] These took the place of the missing financial incentives to patronage, which in turn eased the strain on the official budget. Given bureaucratic willingness to cooperate, therefore, the Imperial Institute's academic proponents could offer social as well as economic incentives to potential contributors. While the old Prussian aristocracy understandably reacted little to social incentives, they could have a strong effect on other potential philanthropists, especially Jews or those of Jewish descent.

Jews did not face legal restrictions in Imperial Germany, but as in many other countries they did face discrimination that varied according to profession, social rank, and even region; moreover, the form and intensity of anti-Semitism had distinctly changed during the decades since 1871. At the height of classical liberalism, during the early years of the Empire, especially in Berlin, many Jews had abandoned their traditional faith and often intermarried with gentiles. Many chose the path of conversion for the social advantage that often came with it.[10]

As racist thinking became more and more fashionable toward the end of the century, however, conversion afforded a less and less secure solution to the social problem confronting Jews. The bourgeois Jewish community chiefly hoped that the principal difference between themselves and other Germans would be seen as confessional rather than racial or social. Such German Jews, while no doubt sympathetic to the plight of Eastern European Jews whose flight from Czarist persecution took them to Imperial Germany during this period, nevertheless appear to have taken pains to distinguish themselves from their much poorer and less "cultured" coreligionists.[11]

Most converts and descendants of converts, under even greater pressure to identify with the Germanism they had embraced, became models of social conventions.[12] Conspicuous philanthropy could help to reinforce their German identity. Wilhelm II and the Prusso-German bureaucracy gladly offered such philanthropists just enough recognition to encourage them to repeat their generosity.[13] The Jewish tradition of family-owned banks and partnerships had tended to concentrate wealth, whereas gentiles had been more likely to become shareholders in giant corporations that distributed their earnings more widely. Hence wealthy assimilated Jews and converts, who were especially plentiful in Berlin but also to be found in Western cities like Frankfurt, seemed outstanding candidates for philanthropic appeals.[14] For those with ties to the chemical industry, social advantages could reinforce economic incentives. As early as February 1906, Nernst had considered Fritz Friedländer, one of the richest men in the country with a fortune of some 40 million marks, as a potential donor to the Imperial Institute. Friedländer was of Jewish descent and one of the very few commoners among the wealthy men with large holdings in Upper Silesian mining and heavy industry; he also controlled a chemical corporation in Berlin. Thus, "for a *title* he might well be had."[15] The official policy, Fischer eventually found, was to avoid the appearance of a trade in ennobling philanthropists. Nevertheless bureaucrats did tend to propose titles for those whose patronage was assured, provided they were otherwise "honorable" men.[16]

Unfortunately the advocates of the Imperial Institute could not count on the bureaucracy to cooperate with titles. Another possibility arose when Nernst and Ostwald met Ludwig Mond in Rome at the International Congress for Applied Chemistry in early May 1906. Mond was a German-Jewish immigrant who had made his fortune in the British chemical industry as cofounder of Brunner, Mond, one of the pioneer manufacturers of alkalis according to the Solvay process. Mond had endowed the Davy-Faraday Laboratory at the Royal Institution in London, and as he approached the end of his life he thought of benefiting science in his original homeland. Thus when informed about the Imperial Institute plan, Mond offered to give a large sum if four or five other philanthropists in Germany came forward to produce a total of one to two million marks. Although that would have met the Imperial government's demand at the time, Nernst rightly thought it would be hard to find such magnanimous benefactors in Germany.[17]

Mond's offer to contribute introduced an element of international cooperation that further complicated the project. The planners now could not afford to use the chauvinistic rhetoric that might otherwise have lent itself to recruiting support in Imperial Germany alone. Of course, by playing up the United States as the chief competitive danger, one had only slightly to modify the original rhetoric in order to address other Europeans. Besides, even an institution with an international character could be viewed as fulfilling German ambitions to organize and lead an eventual European federation.[18]

Clearly, however, it was not a matter of indifference which type of funding predominated. If the institute was to be funded chiefly by the Imperial government, one would have to justify the laboratory's economic benefits in general terms only; this had been the original plan. If it was to be looked upon mainly as an economic investment by chemical corporations, those providing the bulk of the funds would expect at least some direct financial returns, to guarantee which they would naturally want to exercise some control over the research to be done. Philanthropic sources would allow for greater flexibility and the least emphasis on direct economic returns, but in general they could not be recruited without the active cooperation of the government bureaucracy. That, unfortunately, still remained questionable.

Testing the Limits of "Jewish Money" and Corporate Benevolence, 1906–1907

With the preceding considerations at least in part consciously in mind, Fischer and Nernst set out in 1906 to collect the construction costs for the Imperial Chemical Institute. They decided to reduce their estimate to 1.5 million marks and ask the chemical industry for a half-million of this, the rest to be obtained, as Ludwig Mond had suggested, from a few wealthy patrons.

At the 1906 convention of the Chemical Industry Association, Franz Oppenheim, a director of Agfa, announced that his Triple Alliance would set a scale of contributions to the project by their own example (the basis was one percent of the net profits or dividends paid during 1905, which worked out to roughly 145,00 to 500,000 marks for the three firms, or 65,000 each for Bayer and the BASF and 20,000 for Agfa).[19] If every member of the association cooperated, construction could begin in 1908, when the Imperial government was expected to begin supporting the project. The fund-raising committee then elected was dominated by the big concerns: Oppenheim, Böttinger, and (probably Karl) Müller from the Triple Alliance, Lepsius from Griesheim-Elektron, and Gustav von Brüning from Hoechst, besides a single representative of a smaller firm, and the general secretary of the Industry Association (later they also brought in Max Delbrück of the Institute for Commercial Fermentation).[20] Oppenheim became chairman of the new committee and henceforth dominated the financial affairs of the Imperial Institute project.

By October Mond had confirmed to Nernst his intention to donate 200,000 marks.[21] Having succeeded with one Jewish chemical manufacturer, Fischer turned to another Jewish family firm. The Cassella firm in

Frankfurt/Main had until recently been the private partnership of Leo Gans and the Weinberg brothers, Carl and Arthur. Like Franz Oppenheim, they were all apparently well-assimilated, baptized Jews (Leo Gans was related to the Eduard Gans who had taught Karl Marx in Berlin; Arthur von Weinberg, ennobled by Wilhelm II, would die in Theresienstadt). The collective wealth of Gans and the Weinbergs was at least 53 million marks in 1908, perhaps the largest fortune from purely industrial (as opposed to banking or commercial) sources amassed by people of Jewish descent in Germany. In the belief that Oppenheim could persuade the Cassella people to endow the institute, Fischer confided to Nernst that they could probably rely primarily upon "Jewish money."[22] Among the gentile capitalists, the Krupps seemed to be the best prospects.[23]

Fischer realized that his assumption was wildly optimistic when Leo Gans joined Carl Martius in intransigent opposition to the project. As discussed earlier, Gans tried to persuade the Hoechst directors to withhold their contribution in order to fight the Triple Alliance. Arthur von Weinberg followed up by telling Hoechst that subsidies for Paul Ehrlich's research would be "placed to incomparably better advantage . . . than our endowments for the Imperial Institute."[24] Ehrlich was in the first place a Jewish scientist working in Frankfurt, whose research on chemotherapy did later produce salvarsan, a useful treatment for syphilis. Although Hoechst reopened its contractual relationship with Ehrlich in 1907, Gustav von Brüning and his colleagues also offered 60,000 marks to the Imperial Institute fund after conferring with Fischer, who as their business partner possessed leverage not to be neglected.[25] Fischer and Nernst failed to reach a similar agreement with Gans, whose firm had set aside an equal amount for "the purposes to be promoted by the Imperial Institute," but not for the institute itself.[26]

Although the industry's goal of 500,000 marks in contributions was realistic, given a conservative estimate of half a billion marks in gross productivity for the other branches and a minimum net profit of 5 percent,[27] it did not take into account the degree of apathy in the industry, the opposition engendered by Martius and Gans, or the oncoming recession of 1907. Thus by September 1907, only some sixty-five different individuals and companies had agreed to contribute a total of about 380,000 marks, of which only forty grants were as much as one thousand marks or more (table 5-1). The mighty Potash Syndicate offered only 500 marks, and several major firms offered nothing at all. Thus, at the convention of the Chemical Industry Association, Duisberg harshly criticized Leo Gans, but the same convention made Gans an honorary member, which suggests the sentiment in his favor.[28]

By this time the government had raised its expectations for industrial

Table 5-1. Firms in the Chemical Industry Association Offering Contributions to the Imperial Chemical Institute Project, ca. September 1907

Firm	Marks Contributed	Representation[a]
Principal Contributors		
Dye concerns		
Triple Alliance	160,000	(F, 3 members; S, 4 members)
Agfa	20,000	
Agfa Aufsichtsrat and Directorate	20,000	
BASF	60,000	
Bayer	60,000	
Hoechst	60,000	(F, 1 member; G, 1 member)
Soda industry: Deutsche Solvay-Werke AG	50,000	(G, 1 member?)
Nobel Dynamite Trust	20,720	(G, 1 member)
Deutsche Sprengstoff AG	2,000	
Dresdner Dynamitfabrik	1,200	
Dynamit-AG vorm. Alfred Nobel & Co.	15,000	
Rheinische Dynamitfabrik	2,520	
Electrochemical concerns		
Griesheim-Elektron (incl. 500 marks from subsidiary Elektrochemische Werke GmbH)	15,500	(F, 1 member; G, 2 members)
Total	*306,220*	
Mid-Range Contributors (1,000–5,000 marks)		
Heavy chemicals, metals		
Allgemeine Thermit-GmbH (Dr. M. Goldschmidt)	3,000	
Chemische Fabrik Kalk, GmbH	5,000	
Chemische Fabrik Rhenania	4,000	
Duisburger Kupferhütte	5,000	
W. C. Heraeus	5,000	(S, 1 member)
Kunheim & Co.	5,000	
Pharmaceuticals, organic preparations		
Pharma IG	5,000	(F, 1 member)
C. F. Böhringer & Söhne	1,500	(S, 1 member)
Gehe & Co. AG	500	
Knoll & Co.	1,000	
E. Merck	2,000	
Chemische Fabrik vorm. Goldenberg, Geromont & Co.	1,000	
(miscellaneous organics)		
Kalle & Co. (also dyes)	3,500	

Table 5-1. Continued

Firm	Marks Contributed	Representation[a]
Oil industry		
AG für Petroleum-Industrie	1,000	
AG für Theer- und Erdöl-Industrie	3,000	(G, 1 member)
Petroleum-Raffinerie vorm August Korff	1,000	
Verein für Mineralöl-Industrie	1,500	
Gunpowder producers		
Vereinigte Köln-Rottweiler Pulverfabriken (Powder Group)	5,000	
Sprengstoff AG Carbonit (Powder Group?)	1,200	
Perfumes, essential oils		
Haarmann & Reimer	3,000	(G, 1 member)
Schimmel & Co.	1,000	
Organic intermediates (for dyes, explosives)		
Chemische Fabriken vorm. Weiler-ter Meer	3,000	
Inorganic preparations		
Chemische Fabrik Hönningen vorm Walther Feld & Co. AG	2,000	
R. Wedekind & Co. GmbH	1,000	
Rudolf Koepp & Co.	1,000	
Product unidentified (5 contributors)	8,500	
Total	*68,700*	
Lowest-Range Contributors (below 1,000 marks)		
Heavy chemicals, fertilizers		
Kaliwerke Aschersleben (Potash Syndicate)	500	
Chemische Fabrik AG vorm Karl Scharff & Co.	500	
Norddeutsche Chemische Fabrik	500	
Inorganic preparations, organic preparations		
Joh. Diedrich Bieber (inorganic)	500	
J. Hauff & Co., GmbH, (inorganic)	750	
Chemische Fabrik Cott, E. Heuer (organic)	200	
Product unidentified (18 contributors)	4,435	
Total	*7,385*	
Total, all 65 contributors	*382,305*	

Sources: "Verzeichnis derjenigen Firmen, welche einen Beitrag für die Errichtung einer chemischen Reichsanstalt gezeichnet haben" (no date), p. 1, HA VCR; note that the total given here is only 382,305 marks, 1,000 marks less than that announced in *Chemische Industrie* 30 (1907): 492–94.
   [a]F = represented in Fund-Raising Committee; S = represented in Select Committee; G = represented in General Committee.

support by demanding an additional endowment fund of two million marks, to be collected "without regard to the question of who is to bear the costs of building and maintaining the institution."[29] As Posadowsky later explained to the Reichstag, the Imperial Institute should be "a kind of cross between a private and an Imperial institution."[30] But Carl Duisberg, who had recently become a member of the Select Committee, probably spoke for all the businessmen who supported the project when he complained to Delbrück, "How and where are we going to collect such great sums? A great deal of water is going to run down the Spree before the requisite donors have gathered in sufficient numbers with the necessary openness."[31]

The results of Fischer's appeals for philanthropy confirmed Duisberg's pessimism. Aside from Mond, the only ones willing to contribute a large sum were the Krupps, who offered only 100,000 marks, and Rudolf Koch (director of the Deutsche Bank), who shied away when no title was forthcoming in return.[32] After Fischer's desperate appeals to the Ruhr coal magnates for philanthropic support also produced no definite offers, Max Delbrück took the initiative.[33] In mid-June 1907 he contacted Fischer and Nernst with a new plan to get around the two million mark endowment requirement.[34] Only one million need be collected if his old standby, annual contributions, be permitted to replace the interest from the missing million. "The Imperial Office of the Interior has completely come over to my point of view," he had told Duisberg in March.[35] The new conditions, he later happily observed, forced the institute's academic supporters into an entirely new position. "Until the Office of the Interior worked itself up to a declaration Nernst, Fischer, and Ostwald, but especially Nernst, counted little on the definite participation of a curatorium in connection with monetary payments."[36]

Delbrück's new plan called for the founding of an "Imperial Institute Association," in effect a kind of joint-stock company for research. Votes in this association would be apportioned, like shares of stock, according to the amount invested; the biggest contributors would gain effective control over the work of the Imperial Institute, and the motivation for contributing would shift decisively from the philanthropic ideal, conditioned by hopes for traditional social status, to the more modern, economically conditioned idea of investment in research with the expectation of practical control and a profitable return.

Before embracing the new organization, Fischer and Nernst again approached the Imperial bureaucracy. In September 1907 they met with Theobald von Bethmann-Hollweg, who had replaced Posadowsky at the Office of the Interior. They found Bethmann prepared to pay only the president's salary, no more. "As he learned that we expect a considerably larger annual subsidy from the Reich, he became very reserved. In that case, he declared, we should first collect two million in bar and then come back." They pleaded for at least a written assurance that Bethmann would support their cause once they had collected the two million. He was "inclined" to do so, and they left in the hope of soon receiving some definite encouragement. None was forthcoming.[37]

Bethmann-Hollweg did forward to State Treasury Secretary von Stengel the draft of a declaration to Fischer, whereby the government would offer to support an Imperial Institute along the lines Fischer wanted, once the two million marks had been collected and the Prussian government had provided the land.[38] Stengel disapproved, holding firm even when Bethmann forwarded and endorsed a new plea from Fischer for official assurance that might sustain a new round of fund raising and secure the pledges already made. The Reich could not fund an Institute either in 1909 or 1910, Stengel insisted, but perhaps later. In the meantime the "chemical interests" were wealthy enough not only to collect two million marks but also to provide an "appropriate quota" toward the long-term operation of the institution. The Imperial Institute would then have to develop "within the limits of the necessary and in accord with the actual interests of the chemical industry."[39] Bethmann apparently never relayed this reply to Fischer, but with Bethmann's silence it became clear that Delbrück's plan was the only alternative.

The Imperial Chemical Institute Association: A Joint-Stock Company for Investment in Scientific Research

As December 1907 arrived with no official assurances, Fischer, Nernst, and Ernst Beckmann thought to pressure Bethmann-Hollweg with the "weightier influence" of the chemical industry and its "other means" of persuasion. In view of "the Reich's miserable financial circumstances," Duisberg was not encouraging, but he offered to approach his wife's uncle, Baron von Gamp-Massaunen, the Free Conservative leader who was chairman of the tax committee in the Reichstag.[40]

Duisberg first arranged a meeting between himself, Fischer, and Max Delbrück, who proposed the following plan of action: an Imperial Chemical Institute Association must be constituted whether or not Bethmann produced a guarantee of support for the project; fifty thousand marks in annual dues, representing fifty votes, should be collected by August 1, 1908; by that time the association should have prepared detailed plans and cost estimates for the proposed institute. It would also provide up to one million marks in endowment; every 25,000 marks of capital meant one vote, and every 1,000 marks of annual dues, also one vote, with a maximum of ten votes per member. The chemical industry would thereby have sufficiently demonstrated the sincerity of its interest in the Imperial Institute to get funding for the proposal in the Imperial budget of 1909; they hoped for an annual subsidy of 150,000 marks and a construction capital of 1.5 million.[41]

Duisberg's response to the new situation was simple. Regarding the statutes for what he now called the "technical institute," Duisberg wrote Fischer and Delbrück: "I urgently recommend bringing in industry more and physical chemistry less."[42] Two weeks later, Wilhelm Ostwald resigned from the Select Committee for the Imperial Institute. Ernst Beckmann, the applied chemist, took the physical chemist's place, in a possibly coincidental manifestation of Duisberg's recommendation. Ostwald later explained in his memoirs that the institution would not have accomplished what he had intended, presumably to promote physical chemistry in the universities.[43]

Despite some opposition—for example, from Merck, who resented the government's assumption that "the rich chemical industry can pay"—the Select Committee approved Delbrück's draft statutes for the new Association.[44] Fischer, Nernst, Oppenheim, and Delbrück then revised them. The legal form of the proposed Association presented some problems. Although in essence Delbrück had proposed a joint-stock company for research, with the votes equivalent to shares, the dignity of academic science did not lend itself to commercial incorporation. Worse, the taxes would have been far too high—30,000 marks to set up. The appropriate choice was the "registered association," but in that case the duration of membership was limited to two years, too short a period to please the government. At least five years of dues could be guaranteed, however, by establishing as the minimum share an "entry fee" that equaled five years' worth of dues but did not depend upon the actual length of membership.[45] The legal requirements for this type of association also resulted in a small managing directorate with a larger "council of directors" (similar to a corporate council of supervisors), which was intended to become the curatorium (or board) of the institute. It was to approve the annual operations plan and the applications of research results (implying a control over patents).[46]

The new approach met with initial skepticism even within Duisberg's Triple Alliance; the BASF, whose directors evidently still saw the institute as a chiefly academic, "pure-scientific" institution, argued "that it is actually not legally permissible for a joint-stock company to enter into obligations of this type for such a long period, all the more as we can hardly expect equivalent benefits from them." Their participation came reluctantly, in deference to "prominent scientific authorities," especially Fischer.[47]

Fischer responded by emphasizing that industry would dominate the association and through it "exert a considerable influence on the practical leadership of the institute."[48] Although he and Nernst wanted the businessmen to take the lead in the new association, the two academic chemists were nevertheless persuaded to accept the first two positions in the directorate with Oppenheim as treasurer.[49] "We three," Fischer assured Duisberg, "will naturally do nothing unacceptable to the council of directors."[50]

Thus the old General Committee dissolved itself on March 7 to make way for the Imperial Chemical Institute Association.[51] The council of directors, elected at the same time, consisted of four directors of the Triple Alliance (Böttinger, Brunck, Oppenheim, and Duisberg), Brüning of Hoechst (who had insisted that his firm's share of control equal those of the other principal dye factories),[52] Lepsius of Griesheim-Elektron, and Ehrensberger of Krupp. The elected council also included eight professors, among them Beckmann, Delbrück, Fischer, Nernst, and Carl Harries. Delbrück's Institute for Commercial Fermentation had purchased only one vote, the other agricultural groups nothing, but his symbolic importance was too great for him to be omitted. Later the council was enlarged to include six more professors and five government officials (three Prussian, one Bavarian, one Saxon), thus creating a triumvirate of big industry, big science, and government (see table 5-2).

In contrast, middle and small industry played almost no part. Heraeus and Merck especially resented their "exclusion" from the new organization by its high dues requirements. After speaking with Heraeus and others, Ernst Beckmann concluded "that big industry values not a little its influence on the operation of the institute and considers insufficient the influence of, for example, the curatorium of the Imperial Physical and Technical Institute."[53] How much influence did "big industry" actually possess in the Institute Association? The three concerns represented on the council of directors controlled more than half of the regular votes, and they also represented 483,000 marks in endowment (considering Lepsius as chairman of the Chemical Industry Association). Thus their weight increased as the capital donors began to convert their endowments into permanent votes, which had the welcome side-effect of evading the gift tax. Of the academic chemists only Harries could offer a similar capital endowment of 100,000 marks, having married into the Siemens family while he was Fischer's assistant in Berlin.[54] The others also represented only one vote each, but they were there to guarantee the Institute's "scientific character."[55]

The imbalance of power in the new association caught the attention of the institute project's old enemies. In rhetoric undoubtedly designed to appeal to the most conservative traditions of the bureaucracy, Adolf Martens warned the Prussian education minister against the "capitalist interests of the chemical industry," which threatened to compromise the

Table 5-2. Membership of the Imperial Chemical Institute Association, March 1908–March 1913

Member	Regular Votes[a]	Permanent Votes[a]
Academic chemists, Berlin (R = 7, P = 0)[a]		
Emil Fischer (Chairman)[b,c]	1	—
German Chemical Society[b]	1	—
(Max Delbrück)[c]	(see Agricultural industry)	
Instructors, Berlin University Chemical Institute[b]	1	—
Carl Liebermann[b,c]	1	—
Walther Nernst (Secretary)[b,c]	1	—
Robert Pschorr (joined 1912)	1	—
Hermann Wichelhaus[b,c]	1	—
Academic chemists, elsewhere (R = 5, P = 4)		
Ernst Beckmann, Leipzig (1912 Berlin)[b,c]	1	—
Carl Harries, Kiel[c]	1	4 (1912)
Ludwig Knorr, Jena[b,c]	1	—
Karl Schall, Leipzig (joined 1912)	1	—
Wilhelm Semmler, Breslau[b]	1	—
Industrial chemists, organizations (R = 2, P = 10)		
Chemical Industry Association	1	10 (= 380,000 marks; see table 3-1)
Association of German Chemists	1	—
Organic chemicals industry (R = 35, P = 1)		
Triple Alliance Firms, Directors, Stockholders		
Total	23	1
Agfa[b]	2	—
Franz Oppenheim (Treasurer)[b,c]	1	—
BASF[b]	5	—
Heinrich von Brunck[b,c] (Chairman of council to 1911)	1	—
Gustav von Siegle heirs	1	1
Alfred von Kaulla	1	—
Gustav von Müller	2	—
Eduard von Pfeiffer	2	—
Bayer[b]	5	—
Fritz Bayer	1	—
Henry von Böttinger[b,c]	1	—
Carl Duisberg	1	—
(Duisburger Kupferhütte: see Primarly Inorganic Chemical Industries)		
Hoechst-Cassella	6	—
Hoechst[b]	5	—

Table 5-2. Continued

Member	Regular Votes[a]	Permanent Votes[a]
Gustav von Brüning[b,c] (Chairman of council 1911–13)	1	—
Degussa[b] (cyanide processing)	1	—
Fritz Roessler	1	—
Heine & Co.[b] (perfumes, essential oils)	1	
C. A. F. Kahlbaum (Schering subsidiary, preparations)	1	—
Haarmann & Reimer[b] (perfumes)	1	—
Schimmel & Co.[b] (perfumes, essential oils)	1	—
Primarily inorganic chemicals industry, metals (R = 10, P = 19)		
Griesheim-Elektron	3	—
Bernhard Lepsius[b]	1	—
Ignatz Stroof	1	2 (July 1911)
Duisburger Kupferhütte (joined 1912)	1	—
Th. Goldschmidt (joined 1911)	1	—
Krupp (Emil Ehrensberger)[b]	—	4
Tellus Corporation for Mining and Metallurgy	1	—
Oberschlesische Kokswerke & Chemische Fabriken (Friedländer; owned Schering)	1	1
Erich Kunheim (Kunheim & Co., Berlin) (also Upper Silesian mining interests)	1	—
Ludwig Mond (Brunner, Mond) (d. 1909)	—	8
Ernest Solvay (Solvay & Cie, Brussels)	—	4
Agricultural industry (R = 1, P = 0)		
Institute for Commercial Fermentation[b] (Max Delbrück)[c]	1	—
Unidentified and miscellaneous (R = 5, P = 0)		
Hans Clemm (joined 1912), Mannheim	1	—
Paul Hoering, Berlin	1	—
Fritz Schulz jr. AG, Leipzig	1	—
Schott & Genossen, Jena (technical glass)[b]	1	—
F. Vieweg & Sohn, Publishers, Braunschweig	1	—
Total	64 (= 320,000 marks)	34 (= 980,000 marks)
	Combined: 1.3 million marks, 1908–13	

Sources: Fischer and Beckmann, *Kaiser Wilhelm-Institut für Chemie*, pp. 10–12; VCR documents.
[a]Total number of votes for each category of donor is given in parentheses. (R = Regular votes, P = Permanent votes). One regular vote required a contribution of 5,000 marks; one permanent vote, 25,000 marks. The maximum number of votes per donor was ten.
[b]Member in March 1908.
[c]Elected to council of directors. Eleven nonmembers were chosen to the Council of Directors in 1908: six full professors/institute directors (Adolf von Baeyer, Munich University; Theodor Curtius,

"scientific character and objectivity of the 'Imperial Institute.' "[56] Carl von Martius came to very similar, albeit not anticapitalist conclusions. He condemned the association's use of the "imprecise and misleading" term "Imperial Institute," proposing instead the prophetic title "German Association for the Advancement of Scientific Research in Chemistry."[57]

Yet the Imperial bureaucracy itself seemed favorable to the Imperial Chemical Institute Association, which Lewald regarded as "thoroughly in accord with the wishes expressed by the Imperial Treasury administration."[58] The Treasury Office did not object to "capitalist interests" in the association, provided they put up the necessary capital; but how many marks would the government put up, and when?

Despite two years of frustration, and the continuing uncertainty as to Imperial support, Emil Fischer expected some political advantages from the long struggle; chemists would, he hoped, "become more conscious of their own strength in dealing with public issues."[59] The proponents did try to make the institute a public issue by emphasizing the small but growing threat of foreign competition in science-based industry. In a newspaper article, Nernst argued that "scientific research . . . resembles a kind of war making and is likewise expensive." Big industry would do its share through the Institute Association, but the government must also provide some support to repay chemistry for its contribution to the national welfare.[60]

In May 1908 Ernst Beckmann completed a much more elaborate pamphlet along the same lines as Nernst's article, showing that recent foreign advances in chemistry depended upon working conditions that the traditional German academic teaching laboratories did not possess. The old method of "sifting through a research area with a large amount of student experimental data must be supplemented by quiet work with reliably trained workers," the kind of work which in Britain had produced Ramsay's discoveries of the noble gases or in France the Curies' refinement of radium from pitchblende. "How could one ever have achieved that with the work of students?" Beckmann asked.[61] As for the chemical industry, Beckmann portrayed the United States as Germany's most dangerous competitor, as well as the nation whose chemical research received the greatest amount of industrial philanthropy. The German chemical industry could not compete with the Americans because the American enterprises were on a larger scale, he claimed, and their tax burdens lighter. But "the Imperial government, industry, and private individuals ought to vie with each other in providing support. Haste is most urgently needed

Heidelberg University; Carl Engler, Karlsruhe Technical College; Walther Hempel, Dresden Technical College; Otto Wallach, Göttingen University; Emil Warburg, Imperial Physical and Technical Institute) and five government officials (E. Knilling, Bavarian Education Ministry; Naumann and F. Schmidt, Prussian Education Ministry; H. Thiel, Prussian Agricultural Ministry; Waentig, Saxon Education Ministry).

here—standstill means retreat. . . . In the peaceful competition of nations, Germany can conquer only in the sign of scientific and industrial progress. . . . With the great sums that must be raised to provide armaments for a possible war, one ought not shrink from small expenditures on facilities for a peaceful contest."[62]

Beckmann's concluding statement had revealed a growing tension between demands for research and armaments spending, as well as the looming threat of a European war. By the spring of 1908 Fischer too had begun to speak of what he called the British government's realignment of European powers, which he feared would lead to war, and by the following year of British fears that "Germany is preparing a war of aggression; but no serious man among us thinks of it."[63] In this atmosphere of growing international tension, the leaders of the Institute Association had reason to fear the loss of their British contributor, Ludwig Mond. After Fischer and Nernst offered Mond an honorary membership in the German Chemical Society, he finally agreed to sign over his pledged 200,000 marks to the association.[64]

Fischer had also appealed to Ernest Solvay, another great European philanthropist and leader of the chemical industry. Pointing out the involvement of Solvay's German affiliate and of Mond, whose firm was close to Solvay's, Fischer argued that the institute was really a European enterprise designed to keep chemistry in Europe ahead of the United States, "where giant institutions with almost unlimited means are being developed for the sciences." Solvay was most obliging. "In the current stage of scientific and social organization," he favored the project and, agreeing that "Germany is by all indications the country to take the initiative in Europe," offered 100,000 marks, which pleased Fischer so much that he and Nernst arranged to have the Berlin Academy award its Leibniz Medal to the Belgian.[65]

Although the association's capital thereby reached some 900,000 marks, it still could not attract support from Leo Gans's firm, Cassella. Its endowment of 60,000 marks went to Prof. Paul Jacobsen, general secretary of the German Chemical Society, as a fund for a systematic chemicals register and formula index in conjunction with the preparation of a new edition of the Beilstein handbook of organic chemistry. Jacobsen's competition infuriated Duisberg, but there was nothing to be done.[66]

In the meantime the association had asked Ernst Beckmann to draw up preliminary building plans, with the advice of the directorate and the assistance of Baurat Max Guth, who had previously designed Fischer's own institute as well as the Prussian Materials Testing Office Laboratories in Dahlem. The total cost they estimated for a simple, expandable structure and separate official residences for staff was one million marks, less than the cost of Fischer's Berlin University Chemical Institute of 1900—but still more than the cost of any other university chemical laboratory in Germany.[67]

In response to Delbrück's suggestion that the Association go ahead with construction of the main building by April 1, 1909, with or without support by the government, Fischer lamented that the institute was "not as popular in the industry as we had originally assumed. . . . As long as they thought they could buy themselves off with a small sum, leaving the lion's share of the outlays to the Reich, they were rather enthusiastic. But now a decided indifference has set in. I fear that it will become still worse."[68] Delbrück was thereupon elected to a formal position of leadership as vice chairman of the council of directors, but the association decided to delay construction pending a new petition for a subsidy from the Imperial government.[69]

Fischer, Nernst, and Oppenheim then distilled all the arguments and debates of the preceding three years into a concise plea to the Imperial government for an annual subsidy, beginning in 1910. While they painted the foreign threat, especially from America, more garishly than ever, their petition's chief novelty was an itemized budget of 50,700 marks for salaries (to be paid by the Association) and 130,000 marks for operation (to be paid by the government). The cost, admittedly "rather large" compared to the chemical teaching laboratories, was justified because the institute's work was that "for which the usual chemical laboratories possess insufficient furnishings and means," while the industrially oriented experiments would often be "on a much larger scale and with greater precision than was possible in academic laboratories up to now." The institute must also have "complete flexibility" in allocating this budget "if it is, according to the modern tendency, swiftly to follow up all advances." The association could only guarantee to keep the total budget at the given level during the first five years; nevertheless, the institute would be "productive" and would "more than pay for itself through direct or indirect benefits to the chemical industry."[70]

Once again, Bethmann-Hollweg endorsed the plan on paper, pointing out that the government was not creating another Imperial Institute for Physics and Technology, but the new treasury secretary, Reinhold von Sydow, evidently still smelled a Trojan horse. The government had no "essential interests" at stake, Sydow insisted, and the chemical industry could pay for the entire project. "I therefore request that the matter be pursued no further."[71]

The Imperial finance reform in July 1909 brought new evidence of the government's insensitivity to scientific research institutions, which lost their exemption from the alcohol tax. Despite the energetic lobbying efforts of Fischer and others, Duisberg's wife's uncle, Baron von Gamp, gave no help; it took a last-minute intervention by Max Delbrück's friends in the alcohol industry to save the tax exemption, if only for teaching laboratories.[72]

The depressing climax of the finance reform nevertheless offered some hope in the form of Bülow's resignation after the defeat of his inheritance tax proposal. His departure brought Bethmann-Hollweg to the chancellorship and Clemens Delbrück, Max Delbrück's cousin, to the Office of the Interior. Clemens told Fischer that the Reichstag and Bundesrat would eventually approve a grant of 100,000 to 150,000 marks for the Institute Association.[73] When Nernst and Emil Warburg went to see the new secretary of the Imperial Treasury Office, Adolf Wermuth, however, he gave them little or no hope for "any sort of subsidy . . . in the near future" due to the Reich's budget problems.[74]

This news outraged the Chemical Institute Association. "The directorate wanted to proceed much more cautiously," Fischer explained to Duisberg, "but indignation over the treasury secretary's completely negative attitude threw all caution to the winds, and so we have unanimously decided to build, if at all possible, next year. . . . At the moment," Fischer continued, "there is another plan in the air" that might produce "some support for the institute from Prussia" and perhaps also from the Reich as well.[75] Although Fischer had accordingly tried to delay action by discreetly intimating that "higher circles" might take a special interest in the institute, in connection with pending plans to develop Dahlem, he could say nothing more because Adolf Harnack had not yet submitted the relevant memorandum to the Kaiser.[76]

Unfortunately, the association was hardly in a good position to establish an institute. Its total existing assets and expected income for 1909 would barely cover the capital costs of 900,000 marks, omitting the staff residences. If the membership dues for 1910 were applied to salaries as planned, what would be left over for maintenance and materials? Some of the costs could be recovered from fees and various small grants, but even so, the institute could not be fully furnished, and it could only have operated at half its capacity. These plans became moot when the Prussian bureaucracy finally took the matter in hand; only one point is worth mentioning.

Evidently in order to propitiate Max Delbrück, the building committee agreed to widen the distillery room at a cost of 20,000 marks, which would have repaid many times over the monetary contribution of Delbrück's supporters to the institute fund.[77] Delbrück's political services perhaps made it worthwhile. He acted as liaison in drafting the Dahlem land-grant contract with the Prussian bureaucracy, including the Ministry of Agriculture, whose approval would be required both for the agreement itself, as well as for any changes in plans after the contract was signed.[78]

Fischer and Nernst had already taken steps to ensure Beckmann's appointment as president by arranging a research professorship for Beckmann with both the philosophical faculty and the Education Ministry, then proposing him to the council of directors.[79] The Prussian government had long wanted Beckmann in Berlin, but he represented no research program of particular value to the Triple Alliance. Although Fischer and Nernst had therefore intended to push Beckmann's appointment through without a meeting of the council, Fischer held one anyway in order not to alienate Brunck of the BASF, one of the few people who was bringing new members into the Association in late 1909.[80] Fischer assured him that the directorate "in no way want to infringe on the rights of the council of directors." Fortunately, the council accepted Beckmann.[81]

Oppenheim and Duisberg did see a valuable research program in the man they wanted as deputy director, the organic chemist Richard Willstätter,[82] who characterized his work at this time as the study "of the relationship between color and constitution of organic compounds." His work on benzene derivatives, particularly aniline black, lay in the mainstream of classical organic chemistry and its industrial applications, while his pioneering structural analysis of chlorophyll opened new insights into biochemical pigmentation. Willstätter might be open to a call, because he was one of Baeyer's most talented former students, but he was also a Jew who had adamantly rejected Baeyer's urgent suggestion that he convert to advance his academic career. Thereby lacking opportunities for advancement in many German universities, Willstätter had gone to more tolerant Zürich in 1905. By appointing him, at one blow Fischer could encourage Jewish philanthropy and satisfy the businessmen who wished to emphasize organic chemistry.[83] Without official support, however, the association could not yet approach Willstätter. Nevertheless, he and Beckmann represented the nucleus of the future institute.

Taken together, the efforts of the various fund-raising organizations for the Imperial Chemical Institute had resulted in a limited success at best. Fischer and his academic colleagues had ultimately raised a sizable sum, but through the method least acceptable to them. They had had to grant effective control over the future institution to the big concerns of the chemical industry in order to get them to invest in the potential results of its research, and they would consequently have to pay special attention to industrial demands. They had also made significant concessions to Delbrück's agricultural interests for limited political gains that did not include much financial support. Their attempts to obtain disinterested philanthropy had been almost wholly unsuccessful within Germany, except perhaps for the Krupps' pledge obtained through Fischer's former student Ehrensberger. The successful appeals to Mond and Solvay, couched in internationalist rhetoric, had been strengthened by the kind of honors that Fischer could offer: an honorary membership in the German Chemical

Society and the Leibniz Medal of the Berlin Academy. Others withheld their patronage for lack of the honors that only the Prusso-German bureaucracy could have offered. The Imperial Treasury Office, ignoring the demands of the academic scientists and the ineffectual endorsements of Interior Secretaries Bethmann-Hollweg and Clemens Delbrück, was perfectly willing to let the project either collapse or fall completely into the hands of industry. (Bethmann's performance here foreshadowed in a small way his later, equally ineffectual performance in greater matters as Imperial Chancellor.) In any case the treasury officials believed that expenditures for a "peaceful contest" in chemical research did not belong among the "essential interests" of the Imperial government, at a time of budget deficits and concessions to the military and the most conservative sectors of agriculture and industry.

Finally, consider the results of the chemists' search for funds in the context of modernization in Imperial Germany. The bureaucracy appears to have seen its power to reward donors as an effective way to promote the integration of the business and aristocratic elites. Unfortunately for the chemists, that made it very difficult to encourage philanthropy without active bureaucratic cooperation, which might have been less necessary had the incentives taken the form of tax deductions. The chemists had no other choice but to appeal to the most naked financial interests of the big corporations. Even so, the latter did not see the possibility of returns clearly enough to provide all the necessary funds—probably because their own factory laboratories were easier to control and make profitable. In contrast, the academic chemists wanted to mitigate the policy that money would buy scientific power, partly because they would no doubt rather have seen research go on without any financial pressures, but also because a research institution organized as a purely capitalist venture would have had an extraordinarily difficult relationship with the rest of the German academic system and its tendency to "quarantine modernity."[84] Martens's hostility was only a foretaste of how the universities might react. Fischer now hoped to regain the initiative by working through the Prussian educational bureaucracy and with the Kaiser's support.

6

The Kaiser's Call Resounds: The Kaiser Wilhelm
Society for the Advancement of the Sciences
as Orchestrated Philanthropy

It would not do to make a leap in the dark, to have the Kaiser call upon the
German willingness to sacrifice and then to face results that would fully pre-
clude the completion of the great plan.
—Official memorandum on the founding of research institutes, February 1910

I am persuaded that our expectations will everywhere be exceeded, and a
golden rain will pour down as soon as the Kaiser's call resounds.
—Civil Cabinet Chief Valentini to Friedrich Schmidt, June 1910

The Kaiser Gets Involved

It may seem paradoxical that after initially dismissing the idea of building a research institute with support from the Prussian government, Fischer hoped in 1909 to do so after all. If the Kaiser expressed an interest in
the plans, support for new research institutes could potentially become an
official priority, except that all the other official priorities with their financial constraints remained unchanged. This raised once again the characteristic problem of conservative modernization: how to create a new institution without infringing on the rights of any existing ones. The Kaiser's
interest could not magically create the funds—or could it?

When Friedrich Althoff died in the fall of 1908, the Prussian Ministry of
Education was still far from realizing his old dream of a "German Oxford,"
a complex of academic research institutes in Dahlem. The Kaiser then
revived hope for the plans; at the request of Rudolf von Valentini, the
chief of Wilhelm's Civil Cabinet, Friedrich Schmidt, Althoff's successor in
charge of academic affairs, dutifully sorted through Althoff's papers and
summarized all the requests that Althoff had received over the years from
Fischer, Nernst, and other scholars desiring land and facilities in Dahlem.
In the summer of 1907 Fischer had worked out a brief memorandum for

the Prussian education minister. Referring to the relevant arguments in the Imperial Institute memoranda, he proposed establishing a complex of small "academic research institutes for chemistry" in Dahlem, but connected to the university. Each institute would be led by one or two researchers, each with minimal teaching duties and supported by four or five assistants as well as ten or twelve advanced students. Fischer referred to the research laboratories of Germany's major foreign competitors—the United States, Great Britain, France, and Russia—as well as to his own earlier requests for academic research institutes since 1899–1900. In April 1908 Nernst had followed up Fischer's memorandum by specifying four academic research institutes to be set up: radioactivity and electron research, inorganic chemistry, serum research, and physiological chemistry.[1] Thus both chemists hoped that, even without an Imperial Institute, academic research institutes might still find a place in the Dahlem complex.

What was the immediate source of Wilhelm's interest in the Dahlem plans? Coincidentally with Althoff's death, a political storm had broken over the Kaiser's embarrassing interview with the London *Daily Telegraph* in late October 1908. His tactless remarks, indiscretions, and demonstrably false statements, passed without change by Chancelor Bülow and the German Foreign Office, testified to incompetence and irresponsibility in the conduct of German foreign policy. After being openly censured by the Reichstag and by the educated middle classes, normally his fervent admirers, the Kaiser was casting about for ways to regain some of his tarnished luster. Rejecting the bellicose diplomatic offensive in the East wanted by the "war party" on the general staff, Wilhelm hoped instead to rally middle-class support with a magnificent gesture for German education and scholarship.[2] Althoff's plans, in the form submitted by Friedrich Schmidt in early 1909, offered vague but interesting possibilities, and Wilhelm initially decided to increase the total amount of land set aside for academic facilities in Dahlem to one hundred hectares, more than three times the amount previously set aside and a fifth of the entire area of the tract. Immediate objections came from other ministries, especially finance and agriculture, which had intended to subdivide Dahlem into villa-size lots for profitable sale to Berlin's financial elites. When it became clear that the government lacked funds to build so big a complex, the scientific sections were reduced to fifty hectares, which still represented a substantial increase.[3]

Nevertheless Schmidt's memorandum still lacked a compelling, unifying idea that could produce the dramatic gesture the Kaiser wanted to make at the centennial of the University of Berlin in the fall of 1910. Otto Jaekel, a paleontologist at Greifswald, had been lobbying through one of the Kaiser's military aides for a "biontological academy," which was at least something new. Schmidt responded by again advocating the Dahlem research complex, and he believed that Adolf Harnack would be the "right man" to bring it to life.[4]

Harnack, one of the Kaiser's favorite scholars, was an ideal choice. Although Harnack was a liberal theologian and heir to Theodor Mommsen's reformist leadership in the Berlin Academy, Wilhelm admired Harnack's efforts to rejuvenate Prussia's hidebound established church and to create in the Evangelical social movement a counterforce to Social Democracy. Wilhelm also appreciated Harnack's subtle flattery and what Prince Bülow recalled as "that reverent devotion he always accorded the powerful"; Harnack's first reward was to be made head of the Royal Library.[5]

Although Harnack had apparently been sympathetic to Althoff's Dahlem plans and was to be placed on the Dahlem land commission at the Education Ministry's request, he lacked a scientist's stake in the project.[6] Schmidt thus enlisted Emil Fischer, among others, to discuss it with Harnack and persuade him of its importance. Fischer drew up a short memorandum outlining a research institute that would be connected both to the university and to the planned Imperial Chemical Institute. He added that if the Imperial Institute itself were not approved, the Institute Association's funds might go to the new institute. Schmidt then provided Harnack with a comprehensive memorandum as a basis for his petition to the Kaiser.[7]

Schmidt was assisted by a new subordinate, Hugo A. Krüss. For a Prussian bureaucrat, Krüss was unusually well qualified to deal with the task now unfolding: his father owned a prosperous optical company in Hamburg, his late brother Gerhard had worked with Emil Fischer and later headed the inorganic section in Baeyer's institute, and he himself had not only studied science and mathematics but also had lived for a year in the United States.[8]

Mostly Krüss's work, the memorandum given Harnack thus accepted the arguments of Fischer and the Institute Association, simply extending them to other fields. The idea was to create a new institution to support research, chiefly by building its own laboratories in Dahlem but also through grants to researchers elsewhere, in the manner of the Carnegie Institution in the United States. On this analogy as well as the example of the Chemical Institute Association, it was proposed to collect part of the necessary funds in the form of "private endowments." Nevertheless the Prussian government was also to contribute a "considerable" portion. All the funds would be brought together in a central "foundation or association" to be called the "Kaiser Wilhelm Institution for Scientific Research"; within the central organization there would be subdivisions for chemistry, physics, and biology, and funds could be specified for each. This evidently offered the Chemical Institute Association a way of maintaining its integral organization and capital. The first project was to be a chemical research institute, for which the government would donate a building site, create a new position in the Academy for the director, and subsidize the initial and long-term costs. In return, the Prussian Education Ministry would have overall administrative control.[9] Hence it appeared that the Prussian government would step into the breach left by the Imperial government's refusal to cooperate.

Harnack had long supported the general idea that wealthy philanthropists should support cultural activities, and he grew more enthusiastic about the new project when the defeat of Bülow's inheritance tax in the summer of 1909 made it clear that additional funds for research were unlikely to be forthcoming from the government. The essential thing though was probably that the ministry let him incorporate at least a token reference to the humanities into the memorandum he submitted to the Kaiser.[10]

Wilhelm II read Harnack's memorandum "word for word" and gave it his "liveliest, unrestrained applause."[11] The good news swiftly passed to Fischer, whose association's plans occupied a central place in Harnack's memorandum. Harnack had requested that the Prussian and Imperial governments together appropriate 90,000 marks annually, beginning with the fiscal year 1911–12, to supplement the operating budget of a chemical research laboratory to be built by the association.[12] Trusting that the Kaiser's backing for these measures might finally break the bureaucratic resistance against them, Fischer and his codirectors now prepared to cooperate with the Prussian state and perhaps even with the Imperial government as well.[13]

Fischer, Nernst, and Oppenheim thus took part along with Harnack in the policy debates within the bureaucracy, which began in earnest in late December. Bethmann-Hollweg, as president of the Prussian Ministry of State, authorized August von Trott zu Solz, the education minister, to prepare a comprehensive plan for implementing the Harnack memorandum.[14] Friedrich Schmidt, assisted by Krüss, assumed the responsibility for the Education Ministry. Theodor Lewald spoke for the Imperial Office of the Interior, two representatives came from the Prussian Finance Ministry, and Bethmann was represented by Undersecretary of State von Guenther. The lines of conflict among these parties emerge from the memorandum that Schmidt and Lewald finally prepared in February.[15]

A major issue was the Harnack memorandum's phrase, "cooperation of the government with wealthy private citizens who are interested in science," by which he meant that the government should match every million marks raised from private sources. Thus, given the million available from Fischer's association, Harnack wanted Prussia to appropriate a million marks toward the subsequent biological institute. The Finance Ministry opposed not only this level of funding, but also even giving official sanction to the building of new institutes, in view of the uncertainties of long-term private support.[16] Only the Education Ministry's representatives were prepared to support Harnack's interpretation. Even Schmidt's own chief, Trott zu Solz, needed persuading by Harnack's warning against "the danger of the dependence of science upon *Clique* and *Capital*." While the new institution should feature "self-administration," the government must be able to prevent the "dangers of one-sided developments" through its financial involvement and through "trusted scholars" who would represent official interests and help tie the new institutes to the universities.[17]

Lewald argued instead for withholding any guarantees of government subsidies pending the collection of six million marks in donations to an endowment fund like the one previously demanded for the Imperial Chemical Institute. With some 210,000 marks in annual interest, this fund could be used to cover the 90,000 for the chemical institute's budget as well as an additional 120,000 projected for a biological institute. Additional support could come from "annual contributions of several hundred thousand marks."[18]

How were these funds to be raised? Harnack had suggested the Kaiser make an "appeal to the nation" for a "great common effort" of scientific patronage in its "highest interests,"[19] but in Lewald's opinion, "It would not do to make a leap in the dark, to have the Kaiser call upon the German willingness to sacrifice and then to face results that would fully preclude the completion of the great plan." To ensure that the government need not pay the bills after all, the required philanthropy would have to be orchestrated well in advance of the Kaiser's address at the Berlin University jubilee. "Carefully chosen confidants, especially . . . discreet members of the propertied classes" would carry on an "agitation" [*sic*] based upon "information on the location of the great fortunes and the interests of their owners" supplied by the tax authorities, by the various levels of regional and local officialdom, and by "suitable industrialists." At least a half million marks each might come from a few donors, who would join the senate at the core of the society of patrons. Additional titles were to be granted only in "special cases"; however, membership in the society or its senate was to be considered a reward in itself.[20]

Lewald probably spoke for the majority of ministers in viewing the society as a means to effect a "considerable reduction in the burdens on both the Imperial and Prussian disposition funds of the Kaiser."[21] When a commission of ministers under the chairmanship of Bethmann-Hollweg subsequently discussed the plans in February 1910, they agreed to reject the idea of "cooperation" in Harnack's sense of matching funds, and to await the results of private contributions before settling the issue of government support.[22]

The Education Ministry had thus still not given up hope for some government assistance when Schmidt reported to the Imperial Institute Association's council on March 5, 1910. He explained that while the association would have an "essential share in the control of the future Chemical Institute," which would be considered a German rather than simply a Prussian institution, the chemists must also work "in cooperation with the authorities of the Reich and Prussia to raise the funds still lacking." He did not, however, promise support from the Reich in return for such "cooperation."[23]

When Schmidt admitted that no acceptable name for the institution had yet been selected, Carl Engler, the association's representative from Baden, suggested "Kaiser Wilhelm Institute," which Harnack had suggested in his original memorandum and which at least conferred an Imperial aura.[24] Schmidt relayed this to Bethmann-Hollweg, who however also suggested to the Kaiser that the patronage organization be designated the "Imperial [Kaiserliche] Society for the Advancement of the Sciences," so as to encourage other German state governments to participate.[25] The Kaiser was doubtful, ostensibly because the smaller state governments might object to Imperial and Prussian infringement upon their prerogatives in the area of science policy. Of course he also wanted the organization to bear his name, and so the bureaucrats finally settled on "Kaiser Wilhelm Society," which seemed to possess "neither constitutional nor territorial significance" and thus to satisfy all parties. Nevertheless the smaller state governments neither aided in the collections nor themselves contributed to the society, which before 1918 remained essentially Prussian, in fact if not in name.[26]

The Orchestrated Philanthropy

The Kaiser had accepted Bethmann-Hollweg's suggestions for fund raising, which essentially followed Lewald's ideas, including the premise that six million marks must be collected from private sources before announcing the new society. At this point Fischer must have felt as if he were reliving a bad dream. "Neither the Reich nor Prussia has money" for the Imperial Institute, he complained to Baeyer, and there would be "no sense" in trying to build it without adequate support. That was unlikely to be forthcoming, though he hoped for the best. In the meantime, the association's plans would have to wait.[27]

In May the government undertook the actual search for contributors by holding a series of meetings with the principal administrative bureaucrats for the wealthiest districts and cities in Prussia, as well as several of the most prominent capitalists from Berlin and the Western industrial regions.[28] The initial results were not especially auspicious, partly because the divisions within the bureaucracy quickly became all too evident.[29]

Harnack thus revised his memorandum to make it a more effective tool for recruiting donors. In order to make the society seem a more national endeavor, he changed the previous references to Prussia into references to Germany; and to counteract fears of overcentralization in Berlin, he also implied the possibility of concessions to special or regional interests and mentioned the necessity to avoid anything that might threaten the scientific enterprises pursued by the separate state governments. Yet the principal emphasis continued to be upon the central organization and institutes to be founded in Berlin along the lines already laid down by the Chemical Institute Association: establishing "large central institutes . . . in those areas of knowledge where strong and productive industries work in dependence upon science."[30] For this reason the conferences had involved representatives of the chemical industry (Böttinger), electrical industry (Walther Rathenau and Wilhelm von Siemens [Werner's son]), steel and armaments industry (Krupp, represented by Alfred Hugenberg as chairman of the board of directors), and gas industry (Leopold Koppel, chairman of the council of supervisors of the Auergesellschaft of Berlin). There was also Eduard Arnhold, a representative of the Upper Silesian coal industry, who had previously contributed to the Göttinger Association for Advancement of Applied Physics and Mathematics. Several other participants came from the banks, which might expect increased returns to their industrial investments from scientifically based technological developments.[31]

Not all these men were satisfied with the proposed organization of the Kaiser Wilhelm Society.[32] The government rejected Siemens's proposal to make the enterprise more truly national by founding regional groups in Leipzig, Munich, and perhaps also Breslau and Heidelberg, as well as Berlin. No more acceptable was Rathenau's idea, backed by Siemens and by Ludwig Goldberger of the Dresdner Bank, that the society be made into a mass organization by allowing lower dues levels. Hugenberg, who was already active in a mass organization, the Navy League, probably also supported the others; his boss, Gustav Krupp von Bohlen und Halbach, thought that the "main goal" should be to mobilize the "widest possible circles" to support the society's institutes.[33]

Yet the bureaucrats and scholars involved with the Kaiser Wilhelm Society insisted on an elitist approach to patronizing science, so that far from becoming a mass organization, the Kaiser Wilhelm Society never gained more than a few hundred members. How much mass support could have been expected, anyway? Although Harnack's revised memorandum contained the passage, "Military power and scholarship are the two strong pillars of Germany's greatness,"[34] the Imperial German middle classes saw the two more in the terms of Carl Zuckmayer's 1930 satirical novel *Hauptmann von Köpenick*: "The doctorate is the visiting card, but the reserve commission is the open door."[35] Böttinger's Friedrich Althoff Foundation, established in 1908 with annual dues of just three marks to provide grants to scholars and secondary-school teachers, had barely 3,500 members by 1912.[36] The Navy League, established at the turn of the century, had about 300,000 members, while the Army League, founded in January 1912, had 40,000 members and 100,000 affiliates by autumn, despite criticism from the left-liberals and Social Democrats.[37] Harnack, who was chairman of the board of directors for the Althoff Foundation, thus had reason in the case of the Kaiser Wilhelm Society to reject what he called a "scientific Navy League, which would call upon the last man in the nation to promote its purposes."[38] No mass organization favoring science and academic culture would emerge to balance the promilitary pressure groups in Imperial Germany.

The society thereupon lost some potential support in Rathenau, who withdrew from the project entirely, although he had been involved with Harnack in the planning since 1909. Similarly, despite a personal invitation to contribute from Valentini on behalf of the Kaiser, the Krupp family decided to cut its initial offer of one million marks in half.[39] Siemens stayed in to contribute 100,000 marks, for which he was made a senator, but even after this he continued to favor an organization that might attract 100,000 members.[40]

Such responses from industry as well as the provincial bureaucracy forced the central government to reduce its expectations. Eventually the minimum initial contribution for a regular member in the society was set at 20,000 marks.[41] On this basis (with a few exceptions) the society was to gain about two hundred members by August 1, 1914.[42]

Before the bureaucracy could swing into action throughout Prussia in June 1910, however, the Kaiser began to have second thoughts about orchestrating the whole philanthropic response to his "appeal to the nation" before he had even made it. He did not want "the affair . . . pursued too 'bureaucratically.'" Therefore each provincial governor was to approach a very small number of potential contributors in "strictest confidence" to get preliminary commitments only.[43]

Although the Kaiser was not even supposed to be told about offers until after his proclamation, the bureaucrats proceeded to disregard this policy on the advice of Ludwig Delbrück, Wilhelm's personal banker, who thought it better to have donors respond immediately and directly to the Kaiser.[44] When he did so, offering the first 100,000 marks, the Kaiser was "delighted," Valentini told Schmidt. "I am persuaded," he went on, "that

Table 6-1. Capital Grants to the Kaiser Wilhelm Society and Its Institutes from Sources in Germany, by Economic Branch, to August 1, 1914

Branch[a]		Marks Contributed (in millions)	Percentage of Total Grants
Agriculture		.6	4
Heavy industry		3.8	28
City of Mülheim[b]	.7		5
Krupp family	1.4		10
Others	1.7		12
Chemical and electrical industry		2.1	15
Institute Association[b]	1.0		7
Others	1.1		8
Trade and commerce		.9	7
Banks		3.5	26
Koppel Foundation[b]	1.0		7
16 other Jewish bankers	1.6		12
20 non-Jewish bankers	.9		7
Others and not identifiable		2.7	20
Total		13.6	100

Sources: Burchardt, *Wissenschaftspolitik*, Tab. 4, p. 78, modified by inclusion of additional material from pp. 79–80, 100, 102, and from printed minutes, VI. Sitzung des Verwaltungsrates des Kaiser-Wilhelm-Instituts für Chemie, (March 14, 1914), pp. 2–3, in BA, Nr. 142, Sitzungen.
[a]Grants from members involved in more than one economic branch were divided between the relevant branches, so total grants from all individuals connected with a single branch may be higher than shown in this table.
[b]Direct grants to Kaiser Wilhelm Institutes (not through the Kaiser Wilhelm Society): Koppel Foundation, for physical chemistry; Imperial Institute Association, for chemistry; city of Mülheim, for coal research.

our expectations will everywhere be exceeded, and a golden rain will pour down as soon as the Kaiser's call resounds."[45]

The "golden rain" fell from well-seeded clouds. Wilhelm's "appeal" in October really consisted of a proud proclamation that the endowments promised for the Kaiser Wilhelm Society already ranged between nine and ten million marks.[46] During the following three years fewer than three million marks came in that had not been prearranged by the government during the summer of 1910. Table 6-1 summarizes the sources of these grants, including funds that went to Kaiser Wilhelm Institutes from sources that cooperated with the society without belonging to it.

Who was most willing to give? And who was least willing? It is clear that the Prussian government was able to achieve what the Imperial Chemical Institute Association had failed to do: attract large numbers of benefactors from banking and heavy industry. It also appears that "Jewish money" predominated among the bankers and that the Jewish bankers gave, on the average, a larger proportion of their means.[47] These results seem to confirm the hypothesis that political and status considerations, rather than expectations of direct economic gain from scientific research, motivated many of those in the wider circle of donors that became the Kaiser Wilhelm Society. Those businessmen and bankers whom the Kaiser had accepted among his friends could now advertise their acceptance, but he was obliging them to pay for the privilege. Some of the Jews evidently also hoped to use their contributions as leverage, to induce the Prussian government to lower the social obstacles facing their coreligionists. Paul von Schwabach, director of Bismarck's old ally, the Bleichröder Bank, complained "bitterly" to Friedrich Schmidt "about the snubbing of Jews in the officers' corps."[48] Baroness Mathilda von Rothschild and Baron Max von Goldschmidt-Rothschild told the district president in Wiesbaden "that in their view the state government constantly avoids appointing Jews as full professors in the universities." They cited both Paul Ehrlich and Jacques Loeb, the latter a German-born biologist who had emigrated to the United States during the 1890s. Harnack's memorandum had used Loeb to illustrate the way in which German biology was falling behind for want of "work places and funds." The Rothschilds disagreed; the "only" reason Loeb had gone to the United States was that, being a Jew, "he could not have become a full professor in Prussia."[49] Nevertheless these complaining Jewish bankers loyally provided some of the largest grants to the society, 300,000 marks from the Bleichröder Bank and the same amount from the Rothschilds. The largest initial grant of all, 700,000 marks, came from another Jewish financier in Berlin, Leopold Koppel. It was exceeded only when the Krupps added another million to their initial sum of 400,000 marks after Gustav Krupp von Bohlen was made first vice president of the society in honor of his family's standing as the Kaiser's closest associates among the Western industrial elite.[50]

No social hopes or obligations attached to grants from the landed nobility, who thus became the propertied group least likely to contribute. Even those members of the aristocracy whose incomes were demonstrably equivalent and whose industrial interests were similar to those of the wealthiest bourgeois industrialists and bankers did not favor the Kaiser Wilhelm Society with donations on anything like the same scale.[51] The earliest reports of potential donors, provided by the provincial bureaucrats in May, had listed many names in the East-Elbian Junker strongholds as well as in Berlin and the Western industrial districts. The bureaucratic funding campaigns then produced, by October 1910, over 2.5 million in promised grants from Berlin and 4 million from the Western provinces; but from the East-Elbian provinces came less than 900,000, and the three eastern-most of them offered nothing at all. The *Kreuzzeitung*, voice of conservative Junkerdom, epitomized their attitude with the recommendation that the society promote the "occult sciences."[52] This indifference was not for lack of wealth. Among Silesia's aristocrats, with their extensive mining and heavy industrial interests as well as extensive landholdings, could be found the five richest nobles in Prussia. Only the wealthiest of these, Prince Henckel von Donnersmarck, provided more than the minimum required to join: 100,000 marks, and that in response to an urgent request from Harnack. Of the next three richest nobles, two gave nothing, while the third offered less than the membership fee. Finally Count von Tiele-Winckler, the fifth richest, raised his offer from 6,000 marks to the minimum membership level "with the precondition that the only goals set for the Kaiser Wilhelm Society be those in the areas of industry and the various branches of the natural sciences."[53] Nor was Tiele the only wealthy aristocrat who sought to influence the society on the grounds of a slim donation. Duke Engelbert von Arenberg of Westphalia, the sixth richest noble in Prussia, declined to join after his prospective grant of 30,000 marks did not lead to a research institute in Westphalia.[54]

These six aristocrats, together with a seventh (who also did not contribute), enjoyed an annual income of some 35 million marks. They felt inclined to offer 160,000 marks in all for the society, which ultimately received even less. Of their seven opposite numbers among the industrial and banking bourgeoisie, with a total income of about 37 million, the first three alone, the Krupp family and the two Rothschilds, contributed more than ten times as much. Nevertheless the four next richest members of the bourgeoisie were hardly more inclined to support the society than the nobles. August Thyssen withdrew his early offer when the government refused to exchange his donation for a railroad concession, and although he ultimately helped to fund the Kaiser Wilhelm Institute for Coal Research in his home city of Mülheim, he never actually became a member of the society itself. Two others joined with minimal contributions of 20,000 marks, and a third, Eduard Beit von Speyer, who came from a Jewish family, did not participate in the society at all. Although the Speyer family supported Paul Ehrlich and the Frankfurt "endowment university" project, Beit von Speyer had made a title of nobility his condition for a contribution to the Kaiser Wilhelm Society.[55] That did not fit the Prussian government's criteria.

Levels of response to the Kaiser Wilhelm Society thus did not vary in close relationship to the donor's wealth alone. Nor did a large contribution necessarily indicate that the donor expected to reap economic benefits from the research work of the society. The Krupps had, it is true, given

100,000 marks to the Imperial Chemical Institute Association; but their truly large grant to the Kaiser Wilhelm Society was specified for biology, and particularly neurobiology, from which they were far less likely to gain direct economic rewards. Many other businessmen and bankers also specified their grants for purposes related to the racial, eugenic, and Social-Darwinistic theories popular at the time.[56] For others like Emil Kirdorf, the whole effort was little more than a bureaucratic subterfuge to extract money from the business corporations without an official tax.[57] That was also the reaction reported of the businessmen in Prussian Saxony by the provincial governor, who encountered outrage by National Liberals and left-liberals against the recent finance reform. He added that some had told him that there was little economic usefulness to be expected of a laboratory in Berlin, because most research-oriented industries already possessed their own laboratory facilities. Prussian Saxony, it may be noted, was the center of the beet-sugar industry, which had likewise refused to contribute to the Imperial Chemical Institute. Nevertheless, the Prussian government did obtain from the largest sugar firm, Giesecke & Rabbethge, a total promised endowment of 150,000 marks, and Saxony's 350,000 marks in grants by October 1910 was the largest available from the Eastern provinces, making up more than a third of their total.[58]

There were of course some industries whose businessmen might reasonably have joined the Kaiser Wilhelm Society knowing that scientific research paid dividends; that had certainly been true for the chemical and electrochemical industries. Yet both groups together constituted less than 10 percent of the membership of the society, and their contributions were exactly in proportion to their share of the membership.[59] Does that mean that these businessmen showed no unusual interest in the society's goals? No, because the figures are slightly misleading. One has only to recall that both of the prime potential contributors from the electrotechnical industry in Berlin had alternative projects or plans for the society that were not accepted. Hence the Rathenaus, directors of the AEG, contributed nothing and Wilhelm von Siemens only 100,000 marks. Yet Theodor and Max von Guillaume, controlling one of the largest electrical firms in the West (Felten & Guillaume, Cologne), together very early offered a total of half a million.[60]

On the other hand, most leading firms in the chemical industry had already contributed to the Imperial Institute Association. Thus men like Carl Duisberg initially saw no need to join the Kaiser Wilhelm Society as well.[61] Although a total of 230,000 marks eventually came from the leaders of the Bayer corporation, above all from Böttinger, the directors of the other companies in the Triple Alliance gave no more than the minimum membership fee. Yet 350,000 marks came from the directors of Hoechst, and even 100,000 each from the Weinberg brothers and Leo Gans of

Cassella. The leaders of Cassella gave in to bureaucratic pressure, even as they again denied the industry's need for new chemical research institutes. Gans in fact specified that his endowment be used for research grants in the sense of his earlier proposal. Even that long-standing enemy of the Imperial Institute, Carl von Martius, joined the society with a minimum payment of 20,000 marks.[62] Several other leaders of the chemical industry contributed, including some who were not members of the Institute Association.[63]

The total amount of money that the Kaiser Wilhelm Society obtained from its sources in the German chemical industry was 1,160,000 marks, including 100,000 from Fritz von Friedländer-Fuld. In other words, the Prussian government was considerably more successful than the association had been in tapping the richest men in the chemical industry and attracting previous opponents of the research institute idea. This conclusion applies, of course, only to Prussia. Heinrich von Brunck's contribution to the society was far below his firm's stake in the association. Brunck probably would not have contributed at all without Emil Fischer's invitation stressing that the society would be not Prussian, but German.[64] As for the academic chemists, very few could afford to join. Carl Harries and Emil Fischer were the only active scholars to pay the minimum fee of 20,000 marks. Fischer made only perfunctory efforts to recruit members to the society, aside from Brunck, despite the commitment made by the Institute Association council in March.[65]

The largest single contribution for the purposes advocated by the Institute Association came from Leopold Koppel, who had previously had no contact whatsoever with Fischer's group. But the society gave him the opportunity to pursue social as well as economic goals; not only was he Jewish, he also controlled the Auergesellschaft, the Berlin gasworks, which might benefit from technical advances emerging from physical chemistry. Koppel's 700,000 marks could have been combined with the Institute Association's funds to produce a truly stately Imperial Chemical Institute. But Koppel insisted on endowing a separate Kaiser Wilhelm Institute for Physical Chemistry and Electrochemistry, to be supported and controlled through his own Koppel Foundation, not the association or even the Kaiser Wilhelm Society. He also wanted to name his own director. Koppel also made his grant conditional on the government's financial participation, possibly at the suggestion of the Education Ministry, which still hoped that the government would provide one-third of the operating costs of all institutes to be founded by the Kaiser Wilhelm Society.[66] Koppel's demands gave substance to Harnack's argument about the "dangers of one-sided developments" threatening from "the dependence of science upon *Clique* and *Capital*." Many years later Schmidt explained these "dangers" to a historian of the Kaiser Wilhelm Society; government financial influence was supposed to "protect the society, in the . . . case of worsening circumstances, from Jewish or generally unobjective patrons and their influence."[67]

Thus, although the Finance Ministry resisted the Education Ministry's more general demands for regular budget subsidies to all future Kaiser Wilhelm Institutes, it did agree to provide 50,000 marks of the operating costs for the institute Koppel had proposed. The director's salary of 15,000 marks was to be included in the government's share, and the institute would be set up on royal land in Dahlem adjoining the institute planned by the Imperial Institute Association, which was also to receive a smaller subsidy in the form of two new professorships.[68]

The centenary of the University of Berlin was celebrated with great pomp on October 11, 1910. The plan to found Kaiser Wilhelm Institutes naturally occupied a prominent place in the proceedings. Fischer, one of the originators of the plan, was among the five representatives of the various university faculties to be awarded the title "Excellency," and he was much pleased by the Kaiser's address,[69] which had been drafted by Harnack and Schmidt. No doubt especially pleasing was the section in which Wilhelm announced: "My government will take care that the institutes to be founded will not lack state assistance where necessary." In the face of the Kaiser's guarantee, which he ultimately confirmed by criticizing the Finance Ministry's continuing resistance, the Prussian finance authorities were grudgingly forced to concede at least some, albeit minimal, support in the form of land and directors' salaries to future institutes.[70]

And so the Imperial Institute plans would have to be revised once more. It could hardly be doubted that the new form that the would-be Imperial Institute was about to take under the auspices of the Prussian bureaucracy and the Kaiser Wilhelm Society was to be very much different from the original conceptions of Fischer and his friends. Yet the new situation might offer them new opportunities as well. First, though, consider the sociopolitical significance of the society as such: it was no quasi-corporation for investment in scientific research, like the Imperial Institute Association, nor a "scientific Navy League," but a quasi-aristocratic status symbol set up by a Prussian bureaucracy that was unwilling or unable to alter the priorities in the government's budget. By using the aura of the Kaiser's name to entice philanthropy from the often reluctant elites of banking and technologically advanced industry in Prussia, by playing on the social ambitions of the wealthy whose bourgeois origins or Jewish ancestry had so far hindered their advancement into a status-conscious upper class, the bureaucrats had solved the problem of how to produce large amounts of capital for scientific research. And they had done it selectively, so that those who were already in the inner circle, and those who were opposed or indifferent, had had to yield practically nothing: no taxes raised, and almost no need for concessions from the conservatives dominating the Prussian legislature. And at the same time, thanks to the Kaiser's "appeal," Prussia had become just a bit more "Americanized" by emulating the Rockefellers and Carnegies. In 1913 the Kaiser's government celebrated "his" society as the culmination of a quarter-century of "social culture" in Wilhelm's reign, and rightly so, for it was a triumph of conservative modernization.[71]

7

The Prussianization of the Imperial Institute: Shaping Chemical Research Institutions through the Kaiser Wilhelm Society

---

If I am replaced by Excellency Fischer—the obvious choice—the change would appear understandable and pleasing to everyone.
—Adolf von Harnack's offer to resign as president of the Kaiser Wilhelm Society, January 1913

The form must correspond to the dignity of the parties involved and to the significance of the goals being pursued.
—"Comments on the Legal Form of the Chemical Institutes," Adolf von Harnack Papers, ca. 1911

You will be completely independent.
—Emil Fischer's promise to Richard Willstätter, ca. 1911, regarding conditions for research in Dahlem

---

Separate Institutions, a Unifying Vision: The Leadership of Emil Fischer

The Kaiser's approval of Harnack's memorandum and the subsequent creation of the Kaiser Wilhelm Society presented the Imperial Chemical Institute Association with prospects that did not please all concerned. In January 1910 Nernst seemed a little doubtful about the "Prussianization of the [Imperial] Institute"[1] that must result from the new arrangements. Among the many changes that posed new opportunities and problems, three areas are especially worth discussing here.[2] First, could the Institute Association's plans be carried over into a cooperative relationship with the new society? By 1914, three separate Kaiser Wilhelm Institutes and a fund for research grants in chemistry had emerged instead of a unified Imperial Chemical Institute; the added support for these projects came from groups that had hitherto avoided or opposed the Institute Association, and were scarcely more willing to cooperate within the framework of the new society. To the extent that any single vision could be imposed on these disparate interests, that vision was Emil Fischer's. As the only scientist on the society's administrative committee, Fischer obtained unprecedented authority to influence the direction of its support for research. Second, how much of the Imperial character of the original plans could be preserved? Under the oversight of the Prussian government, the new institutes took on a characteristically Prussian legal and architectural form, implying a particular social status commensurate with their origins and source of support. Finally, how much control would the private donors have over the new institutes, and how much scientific autonomy and "purity" could be retained for their principal staff members? Fischer's answer was to minimize direct technological work in some of the institutes and uphold the ideal of "free research" in all.

The process of Prussianizing the Imperial Institute had begun early in 1910, when the leadership of the Institute Association worked out a preliminary set of guidelines for cooperating with the Prussian government and the projected society of donors.[3] At that time it was assumed that Prussian funds would make possible maintaining the original plans more or less intact. Fischer, however, privately told the Prussian Finance Ministry that financial limitations necessitated eliminating two of the sections originally planned in 1908, including the technical section. Now it would be a smaller "pure scientific institute,"[4] and thus presumably more acceptable to the Prussian bureaucracy. Although the association never formally agreed to eliminate the technical section, there was also never enough money to build it. Leopold Koppel's offer to build a separate institute for physical chemistry and electrochemistry made up for the elimination of the other section Fischer had mentioned to the Finance Ministry.

Koppel's insistence on Fritz Haber as the director for his own institute probably made for some difficulties with the Institute Association, because of Haber's rivalry with Walther Nernst.[5] Since 1906 Haber had been full professor of electrochemistry at Karlsruhe, where he had developed one of the best-equipped laboratories for physical chemistry in Germany. Nernst and Haber had had a dramatic confrontation at a meeting of the Bunsen Society in 1907, when Nernst had disputed Haber's experimental results on the ammonia synthesis and temporarily appeared to have demolished Haber's reputation. Nernst himself had then abandoned the quest for a commercial ammonia synthesis, but Haber and an assistant had nevertheless gone on to solve the problem and then sold the process to the BASF, whose researchers were still working on its technical development in 1910–11.[6] Koppel had heard of Haber because of ammonia, but had he been persuaded instead to appoint Nernst, it would have made for much closer relations between the two new institutes. Before accepting Koppel's demand, Friedrich Schmidt therefore went to Stockholm for an authoritative outside opinion from Svante Arrhenius, who endorsed Haber.[7] As it turned out, Haber's work and interests were to fit perfectly into the vision Emil Fischer was forming of the society's research policy.

In the fall of 1910 Fischer was already on his way to becoming the most influential scientist in the Kaiser Wilhelm Society. With his new title of "Excellency," which Imperial Chancellor Bethmann-Hollweg had told him was a mark of the importance of science in "modern culture and in the flourishing of our Fatherland,"[8] Fischer had authority in symbol as well as substance. He took part in the discussions over the society's statutes and was one of those whom Schmidt asked to suggest nominees for election to the society's senate.[9] After promising to assure to the Institute Association both a high degree of autonomy in developing its own plans as well as a voice in the administration of the Kaiser Wilhelm Society itself, Schmidt placed Fischer on the other list of senators, the one chosen by the Kaiser. Fischer also asked Schmidt to place Nernst on this list, but Schmidt stood by his original choice of the better-known but fatally ill van't Hoff, who was already dying of tuberculosis.[10] Two businessmen from the association also became senators: Gustav von Brüning of Hoechst and Henry von Böttinger of Bayer, the former elected and the latter appointed by the Kaiser. This gave a disproportionately large voice in a senate of only twenty members to the interests of the chemists.[11] Koppel too became a senator through royal appointment, which was one of the conditions he had set for his own grant.[12] The senate then proceeded to elect Böttinger and Fischer to the society's administrative committee, which consisted of only seven members; the others were Krupp von Bohlen, Ludwig Delbrück, Franz von Mendelssohn, Eduard Arnhold, and of course Adolf Harnack as president.

Fischer's original position in the committee was second secretary,[13] nominally the lowest of the seven, but in fact he was already one of its most influential members. Through his leadership of the Imperial Institute Association he had a strong base of industrial support. He also enjoyed enormous respect among his scientific colleagues in the Berlin Academy and the university. Hence he could approach the Kaiser Wilhelm Society with confidence, whereas Harnack did so with uncertainty and self-doubt. Harnack, theologian and son of a theologian, seems indeed to have disliked and distrusted most of the businessmen and financiers with whom he had to associate in the society. He accepted the presidency, it appears, mainly out of a sense of duty. He felt, moreover, that his academic colleagues turned against him and denied him the secretaryship of the Berlin Academy chiefly because of his involvement in the society. As a result Harnack, unlike Fischer, found himself isolated in the society and cut off from his previous sources of strength.[14] He was forced to depend heavily upon those few men to whom he felt some kinship: Friedrich

Schmidt, in the bureaucracy, and increasingly also Emil Fischer, whose views on academic organizations closely matched Harnack's.[15] In January 1913, in fact, Harnack concluded that he had lost the confidence of the Kaiser through an unrelated matter of church politics, and he offered to resign the presidency. "If," he wrote to Schmidt, "I am replaced by Excellency Fischer—the obvious choice—the change would appear understandable and pleasing to everyone." In March a relaxed evening and dinner with the Kaiser reassured Harnack, and he wrote no more of resignation.[16] By retaining Harnack as head of the organization, the government assured doubtful scholars that humane values and "pure" science would continue to have a place in the society's research. Fischer meanwhile advanced to the second vice presidency after the death of Ludwig Delbrück that same month.[17] No doubt it was a position that appealed to him: prestigious and influential, but without the time-consuming administrative responsibilities of a president. Thus, although the defeat of the Imperial Institute proposal had prevented the creation of a "president of German chemistry," Fischer through his influence in the society assumed the de facto role of a "president of German science."

Recent Successes and Problems of Chemistry

How was Fischer going to use his influence? Even before his appointment as senator became official, Fischer had given the featured address to the constituent meeting of the Kaiser Wilhelm Society on January 11, 1911. His remarks, profusely illustrated by examples of the latest achievements of German academic industrial chemistry, amounted to a scientific manifesto.[18] All the fields of science, he assured his listeners, were in a state of rapid and profound change. The old mechanistic views of nature that the nineteenth-century physicists had held sacred could no longer explain new discoveries like radium and the transmutation of elements.[19] At the same time the general progress of knowledge benefited a wide range of industries, from chemicals to agriculture. German scientists appeared to be playing a leading role in this process, as measured by the number of Nobel Prizes in the first ten years going to Germans for chemistry (six), medicine (three and a half), and physics (two and a half). Obviously, Fischer could not portray the situation in chemistry bleakly. In fact, Fischer had warned Harnack in November 1910 that he should tone down the references to the "state of emergency in chemistry" in his original memorandum before bringing it before a wider audience. Now he emphasized the dangers of too much complacency. Most of the work for which the prizes had been awarded was already old, dating from the nineteenth century. The younger generation of scientists faced a heavy teaching load that allowed them, as assistants or lecturers, to perform experimental research in the academic laboratories "only through an unusual ability to work." The Kaiser Wilhelm Institute for Chemistry, he explained, had been designed to alleviate this situation and to meet the threat of scientific competition from the United States.[20] In these arguments Fischer indicated the fundamental similarity between his goals for the society and his original goals for the Imperial Institute.

Fischer went on to discuss the current situation of chemistry in greater detail, making pointed references as he did so to the growing significance of large capital donations, which were becoming indispensable to progress in the newer areas, as well as to the ways in which chemical research was providing domestic substitutes for products previously imported from colonies and foreign competitors. Germany had, for example, no natural source of raw materials from which radium could be refined for scientific or technical uses. Recently, however, Otto Hahn, a young researcher working in Fischer's institute, had discovered a cheaper, domestically available substitute in mesothorium, a decomposition product of thorium. Hahn's process was nevertheless still extremely expensive, 100 milligrams alone costing 11,000 marks, and it was only through Henry von Böttinger's generosity that the Prussian Academy could purchase 250 milligrams for loan to researchers. Fischer did not mention that he himself had directed Böttinger's 30,000-mark grant to this purpose.[21]

Fischer then referred to recent advances that had made it possible to carry out experiments at much higher and lower temperatures than previously. Although a grant from the Kaiser had put an air liquefaction machine at the disposal of the University of Berlin, to liquefy hydrogen required more expensive equipment.[22] Fischer's audience was astonished to learn that the necessary apparatus was still unavailable in Berlin,[23] yet he could not guarantee to them that the new chemical institutes would remedy the situation (Fritz Haber later promised to do so).[24]

The study of high temperatures had solved the problem of synthesizing nitrates from atmospheric nitrogen so that they could be used in agriculture and in explosives. As Fischer entered on this topic he saw the Kaiser nod in approval.[25] Wilhelm was apparently well aware of Germany's dependence upon the dwindling supplies of Latin American nitrates. Potentially the most significant advance in this area for Germany was the BASF's recent work on the Haber process for synthesizing ammonia, which required no electricity and thus utilized only domestically available energy resources. This could triple the supply of nitrogen compounds available to agriculture, Fischer explained, and lead to a rise in harvests sufficient to make Germany "independent from foreign countries in relation to products of the soil."[26]

The problem of conserving energy brought Fischer to the subject of coal technology. He suggested that the potential value of coal could be improved by converting it to coal gas for power production and to obtain the valuable by-products tar and ammonia. A future Kaiser Wilhelm Institute for Coal Research could pursue the research opportunities in this area.[27]

The fossil fuels were Fischer's bridge from mineral chemistry to organic chemistry and the burgeoning development of synthetic organic products.[28] Some of the substances he displayed, like chlorophyll, were still the subjects of academic research by scientists like Willstätter. Others, like camphor and indigo, commercial products of long standing that originally had had to be imported, had been recently synthesized and could now be mass-produced domestically and even exported at enormous profit. Thus although Japan had conquered Formosa to obtain a monopoly on camphor, German chemical research had broken the monopoly. Another class of synthetics that Fischer stressed were substances that, like artificial silk, differed from the naturally occurring materials in their chemical composition but that could perform the same functions and thus replace the natural product. Fischer himself was working on an attempt to produce synthetic substitutes for the aromas of coffee and tea.[29] Since Germany already manufactured synthetic caffeine, success with the aromas would liberate the Germans from their dependence upon foreign sources for these drinks. Fischer was also certain that artificial rubber was only a matter of time. Natural rubber, another colonial product, was likely to go the way of natural dyes like alizarin and indigo, driven off the market by synthetic competitors.[30]

Fischer thus painted a vivid picture of vigorous academic and industrial research in which the Kaiser Wilhelm Institutes would play their part. All the elements of the chemical institutes' initial programs were present in his speech. In his conclusion he implicitly returned to the theme of foreign competition, speaking not of great opportunities in vast overseas empires, but of the "hidden treasures" that the "Kaiser's godchildren," nourished by their benefactors in the society, would help to find in chemistry's "true land of unlimited possibilities."[31]

Thus by January 1911 the main lines of what Nernst had called "Prussianization" had been sketched out: there would not be an integrated Imperial Chemical Institute, but rather two or more Kaiser Wilhelm Institutes for various branches of chemistry. Nevertheless, though there was to be no single large chemical institute and no "president of chemistry," Emil Fischer's unique position in the society was to make him a de facto "president of science." He had already indicated the direction in which he wanted the society to go: toward research centered on chemistry, in all its wide-ranging relationships with the other sciences, and with a special emphasis on what German chemists already did best, the substitution of scientifically transformed domestic resources for imports from foreign colonies or competitors. The difference in emphasis between Fischer's manifesto of January 1911 and the earlier memoranda and brochures advocating an Imperial Chemical Institute reflects the considerable increase in international tensions since 1905–6. Fischer even had to apologize to his British friend William Ramsay for the chauvinism implicit in the picture of chemistry he had presented to the Kaiser Wilhelm Society.[32]

By October 1912, two years after the Kaiser's proclamation, the first two Kaiser Wilhelm Institutes were opened in Dahlem on sites provided by the Prussian government. One was the Institute Association's project, now called the Kaiser Wilhelm Institute for Chemistry, built at a cost of 1.1 million marks, of which the association provided 850,000 and the society the rest. Annual operating expenses were to be divided equally, 60,000 marks coming from each organization. Besides Ernst Beckmann as director and analytic chemist, the principal scientists in the Kaiser Wilhelm Institute for Chemistry included Richard Willstätter in the section for organic chemistry and Otto Hahn and Lise Meitner in a smaller section for radioactivity chemistry. Beckmann and Willstätter represented the surviving parts of the original Imperial Institute plan; the radioactivity section was evidently added at Fischer's request, to give Hahn and Meitner better facilities than the old workshop of his Berlin institute. The neighboring Kaiser Wilhelm Institute for Physical Chemistry and Electrochemistry was built entirely at Leopold Koppel's expense. Besides Haber, its principal staff included Gerhard Just as deputy director and two other younger researchers. Despite a relatively small number of researchers, Haber obtained the best available equipment and instruments for physical and chemical research, on the assumption—in line with the original conception of the Imperial Chemical Institute—that his institute would deal with problems that existing academic institutes could not afford to approach. Accordingly, Koppel's capital costs ultimately approached one million marks, while the annual operating costs, shared by Koppel and the Prussian government, were apparently about 100,000 marks.[33] Hence, Haber's institute was closer to the size of its neighbor than originally intended.

The Tasks of the Kaiser Wilhelm Institute for Coal Research

Fischer soon became actively involved in the plan for a coal research institute in the Ruhr, which he had suggested in January 1911 and had considered several years earlier, when trying to get support from the coal industry for the Imperial Chemical Institute. A coal institute only became a practical possibility several months later, however, as a result of the efforts of the Düsseldorf District governor, Francis Kruse. Kruse had tried unsuccessfully to persuade several of the leaders of the Ruhr coal industry to join the Kaiser Wilhelm Society. One of those who did join, Hugo Stinnes, had suggested establishing a Kaiser Wilhelm Institute in the

Ruhr. Kruse had apparently welcomed this idea as a focus for the efforts of local scholars who wanted to set up a regional academy in his district. Until fall 1911, however, he had been unable to find an approach that would be satisfactory to all parties involved, including the Kaiser Wilhelm Society's leaders in Berlin. At the invitation of Krupp von Bohlen, Kruse met over dinner with the society's senate and administrative committee. Within two weeks Fischer met with the mayor of Mülheim in the Ruhr, home of Stinnes and other leaders of the coal industry, to discuss the possibility of establishing a coal research institute in that city. The idea evidently appealed to Kruse as an extension, at least in part, of his earlier efforts; investigation of coal and its derivatives had already been considered by the scholars in Düsseldorf as a potential area for research.[34]

As Kruse put his subordinates to the task of finding potential donors for such an institute, Emil Fischer outlined a preliminary proposal for its organization and funding. After that had been approved by the society's leadership, Fischer began to draw up a program of research. Besides his conversations with Stinnes and Kirdorf in 1907, Fischer had discussed problems of the fuels industry with Ludwig Mond, who had experimented with the by-product coking process and found it possible to triple the output of ammonia. Convinced that systematic study of the fuels could produce many more such gains, Fischer hoped an institute in this area would finally interest the Rhenish-Westphalian Coal Syndicate.[35]

Fischer took charge of outlining a program, beginning with the director, whose personality would shape the research. Normally, of course, the administrative organizations in charge of the institute would have to confirm the appointment; since none had yet been constituted, Fischer proceeded on the apparent assumption, which later proved justified, that any reasonable suggestion by him would be approved. The man who seemed most suitable was one of his former students and assistants for inorganic chemistry, now a professor of electrochemistry at the Berlin College of Technology. It was Franz Fischer (no relation), whom Emil had praised in January 1911 for developing strongly electromagnetic alloys for motors. Franz might therefore be considered an expert in one form of power production, but he was as yet virtually a stranger to coal or fuels. When the two men met to discuss the project, probably in June 1912, Franz pointed this out. No matter, Emil replied. The astounded Franz Fischer learned that he was expected only "to approach the chemistry of coal, above all its chemical processing, from new and original points of view and to apply methods similar to those [he] had already brought to bear on other subjects."[36]

A prospective director customarily worked out his own research program, but in view of the need for haste, Emil Fischer disregarded this formality also and sketched out a preliminary program himself, based on

consultations with various experts. These included Adolf Frank in Charlottenburg, one of the developers of the calcium cyanamid process for
nitrogen fixation; Hans Bunte, who had established a laboratory for the
study of fuels at Karlsruhe; Gustav Kraemer, an old friend in the petroleum industry and director of the AG für Theer- und Erdölindustrie in
Berlin; and his colleague Walther Nernst.[37]

Fischer could have learned from either Bunte or Frank about details of
recent work on the catalytic hydrogenation of poisonous carbon monoxide
to produce useful methane gas or other fluid hydrocarbons. Although the
process had been demonstrated in the laboratory, it was not yet commercially practicable. If so, it would greatly enhance the value of the by-
products of the coking industry. The BASF was already exploring this
area, using the company's newly won expertise in hydrogenation technology (the method used in the Haber-Bosch ammonia synthesis) and
thereby taking its first step toward the synthesis of liquid fuels.[38]

The idea of producing liquid fuels from coal especially excited Fischer's
friend Kraemer, whose company competed with the American oil-produc-
ing giants. Germany had almost no domestic sources of petroleum, whose
high cost limited the scale of the German automobile and aircraft industries. Kraemer would have liked nothing better than to reduce Germany's
dependence on the Americans, and he thus endorsed the idea that the
new institute work on a conversion process using the country's volumi-
nous supplies of bituminous coal or lignite. Hydrogenation could also be
applied to the more volatile components of coal tar to produce a variety of
products. Moreover one of Kraemer's former trainees, now working with
a company in the Ruhr, had recently discovered in coal tar significant
quantities of butadiene. This could be useful as a raw material for synthetic rubber from a process recently found by the Bayer dye firm.[39]

Walther Nernst endorsed the last element in Fischer's program, the
"electrification" of fuels. Theoretically, one could design a thermoelectric
element capable of producing electricity at least twice as efficiently as the
best existing motors. Unfortunately the practical results thus far obtained
were only a fraction of this. Another way of approaching the problem
would be to develop a fuel cell to produce electricity from the oxidation of
hydrogen or other gases. Nernst assured Fischer that recent work on the
subject was rife with possibilities, and that it would be necessary only to
conduct "numerous systematic experiments" to determine the best technique.[40] If successful, of course, the benefits to German industry would be
enormous, particularly given the lack of cheap domestic hydroelectricity.

The information he had collected by the end of July made altogether a
deep impression on Emil Fischer, who found himself "quite astonished"
as he realized "how many and how great are the problems to be solved in
the fuels industry."[41] On July 29, 1912, he presented his findings to some

120 leaders of Ruhr industry, whom Kruse had assembled in Mülheim. He used the slogan "Multiplying the Inherent Value of Coal" to tie together his many suggestions for the proposed coal institute's research program. "Many other industries now complain about their high expenditures for coal," he admitted. "But if they could gain twice as much from it, they would gladly pay one and one-half times the price."[42] Although much wrangling remained to be done over administrative and financial details, Fischer could be justly proud of the meeting's results. The assembly accepted the institute as such, together with his programmatic ideas, virtually without discussion.[43] As the only chemist eventually appointed to the curatorium or administrative board of the coal research institute, Emil Fischer retained an authoritative if not a commanding influence on the development of the institute.

Emil Fischer's interest in coal research was hardly just academic. It is clear from his program that he was becoming increasingly concerned about the problems facing Germany in regard to strategic resources, not merely in peaceful international economic competition but also in the event of an approaching world conflict. Fischer had announced the Bayer company's preliminary solution to the problem of synthetic rubber in his 1911 speech to the society, but by 1912 the price of natural rubber had fallen so drastically that Bayer suspended its development program, despite having already invested some 150,000 marks.[44] The problem of petroleum was even more critical. Without domestic sources, the German military would be unable to make extensive use of airplanes or automotive transport, essential weapons in twentieth-century warfare. Yet while the military authorities showed considerable interest in the establishment of a Kaiser Wilhelm Institute for Aerodynamics in Göttingen, they ignored the Institute for Coal Research.[45] Any major war would, of course, be over so quickly that strategic resource questions could scarcely arise. Yet in January 1913 Fischer openly worried to his American friend T. W. Richards about the possibility of Germany's producing fluid fuels from coal in case of war.[46] The institute he advocated was ready to begin operations by July 1914.

The Connection of Organic Chemistry and Biology

Besides the first three chemical institutes in which Fischer played a central role, there were two other early projects fostered by the other two scholars who had contributed to Harnack's memorandum, August von Wassermann and Max Rubner.[47] Wassermann became director of the Kaiser Wilhelm Institute for Experimental Therapy, which opened in Dahlem in 1913 as the society's third major project to be completed. Although Fischer had relatively little to do with this institute, he may have seen to it that it would have a section for biochemistry, whose director was Carl Neuberg, one of his former students. Rubner opened a Kaiser Wilhelm Institute for the Physiology of Work, provisionally located in his own Institute for Physiology at the University of Berlin; it thus did not require a separate building at first. While Fischer was not directly involved with this institute, he was interested in developing a Kaiser Wilhelm Institute for Physiology, which was to be funded by the Krupps and whose director was to be his former collaborator in protein research, Emil Abderhalden, now professor of physiology at Halle University. Because it was not possible to begin building the institute before or during the war, Fischer saw to it that the society would provide Abderhalden with regular subsidies.[48]

Although a Kaiser Wilhelm Institute for Biology also could not be completed until the spring of 1915, Fischer also took a special interest in its organization and construction, and he became the chairman of its curatorium. The institute's areas of greatest concentration were to be in genetics and development, which Fischer believed might prove to be influenced by chemical changes in the cell. The institute's section for physiology was to be headed by Otto Warburg, another of Fischer's students in what was already beginning to be called biochemistry. Outside this area, however, Fischer evidently did not feel comfortable about setting scientific priorities. Lacking authoritative leadership in the field, the Kaiser Wilhelm Society was forced to the unusual step of surveying the opinions of some thirty specialists in various related biological disciplines. The society then invited these men to a conference to discuss the scientific goals of a general biological institute; only then did the leadership actually attempt to recruit scientists and establish the institute.[49]

By the fall of 1915, despite delays in development resulting from the First World War, Fischer had gained an even deeper vision of the fundamental scientific goals of the Kaiser Wilhelm Society than he had had in 1911. In another programmatic speech, while acknowledging that there was no "fixed plan" to the development of the institutes, so that the primacy of research in chemistry and biology was more or less accidental, he also voiced the hope that the Dahlem environment would promote fruitful interdisciplinary work by chemists and biological or medical scientists across a wide spectrum of problem areas. Just as biologists had experimented with artificial selection and other ways of altering life forms, while chemists had hitherto synthesized and then created artificial varieties of such natural products as vegetable dyes or sugars, so might scientists eventually synthesize the complex molecules of life, the proteins and nucleic acids, and then chemically modify them to produce new artificial life forms as well. He showed the audience samples of the protein-like polypeptide and of the nucleic acid that he had already synthesized as steps toward this goal. "So I see, half in a dream, the emergence of a synthetic-chemical biology, which will encroach as fundamentally on the living world as chemistry, physics, and technology have done for so long on lifeless nature."[50] Thus Fischer envisioned the Dahlem institutes participating in one of the farthest-reaching of science's unlimited possibilities, the creation of what would today be called molecular biology and genetic engineering.

True to his nature, Fischer had stamped the scientific program of the Kaiser Wilhelm Society with a dual character. On the one hand, it was aimed at the most fundamental problems of natural science; but on the other, it was intended to produce solutions to technological problems of the highest national interest, particularly with regard to providing domestically available synthetic or artificial substitutes for imported materials. Others made their voices heard on theses issues as well, of course, but Emil Fischer's was unquestionably the strongest influence on the overall scientific goals of the early Kaiser Wilhelm Society. This was the scientific sense of the "Prussianization" of the Imperial Chemical Institute.

Shaping the First Kaiser Wilhelm Institutes:
Form, Function, and "Dignity"

Besides putting Emil Fischer in a position to influence the society's scientific goals, the "Prussianization" of the Imperial Institute also brought changes, both legal and architectural, in the form of the research institute. Different as these two aspects of form may seem, they can nevertheless be examined together, because both involved issues of practical function vs. social status or "dignity," as well as the straightforward political problems of converting from an Imperial to a Prussian-oriented institution.

The last issue arose at once because Brunck and other key members of the Imperial Institute Association were not Prussians, and they still wanted their institute to be at least a quasi-official agency of the Imperial government. In March 1911, however, the Kaiser Wilhelm Society's leadership, excluding Fischer (who was then ill and on vacation), decided against the participation of the Imperial government. The association therefore "temporarily" abandoned its proposal that their institute bear an "Imperial" title in return for a small annual subsidy from the Imperial government.[51]

If the institute was not to be an Imperial agency, what then would it be? Emil Fischer wanted the legal form of the new institute to be a foundation, but Duisberg complained that all contributions would then be subject to a 5 percent gift tax. Instead, the Kaiser Wilhelm Society should simply join the Imperial Institute Association with annual dues of 60,000 marks. The Kaiser Wilhelm Institute for Chemistry could then be organized as a contractual partnership (*Gesellschaft des bürgerlichen Rechts*).[52] The Kaiser Wilhelm Society's administrative committee considered both of these possible legal forms for the chemical institutes, as well as the registered association and the limited-liability corporation. To be acceptable, "the form must correspond to the dignity of the parties involved [i.e., society, association, and Prussian government] and to the significance of the goals being pursued." And it had to be cheap. The registered association, despite its low initial taxes of five marks, was designed for large groups with fluctuating memberships; it was thus inappropriate for a long-term, tripartite relationship. The corporation, a form designed for profit-making enterprises, could not properly be employed for an institute bearing the royal name. Besides, the taxes required to establish it, 30,000 marks, were far too high. In the case of the contractual partnership, the taxes were negligible, but the partnership lacked the desirable qualities of limited liability and legal personality possessed by the foundation. The foundation, moreover, met the criterion of "dignity" and seemed best to reflect the charitable and scientific goals of the Kaiser Wilhelm Society. Unfortunately, the initial taxes would exceed 150,000 marks. Hence the administrative committee decided to request the government to defray these costs through the royal disposition fund.[53]

The response of the Prussian finance minister to the society's request for tax exemption was not encouraging. Three-quarters of the tax on a foundation was supposed to go to the Reich and only one-quarter to the Prussian government; but the minister not only offered no exemption from the Prussian share, he noted that the Bundesrat so far had denied all Imperial exemptions, on principle. The society's contributions would be subject to tax unless the Kaiser Wilhelm Institute for Chemistry were founded as an administrative section of the society, not an independent foundation.[54]

The society's administrative committee rejected the idea of making the chemical institute an administrative dependency. It would not be possible to justify the Imperial Institute Association's contributions as compensation for services rendered as the finance minister had suggested; that was not the sort of arrangement that suited their vision of the Kaiser Wilhelm Institute. The committee continued to prefer the foundation, but pending a tax concession they adopted the expedient of a partnership as the legal form for the institute.

While the Prussian Finance Ministry rejected formal participation in the contract establishing the Chemical Institute, it demanded revisions that to Fischer seemed "quite unreasonable."[55] The ministry wanted the institute to be endowed with sufficient capital to maintain its operation without the dues of the association, inasmuch as no one could be certain how many members the association would have when the first five-year term expired in 1913.[56] The final version of the contract retained the ministry's obligation to provide land and a professorship, but specified that the ministry could withdraw its support (i.e., land and professorship) if the institute's operation "no longer appears to be secure."[57] Moreover, the Prussian finance minister, Dr. August Lentze, informed the society that "I—like my predecessor in office [von Rheinbaben]—would not consider the Finance Ministry's special involvement in the further activity of the society to be in keeping with the main idea in founding the society: to create and maintain economically independent research institutes from private funds, in order as far as possible permanently to free the heavily burdened general government finances from new tasks of this type." The society's endowment was to be expanded to cover all expenses.[58]

The society's leaders immediately protested to the Kaiser, recalling His Majesty's promises of October 1910.[59] Wilhelm then confirmed the principle that future Kaiser Wilhelm Institutes in Dahlem were to receive free land, and their leaders, government salaries. The salaries were not necessarily to come in the form of full professorships; in fact Beckmann's was the only such appointment among the directors brought in from outside Berlin for the early institutes.[60]

The contract formally establishing the Kaiser Wilhelm Institute for Chemistry for an initial term of fifty years was finally concluded between the Kaiser Wilhelm Society and the Imperial Institute Association on December 23, 1911.[61] Hopes for transforming the partnership into a foundation did not wholly vanish until a few years later.

On the other hand, the other two chemical institutes opened during the prewar period were closer to the legal form that Fischer continued to prefer; although neither was made into a foundation as such, both were supported by foundations.[62] Koppel established his institute within the framework of his own foundation, created in 1905 to foster international cultural exchange. He had thus already paid the discouraging start-up taxes faced by the association, but he still had to pay a gift tax on his donation to build the institute.[63] Similarly Mülheim already had its own Leonhard Foundation, which conveniently fell into the city's hands with the death in October 1911 of the widow Margarete Leonhard, Hugo Stinnes's sister. From the foundation's endowment of nearly five million marks, the city was able to provide the Coal Research Institute's entire capital—land, buildings, and furnishings, estimated at a total of some 850,000 to 900,000 marks—in the form Fischer had recommended.[64] The gift tax of 5 percent on all this was eventually avoided through the legal formality of having the institute's capital remain the property of the foundation, not of the Kaiser Wilhelm Society; at Fischer's suggestion, the institute's director became a salaried employee of the city, so the Prussian Finance Ministry would not have to support the enterprise at all. The

Kaiser Wilhelm Society then contracted with the city of Mülheim for tax-free use of the site. The society's administrative committee accepted this arrangement "in order not to weaken the coal-lords' sense of duty" to subsidize the operating costs, as Harnack explained to Friedrich Schmidt (a "Committee" of mining companies and other interested groups had been organized for the latter purpose).[65]

Architectural Form and "Prussianization"

The Kaiser Wilhelm Institutes for Chemistry and Physical Chemistry had begun to take physical form well before their legal form was settled. The shaping of these buildings also reflected the "Prussianization" of the Imperial Institute.

In November 1910 the council of the Institute Association had appointed a planning commission whose six members included the three directors, Fischer, Nernst, and Oppenheim, plus Heinrich von Brunck, Max Delbrück, and Carl Duisberg. The commission was to work out the necessary contractual arrangements and, in cooperation with Beckmann, design the chemical institute.[66] Fischer wrote to Richard Willstätter, who had been already contacted about a position in the chemical institute, explaining that preliminary building plans would be sent to him in order that his ideas might also be incorporated into the construction.[67] Under the new circumstances it was inevitable that the master architect would be Ernst von Ihne, who had renovated the royal palace in Berlin and who had joined the Dahlem planning commission along with Harnack. Ihne was the man guaranteed to produce buildings of which the Kaiser would approve;[68] hence Fischer could hardly object to Ihne's taking charge, even though the result might be more expensive than the association would prefer. Fischer took care, however, to bring in his own trusted builder, Max Guth, to take responsibility for the technical aspects of the design.[69] The preliminary plans for the Kaiser Wilhelm Institute for Chemistry were the product of the two architects and Ernst Beckmann.[70] Haber and Ihne independently designed the Kaiser Wilhelm Institute for Physical Chemistry and Electrochemistry.[71]

Ihne had presented his preliminary building plans to the Imperial Institute Association in February, when the directorate and building committee approved them "in principle." A few days later the administrative committee of the society also approved them along with the plans for the Institute for Physical Chemistry. Some of the leading industrial members of the Imperial Institute Association, however, were by no means prepared to accept Ihne's plans. On March 15 there was a "rather stormy" session of the directorate and building committee, to which Brunck had brought his chief construction engineer. Fischer was recuperating from influenza in the south of France and so could not attend; without his calming influence, Beckmann found himself under attack from several quarters. Objections were raised both to the "external design in general" and to "details of the internal furnishings." Beckmann found himself virtually ordered to visit the BASF's laboratory in Ludwigshafen as well as other industrial research facilities of "modern" construction and furnishings, after which he was to revise the plans. Franz Oppenheim, whose idea this was, reported his principal objections to Carl Duisberg a few days later.[72] Duisberg's first impression was that Oppenheim's objections sounded "so important, that we must bring down the present plans."[73]

In place of the one Imperial Institute building, there were now two institute complexes on adjoining land. The symmetrical, vaguely neoclassic facade of the old plan, which had been criticized as "too simple for an Imperial Institute"[74] (see illus. 7-1), found no echoes in the new institute for chemistry, which presented the outward appearance of a turreted suburban villa (see illus. 7-2) with high peaked roof and multiple chimneys. To the rear was planned a smaller adjoining building that seemed to be a stables but was actually the section for large-scale technical experiments. The technical section's external appearance and separation from the main building symbolized the subordinate role technological investigation was to play in the Kaiser Wilhelm institutes at Dahlem, contrary to the earlier expectations of the Imperial Institute's planners.

Beckmann claimed in his initial description of the new plans that they corresponded to "nearly all expressed wishes" far better than had the old Imperial Institute plans, and in some respects he was clearly right. The waste of space on corridors in the new plans was, for instance, only half that of the old (12.5 vs. 25 percent of the floor area). Beckmann also emphasized that Ihne had made "great sacrifices from his point of view as architect" to adapt himself to the chemists' desires.[75] That was hardly surprising, since Ihne was far more experienced at designing palaces than laboratories.

From the businessmen's perspective there were substantial problems with the design, such as the many small rooms that split up the work area (see illus. 7-3).[76] Brunck's staff had thus presented an alternative plan involving a few large, central laboratory halls similar to an industrial laboratory. But Nernst had warned Duisberg, and presumably Brunck as well, that Fischer had originally wanted Ihne involved, and that both Ihne and Beckmann would withdraw unless the association accepted the main principles of their plan.[77] Duisberg assured Nernst that he saw far fewer faults in the plans than he had been led to expect;[78] nevertheless he had also prepared and presented to Beckmann an alternative plan for the institute, which preserved only the external form while proposing a quite different interior layout based on his favorite "box system," an arrangement of laboratory cubicles he had devised two decades earlier for the main factory laboratory of the Bayer company (see illus. 7-4).

Beckmann also visited the laboratories at Hoechst, where Gustav von Brüning gave a more sympathetic ear to Beckmann's complaints about the alternative plans put forward by Brüning's competitors. Although Brüning, too, objected to the amount of space given to small, special-purpose rooms in Ihne's plans, he also rejected the large, factory-style laboratories proposed by the leaders of the Triple Alliance.[79] Because Fischer was still recuperating, Brüning contacted Friedrich Schmidt in the Prussian Ministry of Education, to whom he wrote as senator of the Kaiser Wilhelm Society.

Schmidt welcomed Brüning's letter, not the least because Schmidt had gained the worrisome impression from "the latest communications out of the circles of the Imperial Chemical Institute, that a unitarily directed giant institution in the sense of the Imperial Physical and Technical Institute could develop out of the pure research institutes with self-contained laboratories." Schmidt had therefore insisted on making the building plans "subject to approval by the administrative committee of the new institute."[80] That, of course, gave the government the opportunity to veto any major changes, if necessary. The combination of Schmidt's and Brüning's support may have given Beckmann the impetus he needed to dismiss both Duisberg's and the BASF's proposals.[81]

Beckmann's principal concession in the internal design was to accommodate Richard Willstätter, who later recalled that when he met Beckmann to discuss the building plans, "I was interested in the arrangement of the available space, and Beckmann in the equipment."[82] Like the businessmen, and for similar reasons—given their common experience in organic chemistry—Willstätter found the small rooms in the original plan inadequate and consequently had his section redesigned to convert three individual laboratory rooms into one large area for organic preparative work. Besides this general work room, he had space for more than a dozen researchers in his central laboratory and four more in each of two smaller laboratories (see illus. 7-5).[83]

One more change should be noted, minor in itself, but characteristic of the "Prussianized" form the institute had taken. Ihne's original conception of the exterior appearance of the Institute for Chemistry called for a simple, conical roof on the turret. When the building was completed, however, the turret bore a much more elaborate cupola, remarkably similar to a *Pickelhaube*, the traditional spiked helmet of the Prussian army (see illus. 7-6).[84]

The leading chemists of the Institute Association were unimpressed by such decorative touches, which led to excess costs. Nernst complained to Fischer about Ihne's "grandiose" style, which took money away from the research equipment itself.[85] Nernst was at least happy that the "combination of H[is] M[ajesty]'s and Ihne's ideas" had not produced even worse ornamentation than he expected.[86] Even so, when Ihne and Max Guth undertook a more precise estimate of the total cost of the plans in their original form, they came up with the appalling figure of 1.33 million marks. Even after simplifications, the total cost estimate exceeded by 100,000 the one million marks available to the Institute Association. Accordingly Fischer pursuaded Harnack to increase the society's contribution by 50,000 marks to a total of 200,000 marks, while the association raised another 50,000 marks with the help of Ignatz Stroof of Griesheim-Elektron.[87] Even with additional gifts of equipment and furnishings from several sources, it was not yet possible to provide complete furnishings for all the rooms, except in Willstätter's section. The cost problem also put an end to any of the businessmen's lingering hopes for a technical section, which remained unbuilt.[88]

The sister institute for physical chemistry also encountered cost problems, but the fact that a single man was paying for everything in the building evidently simplified matters. In October 1912, just before the institutes were scheduled to open, Haber informed Koppel and the government that the initial construction budget of 700,000 marks had been exceeded by 230,000 marks; he also requested an additional reserve fund of 120,000 marks.[89] (Ready to grant Haber all but 50,000 marks, Koppel requested that the Prussian government cover this by reimbursing the gift tax his foundation had already paid. The Finance Ministry apparently refused.)[90] Trott zu Solz, the education minister, therefore announced at the opening ceremonies on October 23 that Leopold Koppel was donating an additional 300,000 marks toward the construction and furnishing of Haber's laboratories.

Koppel, said Trott zu Solz, had been moved to generosity "in deep thanks for Your Majesty's presence at today's celebration."[91] Then, as previously arranged with Koppel, Wilhelm repeatedly singled out the Jewish banker for special thanks and praise.[92] This one incident epitomized the Prussian style of modernization through the Kaiser Wilhelm Society; the gleam of Koppel's gold had combined with the aristocratic aura of the Kaiser's person to produce the special brilliance of a new institute.

Emil Fischer's speech on this occasion pointedly referred to the related combination that had produced the other institute. The Imperial Institute Association had initiated the plan and owned the building, but the Kaiser had made it possible for the institute to come into existence through founding the society. Disguising the problems in construction, Fischer explained that the institute could not be a "monumental building, because the architecture had to be adapted to the purposes of the institute. But

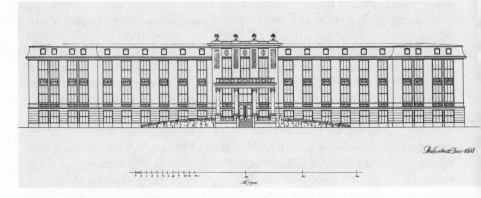

Illus. 7-1. Max Guth's conception of the facade for the planned Imperial Chemical Institute, dated June 25, 1908 (BA 46/6, VCR/B)

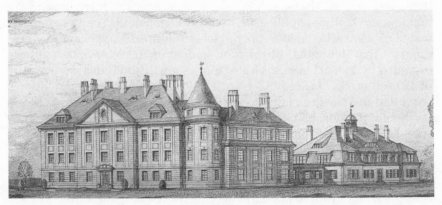

Illus. 7-2. Ernst von Ihne's perspective drawing of the main laboratory (center) and technical section (right) for the planned Kaiser Wilhelm Institute for Chemistry, Berlin-Dahlem, 1911. Compare illus. 7-6. The technical section was never built. (BA, Nr. 144, Baupläne)

simplicity is characteristic of all experimental science. . . . Therefore the workshops of experimental research should also be free from any splendor, but equipped with all the means of advanced technology and wholly adapted to serious, dispassionate observation."[93] Nevertheless Ihne had done his best to encase the institutes with their modern research facilities in shells that could pass for examples of the upper-class villas of Dahlem. The result may not have been the palaces some would have preferred, yet some outside observers were impressed all the same. French scientists, for example, contrasted the modern "country houses" of the society to their

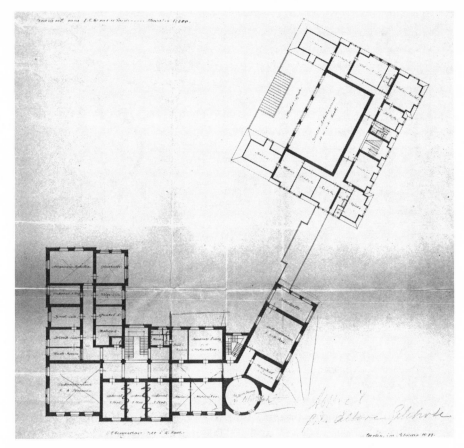

Illus. 7-3. First-story plan of the Kaiser Wilhelm Institute for Chemistry, Berlin-Dahlem, as proposed by Ernst von Ihne, February 1911. The main building is at the lower left, the technical section, at the upper right. (BA, Nr. 144, Baupläne)

own ornate, but obsolete "palaces of science"—too monumental to be torn down and rebuilt.[94]

Emil Fischer seems to have taken greater care to keep the building costs to a minimum in the case of the coal institute in Mülheim. He also had the powerful backing of Krupp von Bohlen, who agreed that "Ihne builds too dearly,"[95] as well as of Hugo Stinnes, who was opposed to collecting large sums of capital from the coal industry beyond what was available from the city's Leonhard Foundation.[96] Fortunately, although the coal institute too bore the Kaiser's name, its remoteness from Berlin made it less necessary for the Kaiser to put his personal stamp on the building. The Kaiser's architect therefore seems to have played no part in the planning. Emil

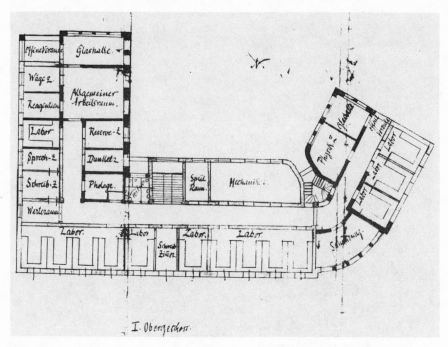

Illus. 7-4. First-story plan of the main building, Kaiser Wilhelm Institute for Chemistry, Berlin-Dahlem, as proposed by Carl Duisberg, 1911. Compare Ihne's plan, illus. 7-3. (BA, Nr. 144, Baupläne)

Fischer himself had estimated that the building and furnishings alone would cost between 600,000 and 700,000 marks, of which the greater part (400,000 marks) was to go for furnishings including apparatus, chemicals, etc.[97] When Franz Fischer designed the building, with the assistance of the mayor and the architect of the city of Mülheim,[98] he was apparently able to keep within these prescribed limits.

The resulting style differed from that of the institutes in Dahlem, betraying a more neoclassic approach favored by Franz Fischer, and reminiscent in some ways of the original plans of the Imperial Chemical Institute. Yet as with the Dahlem institutes, the layout of the Coal Research Institute had the appearance of a country estate; thus its architecture also epitomized the ambiguities in the relationship between science and its industrial patrons. Emil Fischer noted during the opening ceremonies in 1914 that a superficial glance at the exterior might give a stranger the impression that it was a "monument" to the success of the German coal industry, perhaps even a "temple of conspicuous display," an impression belied only by the well-equipped laboratories inside and the "modest men of science" working in them. The institute's location, on a hill overlooking

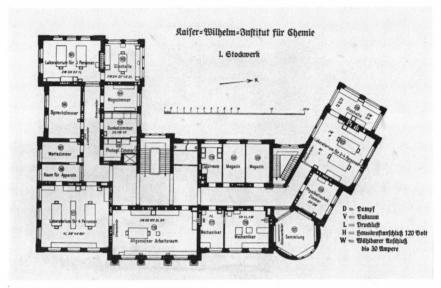

Illus. 7-5. First-story plan of the main building as completed (Willstätter's section). The principal laboratory rooms were 101, 111, 113, and 127; the large general work area (113) had been created by merging three smaller laboratory rooms in the original plan, and the office (105) enlarged by eliminating another small laboratory. Compare illus. 7-3 and 7-4. (Max-Planck-Gesellschaft Photo Archive)

the industrial works crowded around the city, also suggested a degree of aloofness in the scientists' "higher goal" of research, even though its purpose was to open "new pathways" for industrial development.[99] As the following section will show, the ambiguities in the relationship manifested themselves in the administration of the institutes as well.

Agencies of Administrative Control: The Problem of "Free Research"

The conflict over the proper legal form for the institutes seems largely to have been waged between the academics and the bureaucrats. At issue was a question going back to the original Imperial Institute memorandum of 1905: To what degree would the external institutional form manifest the prestige of the scientific research to be enshrined within? By contrast the matter of the internal administrative structure of the institutes and their connections with each other and with the Kaiser Wilhelm Society was a question of power, and in this the businessmen took a much greater interest. The academic chemists and educational bureaucrats were also concerned, however, lest the exercise of business interests in scientific research compromise the autonomy of individual researchers in the new

Illus. 7-6. Photograph of east facade of the Kaiser Wilhelm Institute for Chemistry, Berlin-Dahlem, around 1913. Compare illus. 7-2. (Max-Planck-Gesellschaft Photo Archive)

organization. Emil Fischer was obliged to pursue a difficult course of balancing the demands of his business supporters against the priorities of scientific research; in conjunction with Harnack and Schmidt, he established the principle of guaranteeing "free research" in all the Kaiser Wilhelm Institutes. The preliminary solution of these tricky problems was the final stage in the process of "Prussianizing the Imperial Institute."

Administrative Bodies for the Chemical Institutes in Dahlem

In April 1911 it was decided that the administrative committee of the Kaiser Wilhelm Institute for Chemistry should have five members, two each from the association and the society and one from the Prussian Education Ministry.[100] Fischer accepted this arrangement, along with a contractual provision giving the Education Ministry the right to confirm any subsequent changes in the contract, as a small price to pay for the government's cooperation.[101] The main thing was that the association obtained the effective power to select all four nongovernment members of the administrative committee. Nernst and Fischer decided to have two businessmen and two academic chemists: this was to be the real balance.[102] Fischer and Gustav von Brüning, both senators of the society as well as members of the association, would be the society's representatives; Nernst and Franz Oppenheim would represent the association. Fischer was of course elected chairman of the committee, Nernst its secretary, and Oppenheim its treasurer.[103] The association's directorate was now the Chemical Institute's administrative leadership, assisted by Hugo Krüss as the Prussian government's representative.

The administrative council of the institute, the second and larger of the two directing bodies, could not quite so neatly become an extension of the Institute Association's council. As the main source of the capital, the association claimed one more seat than the Kaiser Wilhelm Society on the institute's administrative council, unless the association's annual contribution to the institute should fall below the agreed-upon level. Brunck wanted to drop the latter proviso,[104] but Fischer retained it as obviously necessary to keep industry contributing to the association. When negotiations to exchange representatives with the Koppel Foundation so as to promote administrative cooperation between the two chemical institutes led nowhere, the administrative council of the first chemical institute was set at nineteen members (in addition to the five members of the administrative committee), including ten from the association and nine from the society.[105]

The two chemical institutes became administratively almost independent, except for their connection with Prussian government. Otherwise their administrative councils were quite different, to the degree that the Koppel Foundation's council contained no chemists. Its members, aside from Leopold Koppel himself as chairman, included Valentini as the Kaiser's representative and two physicists, Philipp Lenard and Emil Warburg.[106] The three directors of the Institute Association selected, for their share of their institute's council, nominees who were "to guarantee a harmonious cooperation of industry and higher education, of foreign and domestic members."[107] The association's choices were evenly balanced between academic, industrial, and foreign representatives, including even nonmembers (Robert Mond had not inherited the membership of his father Ludwig, who had died in the previous year). By contrast, eight of the nine men named by the Kaiser Wilhelm Society were businessmen, seven of them leaders of the German chemical industry. The association's majority was further secured through the fact that two of the society's nominees to the council were also members of the association. On the whole, however, it does appear that those appointed by the association were major contributors to it and not to the society, and vice versa. To the extent that Fischer was responsible for choosing the society's members, it therefore appears that he was trying to select those, like Arthur von Weinberg of Cassella, who had previously avoided supporting the proposal for an Imperial Institute. The resulting apportionment of influence

Table 7-1. Administrative Bodies of the Kaiser Wilhelm Institute for Chemistry, Berlin-Dahlem, March 1912

Body	Affiliation and Selection[a]	Marks Contributed (in thousands)[b]	
		To ICIA	To KWS
Administrative Committee			
Emil Fischer, Berlin University (Chairman)	A-KWS	5	20
Gustav von Brüning, Hoechst	I-KWS	95	200
(Mar. 1913: Herbert von Meister, Hoechst)	(I-KWS)	(95)[c]	50
Walther Nernst, Berlin University (Secretary)	A-ICIA	5	—
Franz Oppenheim, Agfa (Treasurer)[d]	I-ICIA	55	20
Friedrich Schmidt, represented by Hugo Krüss, Prussian Education Ministry; ex officio			
Administrative Council			
Eduard Arnhold, Berlin[d]	I-KWS	—	250
Henry T. von Böttinger, Bayer	I-KWS	100	150
Carl Duisberg, Bayer (Chairman)	I-KWS	(100)[c]	40
(previous: Heinrich von Brunck, BASF)	(I-ICIA)	145	20
Paul Ehrlich, Institute for Experimental Therapy, Frankfurt[d]	A-KWS	—	–
Wilhelm Haarmann, Haarmann & Reimer	I-KWS	8	50
Edmund ter Meer, Weiler-ter Meer	I-KWS	3	100
August Oetker, Bielefeld	I-KWS	—	100
Walther vom Rath, Hoechst	I-KWS	(95)[c]	100
Arthur von Weinberg, Cassella[d]	I-KWS	—[e]	100
Max Delbrück, Institute for Commercial Fermentation, Berlin	A(&I)-ICIA	5	—
Emil Ehrensberger, Krupp	I-ICIA	100	—[f]
Hans Goldschmidt, Th. Goldschmidt[d]	I-ICIA	8	30
Carl Harries, Kiel University (and Siemens)	A(&I)-ICIA	100	20[g]
Bernhard Lepsius, Griesheim-Elektron	I-ICIA	90.5	—
Carl Liebermann, Berlin Technical College[d]	A-ICIA	5	—
Otto Wallach, Göttingen University[d]	A-ICIA	—	—
Carl Müller, BASF	I-ICIA	(145)[c]	—
Robert Mond; Brunner, Mond (Britain)[d]	I-ICIA	200[h]	40
Fritz Roessler, Degussa	I-ICIA	5	—
Totals (=5 A, 18 I, 2 A&I)	All-KWS (12)	211	1160
	All-ICIA (13)	723.5	130
	Entire (25)	934.5	1290

Sources: Minutes, Vorstand VCR, June 15, 1911, VCR-1, pp. 211–12; minutes, Senat KWG, June 23, 1911, AHP, Sect. IV, Box 23, Protokolle.

[a]Affiliation: A = academic; I = industrial. Selection: KWS = chosen by Kaiser Wilhelm Society; ICIA = chosen by Imperial Chemical Institute Association.

[b]Contribution to ICIA includes total from individual, his firm, associates, and to Chemical Industry Association fund; contribution to KWS is that by individual only.

among the big concerns of the chemical industry in the administrative committee and council of the institute was as follows: Triple Alliance, four members; Hoechst-Cassella, three; other major concerns, four. Unlike the situation with the association's council, there were also three representatives of smaller firms. The seven academics, including Max Delbrück, now found themselves in a definite minority; their presence at all reflected close ties to industry or previous work of great economic significance. Fischer's search for "Jewish money" is also evident from the composition of the administrative council (see table 7-1).

Although the administrative council elected Brunck chairman by acclamation in October, he had little time to enjoy the office before his death in December.[108] Fulfilling Fischer's long-standing wish, Carl Duisberg followed Brunck as chairman of the institute's administrative council, while Brüning rather reluctantly replaced Brunck as chairman of the association's council of directors.[109] Although with Duisberg the Triple Alliance retained its controlling position, the BASF as the only major South-German chemical corporation now had only one representative on the institute's council. Similarly the South-German states, which had once been invited into the council of the Imperial Institute Association, would have no say in the affairs of the Kaiser Wilhelm Institute. The representative of the Prussian Education Ministry was the only government official on the institute's council. In fact, the association's council had itself become obsolete; Fischer thus proposed a "simplification" in the association's statutes, whereby the "Imperial Institute" concept was to be buried along with the old council organization.[110]

Accordingly, on March 8, 1913, the Imperial Chemical Institute Association's assembled members unanimously agreed to abolish their council of directors and add an additional member to the directorate to replace the position formerly occupied by the chairman of the council. The new statutes specified that the association was "to promote scientific and technical chemistry, especially through involvement in the establishment and support of the Kaiser Wilhelm Institute for Chemistry." The institute association's new name was "Association for the Advancement of Chemical Research." Carl Alexander von Martius, if he noticed the change, must have chuckled. After five years, Fischer and company had finally adopted one of his suggestions.[111]

---

cAmount of contribution in parentheses has been given in a previous entry.
dJewish or of Jewish descent (8 members).
eLater joined ICIA with 10,000 marks.
fKrupp family gave 1.4 million marks to KWS.
gSiemens gave 100,000 marks to KWS.
hFather's donation.

The timing of the change coincided with the expiration of most of the initial memberships in the association and was intended to forestall the danger that the leading firms, perceiving that the "Imperial Institute" project had finally been abandoned, would themselves abandon the Imperial Institute Association. Their loyalty appeared to be shaken by the deaths of key leaders; first Brunck, then Gustav von Brüning in February 1913. After Brüning's death a letter from the surviving directors of Hoechst appeared to imply that they now contemplated terminating the firm's membership. Fortunately Robert Pschorr, the association's business manager, happened to be a close friend of Herbert von Meister, son of one of Hoechst's founders. Pschorr was able to persuade Meister to join the reconstituted association himself, to accept its chairmanship, and to renew Hoechst's membership. Eventually Meister also agreed to take Brüning's place on the administrative committee of the institute.[112]

Fischer gained an additional success toward the end of 1913 when his old target, Cassella, finally joined the reorganized association, albeit with only two regular votes.[113] Much had changed since Gans had first attacked the Imperial Institute plan; Cassella's directors had, however reluctantly, joined the Kaiser Wilhelm Society, and in return Fischer had equally reluctantly integrated Gans's idea of a national grants fund into the administrative structure of the two Dahlem institutes through their scientific advisory council.

While interring the Imperial Institute as such, the planners of the two chemical institutes had erected an almost purely decorative monument to the departed hope for a single chemical institution with administrative connections throughout Imperial Germany. This was the scientific advisory council, a body consisting of twelve scientists, mostly eminent, selected by eight different organizations (table 7-2). The advisory council was nominally intended to "promote the connection between the [Kaiser Wilhelm] Institute [for Chemistry] and the Kaiser Wilhelm Institute for Physical Chemistry as well as the existing scientific organizations," through such means as providing advice and opinions on the direction of research, the annual budget plans, and the nomination of new directors.[114] It was, however, constituted too late to affect the choice of the first directors of either institute. Moreover, Fischer made it clear to Otto Wallach, the first chairman, that the council "was to be as invisible as possible."[115] Administratively it was so, routinely approving the annual budget plans of the directors without discussion.

Yet in 1912 Fischer had found a real function for the scientific advisory council: to administer grants from Leo Gans's donation to the Kaiser Wilhelm Society of 100,000 marks, which he had insisted be used to provide research grants for any needy chemists in Germany *except* those who might work at the Kaiser Wilhelm Institutes. Each year 3,500 marks,

Table 7-2. Initial Composition (October 1912) of the Scientific Advisory Council of the Kaiser Wilhelm Institutes for Chemistry and Physical Chemistry

---

The Kaiser Wilhelm Society for the Advancement of the Sciences
  Carl Duisberg (Director, Bayer Chemical Corporation)
  Paul Ehrlich (Director, Institute for Experimental Therapy and Speyer House, Frankfurt/Main)

The Imperial Chemical Institute Association
  Carl Engler (Professor of Chemistry, Karlsruhe College of Technology)
  Ludwig Knorr (Professor of Chemistry, Jena University)

The Koppel Foundation
  Philipp Lenard (Professor of Physics, Heidelberg University)
  Emil Warburg (President, Imperial Physical and Technical Institute)

The University of Berlin
  Karl H. Wichelhaus (Associate Professor and Director, Technological Institute)

The Berlin Academy of Sciences
  Emil Fischer (Professor of Chemistry, Berlin University)
  Walther Nernst (Professor of Physical Chemistry, Berlin University)

The Göttingen Society of Sciences
  Otto Wallach (Professor of Organic Chemistry, Göttingen University; elected chairman of the Advisory Council)

The Leipzig Society of Sciences
  Arthur Hantzsch (Professor of Chemistry, Leipzig University)

The Bavarian Academy of Sciences, Munich
  Wilhelm Muthmann (Professor of Inorganic Chemistry, Munich College of Technology)

Sources: Minutes, Vorstandsrat VCR, October 26, 1912, pp. 2–3, in VCR-P.

the interest from the Leo Gans Endowment, was to be apportioned in the form of direct research support to chemists outside the society's institutes. Fischer decided who would receive the first grant in 1912, and he permitted himself a degree of revenge on Gans by selecting Otto Hahn and Lise Meitner,[116] whom Fischer was already preparing to transfer from his own university institute into the Kaiser Wilhelm Institute for Chemistry. Afterward, the scientific advisory council selected the recipients.

The Gans awards averaged about 430 marks in 1913 (eight grants) and 350 marks in 1914 (ten grants). The program probably worked best in 1913, when the council generally picked mature scientists in their forties who had reached the rank of associate professor, mostly at universities. They were well distributed in location and specialty, with a tendency toward the interdisciplinary and toward areas outside classical organic chemistry, the main focus of most directors of German university chemical institutes. Thus their work promoted the original goals of the Imperial Institute project.[117] Although the war and the subsequent inflation destroyed the program, it did demonstrate the value of Gans's proposal for a systematic national grants fund like the American Carnegie Institution, which was later to be tried in Germany on a much larger scale by organizations like the Emergency Community of German Science, in which Fritz Haber of the Kaiser Wilhelm Institute for Physical Chemistry was to play a leading role.

The Gans endowment, along with the reorganization of the Imperial Institute Association, represented a final compromise between the opponents and proponents of an Imperial Chemical Institute. Thus these developments can also be seen as part of the process of "Prussianization." On the other hand, that process also involved the division of the Imperial Institute into three separate Kaiser Wilhelm Institutes, each controlled by competing interests: besides the association and Koppel, governing the first two Dahlem institutes, the coal industry obviously represented the principal interest group that would influence the Mülheim institute. Here too compromises were required in shaping the administrative organs.

Administrative Bodies for the Institute in Mülheim

The original plan called for the Kaiser Wilhelm Institute for Coal Research to be controlled by a director and a curatorium (board); the curatorium would appoint the director, subject of course to confirmation by the Kaiser. Members of the curatorium were themselves to be appointed by the principal groups with interests in the institute: the Kaiser Wilhelm Society (although none of the members actually had to be members of the society), the local donors' organization called simply the Committee, and the city of Mülheim. Kruse, as Düsseldorf district governor, would preside. Trott zu Solz insisted upon adding a member to represent the Prussian Education Ministry,[118] and another seat was added for the Rhenish Society for Scientific Research. Following some heated discussions and disagreements over the relative shares in the governing board or curatorium, its membership was set as indicated in table 7-3. The businessmen had wanted a clear majority for their own representatives (from the Committee and the city of Mülheim) in a smaller curatorium, but Rudolf von Valentini, chief of the Kaiser's civil cabinet, had insisted on adding seats to secure greater influence for the Prussian government and the Kaiser Wilhelm Society. The society's leaders decided to pay for their two extra seats with a capital donation of 10,000 marks and annual contributions of 20,000 marks promised for at least five years. Valentini seems also to have received a price for his intervention. Emil Fischer drafted a petition to have the philosophical faculty of Berlin award Valentini an honorary doctorate, specifically in recognition of his services to the Kaiser Wilhelm Society.[119]

Valentini acted of course in the name of the Kaiser, who was evidently

Table 7-3. Members of the Curatorium, Kaiser Wilhelm Institute for Coal Research, 1912

Member	Representing
Governor Francis Kruse (chairman)	District of Düsseldorf, Prussia
Mayor Lembke (deputy chairman)	City of Mülheim/Ruhr
Hugo Stinnes (deputy chairman)	City of Mülheim/Ruhr
Beukenberg	Committee
Franz Haniel	Committee
Emil Kirdorf	Committee
Möser	Committee
August Thyssen	Committee
Eduard Arnhold	Kaiser Wilhelm Society
Henry T. von Böttinger	Kaiser Wilhelm Society
Emil Fischer	Kaiser Wilhelm Society
Ernst Trendelenberg (Secretary-General, KWS)	Kaiser Wilhelm Society
Friedrich Schmidt	Prussian Ministry of Education
Gustav Steinmann	Rhenish Society for Scientific Research, Bonn

Sources: Minutes, First meeting of the Curatorium of the Kaiser Wilhelm Institute for Coal Research, November 4, 1912, reproduced in Rasch, *Vorgeschichte*, pp. 204–5.

taking a personal interest in the project following Kruse's report to him about the meeting of July 1912 in Mülheim.[120] The Prussian education minister later reported to the Kaiser that the project was successfully in motion and that the participation of industry would bring "no harmful influences whatsoever" to bear on the institute. This did not negate Kruse's similar assurance to the Committee at its first meeting in October 1912 that the administrative structure provided "a sufficient guarantee that the wishes of the participating works of the Rhenish-Westphalian industrial district would always be given the greatest possible attention, and that the influence of the latter would never be resisted."[121]

By this time there were already fifty "participating works" in the Committee, whose resources totaled 117,000 marks in annual donations and 41,000 marks in capital. The minimum contribution required for membership was 1,000 marks annually over ten years or a 10,000-mark capital

Table 7-4. Members of the Donors' Committee for the Kaiser Wilhelm Institute for Coal Research, October–November 1912

Member	Regular Votes[a]
Major contributors (10 or more votes each), 53, including:	
Hugo Stinnes (deputy chairman): 5 Stinnes Mines	7
3 other firms represented by Hugo Stinnes	16
August Thyssen (deputy chairman): Thyssen Concern (6 firms)	10
Franz Haniel: 3 mines	10
Emil Kirdorf (chairman): Gelsenkirchener Bergwerks-AG	10
Middle contributors (3–8 votes each), 37.5, including:	
6 mining and steel firms with 3–7.5 votes each	29.5
Hoechst Dyeworks	3
Rhenish Society for Scientific Research	3
Smallest contributors (2 or fewer votes each), 26.5, including:	
14 mining firms	17
5 miscellaneous firms, including chemicals and tar refining:	8.5
Association for Mining Interests in the Upper Mining	1
District of Dortmund	
Economic Association of German Gasworks	2
Total, all annual contributors:	117
3 one-time contributors:	41,000 marks

Source: "Verzeichnis der für das künftige Kaiser-Wilhelm-Institut für Kohlenforschung in Mülheim zugesicherten Beiträge," SAK, Nr. 15622, nos. 32–34 (forwarded by Kruse to Rheinbaben, November 2, 1912; cf. nos. 13–15).
[a]One vote represents the payment of 1,000 marks in dues annually.

donation.[122] Despite the fact that the coal firms had no tradition of support for scientific research, they willingly accepted these terms; in fact, the pledges continued to come in, so the annual income exceeded 140,000 marks by 1914. This was twice as much as the Imperial Chemical Institute Association had been able to obtain for a commitment to only half the time, despite the much stronger tradition of support for academic chemistry in the chemical industry. Of course a few major concerns held the balance of power in the Committee, because, as in the Imperial Institute Association, each 1,000 marks of dues counted as one vote (see table 7-4). Kirdorf was elected chairman of the Committee, with Thyssen and Hugo Stinnes as his deputies.[123]

The Institute's curatorium held its inaugural meeting in November 1912 with Kruse presiding; one of its first official acts was to approve Franz Fischer's appointment under exceptionally favorable conditions that Emil Fischer had already worked out, including a salary of 20,000 marks (8,000 of which was payable for life from the city of Mülheim) and permanent employment under the same conditions applying to directors of Prussian university laboratories. Franz was supposed to assume his duties in the spring of 1913, about the time construction was to begin; in fact, he had already begun planning the institute.[124]

A scientific advisory council similar to that established for the chemical institutes in Dahlem was also created for the institute in Mülheim, ostensibly to assist the director and curatorium in scientific work and to "promote contacts between the institute and existing scientific organizations as well as industry"; because of the latter phrase, added after the initial discussions in July, the council had a very different composition than the one connected with Dahlem. Aside from seven representatives chosen by the Committee, the institute's curatorium, and the Kaiser Wilhelm Society, its remaining eight members were evenly divided between industrial interests (those appointed by two regionally based industrial interest groups and the two superior mining offices in Bonn and Dortmund) and academic institutions (the colleges of technology of Aachen and Berlin, and the universities of Bonn and Münster). It had, however, only one practical function, to provide an opinion on the selection of a director, and—at Emil Fischer's suggestion—the statutes even excluded it from doing so for the appointment of Franz Fischer. Evidently Emil Fischer had no wish to see his choices debated in such a forum of experts with potentially clashing interests.[125]

The Principle of "Free Research"

Having involved all the principal leaders of the chemical industry and related branches of heavy industry in the support of the Kaiser Wilhelm Institutes, Fischer and his fellow academic chemists had to deal with their expectations for profit from their research. That meant working out arrangements regarding patents and the direction of research.

From the beginning of discussions over the Kaiser Wilhelm Institutes, Fischer, Harnack, and the bureaucrats in the Prussian Ministry of Education evidently agreed that "pure scientific research, not aiming at practical goals, can also be of the greatest economic significance," and that results of research which "seemed to possess solely a scientific value" had "become the basis of the greatest technological progress."[126] How were they to express this in a pithy phrase that could be written into the statutes? A decade or two later they might have simply spoken of "basic research"; unfortunately, the term had not yet become popular or perhaps had not even been coined. In any case, the phrase "pure research" alone did not produce quite the image of autonomous scientific work with potential industrial relevance that Fischer and his associates wanted to convey.

They settled on "free research," which suggested the German scholarly tradition of academic freedom. In 1900, in discussing the principles of operation in his own institute, Fischer had emphasized that a large-scale enterprise in science, as opposed to industry, needed "as free an organization . . . as possible."[127] The freedom of research for the principal scientists in the Kaiser Wilhelm Institutes was therefore guaranteed in writing in the founding statutes of each institute, the idea being that they would not only be free from routine duties like teaching and examinations, but also free to choose any subject for investigation they wished.[128] Fischer also used the idea to recruit Richard Willstätter to join the Institute for Chemistry, telling him, "You will be completely independent. Nobody will bother about you or interfere with you." And indeed, in order "to preserve complete independence" Willstätter rejected "favorable consulting contracts" offered by two large firms.[129] Harnack further emphasized this point in his speech at the opening of the first two institutes, promising that the society's "main task" would be "to watch over the institute's scientific independence and freedom."[130]

But how was "free research" to be guaranteed in practice? One way taken by the academic leaders of the Kaiser Wilhelm Society and the Prussian Education Ministry had been to give the institutes' senior scientists officially salaried positions of one kind or another, thus lessening their dependence on the industrial donors' groups. Another indication of the approach Fischer wanted to take can be seen in the compromise worked out in regard to patenting results of research. The question had long been discussed in private, going back to the early stages of planning for the Imperial Chemical Institute, though patents had deliberately been omitted from the contract between the society and the association in order not to divide the businessmen and drive out current or potential supporters. The patent issue finally surfaced in conjunction with the discussions over terms of appointment in the Kaiser Wilhelm Institutes. Having abandoned the Imperial Institute model, the planners need not necessarily follow Imperial policy, which prohibited scientific officials from taking out patents on work done with its facilities.[131] (It was assumed that research done in official government research institutions would have enough general significance to be made available to the entire industry of the country without patent restrictions.)

What would be the case with the Kaiser Wilhelm Institutes? The Prussian Finance Ministry wanted the directors and members of the Kaiser Wilhelm Institutes to have the right to take out patents, a third of the royalties from which should go to support their institutes (thus minimizing the need for official support). In the case of the Institute for Physical Chemistry, Koppel's firm agreed, since this would also give it the right to profit from Haber's work; Haber's contract thus contained a clause to this effect, despite Haber's own hopes for a contrary provision that from a "humanitarian perspective" or "for ethical reasons" the government could prohibit the patenting of inventions.[132]

On the other hand, the Imperial Institute Association represented a much wider range of interests, and it was not clear who, if anyone, should have the principal rights to patents from the Institute for Chemistry: the individual researchers, the administrative council of the institute, the association, the society, or perhaps certain industrial firms that supported certain research projects? Both Heinrich von Brunck and Gustav von Brüning had thought that individual members of the institute staff should be permitted to take out patents under their own names, which would of course also give them the right to transfer the rights to a private company for profit, while as in Haber's case the institute should be entitled to a share of the royalties.[133] At the institute's first council meeting, it was proposed that each permanent member of the staff be required in his contract of appointment to share with the institute 25 percent of his earnings from any patents taken out as a result of research done in the institute. The professors feared, however, that the government would use the provision as a precedent for carrying over a similar obligation to the chemists of the universities and colleges. Besides, the provision would imbue an institute "devoted to the cultivation of pure science" with "the character of an inventing laboratory."[134] There were only five academic members at this meeting; yet a straw vote went eleven to six against the idea of obligatory profit sharing. Clearly several businessmen had opposed Brunck and Brüning. Nevertheless a compromise was reached that satisfied the latter men by keeping open the possibility of profit sharing in the future. Beckmann's contract included a clause stating that he might be obligated by decision of the administrative council to pay 25 percent of his profits to the institute. Willstätter, who in his memoirs rather proudly called himself a poor negotiator, had the provision altered to state that he would have to give up a share of patent royalties only on such discoveries made after the council decided to obligate him. Furthermore, the money thus given to the institute must "primarily" be reinvested in Willstätter's own research section.[135]

The Coal Research Institute, representing in a sense the missing technical side of the would-be Imperial Chemical Institute, necessarily raised even greater expectations of profit, which had to be balanced against scientific autonomy. In his initial proposal for the institute, Fischer had therefore stressed that its close connection to industry should neither limit the "freedom of research" for the director and members, nor permit the institute to come under control of any single firm. These principles were confirmed by discussions between Böttinger and Kruse in July 1912,[136] then affirmed in Fischer's speech introducing the proposal to the coal industry. The director and his principal subordinate would enjoy their academic freedom, but "naturally within the limits given by [the institute's] name." The director was also to be selected in consideration of the need to ensure a "friendly relationship" with industry. Although devoted to a technical area, fuels, the institute would be scientific in the sense that "in general" its results would be publishable and its administration independent of "any single industrial works." Individual staff members would be permitted to take out patents on their results, but they must give up a share of the profits to the institute as in the case of the society's other enterprises. It might be necessary to add other restrictions, Fischer suggested, to avoid the "monopolization" of such patents. By this Fischer stigmatized only monopolization by a single firm, not by German industry as a whole. He did not think it "right" to "hand over by publication inventions that would guarantee an advantage to German industry" against its foreign competition.[137]

The principle of "free research" as defined by Fischer was thus written into the statutes of the Coal Research Institute; and as with the Dahlem institutes, the patent issue and the related question of sharing profits were defined in the contracts of the director and individual scientific members. By referring to the precedent of the academic laboratories and the Dahlem institutes, Fischer persuaded the leading business members of the curatorium at its first meeting to accept the idea that the scientists should give up no more than 30 percent of the profits from their patents, and that this share should go to the institute. Unlike the situation with the Dahlem institutes, however, the curatorium insisted that additional provisions regarding patents be established through private correspondence between Emil and Franz Fischer. The members of the donors' Committee were to obtain favorable rates for licensing the patents, thus giving them an advantage over domestic competitors; additionally, all German firms were to be given advantages over their foreign competitors, as Emil Fischer had already suggested in his July speech. Although in these discussions Kruse, the district governor, tended far more to support the businessmen's interests than the scientists', Emil Fischer (backed of course by Berlin) won on the points he deemed most vital.[138]

Emil Fischer's talk at the opening of the institute revealed some of the problems he must have had in getting the leaders of the coal industry to invest in "free research." He compared their enterprise to a "marriage of convenience" between science and industry, with the contract initially limited to ten years at the latter's insistence, and he acknowledged that many of the coal magnates doubted that their investments would fully pay off even in that much time. Nevertheless, even if no "great inventions" emerged from the new institute, its expense should be justified by the profits arising from its mere presence as an adviser to the industry for chemical questions and as a center for mutual interchange among local chemists and engineers. Having decided to found a research institute, the industry had shown a willingness to accept the risk of a novel approach. As "the first special institute for a specific material" to be established with the help of the Kaiser Wilhelm Society, it had been "created on a basis far freer than any previous institutions of its kind." In fact, Fischer described its primary task as "opening new pathways" for the coal industry, a phrase almost identical to the one Werner von Siemens had used a generation earlier to express the purpose he envisioned for an ideal Imperial Institute. As director of the new institute, Franz Fischer accepted this characterization of his duties, at the same time recognizing that the "new paths" that could be followed in the coal industry were limited by the degree of engineering sophistication in that industry. For example, whereas the BASF chemical firm could pursue hydrogenation techniques using high-pressure autoclaves on a large scale—the basis for the Haber-Bosch ammonia synthesis and the later Bergius process for synthesizing oil from coal—the coal industry would have to limit itself to the "technically simpler" processes using only heat without high pressure. Franz Fischer eventually chose to work toward a coal-oil conversion process under these conditions, as his way of fulfilling his contract with the coal industry.[139]

Concluding Observations

The founding of the coal institute completed the "Prussianization" of the Imperial Chemical Institute, which had begun with the establishment of the first two chemical institutes in Dahlem. The capital costs of these three institutes together amounted to more than 2.7 million marks, and their operating budgets totaled more than 370,000 marks by 1914, including the professorial salaries of Beckmann and Willstätter. These amounts compare favorably to the high demands made by Duisberg and Oppenheim in the February 1906 discussion of the Imperial Institute plan, when they had estimated the capital and budget costs at 2 to 3 million and 400,000 marks respectively, much to the chagrin of Emil Fischer.

The main difference between 1914 and 1906, of course, was that not a pfennig had come from the Imperial budget, and very little from the Prussian state government. That significant capital funds had come from the municipal budget of Mülheim, controlled by the coal magnates, only underscores the chemists' own inability to loosen official purse-strings. It had thus been possible to obtain sufficient funds only by making the series of compromises discussed in this chapter, the most important of which entailed the division of the originally planned institute into three smaller ones that more closely resembled existing university institutes. This necessitated abandoning the old dream of a modern institute for "analytical chemistry in the widest sense," with science and technology interacting on the frontiers of all the principal subdisciplines of chemistry.

Yet the Kaiser Wilhelm Institutes did correspond to the model of an academic research laboratory that Emil Fischer had apparently preferred before embarking on the quest for an Imperial Chemical Institute. His influential position in the Kaiser Wilhelm Society also made it possible for him to shape its initial scientific policies along the lines of his own interests. Although he subordinated technological aspects at Dahlem, a result confirmed in any case by financial limitations, he did propose a technologically oriented research institute at Mülheim and thereby obtained from the coal industry the kind of support that had been denied in 1906–7. The coal industry's Committee was set up even more explicitly as a joint-stock company for scientific investment than the Institute Association had been. And although many powerful members of both organizations demanded specific returns on their investments, as apparently did Leopold Koppel in the case of Haber's institute, Fischer was able to persuade enough far-seeing businessmen to establish the principle that in general the scientists supported should be left as free as possible to pursue long-term scientific research, which eventually could—but not necessarily would—be profitable. The new institutes thus occupied a middle ground between the "pure-science" ideology of the traditional academic institutions and the profit-making ethic of individual capitalist firms and businessmen, a marriage blessed by the Kaiser's name with its connotations of Imperial loyalty. The combination of a theologian and a chemist in the society's leadership, the legal form and the make-up of administrative bodies of the research institutes, even aspects of their physical form, reflected the resulting dualities in their nature.

While the Kaiser Wilhelm Institutes thus represented a significant change in the understanding of the role of research in Imperial Germany, as well as a significant addition to German research facilities, the effectiveness of their scientists' work was limited by the circumstances of the institutes' creation. It exemplifies the process of conservative modernization that the Prusso-German bureaucracy was so little prepared either to provide them material support or, as the next chapter will demonstrate, to integrate them sufficiently into the existing network of academic institutions.

8

The Promises Were Not Kept: Limits to the Development of the New Institutes before the War

There were ... drawbacks at Dahlem which seem to beset the establishment of research institutions in Germany permanently and immutably. ... The promises proclaimed ... were not kept. ... Disadvantages ... follow from the isolation and the special position of research establishments.
—Richard Willstätter, *From My Life*

Institutional Limits

By 1914 the Kaiser Wilhelm Institute for Chemistry already faced difficulties, not just in hiring new staff but even in holding the researchers it already had. The root problems were only partly financial. Rather the budgetary complications were exacerbated by a deeper flaw, the inability of the Kaiser Wilhelm Institutes to gain full acceptance into the existing structure of academic institutions supported by the Prussian government.

From the beginning the Kaiser Wilhelm Society encountered resistance from within the Berlin Academy and the universities. Let Ulrich von Wilamowitz-Moellendorf present his reasons for fomenting opposition: "first because the Emperor only lent his name and the money chiefly came from industrial sources, secondly because they [the Kaiser Wilhelm Institutes] had nothing to do with the University, and lastly because if industry creates anything of the kind, it expects practical results for itself. We cannot blame industry for that, but it is very American. . . . A friend of the Academy may become anxious if he pictures to himself that all these richly endowed and successful institutes might be combined in one union for natural science, so that our department [i.e., the *Geisteswissenschaften*, or humanities] would be quite overshadowed."[1] The Kaiser, it should be noted, had done somewhat more than just "lent his name"; but his participation in the opening festivities of the first two chemistry institutes would have more than confirmed Wilamowitz's fears that industry expected "practical results." Wilhelm had, on behalf of the Ruhr coal industry, challenged the chemists to produce some means of detecting the deadly, explosive "fire damp" in the coal mines (there had recently been great loss of life from this cause). The chemists had in fact dutifully complied with the imperial orders. Both Haber and Beckmann produced devices, Haber's in time for the "social monarch's" jubilee in 1913.[2]

Wilamowitz thus spoke in one guise as the representative of "pure scholarship," opposed to the corruption of science by practical, "American-style" industrial applications. He had a worldwide reputation as a classical philologist and, therefore, the right to argue in this fashion. But he also had a personal reason for his opposition to an enterprise led by his rival Harnack, whom he must have regarded as a renegade from the humanistic section of the academy.[3] Harnack, for his part, resented the section's dominant "philological clique" and especially its leader. Wilamowitz "lets nothing pass that he has not himself brought about," Harnack told Schmidt in 1911; "he is immoderate and an extremely harmful influence." His "mistrust against the Kaiser Wilhelm Society . . . is extremely strong and is transferred to others through the suggestive power which he exerts upon his friends."[4]

Beyond this, however, Wilamowitz also spoke as a representative of the Junker aristocracy of Posen, the province that had contributed the least—nothing—to the Kaiser Wilhelm Society. He did not conceal his contempt for "the well-fed bourgeois, who only think of earning money and whose god is their belly."[5] Apparently for Wilamowitz "America" meant preeminently the land of the fat bourgeois without culture; he therefore, unlike Harnack and Fischer, opposed Althoff's plan for a German-American exchange professorship. He also fought unsuccessfully to keep the bourgeois spirit out of the universities by keeping the *Gymnasium* and its classical curriculum, including Greek, as the sole acceptable condition for admission, and he still believed in 1910 that it would be better to restrict access to the universities rather than to build new ones (as planned in Frankfurt and Hamburg) that might "receive elements . . . which either find our instruction unpalatable or would drag it down to the level of the eighteenth century." These "elements" were best shunted aside into "quite new institutions," by which he meant the colleges of technology, business colleges, etc.[6] The Kaiser Wilhelm Society with its "American" bourgeois philanthropists fell into the same category. Ironically, here he joined forces with the Social Democrats, who opposed "Americanization" for analogous reasons: they did not want to see the industrial bourgeoisie using money to gain control of German scientific institutions. Yet the two groups differed in that the Social Democrats wanted the government to pay by further taxing the rich, which the Junkers of course rejected.[7]

Harnack and Emil Fischer on the other hand thought in terms of integrating old and new "elements." On the eve of the opening of the Kaiser Wilhelm Institutes for Chemistry and Physical Chemistry, Harnack contemplated the need for modernizing the academy by introducing three or four dozen businessmen into its ranks, at least as honorary members. He had in mind those friendly with the Kaiser like Albert Ballin and the Krupps, philanthropic bankers like James Simon, and the directors of the giant chemical and electrical concerns whose works employed large scientific staffs, and who could thus discuss "issues of the progress of the sciences." This might lead to cooperation between the academy and the Kaiser Wilhelm Society, perhaps to the union of the two organizations, each of which had what the other lacked: businessmen, money, and institutes on the one hand, scholars on the other. But could the academicians be persuaded to accept nonscholars, or the businessmen, to support an official institution like the academy?[8]

Early on, the Prussian government had assumed that the answer would be negative.[9] Then in 1911 the Prussian Education Ministry had made its first effort to open a connection between the Kaiser Wilhelm Institutes and the academy. It arranged to have all German academies represented on the scientific advisory council of the chemical institute. Moreover, at the ministry's suggestion, the Kaiser decreed that three posts be created in the mathematical and scientific section, to be reserved for directors of the new institutes. To minimize the resulting imbalance between the humanistic and scientific sections, the voting rights of the new posts were to be limited.[10]

Tempers flared as the scientific and humanistic sections, meeting separately, discussed and rejected the government's proposals in the searing furnace of a mid-July heat wave.[11] In the humanistic section the discussion coincided with the election of a new secretary, an honor Harnack had expected but was denied as Wilamowitz and his outraged followers wildly attacked the Kaiser Wilhelm Society and its institutes, as well as Harnack's role in creating them. Harnack was forced to defend the society and himself, and to assure his detractors that he acted in the best interests of the academy and that their fears were "unjustified and thoughtless." Finally, he accepted an amendment to the effect that the three new scientific posts be regarded as "preferably," but not necessarily, for the institute directors.[12]

By the following week, tempers had cooled along with the weather, and the academy in its joint meeting approved the new scientific positions in the amended form provided by the humanistic section, requesting in addition three new humanistic posts in order to restore parity between the sections.[13] Apologies were made to Harnack, but the underlying tensions remained.

To relieve the tensions, Friedrich Schmidt found it necessary to invite all the secretaries of the two sections to a private discussion in the fall of 1911. With Harnack, Fischer, and Nernst present, Schmidt made it clear to all that Harnack was acting in accordance with the Kaiser's wishes, and that the new society would not be integrated into the academy. Despite Harnack's private inclinations in this direction, moreover, he and Schmidt rejected suggestions by Fischer and Nernst that would have given the academy a role in selecting directors or a voice in approving projects for future institutes.[14] Thus the Prussian government preferred to keep the academy and the society apart, rather than trying to remove the financial and social obstacles to integrating the two institutions.

A similar problem was encountered in the relationship between the institutes and the universities. When the founding of the society was announced in 1910, the university professors who had not been involved in the initial planning seem to have been uncertain as to the new institution's purpose. Some reactions reported in the press at the time forecast a quite limited role for the institutes, supplementing the research capabilities of the universities.[15] Gradually, however, a debate developed over the possible threat that research institutes posed to the universities, perhaps by draining off the best scientists and the bulk of the research funds from the latter and forcing them to become little more than teaching colleges.[16] Wilhelm Ostwald argued on the contrary that the institutes should become "highest schools," designed to teach and carry out research above the level of the existing institutions for higher education.[17]

The fact that most of the directors and senior staff members of the earliest Kaiser Wilhelm Institutes came from non-Prussian institutions[18] must also have created the impression that the Prussian government would use the society chiefly to drain off talent from the smaller German states (hence the Saxon government refused to let Beckmann go in 1912 until he had been replaced by a Prussian scholar).[19] Even the Prussian universities, however, could be jealous of the society's concentration of talent and facilities or fear the influence of its industrial members on scientific research. By March 1911 the Conference of German University and College Teachers had relayed the resulting professorial criticisms to the Prussian minister of education, Trott zu Solz. During the legislative debates over the Prussian government's financial support of the two Kaiser Wilhelm Institutes for Chemistry, Trott zu Solz took the opportunity to assure the Prussian House of Deputies "that in the first instance an actual *organic connection between the institutes of the Kaiser Wilhelm Society and the universities* is *not* planned." By serving as a link between the two institutions, the Education Ministry would ensure that the society benefited the universities.[20] This assurance did not, however, persuade all the deputies that the society would not damage the provincial universities by luring their hard-pressed teachers to the quieter research centers.[21]

The education minister responded by reaffirming that the universities would remain "places not only of teaching but also of research." The society would act solely to supplement their research efforts, and it would employ only those few, "suitable" scholars who were chiefly inclined to work on long-term research problems, not teaching, along with a few younger scholars who wanted to spend shorter periods in temporary, full-time research. Thus most scholars would continue to work in the universities, and Trott zu Solz promised "close relations" as well as "lively interaction" between the two institutions. "Universities and research institutes should go hand in hand."[22] Only a month earlier Friedrich Schmidt had berated Harnack for not having kept him informed of the internal affairs of the society since Harnack had assumed the presidency. Schmidt warned Harnack that the effective development of the society would be "unthinkable, unless it maintains a friendly, regulated, lasting connection with the government authorities and through the latter with the other great scientific institutions. . . . There could be very undesirable consequences, were this not to happen."[23]

And what was the result? By Richard Willstätter's testimony "there were . . . drawbacks at Dahlem which seem to beset the establishment of research institutions in Germany permanently and immutably. . . . Those establishments which have no connection with universities, or only a loose one, lack a regular influx of collaborators. . . . There is no advancement for the associates, no secure route by which they can enter an academic career without difficulties and obstacles. In general the universities were of little help to the research institutions and have remained so. The promises proclaimed . . . were not kept. The disadvantages which follow from the isolation and the special position of research establishments are the inability to confer the doctorate or permit qualification of instructors."[24] Why not? One of the most important reasons was that the philosophical faculties denied full professorships to most of the society's scientists, even the institute directors. In Berlin, Wilamowitz's "Göttingen clique," which dominated the councils of the philosophical faculty as they did the academy, were equally unwilling to create new senior posts for scientists in either institution.[25] Even scientists, if they were full professors, showed little enthusiasm for creating additional full professorships in their own fields.

Willstätter was able to avoid some of these difficulties because his call to Berlin coincided with the death of van't Hoff, opening an honorary full professorship for Willstätter. He was able to attract students from foreign countries to supplement the ten or so collaborators he brought with him from Zurich, but at first even he could not recruit any new assistants from inside Germany, to say nothing of Berlin. Good talent among younger chemists was particularly scarce after a decade or more of stagnant and declining enrollments in the teaching laboratories, and the problem was complicated by "the rapid absorption of trained chemists" into the now booming chemical industry.[26] Beckmann and Haber undoubtedly had similar difficulties. Even Emil Fischer complained about the shortage of assistants during this period; industrial demands were so great "that many laboratories can hardly occupy their assistantships."[27]

The same kinds of problems that developed in connection with the chemical institutes continued to crop up as other Kaiser Wilhelm Institutes were established, particularly the Institute for Biology, which was delayed in part because of hostility in the university faculties. Emil Fischer and his colleagues did little to improve interinstitutional relations. Hence Theodor Boveri, the government's first choice for director of the biological institute, apparently had to withdraw his first request to Friedrich Schmidt for a full professorship of general biology in the philosophical faculty at Berlin.[28] The position was unacceptable because it would have claimed some of the teaching competence claimed by professors on the medical faculty as well as those for botany and especially zoology on the philosophical faculty. Then Boveri asked Schmidt to guarantee that two of his assistants would be certified for lecturing by the philosophical faculty.[29]

At Schmidt's request, Emil Fischer informed Boveri that the two assistants could not count on certification in the field of general zoology, though possibly in a more specialized field in which Boveri alone could claim expertise rather than one of the existing professors on the faculty. Fischer went on to express the hope that the institutes and the universities could be formally independent from each other, but still have interchangeable staffs. Doctoral candidates trained at a research institute could be examined by the university even without the director's being present on a faculty, because if one faculty proved troublesome the students could always be sent to another. Only the quality of research mattered, not the personal connection between student and professor. Fischer conveyed this suggestion to Boveri with an appeal not to disrupt the faculty and cause further problems for the research institutes by attempting to exert pressure through the Ministry of Education.[30] This was Fischer's solution to the problems posed by faculties and professors jealous of their rights and younger researchers anxious for their academic careers. The research institutes might open opportunities to the younger men without too much infringement on the rights of the established hierarchies. It meant, of course, that the new institutes would not be likely avenues to bring fundamental institutional reforms into the universities.

Fischer later consulted Nernst on Boveri's demands. Nernst was not optimistic for Boveri's chances to control the issuance of doctorates or lectureships if he only directed a research institute without simultaneously occupying a full professorship. The faculty would not and should not give up the *slightest* control over these matters to an outsider, Nernst believed, probably thinking of Haber. Hence a directorship without a concurrent full professorship would be an exception and "generally undesirable."[31] Boveri's subsequent decision to break off negotiations for the appointment appears to have arisen from a combination of these potential problems with the faculty in Berlin as well as a sudden deterioration in his health.[32] One may wonder whether the connection was more than coincidental; he had suffered a stroke following a negotiating session in Berlin.[33] Carl Correns, a botanist rather than a zoologist, eventually became the biological institute's first director.

The Kaiser Wilhelm Society cannot be said to have developed a very close relationship between its early institutes and either the university or the academy by 1914. Besides Beckmann, only one director, Max Rubner, held a full professorship, and he had had it before his Kaiser Wilhelm Institute for the Physiology of Work was created, initially as a section within his existing university institute for physiology; no other new full professorships were created before the First World War. This was not for lack of government financial support, because the Prussian Finance Ministry agreed to establish government-salaried directorships for August von Wassermann in the Institute for Experimental Therapy and for both co-directors, Correns and Hans Spemann, in the Institute for Biology.[34] The salaries, 15,000 marks annually, were made comparable to the highest full professorships,[35] though of course without the student fees that made those professorships really desirable. It was precisely to retain their monopoly over the bulk of student fees that the university faculties opposed the creation of new full professorships for the directors of the research institutes.

As opposed to directors' positions, senior scientific members of the institutes, except perhaps for Willstätter, were generally not as well compensated as full professorships; however, Willstätter recalled that he and Haber worked to have memberships rather than the Prussian university-style section headships established in all the Kaiser Wilhelm Institutes. The idea of a scientific member of an institute was, however, "un-Prussian."[36] The universities would not have approved, because an institute with "members" rather than subordinate section heads or subdirectors resembled a department in a college of technology, or worse yet, an American university, and it thus implied a breach with the hierarchical tradition of university institutes. In the universities a section head was generally an associate professor or lower, but the members of the Kaiser Wilhelm Institutes could and, like Willstätter, did claim a status equivalent to full professors and the directors of university laboratories. Moreover, their compensation was at least higher than the base salaries of section heads, if not always higher than the latter's total incomes.[37]

The sacrifice of financial achievement for status in the institutes perhaps helps to account for Willstätter's observation that in Dahlem "a conspicuously and disproportionately large fraction of the appointments went to Jewish or non-Aryan scientists—too large, in my opinion. They just happened to be available, since the universities certainly did not make it hard to lure them away."[38] Harnack and Schmidt knew as well as Fischer that, at least in some areas, a Jew's chance of reaching a full professorship were far below average,[39] just as they knew that some of the "Jewish money" in the society had been contributed in the expectation that Jewish scholars would thereby benefit. How many "Jewish or non-Aryan scientists" were in fact attracted to the institutes? In the biological institutes one may cite Wassermann, Neuberg, Goldschmidt, and Warburg; in the chemical, Willstätter, Meitner, and Haber.[40] Two out of the first three institutes built in Dahlem were directed by men falling into the "non-Aryan" category. In early 1914, until the coming of war forced a postponement and eventual modification of plans, the society also intended to use part of the grounds of the Kaiser Wilhelm Institute for Chemistry to establish a physics institute for the most famous "non-Aryan" scientist of all, Albert Einstein, who had been elected to the Berlin Academy in 1913. The new institute would have been supported by the Prussian government, the society, and the Koppel Foundation.[41] Thus were the tendencies born that two decades later led the Nazis to speak of the "Jews' Society."[42] Much the same pattern of Jewish involvement simultaneously appeared in the case of the "Endowment University" of Frankfurt/Main, where the donors were also offered some potential influence on the appointments.[43]

Despite its relationship with the Prussian government and its support for scientific research, the Koppel Foundation unfortunately went virtually unrecognized at first by the official German academic community, which could accommodate it even less than it could the Kaiser Wilhelm Society proper. The most striking evidence for this is the fact that the academic yearbook *Minerva* [23 (1913/14)], listed the Kaiser Wilhelm Society and Beckmann's Institute for Chemistry as a research institution in Berlin, but nowhere did it mention the Koppel Foundation or Haber's Kaiser Wilhelm Institute for Physical Chemistry—even though the two chemical institutes had been founded simultaneously on adjacent sites!

Indeed, relations between the two institutes had been somewhat less than neighborly since the beginning, when efforts to establish administrative cooperation between the directors of the two chemical institutes had failed because each director refused to invite his counterpart to take part in his own institute's discussions. While stiffly insisting that Haber's institute be granted no privileges not also accorded his own, Beckmann had disingenuously asserted that he was "on the best of terms" with Haber.[44] One could in fact find plenty of personal differences between the two men:

Beckmann was apparently a devout Christian, Haber a religious opportunist who had converted from Judaism to Christianity to further his career; Beckmann was nearing sixty, Haber in his early forties; Beckmann was close to Haber's rival Nernst; and of course Beckmann had been a full professor at a university for two decades, while Haber had only recently become a full professor at a technical college.[45] Above all, however, Haber's institute represented the dissolution of the Imperial Institute that Beckmann had expected to lead, whereas Haber, having finally achieved an independent position as an institute director on nominally the same level as a university professor, had no intention of surrendering any of the personal power that a director normally would have.

Fortunately, there were other mitigating factors that lessened tensions between the institutes at Dahlem. One was the growing friendship between Haber and Willstätter, which had begun when Haber assisted the Institute Association in its hiring negotiations with Willstätter in 1910–11.[46] Another point not to be overlooked was that Haber's institute possessed the only dining hall in the complex; there were still no restaurants in Dahlem, and Emil Fischer adamantly opposed investing the Kaiser Wilhelm Society's money in "pubs."[47]

The war and the half-hearted revolution that followed it were to produce few essential changes in the structure of German academic institutions; the research institutions remained only partially integrated and thus handicapped, mainly attracting those like Otto Warburg and Otto Hahn who, because of personality or discipline, did not fit well in the universities. No less an authority than Harnack himself testified to this in 1929: "In the nineteen-year history of the society my original worry that the university and teaching could suffer from the research institutes has dissipated. I have learned that the full professorship possesses a maximal power of attraction. . . . Over against the universities, the research institutes have even found it difficult to find suitable personages."[48]

Financial and Political Limits on the Kaiser Wilhelm Institutes of Chemistry

Some of the problems of the Kaiser Wilhelm Institutes derived from the irritating refusal of the Prussian and Imperial financial bureaucracies to grant them rights that traditional academic institutions already possessed, but that would have required some financial concessions from the government. The Kaiser Wilhelm Institute for Chemistry was also financially dependent upon a contractual agreement between two different organizations, both relying upon ultimately voluntary contributions from virtually the same potential sources, which made it nearly impossible to effect steady budget increases. Again this placed the institute at a relative disadvantage, compared with the academic institutions supported by the government.

The disadvantageous results of this situation soon became visible in the case of the alcohol tax. "I had not expected to have to pay the full, high tax on alcohol," Willstätter recalled later. "This sum used up a large part of the equipment appropriation. I encountered no understanding . . . at the tax office. Only educational establishments, i.e., university laboratories, could obtain alcohol tax free. The fact that the research institute was also a professor's laboratory and served for postgraduate training of university-educated men was not appreciated." Yet Fischer's request to the education minister to appoint Willstätter to an honorary professorship had emphasized that although his primary duty was to be a researcher, he would also perform an educative function through holding colloquia and providing research training to his assistants. Willstätter was also expected to attract other students from the university.[49] After mentioning his problems with the tax office, Willstätter went on to recount that "the alcohol problem was settled" after he mentioned it to the Kaiser at the dedication of the Institute in 1912.[50] If only it had been so simple!

Despite several attempts, the institute's leaders failed to get either a tax exemption or compensation from the Imperial government for their expenses. According to the Chief Tariff Office in Charlottenburg, a tax deduction for using denatured alcohol was allowable "only for commercial, but not for scientific purposes."[51] In 1914 the alcohol tax alone cost the institute 4,000 marks (about three quarters of which resulted from Willstätter's work).[52] By 1915 Fischer was forced to concede that no exemption would be granted, "because the law provides such . . . only for teaching institutions."[53] The Kaiser Wilhelm Institute had thus fallen through a crack between the bureaucratic categories "commercial" and "teaching."

One tax concession was finally achieved for the Kaiser Wilhelm Society in 1916, when the Prussian and Imperial governments finally agreed to forgo the 5 percent gift tax on contributions to it. But the concession had required pressure from the Kaiser himself. The tax issue evidently further strained relations within the institute, especially between Beckmann and Willstätter, by exacerbating the budget conflicts between them arising from the differences in their research fields and methods. In a laboratory, Willstätter later reflected, "only one man can direct."[54] In 1912 neither Beckmann nor Willstätter was in the habit of negotiating with a colleague over the allocation of a laboratory budget, and neither had expected to have to learn. Beckmann had every reason to expect that he would be the unchallenged director; Willstätter had, on the other hand, been assured of full independence. Each obtained less than he had expected, and less than he had enjoyed in his previous position.

In 1909 Beckmann had already agreed to become president of the abortive Imperial Chemical Institute, although his income would thereby be cut in half (from 40,000 to 20,000 marks). His disappointments continued in the new situation as he came to see that to many supporters of the Kaiser Wilhelm Institute he was to direct, Willstätter deserved as much if not more support than Beckmann himself, so that as an awareness of the financial limitations on the institute began to set in, it was his budget and not Willstätter's that would mainly suffer. Beckmann's preliminary budget had called for the total operating expenses of the institute during its first year to exceed 150,000 marks, far above the institute's agreed income. Fischer, Nernst, and Oppenheim made it clear to him whose costs were really indispensable.[55] The budget for Willstätter's section was retained at 43,000 marks, while Beckmann reluctantly reduced his own assistants and materials in order to achieve the desired maximum of 120,000 marks, and even more so as to allow for the temporary appointment of independent young researchers besides Willstätter.[56] Beckmann was given one compensation for the cuts, that Beckmann's assistants would receive slightly higher salaries, but on the day after the institute opened in 1912 its administrative committee withdrew that privilege for future appointments.[57] Having already promised Fischer to effect as many savings as possible in paying assistants, Beckmann had little recourse.

The "young researchers" Fischer had had in mind when he insisted on further cuts from Beckmann were of course Otto Hahn and Lise Meitner. Given Beckmann's resistance, it was well that Hahn could be obtained cheaply, with a materials budget of only 1,000 marks per year (later raised to 2,000 marks).[58] His salary of 5,000 marks had to come from direct subsidies offered by Franz Oppenheim and Robert Pschorr for the initial five-year term of appointment.[59] Although Lise Meitner had been Hahn's equal coworker since 1907 and had shared in all his major researches, she was obtained even more cheaply.[60] As an Austrian woman, a Jew, and a physicist, Meitner's presence meant little to the German chemists running the institute, and she had to content herself with the nonposition of unsalaried "guest." Finally in the fall of 1913 Fischer was to get the association to vote her separate compensation of 1,500 marks annually.[61]

Willstätter's demands from the institute were actually higher than Beckmann's and resulted in a long discussion by the administrative council. Beckmann was to be appointed to a full professorship at a standard salary, but the honorary professorship that the Education Ministry offered Willstätter—van't Hoff's old position—carried only an associate professor's salary of about 4,500 marks, including residence allowance. The institute would have to pay him the difference up to 18,000 marks, whereas it had to make up only 10,800 of Beckmann's 20,000 marks. Willstätter's budget for research staff was nearly equivalent to Beckmann's: 10,000 marks for assistants and 15,000 marks for materials. Besides this he requested the right to occupy the entire first floor of the main building.[62] As noted earlier, so near an equality in facilities and remuneration between a director and a mere "member" of an institute was "apparently un-Prussian and repeatedly led to difficulties."[63]

Evidently feeling betrayed by the large cuts in his income and budget as well as the steady erosion of his prerogatives, Beckmann had nevertheless told his colleagues at Leipzig that it was his duty to accept the directorship and finish what he had begun.[64] Yet the Prussian government added insult to injury at the opening ceremonies for the institute by making Beckmann only a Prussian *Geheimrat*, a lower rank than the *"Geheimer Hofrat"* he already held in Saxony. To have awarded Beckmann a higher rank would, however, have been to break with strict equality between him and Fritz Haber, who was also made a simple *Geheimrat*. Willstätter, on the other hand, had also been promised a *Geheimrat* title but did not receive it, evidently out of deference to Beckmann.[65]

Willstätter soon came under pressure to justify his demands, especially after Fischer's efforts to supplement the budget through "Jewish money," soliciting a special grant for Willstätter from Baroness von Rothschild, produced only 4,000 marks for each of the years 1912 and 1913. Fischer hoped that Willstätter would be likely to attract more support once he had achieved some "great successes" in his research.[66] Accordingly, late one evening after an official welcoming party for Willstätter, Nernst warned him that "we need something for show in the Kaiser Wilhelm Institute in a hurry. We expect you to produce some nice things, and especially to produce them quickly."[67]

Willstätter seems to have been somewhat taken aback by Nernst's news, but he at least had incentives and the talent to comply with the wishes of the administrative committee. Beckmann, on the other hand, could offer relatively little to the Kaiser Wilhelm Institute, which no longer resembled the Imperial Institute he had once hoped to lead. Nevertheless both Beckmann and Willstätter probably expected to carry on research at the institute much as they had done in their previous positions, though with less interruption by routine teaching. That was at least the ideal. In some respects it was realized; certainly they did not find it necessary to change their areas of scientific interest. During the summer of 1912, while the institute was still under construction, and during the winter semester of 1912–13, Beckmann worked on determinations of molecular weights and studies of isomeric phenomena. During the winter semester Willstätter worked on chlorophyll and other natural pigments. The most obvious difference they must have found between the new arrangements and their previous academic facilities was that whereas before they would have had a great many doctoral candidates as well as regular assistants to help with research, now they had only a few assistants and few, if any, students.

During the summer Beckmann worked with only two assistants and, after the opening of the institute, with three or four as well as an auditor. He had supposedly been authorized five assistants. Willstätter, who had also been authorized five, worked with six during the first semester as well as with five auditors.[68] "The operating expenses of a laboratory depend entirely on whether the work is predominantly concerned with measurements or with preparative work requiring large-scale use of solvents and other chemicals," Willstätter recalled later. He was engaged in the latter, Beckmann chiefly in the former, and it was clear that Willstätter thought Beckmann's operating costs were set too high and his own too low. "Until the beginning of the war sizable contributions from [Willstätter's] own pocket were necessary" to supplement his allotted "funds for assistants and equipment." The alcohol tax naturally hit Willstätter's work the hardest, and the cost forced him to use a less suitable solvent for some of the work.[69]

Beckmann's disappointments also continued as he had to cut his materials budget during the first year from 15,000 marks (equal to Willstätter's) down to 10,000 marks in order to cover unforeseen expenses in other items of the institute budget.[70] Once Beckmann had reduced his materials budget in 1913, he could not raise it back again to the old level in 1914. He did rearrange the allocations of other items within the overall materials budget to increase the fund for "reagents and materials" for general use,[71] but it is not obvious who benefited most from this change.

Willstätter's completion of his chlorophyll studies and his higher visibility in Berlin in any case soon brought him the leverage to alter the arrangements at Dahlem in his favor. In the winter of 1913–14 the Hamburg authorities approached him regarding a possible appointment with their city's scientific laboratories, which they were planning to convert into a university. Willstätter declined, wisely, because the University of Hamburg was still many years in the future. He used the offer instead, according to time-honored custom, to improve his existing position. Suddenly the Prussian government remembered its promise to make him a *Geheimrat*.[72] The institute's administrative council was likewise constrained, with Fischer's encouragement, to grant three concessions: Willstätter was given complete freedom in handling the sum of 10,000 marks budgeted for his assistants' salaries; his materials budget was increased to defray the alcohol tax; and he received an additional 10,000 to 15,000 marks "for the procurement of apparatus."[73]

Willstätter had thus nominally improved his position, but where were the necessary funds to be found? Beckmann's proposed budget for 1914–15, not including Willstätter's demands, had already reached 126,500 marks (see table 8-1) and thus exceeded the limit nominally imposed by the contractual agreement between association and society. The institute

Illus. 8-1. Ernst Beckmann (with beard) and assistants in his laboratory at the Kaiser Wilhelm Institute for Chemistry, around 1912 (Max-Planck-Gesellschaft Photo Archive)

still had a fair amount in reserve, chiefly 110,000 marks remaining in the furnishings fund and 55,000 marks left over from the operating fund. About half of the former had already been assigned to completing the necessary furnishings of the institute, however, while the surplus in operating funds derived solely from the fact that the Kaiser Wilhelm Society had paid 60,000 marks to the institute in 1911, before it had even been built. From 1912 onward, even though the partially completed institute was not yet operating at full capacity during the first year, it was evidently running at a deficit. Beckmann was paid 180,000 marks for operations from April 1912 to March 1913, when he should only have spent 120,000 marks at most. From May 1913 to February 1914 he was paid 165,000 marks for operations, thus again exceeding the contractual limit. As early as January 1913, Fischer thus realized that the deficit would be chronic.[74]

The administrative council could hardly have been happy to add to the institute's deficit by approving Willstätter's demands. On March 16, 1914, Max Delbrück wrote Duisberg that the previous day's meeting had left him with "a bitter aftertaste" and given him a sleepless night. "Proposals . . . to increase the budget will come every year, in growing proportions. They will not be kindly met . . . , and justifiably so, if it is certain that larger funds can be made available only through renewed collection of capital or dues. . . . A university professor can help himself otherwise. He is freer, because he can replace many assistants by students and doctoral candidates. And, finally, more can be accomplished through the Prussian government than through our administrative council, for whereas the former admittedly has many expenses, it also has a general budget which can be greatly enlarged." Delbrück suggested that the contractual limit of support from the society and association be left intact, but that the institute also be reorganized to permit the development of income sources presently "all but excluded" under the existing arrangements. Laboratory places might be rented out for 3,000 to 4,000 marks annually. Furthermore, patent income could be handled by having the institute join with the Chemical Industry Association, with the Kaiser Wilhelm Society, and with the Institute Association in a limited-liability corporation to which all rights to patents on discoveries made within the institute would be transferred for a fixed annual compensation. In regard to consulting work for fees, Delbrück foresaw "thousands" of opportunities. His own Institute for Commercial Fermentation had a number of agreements with various scientific facilities to do particular tasks for fees. The income from such contractual work could be quite large.[75]

Duisberg agreed with the premise that the basic budget should not be increased, at least not until the institute had time to achieve its full capacity and "so long as one has as little suitable a director as is here the case," but he doubted that any of the other proposals except for the rental of places would "fall on good ground" with Fischer. Nothing "practically useful" had yet been found in the area of patents, nor was it soon to be expected in view of the "purely theoretical level" on which the institute was supposed to work. "Therefore, at least for the present, one cannot speak of fee work either."[76]

The financial problem thus had no immediate solution. Indeed, it became even more serious in May 1914 as Lise Meitner also received a call. Meitner and Otto Hahn's work had not as yet caused much of a drain on the budget of the institute. The radioactivity research they had carried over from Fischer's institute had been in part subsidized by the initial Gans grant of 3,500 marks, and Meitner's salary of 1,500 marks was being paid by the association directly, outside the institute's regular budget. Hahn's salary, one assistant, and materials cost the institute only 7,000 marks annually during the first two years.[77] Then Meitner received her offer to become an assistant in the Prague University physics institute with the possibility of advancing to adjunct. Meitner told Fischer that

Table 8-1. Budget Plan of the Kaiser Wilhelm Institute for Chemistry for the Year 1914–1915 (as approved in March 1914)

Budget Item		Amount Budgeted (in marks)
Personal and Insurance Accounts		
Beckmann		21,700
Director	10,800	
Assistants	10,900	
Willstätter		22,300
Prof. Willstätter	12,300	
Assistants	10,000	
Hahn		6,500
Prof. Hahn	5,000	
Dr. Meitner	1,500	
Lower Officials		10,664
Director's office	1,320	
Willstätter's office	980	
Gatekeeper and custodian	1,500	
Mechanic	2,280	
Machinist	1,800	
Auxiliary stoker	1,200	
Laboratory technician	1,584	
Wage account (Cleaning women)	4,000	
Insurance and security	2,675	
Reserves for personal and insurance accounts	1,661	
Total	69,500	
Materials Accounts		
Gas, water, electricity, heat		16,000
Library		3,000
Director's materials budget		10,000
Willstätter's materials budget		15,000
Hahn's materials budget		2,000
Reagents and materials (general fund)		8,000
Building and grounds maintenance		3,000
Total		57,000
Total costs expected, 1914–15		126,500
Anticipated deficit, 1914–15 (before extra costs)		6,500

Table 8-1. Continued

Summary of Institute Expenditures from 1911 to March 31, 1914

Category	Appropriated	Spent	On Hand, March 13, 1914
Building fund	900,000	894,650.43	5,349.57
Furnishings fund	200,000	90,000	110,000
Operating fund	300,000	245,000	55,000
Totals	1,400,000	1,229,650.43	170,349.57
Interest income			7,226.52
Total Institute cash reserves, March 31, 1914			177,576.09

Source: Printed minutes, VI. Sitzung des Verwaltungsrates des Kaiser-Wilhelm-Instituts für Chemie, March 14, 1914, pp. 2–3. In BA, Nr. 142, Sitzungen.

she would like to stay in Dahlem, but at more than her present salary. Fischer tried to raise money for her among the potential private (Jewish?) donors in Berlin. Frustrated there, he broached the subject to Carl Duisberg. "Beckmann unfortunately does nothing in such cases," Fischer complained. "I am even afraid he will oppose us if we raise Miss Meitner's salary through a special grant without previously satisfying his demands for assistants and such."[78] Nevertheless Fischer and Duisberg ignored any protests Beckmann might have made, and beginning in 1915 Meitner was to receive 3,000 marks within the regular budget without any concurrent increases in Beckmann's personal appropriations. Beckmann's estimate of the regular budget thereby rose to 128,000 marks, not including expenses for alcohol tax and for reprints of institute publications. As no one else had joined the Association for the Advancement of Chemical Research during the first half of 1914, Fischer wrote on June 22 to his former lecture assistant Alfred Stock, teaching inorganic chemistry since 1909 at the new Breslau Technical College, that he was recommending Stock not for the Kaiser Wilhelm Institute but for the full professorship opening at the University of Münster. Nevertheless he would keep Stock in mind for the time when the institute could afford the additional 40,000 marks per year that Stock's research would cost.[79] Some years earlier Fischer had sent Stock to study under Henri Moissan, the French inorganic chemist who had pioneered the use of new methods and apparatus that first isolated silicon and fluorine.[80] With the proper facilities and adequate time to do the research, Stock might develop into a first-class inorganic chemist. This, Fischer thought, was far more likely to happen at Dahlem than at Münster. Stock eventually came to Dahlem, where he was able to return to the analysis of silicon compounds, but only after Willstätter left. The institute could not afford them both.[81]

From April 1914 to March 1915 the institute apparently spent over 60,000 marks of its capital beyond the regular subsidies, and it was therefore necessary for Beckmann to promise further cuts in expenditures.[82] By this time, of course, the situation had begun to change drastically with the coming of the war.

Before the onset of militarization had disrupted work in Dahlem, however, and despite the financial strains involved in the institutional arrangements, the latter had afforded at least some remarkable proofs of their value. Willstätter was able to begin studying the process of photosynthesis in the living leaf, a problem he had been interested in for "years" but until then had had no opportunity to undertake. The completion of his main line of chlorophyll research at Dahlem and its publication in 1913 finally gave him the chance he had been looking for. "During my second year of work at Dahlem," he recalled, "the opportune moment arrived and enough leisure was available in the Institute to permit familiarizing ourselves with the problem. In Dr. A[rthur] Stoll I had a scientifically very gifted, well trained . . . assistant, suited for precision work and of incorruptible reliability in quantitative measurements. We knew nothing about the living leaf. . . . Of course we had to pay dearly for experience. . . . Our results . . . did, however, provide preliminary work for the explanation of the phenomena in question."[83] Willstätter pursued this field for some time before being caught up in war research; it is unlikely that he would have had the time to undertake it at all had he not been at Dahlem. Postwar circumstances did not, however, allow him to return to it.

The work of Hahn and Meitner also benefited dramatically from the new facilities at Dahlem. Because of six years of radioactive "poisoning," their original workplace in Fischer's Berlin institute was almost useless for precise measurements by the time they moved to Dahlem in 1912. The new building was free of radioactivity, and they were able to develop methods to prevent its contamination. Despite the distractions of war, the institute offered opportunities for pioneering new research in radioactivity, leading first to the discovery of the element protactinium in 1917. Without Dahlem, Hahn and Meitner might not have been able to pursue their collaboration in this field. As a specialist in radioactivity, Hahn had little chance for a university professorship in chemistry, while without a position in Dahlem Meitner might well have answered the call to Prague in 1914.[84]

Illus. 8-2. Otto Hahn and Lise Meitner in their laboratory at the Kaiser Wilhelm Institute for Chemistry, around 1913 (Max-Planck-Gesellschaft Photo Archive)

Some additional long-term benefits from the arrangements in Dahlem should be noted, particularly the interdisciplinary contacts that may have been fostered within the small community of scholars there. Despite his tensions with Beckmann, Willstätter at least appears to have gained a greater appreciation for physical chemistry and radioactivity than he might otherwise have had; perhaps this was less a result of working with Beckmann than of his association with Haber, Hahn, and Meitner.[85]

Even with all the financial and institutional limitations they faced, the scientists in the Kaiser Wilhelm Institute for Chemistry therefore achieved some of the goals that had been held out for them. At the end of 1911 Fischer had related to his American friend T. W. Richards both his fears of the powder keg that Europe had become as well as the hope he saw in the progress of the Kaiser Wilhelm Society. "From that you can see that Germany still has some money left over for scientific purposes, despite the powerful military armament which it must bear. The two institutes will be established entirely out of private contributions."[86] He obviously meant this to sound optimistic, rather than to emphasize the government's inability or unwillingness to support the further development of scientific research. As yet he had perhaps not fully realized how limited private financing would be, or how advantageous the use of large numbers of unpaid doctoral students would begin to look, once the institutes were largely cut off from this once-scorned source of research assistance. In any case he had abandoned the earlier hopes of obtaining significant increases in the patronage of science from the Imperial or Prussian government, for as yet he was sharply distinguishing between scientific and military priorities. Hardly more than a year later, however, after considering the program for the Kaiser Wilhelm Institute for Coal Research, Fischer began to abandon this distinction.[87]

On a fine summer's day in 1914, Emil Fischer joined Adolf von Harnack and Francis Kruse in Mülheim to celebrate the opening of the coal institute. The festivities, much delayed due to technical problems, had truly come at the last possible moment. It was July 27, the last day of peace; on the following day, a little before noon, Austria-Hungary declared war on Serbia. The subsequent Russian mobilization in support of Serbia ensured that the war would bring in Germany, whose government could now present the war to its people as a defensive one. And the Kaiser Wilhelm Institutes, built in the name of international competition, promised to be as adaptable to its military as to its peaceful form. Ironically, by proving their military usefulness, the Kaiser's chemists could overcome many of the financial bureaucracy's previous objections to supporting them. Yet could even the crucible of war dissolve the barriers necessarily left between old and new academic institutions by the cautious process of conservative modernization?

For the existing academic institutions, led by tradition-minded humanists like Wilamowitz, had reacted in time-honored fashion by seeking to "quarantine" the Kaiser Wilhelm Institutes as dangerous innovations containing socially unacceptable "elements" like businessmen, especially those of Jewish origins. Those humanist scholars who associated with such "elements" found themselves, like Harnack, ostracized by their former associates. A chemist like Emil Fischer obviously experienced the situation differently, but in a way he had already isolated himself from people like Wilamowitz, with whom he had almost nothing in common.

Yet even Fischer, like his friend Nernst, had vested interests that would have been threatened had the new institutes been fully integrated into the existing academic system. The "un-Prussian" idea that members of an institute could be relatively equal in status to the director was acceptable for Dahlem, but not in Berlin. Nor were the university professors willing to concede unprecedented rights in the philosophical faculty at Berlin to the scientists in Dahlem. Without these rights, however, the scientists in the research institutes who lacked full professorships could not supervise dissertations or vote on lecturing privileges, which meant—especially given the limited budgets of the institutes—they had little to offer the students and young assistants who were still indispensable to a full-scale research program.

Had the corporate donors been willing to invest as much in "free research" as they did in their own industrial laboratories, or had the bureaucrats been willing to take the necessary steps to ensure that the senior scientists in the new institutes were given all the rights and status of full professors, the innovation would have been more successful. But because the new institutes stood, in a sense, halfway between the established industrial and academic institutions, they remained isolated and could not fully share the advantages of either.

9

Military Strength and Science Come Together: The Kaiser's Chemists at War

With deepest thanks to our Imperial Lord we may praise the fate which allowed the Kaiser Wilhelm Society to arise at just the right time.... Create, organize, discipline: in this triad of German spirit and German labor, military strength and science come together.
—Adolf von Harnack, Annual Report of the Kaiser Wilhelm Society, April 1916

In short, modern warfare is in every respect so horrifying, that sensible people can only regret that it draws its means from the progress of the sciences. I hope that the present war will teach the peoples of Europe a lasting lesson.
—Emil Fischer, December 1917

"The outbreak of war overtook us like a natural disaster," Willstätter wrote later.[1] In the first few days of August, the timetables of the Schlieffen Plan pulled most of the bright young chemists from their quiet laboratories and sent them out to chase the dream of victory on the fields of Belgium, France, and Russia. Emil Fischer took what was in those days an unusually realistic view of the war, fearing that Germany's opponents were strong enough to prolong the war into the next summer; after the Schlieffen Plan died at the Marne, he extended his prediction to at least one to one and a half years. His expectations corresponded to the most pessimistic assumptions of the group around Walther Rathenau and Karl Helfferich, with whom Fischer was to agree in other areas as well.[2] Nevertheless Fischer had come to accept the war as an inevitable response to the military threat from abroad, especially from the East. If Germany must fight, he reasoned, it was better to do so before the foe grew even stronger. His reasoning, evidently influenced by exaggerated reports in the German press that summer, approached the idea of "preventive war" circulating among leading circles of the German government and military during the early part of 1914, rather than the "defensive war" line with which the war

180

was officially justified in August.[3] Under the circumstances Fischer and his colleagues found no joy in contemplating their nearly deserted laboratories and lecture halls. Instead they sought out ways to make themselves useful in the war effort.[4] In so doing they discovered that science, and especially chemistry, could play a vital role. The era of the total war was at hand.

In the Service of National Propaganda: Defining Aims and Means

The pressure of events soon obliged Fischer to abandon the illusion that scientists might somehow continue to enjoy a feeling of international solidarity above the conflict. Reluctantly he put aside his correspondence with erstwhile friends on the other side, though he took the opportunity to send Sir William Ramsay greetings via a Swiss scientist when Ramsay asked for help in locating a relative missing in action.[5] As passions on both sides heated up, Fischer and other prominent scientists nevertheless successfully resisted proposals to retaliate against scholars on the other side, either by striking their names from the lists of honorary members of German organizations or by returning scientific honors to the foreign organizations that had conferred them.[6] "You cannot do anything, gentlemen," Einstein recalled Fischer telling the Berlin Academy at one point, probably in July 1915. "Science is and remains international."[7] Yet Fischer had been dealt a hard blow by his old friend Ramsay's vitriolic attacks on German chemists and the German chemical industry in the spring of 1915. With regret Fischer observed that Germany's opponents, like many of his own colleagues, lacked his enthusiasm for scientific supranationalism.[8]

One German scholar whom Fischer scorned for ultranationalism was Wilhelm Ostwald, a leader of the Monist League, which before the war had been pursing a left-liberal campaign of anticlericalism in Germany. Ostwald had even stood on the same platform with Karl Liebknecht, the revolutionary Social Democrat, to promote a "mass strike against the State Church," a movement to strangle official religion by having people renounce their confession (confessionless people paid no church tax).[9] Ostwald then considered himself an internationalist, if not a socialist, and he was involved in various international scientific and intellectual organizations. At Ostwald's suggestion, Ernest Solvay, the Belgian industrialist who had just sponsored the first international conference of physicists, had just agreed to provide the capital for an international chemical laboratory in connection with the recently organized International Association of Chemical Societies (to which Ostwald belonged as a German representative). The initial plans were being made when the German armies marched into Belgium, after which the outraged Solvay excluded the Germans.[10] Ostwald meanwhile drowned his internationalism in patriotic enthusiasm, transforming his anticlerical "Monistic Sunday Sermons" into nationalistic outpourings in support of the war effort and eventually of a peace of conquest. Perhaps his Baltic German origins helped to sharpen his feelings against the Russians. Adolf von Harnack, who was also an Easterner, eventually reacted in this way and by 1917 supported "the most extensive goals" of German war aims "by way of 'liberation' in the East."[11]

In January 1915 Emil Fischer was to write a sharply worded letter to Professor Peter Klason in Stockholm, complaining about Ostwald's Monistic activities there and his unofficial peace proposals. These, along with the public pronouncements of other German scholars, damaged the German cause as Fischer saw it by creating the appearance that "Germany pursues boundless plans. That is all nonsense." In this as in other letters to neutrals, Fischer spoke out for German moderation and for the rationality of the great majority of the German people.[12]

The need to convince the neutrals of Germany's essential righteousness placed Fischer among the ninety-three scholars, scientists, and intellectuals who signed Ludwig Fulda's manifesto "To the Civilized World" in October 1914. In the interest of solidarity Fischer aligned himself with Ostwald, Adolf von Harnack with Ulrich von Wilamowitz-Moellendorf, Richard Willstätter with the anti-Semitic physicist Wilhelm Wien, and all aligned themselves with the cause of German militarism. It was a step that many of them later had cause to regret. After the war Fischer even circulated a countermanifesto among the original signers.[13] As Willstätter recalled, "The professors were convinced that Germany bore no responsibility for the war and that war had taken it by surprise. . . . The war appeared to us to be a defensive one. The search for causes and connections went no deeper."[14] Let the manifesto speak for itself: "*It is not true* that Germany is guilty of having caused this war . . . that we trespassed in neutral Belgium . . . that our troops treated Louvain brutally . . . that our warfare pays no respect to international laws. . . . *It is not true* that the combat against our so-called militarism is not a combat against our civilization. . . . Were it not for German militarism, German civilization would long since have been extirpated. . . . The German army and the German people are one."[15]

A sizable contingent of those who subscribed to these sentiments had also been active in the establishment of the Imperial Chemical Institute Association, the Kaiser Wilhelm Society, and its various institutes. All three authors of the original Imperial Institute memorandum were there, Walther Nernst signing in addition to Fischer and Ostwald. Among the others, Fritz Haber signed as well as Willstätter; Paul Ehrlich and Carl Engler were on the chemical institutes' advisory board. Two other directors of Kaiser Wilhelm Institutes, Max Rubner and August von Wassermann, added their names. While four of the six active directors of Kaiser Wilhelm Institutes joined the proclamation, only one other chemist's name appears among the ninety-three: Fischer's mentor Adolf von Baeyer, whose father had been a Prussian general. These men were indeed the "Kaiser's chemists."

Emil Fischer did not merely subscribe to Fulda's manifesto, he distributed it to neutral colleagues abroad—though perhaps not quite so enthusiastically as Ostwald, who ordered one hundred copies through Fischer in October.[16] Unfortunately Fischer soon discovered that the effect was as much negative as positive.[17] Needless to say, the scientists in countries opposed to Germany reacted with outrage. The result that Fischer had sought to avoid now came to pass. French scientific organizations cut their ties with the Germans, dropping German honorary members from their rolls. "My French colleagues never forgave me for having been one of the signers of the Proclamation of the Ninety-Three," Willstätter recalled.[18] Few seemed able to resist the passions unleashed by the conflict; when Albert Einstein circulated an alternative proclamation with pacifist and internationalist sentiments, he got only four signatures, including his own.[19]

The illusions that led the German middle classes to support this war had captured Fischer as well as Ostwald and his more chauvinistic colleagues, less fanatically perhaps but just as surely. Carl Duisberg had written Fischer in August 1914, full of pessimism because the government's policy of embargo on dyes and drugs had cost his industry its world economic dominance, which might take another decade to restore, but equally filled with outrage against the British, "who are chiefly to blame for all the misery."[20] Fischer in reply forecast a long and bitter economic as well as military struggle, but with one consolation when it was all over. Germany could then create a continental bloc capable of competing with the United States. This was the war aim for which Emil Fischer, like so many of his colleagues, was to expend his talents and energies during the next few years. Essentially the same idea was at the basis of the war aims program that Chancellor Bethmann-Hollweg and his circle, including Walther Rathenau in particular, worked out during August and September 1914.[21] One of the salutary attractions of such a *Mitteleuropa* dream for the German scientists might well have been that if a political-economic unit emerged from the war capable of generating revenues on the same order as American capital, then the fund-raising woes they had been experiencing for the previous decade would finally be over. Whether or not "unlimited possibilities" in chemistry might require imperial conquests after all, however, it quickly became obvious that the conquests would require chemistry.

In the Service of the War Economy: Facing the Crisis in Raw Materials

Initially the war brought research in Germany nearly to a standstill. Two of the four main teaching sections of Fischer's institute were closed in the fall semester, and his own private laboratory was all but deserted. Fischer had just one regular private assistant and four coworkers—including two older men and one woman—where before he would have had several times as many. Overall, Fischer estimated in November that the scientific institutes held only about one-third their normal capacity of students.[22] The pause in German science would allow the United States to take the lead, Fischer told an American chemist.[23]

In the early days of the war the same story had been true of the Kaiser Wilhelm Institutes, with what Richard Willstätter recalled as the "devastation of scientific life at Dahlem."[24] Most of the students and assistants went to war. Thus Fritz Haber's institute, apparently one of the hardest hit, lost all but five members of its staff.[25] Beckmann's institute lost Otto Hahn and many assistants.[26] Under the circumstances, those remaining naturally looked for ways to use their scientific talents in war work. Fritz Haber and Richard Willstätter asked Adolf von Harnack in the first days of August whether the government might need them. Harnack inquired but, as Willstätter recalled, "no use could be made of us." To Willstätter this reflected the lack of technical imagination that the social outlook of the Prussian army had produced at the top of the military hierarchy. Initiatives in the application of science to military problems were to come from outside the military bureaucracy.[27] Emil Fischer was one of the scientists most prepared to participate. While the transition from peace to war may have been traumatic for him, it was not illogical, as he was to acknowledge in November 1914 to a former subordinate then in the army. "I am actively engaged in the business of war. No wonder, because our science interacts very strongly with economic as well as military life."[28]

The administrative committee of the Kaiser Wilhelm Society conferred on August 12, 1914, with the directors and senior members of the institutes, with the society's two principal architects in Berlin, and with two representatives of the Prussian Education Ministry. How, they asked, was the society to act in the war? It was agreed that the institutes should try to pursue their original aims as far as possible within their original budgets, paying salaries to those staff members in service. The society would continue to construct institutes already begun. "It was also indicated," according to the official minutes, "that individual institutes had already begun to take up the solution of questions which would be of direct significance for the war." The administrative committee authorized Wassermann an unlimited budget for biomedical work that he had undertaken in his institute on behalf of the War Ministry, but for the time being it left initiatives to the individual directors rather than attempting to develop a coordinated strategy for war-related research. Prepared by years of struggling to justify their own institutes, the society's chemists already realized how they might be most useful; "Dr. Emil Fischer, Dr. Beckmann, and Dr. Just [representing Haber's institute for physical chemistry] spoke of new problems presented to chemical and physical research by the complete alteration of our raw materials supply."[29]

The problems arose from the illusion that the war would be over in a few months, an illusion that had made it easy to neglect economic preparations before the war began. Of course it had also been a politically necessary illusion, since any other expectation would have implied a lack of confidence in the army while necessitating a greater degree of peacetime bureaucratic involvement in economic planning than the businessmen or even the military authorities were willing to accept.[30] The Imperial German government had of course made some preliminary decisions regarding the wartime trade policy in strategic raw materials, but they do not appear to have been consistent. Thus in 1911 the Schlieffen Plan had been modified to omit the originally intended invasion of the Netherlands. The latter, a major European inlet for overseas raw materials such as oil, was then supposed to be "a country whose neutrality allows us to have imports and supplies," in General Helmut von Moltke's words.[31] Yet the government also made a decision to impose an embargo on products like organic chemicals as well as potash, in which Germany held a near world monopoly. Although damaging to the enemy in the short run, in the long run it was counterproductive—as Emil Fischer foresaw—because it seriously damaged German trade and provoked retaliation from the neutrals. A partial relaxation of the embargo soon followed, especially on behalf of the United States, but within a few months after the outbreak of war, the British blockade would almost wholly cut off trade again.[32]

It is clear that the Kaiser at least took an interest in the Kaiser Wilhelm Institute for Coal Research and in Fritz Haber's ammonia synthesis,[33] but despite the views of Germany's foes, it does not appear that before the war either the military authorities or the government bureaucrats responsible for economic planning systematically examined ways to use chemical substitutes for imported raw materials that might be cut off in time of war. If the problem was considered at all, its solution was left up to private industry.[34] Fritz Haber, on the other hand, had a long-standing interest in the question and the possible uses of chemistry in time of war. Willstätter recalled later that Haber was one of the few professors who as early as 1909 "spoke of the relationship of chemistry to war and emphasized that it is coal for which countries will wage war."[35] He had even tried to establish a connection with the Prussian War Ministry when his Kaiser Wilhelm Institute for Physical Chemistry opened in 1912, but the ministry rebuffed him.[36]

The ministry's attitude began to change rapidly after the war began. By mid-August the shortage of vital imported light metals became obvious, especially copper for the electrical industry and for the production of brass shell-casings. The Th. Goldschmidt chemical firm in Essen had already requested and received an exemption from military service for its research director, Friedrich Bergius, one of whose projects was to attempt to produce synthetic oil from coal. On the day after the war conferences in the Kaiser Wilhelm Institute, Walther Rathenau was commissioned to set up and direct the ministry's War Raw Materials Department, which he had himself proposed.[37] Both Emil Fischer and Fritz Haber were to work with this department on the raw materials problem during the next few months.

Within a week after the military reverse at the Marne, Emil Fischer approached Francis Kruse for help in bringing the Kaiser Wilhelm Institute for Coal Research into the war effort.[38] To do this he had to get Franz Fischer, who had been conscripted at the beginning of the war, back from the Russian front. When Kruse could make no impression on the military authorities, Emil Fischer was obliged to use the Kaiser's influence via Valentini's civil cabinet, which in October contacted the military cabinet to set in motion the relief of Fischer and various subordinates. During the fall and winter they began to come back to Mülheim.[39] Franz apparently took charge of his institute again in late November, when Emil wrote to advise him on the institute's wartime program. The first task would be to coordinate between the War Ministry and the cokeries, giving them technical assistance where necessary to keep up their production of by-product ammonia for explosives and fertilizers.[40] A second task was to find a substitute source for the sulfates normally extracted from imported Spanish pyrites to produce sulfuric acid, the most important industrial reagent. Perhaps by-products from other processes such as coking or the manufacture of explosives could be applied to this purpose.[41] (Eventually gypsum was chosen as the most likely source.) By 1916 the institute would also be working on the synthesis of gasoline from coal and the extraction of oil from coal tar, in accordance with the program that Emil Fischer had outlined in 1912. In 1915 Fischer had already recommended that the government support Bergius's work on the same problem.[42]

Well before Franz Fischer had returned from the front in 1914, Emil Fischer had been working to encourage the output of ammonia and other coking by-products. On September 22, 1914, the coal producers assembled in Essen to hear Fischer presenting the ugly numbers that added up to a critical gap between production and requirements for toluol (for

TNT), ammonia, nitric acid, gasoline and oil, coal and coke. The most serious problem was contained in the fact that whereas Germany normally produced 360,000 tons of ammonium sulfate per year, accounting for about two-fifths of German consumption of nitrates, production had been halved since August simultaneously with the drastically increased military demands for nitrates and the cutting off of overseas imports, which normally accounted for more than half the German consumption. Synthetic sources covered less than a tenth of German needs in 1913. The BASF had promised to produce 30,000 tons of synthetic ammonia by the Haber-Bosch process in 1914 (by the end of the war its annual production would reach 200,000 tons or half of Germany's needs) and the Lothringen Mining Company was using the process developed by Wilhelm Ostwald to produce a small quantity of nitric acid from ammonia contained in coking gas. All these capabilities would have to be expanded as rapidly as possible if the German military machine were not to grind to a halt within a few months for lack of explosives. On October 1 Fischer reported in detail to the Prussian War Ministry on the situation.[43]

At the meeting in Essen, Fischer asked Carl Duisberg to bring the BASF into contact with the acting director of the coal research institute, Professor Hilpert, so that the latter could get information on the development of processes for oxidation of ammonia to nitric acid for explosives. The BASF was experimenting with a process that would compete with Ostwald's Lothringen process, and it naturally wanted to protect its investment. At first its directors refused to see Professor Hilpert, but at Duisberg's urging they finally agreed to receive him.[44] The work of coordination began.

In the following weeks Emil Fischer held a lively correspondence on the ammonia question with scientists and industrialists including August Thyssen, Fritz Haber, Carl Bosch of the BASF, Dr. Adolf Haeuser of Hoechst, Carl Duisberg of Bayer, Gustav Krupp von Bohlen, Walther Rathenau, and Gustav Aufschläger, presiding over the newly established War Chemicals Company.[45] In December he mediated between Rathenau and Haber, in order to settle a difference of views on the raw materials problem so that the common work could continue.[46]

The coordination of ammonia production was in part spurred on by Wichard von Moellendorf, an apostle of state-capitalist enterprise who was one of Rathenau's subordinates in the AEG and then in the War Ministry. Moellendorf, from whom the idea of a war raw materials department is said to have stemmed, apparently hoped to use the ammonia program as a precedent for wide-ranging military and bureaucratic coordination of the war economy.[47] By 1916 the interaction of bureaucrats with industrialists would reach a degree such that Adolf von Harnack could proclaim the ultimate replacement of private enterprise by a "mixed," state-capitalist economy. It was not a conclusion with which Emil Fischer could agree, despite or perhaps because of his participation in the programs that made such a goal possible. He was particularly disappointed in the shortcomings of the Imperial Office of the Interior with regard to economic mobilization for war. Harnack's criticism of private enterprise for war profiteering added insult to injury for the business members of the Kaiser Wilhelm Society, who forced Harnack to issue an eventual retraction.[48]

The chemists' successes led to the Kaiser Wilhelm Foundation for Military and Technical Sciences (*Kaiser-Wilhelm-Stiftung für Kriegstechnische Wissenschaften*), established at Haber's initiative with the support of Koppel and Friedrich Schmidt in 1916, and in 1917 attached to the War Ministry. This organization had no research facilities of its own; rather, it was intended to promote and coordinate war-related work by scientists in academic institutions as well as in the Kaiser Wilhelm Institutes. Fischer and Haber took leading roles in the organization, Fischer as the head of the foundation's Expert Committee I, one of six in various areas. His responsibility was to coordinate the work of seven other chemists dealing with problems in the production, use, and substitution of munitions, foodstuffs, and related war materials.[49]

By the end of 1917 Fischer was to perform the following militarily significant services: experiments on explosives and gas bombs, on the deodorizing of corpses, on the utilization of fatty acids as food, on synthetic tanning agents, on the use of straw as fodder, and on alternate sources for sugar. Other chemists in the Kaiser Wilhelm Institutes followed Emil Fischer's lead and the model of the successful Haber-Bosch ammonia synthesis in attempting to develop chemical substitutes for essential products in short supply. Thus the German *Ersatz* program was born. Ernst Beckmann, for example, belonged to a committee for substitute textile materials and explored the refinement of straw for fodder, though without much success.[50] Other projects were apparently undertaken more in the sense of private business ventures. Into this category might be placed Richard Willstätter's research, in cooperation with the Th. Goldschmidt firm in Essen, which led to a process for producing dextrose sugar from wood cellulose as a means of increasing the food supply.[51]

Naturally a great deal of work was done in industry as well as by individual academic scientists outside the Kaiser Wilhelm Institutes. Only a general impression can be given of these efforts to develop substitutes for strategic materials through chemical synthesis. For the most part, the time and resources were too short to produce adequate *Ersatz* materials, except for those derived from processes (like Haber-Bosch) perfected before the war. Even the Bayer firm's synthetic rubber process, developed before the war but abandoned as too expensive, could not fully meet German needs.[52] The Bergius coal-oil conversion process, also patented but not developed before the war, was never brought into production, and the German government lost interest in it toward the end of 1917 as sources in the East were secured through conquest.[53] As the exigencies of war fostered coordinated research in entire branches of German industry, however, the Kaiser Wilhelm Institute for Coal Research became the model for many similar research centers for strategic materials after 1916: a second coal institute in Silesia, an iron and steel institute, a nonferrous metals institute, a synthetic textile chemistry institute, and a leather institute. None actually opened, except on a small scale in provisional rooms, until 1921–22.[54] Thus although they were too late to affect the outcome of the war, the war accelerated their creation and hastened the integration of industry, science, and military strategy.

In the Service of Weaponry: The Origins and Dilemmas of Chemical Warfare

Whereas the work of the Institute for Coal Research and its analogues was to be mainly in the area of strategic minerals, the Dahlem complex gradually assumed the character of a research center for tactical military science and technology. The man who took the lead in this area was Fritz Haber. Despite his earlier rebuffs, Haber was determined to play a significant role in war work. In a logical outcome of his prewar research, he began by embroiling himself in the ammonia question, in which he also represented the BASF on occasion in the War Ministry. The logic of *Ersatz* led to problems of munitions, and eventually to poison gas. Eventually Haber, who because of his Jewish origins could not obtain a commission in peacetime, headed the section in the War Ministry dealing with all phases of gas warfare, but he was never promoted above the rank of captain. His opposite number in the British Army, also a professional chemist, was made a general.[55]

The bankrupt Schlieffen Plan catapulted the German high command into a situation on the Western front without any precedent in their military traditions. With their lines thinly held and reserves of munitions used up, they confronted an unbroken line of trenches against which conventional weapons "often failed completely. A weapon had, therefore, to be found which was superior to them but which would not excessively tax the limited capacity of German war industry in its production."[56] In other words, innovation in weaponry arose not simply from the unforeseen tactical problems of trench warfare, but also from the crisis in strategic raw materials that produced the *Ersatz* program. Thus the new chemical weapons were to be *Ersatz* themselves—a substitute for conventional munitions. Recognizing this, the generals swallowed their pride and turned to the scientists whose offers of help they had earlier spurned.[57] Haber and other chemists, including Carl Duisberg and Walther Nernst, were asked to devise means of chemically clearing the trenches. In October and November 1914, while Haber's institute was trying unsuccessfully to discover a more powerful explosive for artillery shells, Duisberg and Nernst, using the Bayer facilities, developed various grenades, shrapnel shells, and firebombs. Very early, they began to study nonlethal irritants like sneezing gas or tear gas, which seemed to be acceptable under the international Hague Conventions of 1899 and 1907. Duisberg and Nernst thus developed a gas-filled shell intended to make the enemy trenches uninhabitable only long enough to clear the way for the German shock troops. In the fall and winter of 1914, both sides used such substances in limited quantities, but with no obvious military success.[58]

Chief of staff General Erich von Falkenhayn was disappointed. Although he ordered production of the tear gas shells in December 1914, he also asked the German scientific experts to produce a shell that would either kill or permanently sicken the enemy, forcing them to clear their trenches for an extended period of time after a bombardment. Duisberg believed that if the problem could be solved at all, it would require the cooperation of "all suitable forces in the German Empire," including the chemical institutes in Dahlem. He asked Falkenhayn to consult Fischer, in the hope that Fischer would convince the military authorities not to pursue the task. Fischer was indeed dubious, out of his fear of shortages in raw materials. If the other side could outproduce Germany, the weapon would cut the wrong way. Yet when Duisberg learned that Fischer knew of a substance—probably phosgene—which would kill "even in extraordinarily great dilution," he was all in favor of trying it. Within two weeks Duisberg had set his staff to work on improving the production of phosgene, and by February the Germans had begun to test it in mixtures with tear gas. Initially, however, this extremely deadly gas was not yet available in sufficient quantities or with the proper equipment to use it in combat and protect advancing German troops.[59]

In Dahlem, after a disastrous accident that killed one of his assistants, Fritz Haber had come up with the simple, ingenious solution that induced the Kaiser to break with military tradition and give him a captain's rank: poisonous chlorine gas, to be released under proper wind conditions from canisters in the German lines. The prevailing winds on the Western front went the wrong way, however, which led Fischer to wish Haber "failure from the bottom of my patriotic heart; for if he succeeds, the French will soon figure it out and then turn the tables, which will be very easy for them to do." Duisberg agreed, but the German high command disregarded these doubts, as well as possible objections on the basis of international law or their own discomfort with an "unchivalrous" weapon. Their main question was not whether, but only how soon the English and French could develop the technical facilities that would allow them to "turn the tables." When Duisberg estimated the time at five or six months, Falkenhayn agreed to an "experiment," code-named "Disinfection." Haber told his colleagues in Dahlem that poison gas was more humane than high explosive, and that it might even save lives by shortening the war.[60]

As Fischer had foreseen, wind conditions proved to be a key limitation, causing weeks of delay in the spring of 1915 and the repeated abandonment of planned attacks. Other practical problems also arose, and for some time the gas canisters caused casualties only to the Germans themselves. Perhaps out of frustration, Falkenhayn began shifting his reserves to the Eastern front on April 17 for a major campaign in Galicia. Then, on April 22 before Ypres, "Disinfection" finally worked, producing initial success far beyond what anyone expected; but given the change of plans and lack of reserves and munitions, it could not be followed up by any sort of large-scale offensive. The generals had thrown away the unique psychological and tactical advantage of attacking an unprotected, unprepared enemy.[61]

Allied retaliation came five months later, right on schedule, but even less effective than the initial German attacks.[62] For the remainder of the war, gas weapons became increasingly more sophisticated as both sides raced to find new solutions to the trench warfare problem. Haber continued to lead the German chemical warfare unit, and he gradually expanded the group under his command.

By 1917 Haber had 1,500 people on his staff, including 150 scientific workers in a wide variety of fields who had been recruited, drafted, or militarily reassigned from other positions. All the Kaiser Wilhelm Institutes in Dahlem as well as some other academic facilities set aside space for his work, and his total budget was fifty times that of the prewar Kaiser Wilhelm Institute for Physical Chemistry. Centralization made not only for greater efficiency, but also for the greater secrecy that the military authorities wanted, as they distrusted scientists in the academic institutions. Militarily, the relative isolation of Dahlem and its wealth of talent and facilities for interdisciplinary biological, medical, and chemical research thus made it an ideal place to work on the complex problems of gas warfare, even though its transformation into a military research center was "a purely wartime measure" that was not intended to be permanent.[63]

The organization also placed perhaps too much responsibility on Haber himself. As an academic chemist and specialist in physical chemistry used to directing a relatively small, autonomous institute, managing an operation of this scale and diversity gave Haber some serious problems that he was not fully able to solve. Although he was good at organizing and planning the war effort, he had difficulties dealing with some of his colleagues, perhaps owing to some of the same problems that had divided him from Beckmann, or Beckmann from Willstätter. Yet his biggest problems arose from inability to delegate sufficient authority to his subordinates. As with many German full professors directing big institutes before the war, Haber thus wasted much of his prodigious energy, and toward the end of the war a sense of the approaching disaster helped wear him down. He also had to live with the tragic memory of his wife's suicide in the spring of 1915. She had shot herself with his service revolver, perhaps in part out of despair over Haber's role in developing gas warfare.[64]

Haber and his group nevertheless achieved a great deal, and they kept the lead in what became a race to develop and introduce new defensive measures and new forms of poison gas. On the defensive side, he enlisted his friend Richard Willstätter to solve the problem of developing an effective military gas mask. Before leaving Dahlem in 1916 to take over Baeyer's place in Munich, Willstätter devised a three-layer filtration drum using charcoal and other chemicals. Further study of charcoal filtration led to "one of the few positive results of chemical warfare."[65] On the offensive side, once the munitions crisis had passed by mid-1916 or so, Haber abandoned his own idea of cloud attacks to introduce a variety of gas shells as more effective weapons, and by mid-1917 his group was introducing compounds like mustard gas and arsenicals that worked in ways very different from the earlier cloud gases.

The work involved a combination of his own physical chemistry, inorganic chemistry, physics, physiology, and—not least—the traditional organic chemical syntheses that Germans did so well, but that must have seemed both boring and trivial to the physical chemist in Haber. Nevertheless he was open to suggestions from organic chemists, such as the study of arsenicals proposed in 1916 by Emil Fischer. Fischer's knowledge of the literature was an important factor, because the most successful chemical weapons, like mustard gas, had been discovered in prewar research for peaceful purposes. To make the research more purposive and provide a way of screening the hundreds of compounds resulting from the synthetic work, Haber introduced a degree of quantitative precision in the shape of a formula for calculating and comparing the toxicity of gases. His assistants must have sacrificed hundreds of hapless cats in systematically testing the potential killing agents. The system resembled the way the big industrial firms found new dyes or drugs, but the difficulties of working with the military probably made it less efficient and more frustrating, hence more "amateurish," not unlike the earliest, trial-and-error days of industrial research. In the case of the arsenicals, this led to premature and thus ineffective use, before fundamental problems had been solved. Consequently, all the available reserves of arsenic in Germany were wasted on producing a weapon that could not work or, if it had, might have endangered the German troops themselves.[66]

Overall, however, the Germans had the advantage in the gas war until their final collapse, and for this Haber and his Dahlem group deserve much of the credit. On the other hand, they never produced a decisive breakthrough (though they may have contributed to the Russian collapse), and like the other applications of chemistry on the German side, gas may well have helped to prolong the war and intensify its horrors.

An anti-German work written after the war remarked on the apparent ease with which the great German organic chemical concerns were able to convert from peacetime products to the mass production of chemical weapons, from which the author concluded that it was "the critical factor in this new method of war which almost led to our downfall."[67] The great diversity of German organic chemical production favored flexibility. It turned out that many of the intermediates used for dyes and drugs could just as easily produce explosives and poison gas; hence Germany, or indeed any nation with an advanced chemical industry, could never be absolutely "disarmed." Chlorine and phosgene, the two earliest German gas weapons, were both produced in large quantities by Bayer and the BASF before the war. Later, more complex agents required greater changes in plant, but the process of innovation did not essentially differ from the introduction of any new dye or drug, while it did make use of excess capacity resulting from the wartime blockade. Mustard gas could be derived from an intermediate used by the BASF to produce indigo, and Hoechst was familiar with arsenicals from producing the antisyphilis medications developed by Paul Ehrlich. With few exceptions the gas war put no serious strains on German chemical production. Fischer's early pessimism seems not to have been justified in this respect; although Willstätter believed that "lack of raw materials" limited the German advantage, they were still able to outdo their opponents in producing offensive weapons. The real limitation came in producing gas masks, because the Germans had no good substitutes for rubber and cotton.[68]

Thus Duisberg's original worries about the war being bad for business were to prove wholly unfounded as long as the war lasted. Duisberg himself acknowledged that his industry did well in the war, not only in respect to poison gas but also regarding explosives production. The dye industry by the end of the war was down to 5 percent of its prewar dye production, but it produced 80 percent of all explosives used in the German army. Moreover, he noted that during the war the character of his industry's research interests had shifted decisively in the direction of inorganic chemistry. The unusual demands of the war, which had brought dramatic increases in the production of chlorine, sulfur, nitrates, and other inorganic substances, led the dye companies to invest heavily in these areas and hire large numbers of inorganic experts for them. In peacetime these facilities would not be dismantled, but instead shifted to commercial research and production. Duisberg now estimated that only two years would be required to restore the prosperity of the industry. Hence the war had completed the process of modernization and diversification begun at the turn of the century. His pessimism thus gave way to cheerful optimism, becoming all the greater as he achieved his dream of a nationwide chemical concern, the "Expanded I.G.," in 1916.[69] The chemical industry too had demonstrated its "unlimited possibilities" through war, and the challenges of the war had proved the correctness of the original premises of the proposal for an Imperial Chemical Institute, whereby Fischer, Nernst, and Ostwald had sought more support for research in the nonorganic subdisciplines of chemistry.

A New Symbiosis Defined, 1915–1917

Before the war Adolf Harnack had written of the relationship between *Wehrkraft* and *Wissenschaft*, military strength and science, "the two strong pillars of Germany's greatness."[70] In 1916, in the annual report of the Kaiser Wilhelm Society, Harnack returned to this theme from a new perspective.

> "But our enemies, by their surprise attack, achieved something quite unexpected and, for them, unwelcome: *they brought German science and military strength as close together as possible.* Of course we knew all along that these two pillars . . . , deep down, have a hidden connection; but we did not know that this connection is so immediate that military strength can be directly promoted by science and constantly open new connections with it. . . .
>
> "With deepest thanks to our Imperial Lord we may praise the fate which allowed the Kaiser Wilhelm Society to arise at just the right time. . . . *Create, organize, discipline*: in this triad of German spirit and German labor, military strength and science come together."[71]

Before the year was out, the government awarded Adolf von Harnack the Iron Cross. Emil Fischer had already received his in 1915. At that time he too had expressed similar sentiments in thanking the Prussian government: "One could say that the unity of science and technology, which has become a tradition in chemistry, has again proved itself in the most brilliant fashion during this most difficult time. I consider the award given me to be a recognition of the services to warfare which scientific chemistry has provided behind the fighting front, and for this reason the medal is especially valuable to me."[72] Haber too was happy to see that the old prewar "wall" between academic and military circles had fallen, and in 1917 he hoped that the Kaiser Wilhelm Foundation for Military and Technical Sciences would help to "create a permanent connection" between them. That was in fact Koppel's express purpose in establishing the foundation.[73]

Thus the instruments were fully in place for integrating German science into the war effort; among those instruments the Kaiser Wilhelm Institutes and the leading scientists associated with them played a crucial role both in developing weapons and in coordinating the use, conservation, and substitution of strategic raw materials. Of course similar organizations were created in all the major belligerent nations. What is unusual about the Kaiser Wilhelm Institutes is that they had emerged before the war began, in an atmosphere of intense international competition that was beginning to shape scientific research into the cold-war style of a half-century later.

In 1917 the Prussian War Ministry sought to confirm the pattern of scientific weapons research established within the Kaiser Wilhelm Society by offering to support a permanent Kaiser Wilhelm Institute for Gas Research, to be connected with the Kaiser Wilhelm Foundation's expert committee on gas warfare. The other Dahlem institutes would be freed to revert to their original scientific work after the war, but the experience and the German advantage would not be lost. Because peacetime applications like pesticides were expected to emerge from the new institute, other sources of support might include the Education Ministry and the Agriculture Ministry. Haber worked out the details, emphasizing that there would have to be two sections. The one directly administered by the War Ministry could handle technical problems of specifically military value, but those of more general and fundamental interest would have to be approached in "free scientific activity" by a "research center for applied science," the Kaiser Wilhelm Institute for Applied Physical and Biochemistry. Again he emphasized the need "to strengthen the connection between national defense and science, whose irreplaceable significance we have learned in so many different areas in this war."[74]

Yet permanent institutions integrating science with the military could not fully entrench themselves in a Germany that was about to lose its first total war. The ambitious plans of 1917 receded as Germany crumbled, and just before the collapse the leaders of the Kaiser Wilhelm Society agreed not to establish a separate institute for gas research.[75] Although up to 1916 there had been few chinks in the wall of support among German scholars for the German war effort, the iron crosses and the chauvinistic statements of the early years of the war were not the last word. Emil Fischer, a pillar of militarized science in himself, weakened in 1917 after contemplating the useless deaths of his two younger sons. Overwhelmed by the ongoing horror, he put aside nationalistic shibboleths, reevaluated his own role and that of science in the war effort, and prepared himself to reject the Kaiser and political system that he had served so ably, but which could not halt the insanity. In December 1917—in the shadow of the Bolshevik Revolution in Russia—Fischer reflected that although unlike Haber and Nernst, he had held back from a major part in the development of poison gas, it really did not matter. High explosive—a fruit of his own organic chemistry—caused no less gruesome a death. "In short, modern warfare is in every respect so horrifying that sensible people can only regret that it draws its means from the progress of the sciences. I hope that the present war will teach the peoples of Europe a lasting lesson and bring the friends of peace into power. Otherwise the present ruling classes will really deserve to be swept away by socialism."[76] Before the war, Fischer would have found the last statement unthinkable; it sounded more like the radical Social Democrat Karl Liebknecht, who as a member of the Prussian House of Deputies in 1911 had criticized the Kaiser Wilhelm Society for standing "too much under the protectorate of an all too highly placed personage. . . . Gentlemen," he had warned, referring to the authorization of court uniforms for the members of the Kaiser Wilhelm Society, "*science and research in uniform have hardly ever done good.*"[77]

Epilogue: the Fate of the Kaiser's Chemists

Pleading illness, Emil Fischer scaled back his war work in 1918; after the Kaiser's departure Fischer sent a friendly letter to Leo Arons, the physicist whom the Kaiser had purged from Berlin University two decades earlier for Social-Democratic activism, and who was now calling upon German professors to cooperate with the new regime.[78] But the war's wounds went too deep, and the ensuing revolutionary violence as well as the potential economic consequences of socialism were too frightening; within a few months an acute illness diagnosed as intestinal cancer led Fischer to an apparent suicide,[79] a broken man in a Germany that was disarmed but not truly demilitarized, reluctantly republican but backing away from a brief flirtation with socialist revolution. He could not know how quickly the lesson he had learned would be forgotten.

The other two initial proponents of the Imperial Chemical Institute, Wilhelm Ostwald and Walther Nernst, also regretted their participation in the war's excesses and hoped for better from a more democratic system; neither regretted the Kaiser's fall. Nor did either scientist find much attraction in chemical research after the war. Until his death in 1932 Ostwald promoted a theory of color harmony that he had developed, while Walther

Illus. 9-1. "Science in Uniform": Fritz Haber (pointing) among the German gas troops, probably around 1916–1917 (Max-Planck-Gesellschaft Photo Archive)

Nernst returned to his first love, physics. In 1920 Nernst finally won the Nobel Prize for his heat theorem; two years later, having struggled for so long to achieve an Imperial Chemical Institute, he gained the satisfaction of becoming president—of the old Imperial Physical and Technical Institute. Yet he found it a hopeless place to do research; aside from the financial problems of the postwar era, the earlier complaints about bureaucratization turned out to be valid. After just two years of frustration, Nernst went back to the university. In 1933 he responded to the advent of National Socialism and the dismissal of his Jewish colleagues by retiring to a provincial estate, where he became increasingly disaffected (two of his daughters had married Jews and were forced to emigrate) until his death during the Second World War.[80]

Nernst and Ostwald had had the satisfaction of seeing what Emil Fischer could not: in 1920 the Weimar Republic, its military expenditures almost eliminated by the Treaty of Versailles, could finally afford to create a National Chemical and Technical Institute. The government did not even need to build a new laboratory, because one was already available. The new institute was the old Prussian Military Testing Office under a different name. During the late 1930s it began again to devote facilities to military research, however, and the defeat in 1945 again brought its dissolution.[81]

Ernst Beckmann, who might have become the president of an Imperial Chemical Institute, endured a few frustrating years after the war as director of the Kaiser Wilhelm Institute in Dahlem. At the end of his scientific creativity, he was reduced to seeking advice from the business sponsors of the institute as to what research areas to explore. Carl Duisberg treated Beckmann's request with contempt and was no doubt happy to see him retire in 1921. Two years later, Beckmann was dead.[82]

After the Kaiser's fall, Fritz Haber's institute had also been reconverted to peacetime scientific research, and it was finally integrated into the Kaiser Wilhelm Society after the postwar financial crisis destroyed the capital of the Koppel Foundation. It attracted an outstanding staff and by the mid-1920s became the scene of perhaps the most intellectually exciting, wide-ranging, and open colloquia in Germany. In 1918 Haber had won the Nobel Prize for his ammonia synthesis (despite outcries from critics who associated him with poison gas), and his mind was sharp enough and his interests broad enough—including biology[83]—to make him Emil Fischer's heir-apparent as scientific leader of the Kaiser Wilhelm Society; he had also helped to organize the "Emergency Community of German Science" to deal with the postwar inflation by administering grants to needy researchers. Unfortunately, the influence of men like Carl Duisberg, who vehemently opposed hiring a physical chemist to fill Emil Fischer's chair, had deprived Haber of the chance to use his talents to best advantage within the university itself.[84] Yet Haber loyally served the Weimar Republic, trying for example to extract gold from seawater in order to pay reparations. With the coming of the National Socialist regime, Haber's military service would have entitled him to continue as director despite his Jewish origins. But Haber, whom 1933 broke as much as the war had broken Fischer, resigned his position and left the country, dying within a year. By then the new regime had initiated the remilitarization of his institute; one of the party hacks who now occupied it specialized in gas warfare.[85]

In 1942 Haber's friend Richard Willstätter also died in exile, having fled to Switzerland in 1939. Yet in a sense he had begun his own exile much earlier. After winning the Nobel Prize for 1915 and then refusing to accede to Duisberg's pleas to come to Berlin in 1919, on the grounds that his work in Munich was not over, in 1924 he had resigned the Munich chair in protest against his faculty's surrender to anti-Semitism in professorial appointments. Willstätter henceforth refused to work in a public or corporate research position, or even to set foot in what had been his private laboratory. Yet he also refused to leave Germany until the last possible moment, regardless of the many opportunities presented him. Instead he directed a single assistant from his home by telephone, with less than optimal results. To a Jewish scientific contemporary who believed that the researcher's highest duty was to science, Willstätter's principled attitude produced an incomprehensible result, "the self-destruction of a great genius."[86]

The last and youngest of the Kaiser's chemists was Otto Hahn, who went on to become director of the Kaiser Wilhelm Institute for Chemistry and eventually, after the Second World War, president of the Max Planck Society for the Advancement of the Sciences, successor organization to the Kaiser Wilhelm Society. Although he too had resigned his position at the university after Hitler took power, Hahn remained at his post in Dahlem even as his old scientific partner, Lise Meitner, was forced into exile after the annexation of Austria in March 1938. In the Kaiser Wilhelm Institute for Chemistry, Hahn and his associate Fritz Strassmann went on to provide, in the fall of 1938, conclusive experimental evidence of a puzzling phenomenon that Meitner and her physicist colleagues soon identified as nuclear fission in uranium atoms. The proof had required precise quantitative microanalytic techniques,[87] just the sort of thing that the Imperial Chemical Institute had originally been intended for. Emil Fischer's old vision of the "unlimited possibilities" in modern science to be opened at Dahlem had also found its most spectacular confirmation, followed all too swiftly by another horrifying lesson in the effects of "science in uniform." This time, however, the uniforms would be American.

Conclusion: Reflections on a "Most Instructive Case"

> *A diagnosis of the modern soul*—where would it begin? With a resolute incision into this instinctive contradiction, with the isolation of its opposite values, with the vivisection of the *most instructive* case.
> —Friedrich Nietzsche, *The Case of Wagner*, 1888

Viewed simply as a tale of human striving, achievements, and frustrations, the story of the scientists I have called the Kaiser's chemists would take on qualities of Greek tragedy. Mostly irreligious themselves, the chemists had absorbed enough of the classical education of their era to feel perhaps that the gods of Mt. Olympus were extracting a terrible price from them for their *hubris* in daring to dominate the world of chemistry. How else to explain so many noble intentions bringing so little fruit for so long, so much time and effort wasted in pursuing so many dead ends, so many ironies and tricks of fate played upon the actors, so many of whom came to tragic ends?

Viewed from the perspective of modernization and particularly the "conservative modernization" used throughout this book, at least the general outlines of this story become more comprehensible, if no less tragic. They thereby shed light on the historical issues raised in the opening chapters: the problems of developing a historical frame of reference for understanding the institutional changes associated with the emergence of modern science, as well as the changes in German society from the turn of the century to the First World War. Then come the related questions of what these changes meant to science within Germany and modern science as a whole, and what they reveal about historical continuities across the fateful summer of 1914.

The events that led to the creation of the Kaiser Wilhelm Institutes, together with the subsequent acts of the Kaiser's chemists, present a "most instructive case" of the role of science in the process of modernization not only in Germany, but also in the world as a whole during the twentieth century. Theorists of modernization in general have tended to make science central to that process, almost by definition, but without fully explaining why it should be so. As suggested in the opening chapter of this book, the missing rationale lies in the special character of modern science, whose pattern of development epitomizes a key element in the dynamics of modernization itself. That element is the international framework within which social change has occurred in the modern world, involving the exchange of ideas and institutional models among diverse, competing national units, each striving to retain or improve its position by reforms that may emulate those of its competitors or otherwise meet threats that their development may seem to pose. Such foreign threats, real or perceived, have apparently often helped to overcome domestic resistance to proposals for institutional change.

I have argued that the institutional dynamism of modern science arises from similar reasons related to its dual institutional character, both international and national, and to the dual nature of the international competition, both pure and practical, in which scientists engage. Because the competition for knowledge in pure science is both international and fundamentally esoteric, it has bypassed many political or social barriers to the rapid and systematic diffusion of new ideas and institutional models across national boundaries. Yet, at the same time, the ongoing realization of Bacon's equation of knowledge and power has added practical force to the arguments of scientists in nations like Germany for obtaining increased support and for adopting new foreign ideas and models. The Baconian connection naturally tends to bring scientists together with modernizers in business, government, and other fields where science may affect international competition; as shown in this book, chemistry is an excellent example of a field whose scientific, economic, and political ramifications lent themselves to an alliance of academic and industrial chemists as well as bureaucrats.

The focus in this book has been primarily on the Germans, which has precluded my developing a complete picture of international changes in chemistry during the period. Nevertheless, the German perspective can be justified by the fact that the Germans were probably the world's leading scientific nation at the turn of the century, so that a look through German eyes provides a unique perspective on the international competitive situation at the time. Why, I have asked, did the leading German chemists feel the need for institutional changes, and above all, why did they see the need to emulate a country like the United States, whose scientific accomplishments had until then been far less than theirs? One answer is that the best American chemical work had come in fields like physical and analytic chemistry, where the German chemists believed that their own nation was relatively deficient; all the same, the real reason for emphasizing the potential American "threat" was clearly economic. The Germans realized that many of the areas of scientific research emerging into prominence in the twentieth century would require exponential increases in resources.

As of 1905 the best model for such exponential increases lay in the largess of American philanthropists, to whom the Germans sought to respond by opening new financial sources of their own.

Nevertheless, if the Kuhnian model I have used for the "pure" competition in science is correct, appeals by scientists for support from nonscientists run the risk of impairing the autonomy of science and losing the respect of scientific colleagues. Emil Fischer's sensitivity to this problem explains his apology to William Ramsay for the bias in his 1911 speech to the Kaiser Wilhelm Society, for example; it also explains the care with which he and his allies attempted to ensure the freedom of research in the new institutes. The development of the Kaiser Wilhelm Institutes here exemplifies the origins and dilemmas of what may well be one of the most significant innovations in the institutional history of science during the past century: the creation of institutions for what has come to be called basic research, intended to serve both pure and practical purposes. The exact form and impact of such innovations has varied, of course, depending upon the particular conditions in each of the nations where they have arisen. Yet the fundamental problem that gave rise to the new institutions would seem to be common to all.

Consider scientists like the Kaiser's chemists, who played out their professional lives upon the dual stage of the international scientific community and the national institutions in which they made their careers. Their dual role of research and teaching created dilemmas that account in part for the proposals that eventually led to the Kaiser Wilhelm Institutes. Underlying these dilemmas, however, were more fundamental problems arising from the duality of their audiences, each in a sense interested in only half of the Baconian equation of knowledge and power. Each audience, the world of pure science and the world of practical affairs, had its own values and its own criteria for competitive success. Emil Fischer and Walther Nernst were among the relatively few scientists adept enough to satisfy both. Yet if, in doing so, a few individuals could dramatically enhance the dynamism of modern science, what might be the effect of an entire institution designed for such a dual purpose?

Nernst, Ostwald, and Fischer all had relatively similar expectations from their original scheme for an Imperial Chemical Institute; later, as the plan evolved into the Kaiser Wilhelm Institutes, the principal unifying vision came from Fischer, who was able to use his authority to set the institutes' scientific goals. He did so while arguing that scientific research done for its own good reasons and in its own good time would produce "unlimited" benefits that would certainly be to the advantage of Imperial Germany (as well as to humanity) because they would foster the ongoing substitution of intellectual resources, chiefly scientific and technological, for scarce physical resources. German organic chemists had been among the first successfully to exploit this key idea by applying the scientific technique of synthesis to the economic development of Imperial Germany, in the process satisfying both their scientific and their industrial colleagues. Fischer saw the possibility of promoting its application to other fields as well through the Kaiser Wilhelm Society, and he certainly helped to do so by approving Fritz Haber's appointment to the Institute for Physical Chemistry as well as by shaping the Kaiser Wilhelm Institute for Coal Research. The possibilities must truly have seemed unlimited to a man who, in 1915, expected science eventually to control and modify the ultimate resource, life itself.

Yet in trying to bridge traditional boundaries between pure and applied science, the new institutions could not avoid confronting fundamental dilemmas. Initially the projected Imperial Chemical Institute stumbled over the difficulty of persuading the most influential bureaucrats and businessmen to provide substantial sums to research that could only pay off, if at all, in long-term, generally applicable results rather than in the creation of processes or products that could be monopolized. National and international perspectives did not jibe; opponents wondered, for example, why the tradition of competition within the nation should be sacrificed for the sake of international competition, and they were right to wonder. It was no accident that the principal supporters of the project in the chemical industry had just attempted to create an industrywide monopoly; its eventual emergence would solve the problem of deciding the allocation of benefits from central research institutions like the Kaiser Wilhelm Institutes. Similarly, in promoting the Institute for Coal Research, Emil Fischer had to confront the problem of competing interests, which was probably simplified by the high degree of cartellization in the Ruhr coal industry. The differences in goals and expectations between the international scientific community and German industry, and the compromises in internationalism necessitated by these differences, are exemplified by Fischer's concession that publication of economically significant results might be suppressed to prevent their falling into the hands of foreign competitors. Even in the Institutes for Chemistry and Physical Chemistry, whose patrons were less inclined to place limitations on scientific autonomy, budgetary constraints put restrictions on researchers' potential income from patents while simultaneously putting pressure on them to produce quick, spectacular results to justify the expense of supporting their work.

Such were the limits of "free research" in institutions whose successful operation depended chiefly upon ongoing industrial largess. At the same time, the willingness of German scientists to accept these limits testifies to the combined effects of nationalism and economic need on chemical research just before the First World War. The war itself was of course to suppress internationalism in science almost entirely for a time, while exaggerating nationalism to the point of absurdity. Despite the resulting increases in support for militarily useful chemical research, under such conditions truly "free" research became practically impossible. Thus the optimal development of these research institutions evidently depended upon a balance between internationality and nationality.

The present case study thus amply confirms the patterns and dilemmas inherent in the institutional development of modern science. Many of these dilemmas were accentuated in Imperial Germany by what I have called "conservative modernization." Like modernization in general, conservative modernization takes different forms at different times, but whatever the specific form of social and institutional change, it is undertaken in such a way as to conserve at least part of an established social order and, particularly, to protect the vested interests of its elites from the deleterious effects that are otherwise unavoidable in the process of modernization. As used here, it refers mainly to the Prusso-German bureaucracy's strategy for promoting industrialization and technological innovation while preserving the power and influence of well-established, vested interests like the East-Elbian Junker landlords or the full professors in the universities. Given the near-equal pressures fostering and resisting change, it is not surprising that the plans for something like an Imperial Chemical Institute went through many convolutions nor that the ultimate result, the "Prussianized" Kaiser Wilhelm Institutes, reflected the many compromises that made them possible. They thus took on qualities like those of so many other institutions of Imperial Germany.

The compromises arose in response to resistance not only from the Imperial bureaucracy and conservative academic elites as well as the economic elites of heavy industry and agriculture, but also from within the chemical industry itself. This resistance kept the Imperial government from adopting the first proposal for an Imperial Chemical Institute and led to the creation of the Imperial Chemical Institute Association as an industrial funding organization. In the process, the Imperial bureaucracy seemed indifferent to the danger that Werner Siemens had used to justify his proposal for an Imperial Physical and Technical Institute: that research of general significance would be dependent upon short-term economic calculations by industrial investors. The Institute Association was "modernity" with a vengeance, in a most "American" style; but it was also a natural evolution of an existing German pattern of development, which had produced the great factory laboratories of the chemical industry.

Nevertheless the chemists themselves were unwilling to accept this solution, which only partly solved their economic problems. They might, however, have been forced to do so, had it not been for support "from above," arising from the Kaiser's need to restore his damaged domestic prestige through a magnificent gesture on behalf of science. The Kaiser's involvement made the Kaiser Wilhelm Society and its chemical institutes possible by motivating the bureaucracy and providing the social incentives to philanthropy that the Imperial Institute Association lacked. At the same time, the Kaiser's involvement and the contributors' social goals promoted "Prussianization" and the accompanying compromises with the original plan in order to ensure the proper "dignity" in legal and architectural form.

The importance of social factors in encouraging German philanthropy leads one to wonder how much genuine interest in science there was among the initial members of the Kaiser Wilhelm Society. Still, it must be recalled first that Germans were used to the idea of letting the state governments patronize science; second, the bureaucracy itself had already established the pattern of trading social advancement for philanthropy; and third, the considerable private support for scientific research as already existed in the German chemical industry and elsewhere had paid off handsomely in corporate profits. What reasonable German, then, would give money without expecting some sort of return? For the individual members of the society who did not expect direct business benefits from philanthropy, the obvious returns had to be social, and that was what the Prusso-German bureaucracy intended when it organized the society as a quasi-official extension of the Kaiser's personal circle. Moreover, by setting the policy that additional titles would not be awarded even to major contributors, the bureaucracy sought to use the society as a means to relieve the increasing pressure of newly wealthy Germans for new titles. Because Jews and converts had the most to gain socially from their membership, it is not surprising that they saw significant contributions to the society as particularly worthwhile; nor is it surprising that the old aristocracy and the military found little reason to join. The same was true of the representatives of heavy industry, with a few significant exceptions; Fischer's idea for a coal research institute gave them economic reasons to contribute to the Committee in Mülheim, if not to join the society.

Thus overall it can be said that the Kaiser Wilhelm Institutes involved conservative modernization on three distinct levels. On the level of academic institutions, they protected the vested interests of the full professors and classical academicians while providing an outlet for pressures to increase German scientific research facilities. On the level of social institutions, they protected the interests of established elites in the old social order while providing the new economic elites with "attractive possibilities to win terrain in a subordinate area."[1] Finally, on the political level they protected vested interests by making no significant changes in established budgetary priorities, either of the Imperial or of the Prussian government. In each case, the tendencies toward greater integration between

previously separated groups, principally academic scientists and businessmen, encountered an opposing "quarantine effect," which tended to
limit contacts between the new and old institutions or social groups.
When the war came, however, the enormity of the external threat apparently lowered some of the barriers, most notably making possible much
closer contacts between leading chemists, businessmen, and the military
authorities. In general, therefore, the development of the Kaiser Wilhelm
Institutes provides a "most instructive case" of the workings of conservative modernization in Imperial Germany.

What was the result of this institutional innovation for the discipline of
chemistry? In line with the tendencies of conservative modernization, the
Kaiser Wilhelm Institutes provided a buffer zone in which the newer
subdisciplines of chemistry, such as Haber's physical chemistry or Hahn's
radioactivity, could further develop without infringing directly on the
prerogatives of established subdisciplines, principally organic chemistry.
Similarly, Jews or others who did not fit well into the established academic
system could find better opportunities in the new research institutes.
These opportunities made it possible to bring new talent into chemical
research, even without expanding the number of positions at the very
peak of the academic pyramid. Here, too, the war lowered some of the old
social barriers. For example, before the war Emil Fischer had wondered
whether a Jewish chemist, even as good as Richard Willstätter, could have
obtained a position at the University of Munich. During the war it became
possible.[2]

Social benefits also accrued to the discipline of chemistry as a result of
the innovation. With Emil Fischer, a chemist became the most influential
scientist in the nation, and he was able to ensure that a disproportionate
share of the society's scientific positions went to chemists (especially his
own associates and former students). The spectacle of so many new institutes and so much capital being invested in chemistry must have considerably enhanced the discipline's prestige at a time when the chemical industry was finally beginning to announce such long-awaited innovations as
the syntheses of ammonia and rubber. Could it have been purely coincidental that the numbers of German university chemistry students again
began to rise at this same time, 1911–12, after nearly a decade of decline or
stagnation? Although the war temporarily interrupted this trend, it may
ultimately have served to extend it; the postwar period saw unprecedented enrollments of chemistry students.

Despite the constraints and pressures, some first-rate research had
already emerged from Dahlem during the short time before the war
changed the situation. Willstätter put the finishing touches on his chlorophyll research, and Haber on his ammonia synthesis, both of which were
to win them Nobel Prizes. Then Willstätter embarked on his pioneering

project studying the coloration of living flowers. After the war more first-rate, fundamental work would follow. Nevertheless the Dahlem institutes collectively could not become the German center for analytic chemistry, nor could they quite "educate" chemists in the German academic system, in the ways that Nernst had once envisioned for an Imperial Chemical Institute.

Of course Willstätter and Haber did introduce a significant organizational innovation in the "un-Prussian" membership, which broke with the hierarchical tradition of the Prussian university institutes while carrying over an idea from the colleges of technology. Haber's postwar colloquia were also to be unusually democratic, thus encouraging innovation in an especially creative era of modern science, and their wide-ranging approach to science followed in the integrative spirit of the new physical chemistry that Ostwald and others had pioneered. Willstätter too was to take from Dahlem to Munich a more inclusive and explicitly "modern" approach to teaching his discipline, placing more emphasis than most German organic chemists upon physical aspects.

Even so, these institutional innovations were fundamentally conservative, and their impact was limited by the initial resistance the Kaiser Wilhelm Institutes encountered from university and academy. The Prussian government chose not to try to overcome this resistance, and in the end even Fischer and Nernst joined those full professors who wished to protect the rights of the professorial hierarchies and their own vested interests. One may trace this professorial conservatism to the fact that the German universities owed their social status and functions to support "from above," i.e., from the state bureaucracies, whereas to most professors, society as a whole must have seemed inferior or even hostile.[3] Yet what the bureaucracy had given, the bureaucracy might take away. The university professors' resulting sense of vulnerability is striking; their proud tradition of research must have seemed so fragile to them that, rather than welcoming the spread of this tradition to new institutions, they clearly feared that increased support for others' research could only undermine support for their own. Perhaps they were right; after all, the "traditional" emphasis upon research in the universities dated only from the early nineteenth century, and large-scale bureaucratic financial support for their research was even more recent. Could the university professors afford to risk carrying over to themselves measures like the limitations on patent royalties that applied to members of the Kaiser Wilhelm Institutes? Further research should show whether the war at least temporarily lowered university resistance to the new research institutions by demonstrating their importance to the national cause; the effect of the war's aftermath on the relationship between the Kaiser Wilhelm Institutes and the postwar academic system is another matter.

What, finally, does all this mean for the issue of continuity between the events that preceded the outbreak of war and those that followed, particularly the continuity between the peacetime and wartime development of scientific institutions? In terms of the individual research projects the Kaiser's chemists had been working on in the early summer of 1914, the war certainly spelled discontinuity; yet as already suggested, the war served to promote many of the chemists' institutional goals. Nor did it prove very difficult for them to redirect their chemical work along military lines. The long, frustrating campaign to create Imperial chemical research institutions actually made this redirection more likely. First, it forced Emil Fischer and his allies to think hard about the increasingly complex relationship between scientific research, industrial needs, and state or national policy. Then, as the atmosphere of the decade before 1914 grew increasingly tense, it helped to concentrate attention upon problems with strategic resources. Moreover, amidst the fears of "encirclement," which helped to prepare the German middle classes for the declaration of war in 1914, the scientists' stress on "foreign threats" in order to promote their cause took on a sense they had not originally intended. Hence, even before their wartime scientific service for the emperor defined them as the "Kaiser's chemists," their peacetime struggles to get increased support for science had set them in place and shaped their institutional plans, their thinking about the social implications of chemical research, and not least of all their rhetoric. As a result, many of those who fought hardest to create the new institutes also pioneered the chemists' war.

In view of the Harnack memorandum, the Kaiser's "call" in 1910, and Fischer's speeches in 1911–12, those who joined the society and contributed to its institutes had thereby endorsed the premise that their philanthropy was intended to promote science not for itself alone, but also in the national interest. Indeed, even if a donor's main goal was his own social advancement, he would have attained that best if the scientific work he promoted had the utmost national significance. But what could be more significant than a war?

Although one still cannot conclude from these arguments that any of the society's planners initially had military applications uppermost in their minds, there was a fundamental continuity between the events before and after August 1914 in the idea of making science a pillar of strength for the nation. The same scientific knowledge that could enhance economic competitiveness could also enhance military power, in both cases by making up for scarce material resources. Fritz Haber's work is a perfect example.

In short, the process of conservative modernization readied the Kaiser Wilhelm Society for war by placing the "right" men, with the "right" ideas, into the "right" positions at the "right" time. It did so, however, for the "wrong" reasons: it had conserved the rigid definition of official priorities that prevented the Imperial government from supporting chemical research, and it had conserved the narrow vision of the German military authorities that blinded them to the nature of the coming war and so kept them from adequately preparing for it. In any case, the German chemists only helped to prolong the war, not to win it. Who can say whether a less conservative approach to social change might have produced a different outcome? Yet the deepest problem with conservative modernization, as Emil Fischer and later Richard Willstätter came to realize, was not that it kept Germany from winning the war—it was that by not "clearing away the leftovers of past centuries from the edifice of the German Reich,"[4] the German people had acquired a political system whose inadequate leadership could not prevent the war from occurring. That failure, though, is not Germany's alone.

As usual, the war's shallower lessons proved easier to learn. The Versailles Treaty drove one home by disarming but not pacifying Germany. The effect was to focus greater attention, not less, on the equation of scientific knowledge and potential military power. It is still an open question how much this equation, along with other political considerations, may have helped to justify the Weimar Republic's shift in budgetary priorities, which brought the Kaiser Wilhelm Society its first major subsidies from the national budget.

I conclude with some general reflections. The integration of modern science into warfare remains insufficiently understood, both in its origins and in its implications, but both seem to be closely intertwined with the process of modernization. A fully international and comparative history of the role of science in modernization during the twentieth century would surely reveal how international competition, conflict, and the tensions between internationality and nationality, analogous to those that shaped the Kaiser's chemists and their institutions, have influenced the more recent development of science as well and led to tremendous investments by governments and businesses in scientific research, including a great deal for military purposes.

The results have transformed and continue to transform the world. Perhaps they are even bringing in sight the end of the modern era itself. That end would only come, one might argue, with the end of the system of national states that has provided the fundamental framework of modernization. Some observers would claim that science has rung the death knell of that system by making possible the development of nuclear weapons; others would even argue that international science itself, as the "preeminent transnational community in our culture,"[5] presents the model framework for a united world. That may be; yet if the duality of nationality and internationality in modern science is the key to its institutional dynamism, as suggested here, then the vested interests of scientists would lie in the preservation of the modern state system, irrational as many of its consequences may be. Recall that Wilhelm Ostwald was dedicated as few others could have been in the years before 1914 to an eminently rational program of international scientific organization, yet the war converted him, virtually overnight, to an ultranationalist. A future world might eliminate that sort of irrationality, along with the other inherent contradictions that Imperial Germany so richly displayed. But if it did, would it also eliminate the dynamism of modernization and modern science?

Notes

Abbreviations

AEG — Allgemeine Elektrizitäts-Gesellschaft, Berlin

AHP — Adolf von Harnack Papers, Deutsche Staatsbibliothek, Berlin-DDR

BA — Werksarchiv der Farbenfabriken Bayer AG, Leverkusen

BAM — Bundesanstalt für Materialprüfung, West Berlin

Berichte D. C. G. — *Berichte der Deutschen Chemischen Gesellschaft*

EFP — Emil Fischer Papers, Bancroft Library, University of California, Berkeley

50 Jahre KWG — Generalverwaltung der Max-Planck-Gesellschaft zur Förderung der Wissenschaften. *50 Jahre Kaiser-Wilhelm-Gesellschaft und Max-Planck-Gesellschaft zur Förderung der Wissenschaften, 1911–1961: Beiträge und Dokumente.*

GSA-PK — Geheimes Staatsarchiv Preussischer Kulturbesitz, West Berlin–Dahlem

KBH — Gustav Krupp von Bohlen und Halbach

HA — Firmenarchiv der Farbwerke Hoechst AG, Frankfurt/M.-Hoechst

HD — Hauptstaatsarchiv Düsseldorf

KA — Historisches Archiv Fried. Krupp, Villa Hügel, Essen-Bredeney

KWG — Kaiser-Wilhelm-Gesellschaft zur Förderung der Wissenschaften, e. V., Berlin

KWICh — Kaiser-Wilhelm-Institut für Chemie, Berlin-Dahlem

KWIKf — Kaiser-Wilhelm-Institut für Kohlenforschung, Mülheim/R.

MPG — Archiv der Max-Planck-Gesellschaft, West Berlin–Dahlem

Nr. — Designation of an archival volume or file

no. — *Blatt* (page) number (applied to numbering of documents in an archival volume or file)

SAA — Werner-von-Siemens-Institut für Geschichte des Hauses Siemens, Munich

SAK — Staatsarchiv Koblenz

SAM — Staatsarchiv Merseburg

TGA — Archiv der Literatur-Abteilung, Chemische Fabrik Th. Goldschmidt AG, Essen

VCR — Verein chemische Reichsanstalt, e. V., Berlin

VCR-1 — VCR official documents, vol. 1 [1905–June 1988] (in BA)

VCR-2 — VCR official documents, vol. 2 [June 1911–March 1913] (in BA)

VCR-B — VCR-Briefe (official VCR letters file, 1905–11, in BA)

VCR/B — VCR, Begründung einer chemischen Reichsanstalt 1905–[1910] (in BA 46/6)

VCR-G — VCR-Gesuche um Beitritt als Mitglied (official VCR documents in BA)

VCR-P — VCR-[Protokolle] (printed minutes, 1907–1913, in BA)

VCR-V — VCR-Verein zur Förderung chemischer Forschung, e. V., Berlin (abbreviation used for files of this name in both BA and HA)

VCR-Z — VCR-Zustimmende Äusserungen für die Gründung einer Chemischen Reichsanstalt (1900, 1905–7).

VFCF — Verein zur Förderung chemischer Forschung, e.V. (used to refer to the organization and its own documents)

Zeits. angew. Chem. – *Zeitschrift für angewandte Chemie*

ZSA-P — Zentrales Staatsarchiv der DDR, Potsdam

Chapter 1

1. Emil Fischer, "Neuere Erfolge und Probleme," col. 18.

2. Duisberg to Fischer, Feb. 4, 1911, in EFP.

3. Two book-length studies deal with aspects of these developments: Burchardt, *Wissenschaftspolitik*, and Wendel, *Kaiser-Wilhelm-Gesellschaft*. Both are based primarily on official documents of the Prussian and Imperial German governments in the state archives of the German Democratic Republic; I have been able to verify that their citations from these sources are accurate, although of course their interpretations differ. Unlike Burchardt and Wendel, however, I have used other primary sources such as the Emil Fischer Papers and corporate archives, which contain important materials unobtainable elsewhere.

4. Burchardt, *Wissenschaftspolitik*, pp. 11–29, is good on the bureaucratic politics and patronage of science but has little to say on science as such. Wendel, *Kaiser-Wilhelm-Gesellschaft*, pp. 23–75, in a more extensive analysis,

interprets the Kaiser Wilhelm Society along orthodox Marxist-Leninist lines, bringing out aspects of the social influences on science but still offering little on the inner dynamics of science itself.

5. First published in Düsseldorf in 1961, Fischer's book appeared as *Germany's Aims in the First World War*, an English abridgement omitting some of the most controversial passages in the German original; it was followed up by his *Krieg der Illusionen* (English title, *War of Illusions*).

6. Wehler, *Das deutsche Kaiserreich*, pp. 14, 80, 226, 238, cited with useful criticism in Eley, *Reshaping the German Right*, pp. 8–9, 13.

7. See Willstätter, *From My Life*, p. 241.

8. Black et al., *Modernization of Japan and Russia*, pp. 3–6.

9. Ben-David, *Scientist's Role*, pp. 21–27.

10. Kuhn, *Structure of Scientific Revolutions*, pp. 170–73.

11. For example, Lepsius, *Deutschlands chemische Industrie*, pp. 5, 94–95; Lepsius was a director of the Griesheim-Elektron corporation.

12. Wendel, *Kaiser-Wilhelm-Gesellschaft*, p. 24; Kocka, "Organisierter Kapitalismus oder Staatsmonopolistischer Kapitalismus?," p. 21.

13. Beyerchen, "Stimulation of Excellence," pp. 139, 142–43, 161.

14. "Aus einer Tischrede des Präsidenten v. Harnack auf der 12. Hauptversammlung" (1926), in *50 Jahre KWG*. For Harnack (1851–1930), see Zahn-Harnack, *Adolf von Harnack*; for his prewar interest in scientific exchange, see Harnack, "Grossbetrieb der Wissenschaft," in *Aus Wissenschaft und Leben*, 1:10–20. The word *Wissenschaft* will hereafter be translated as "scholarship," unless the narrower sense of *Naturwissenschaft* is clearly indicated, in which case it is rendered as "science."

15. Price, *Little Science, Big Science*, pp. 20–30.

16. Kuhn, *Structure of Scientific Revolutions*, pp. 36–38.

17. Merz, *A History of European Scientific Thought*, 1:16–20, 156; see Forman, Heilbron, and Weart, "Physics circa 1900," generally, and esp. pp. 127–28.

18. For the prewar international system of organizations in general, see Fried, La Fontaine, and Otlet, *Annuaire de la vie internationale*, 1908-09, 1910–11; Schroeder-Gudehus, "Caracteristiques des relations scientifiques internationales," pp. 161–71, and her "Division of Labor and the Common Good," pp. 3–20. For the situation in chemistry, see reports of the International Congresses of Applied Chemistry (Paris, 1889, Geneva, 1892, etc.) as discussed in Ihde, *Development of Modern Chemistry*, pp. 338–40.

19. Kuhn, *Structure of Scientific Revolutions*, pp. 20–21, 164; this discussion is framed in general terms, but the overall picture in Forman, Heilbron, and Weart, "Physics circa 1900," appears to confirm its applicability here.

20. Dupree, "Nationalism and Science," p. 50.

21. Ben-David, *Scientist's Role*, chaps. 6–8; Ringer, *Education and Society*; Jarausch, *Transformation of Higher Learning*; Forman, Heilbron, and Weart, "Physics circa 1900," pp. 49–56; Merz, *A History of European Scientific Thought*, 1:89–301; Bernhard, Crawford, and Sorbom, *Science, Technology and Society*, pp. 307–400; Crawford and Heilbron, "Die Kaiser Wilhelm-Institute."

22. Ben-David, *Scientist's Role*, pp. 18–19, 107, 146; for the view from Brit-

ain, esp. of Germany, see Alter, *Wissenschaft, Staat, Mäzene*, pp. 115–56, 160–61, 173, 180–85; for the issue of imperialism, see Pyenson, *Cultural Imperialism and Exact Sciences*, pp. 9–12, 312–16.

23. Alvin Weinberg, *Reflections on Big Science*, pp. 72–82, gives contemporary American examples.

24. E.g., Emil Fischer, "Neuere Erfolge und Probleme," cols. 3–4.

25. Kuhn, *Structure of Scientific Revolutions*, p. 168.

26. Note the rhetorical and functional similarities of the arguments in Bush, *Science—The Endless Frontier*, esp. pp. vi, 6–7, 26–27, to those of Emil Fischer in "Neuere Erfolge und Probleme," cited above and in Chapter 7.

27. Classically argued by Dahrendorf, *Society and Democracy in Germany*, pp. 41–51, in a deliberately extreme form (see pp. vii–x), echoed perhaps too uncritically by some later historians of the *Kaiserreich*.

28. Gerschenkron, *Bread and Democracy in Germany*, pp. 19–88; Landes, *Unbound Prometheus*, p. 330.

29. Kitchin, *German Officer Corps*, pp. 24–27; Craig, *Politics of the Prussian Army*, pp. 234–38; Herwig, *German Naval Officer Corps*, pp. 39–59, 69, 75–80 109–17, 135; Tipton, *Regional Variations*, pp. 114–17; Perkins, "Agricultural Revolution in Germany," p. 114; Gillis, "Aristocracy and Bureaucracy," p. 105–29; Ben-David, *Scientist's Role*, p. 135 n. 48; Schumpeter, *Imperialism and Social Classes*, pp. 117–25; Dahrendorf, *Society and Democracy in Germany*, pp. 49–50; Roth, *Social Democrats in Imperial Germany*.

30. Pinson, *Modern Germany*, pp. 276–80; Craig, *Politics of the Prussian Army*, pp. 238–42; Cecil, "Wilhelm II. und die Juden," pp. 313–47.

31. Herwig, *German Naval Officer Corps*, pp. 19–22; Fritz Fischer, *Germany's Aims in the First World War*, pp. 19–20 n. 1; cf. McNeill, *Pursuit of Power*.

32. Moore, *Social Origins of Dictatorship and Democracy*, p. 438.

33. Willstätter, *From My Life*, pp. 126–27.

34. Pyenson, *Neohumanism and the Persistence of Pure Mathematics*, pp. 4–7; for nonscientists, Ringer, *Decline of the German Mandarins*.

35. Cited in Zahn-Harnack, *Adolf von Harnack*, p. 329; emphasis in the original.

36. Ben-David, *Scientist's Role*, p. 123.

37. Useful overviews of academic institutional development in Imperial Germany are Lexis, *Das Unterrichtswesen im Deutschen Reich*, summarized in Lexis, *A General View of the History and Organisation of Public Education*; McClelland, *State, Society, and University*; Karl-Heinz Manegold, *Universität, Technische Hochschule und Industrie*; and Ringer, *Education and Society*, esp. pp. 3, 37–40, 51–54. Pfetsch, *Zur Entwicklung der Wissenschaftspolitik*, pp. 43–102, provides figures for budgetary expenditures for the academic system and official scientific enterprises. Note that in the present work *Technische Hochschule* will be translated "college of technology" or "technical college."

38. Ruske, "Reichs- und preussische Landesanstalten in Berlin," pp. 21, 25–26; Lundgreen, "Measures for Objectivity," pp. 2–7.

39. Minutes, "Kommission zur Berathung der Organisation und des Kostenanschlags für das mechanisch-physikalischen Institut," Oct. 29, 1884, p. 6, copy in SAA 61, Lc 973, vol. 1, no. 37; Cahan, "Werner Siemens," pp.

259–60, 264–65; Cahan, *An Institute for an Empire*, also citing much additional secondary literature.

40. Cahan, "Werner Siemens," pp. 255 n. 6, 261, 269–73, 280–82.

41. Lundgreen, "Measures for Objectivity," pp. 33–36; Warburg, "Die Physikalisch-Technische Reichsanstalt" (reprint in SAA 61, Lc 973, vol. 4, no. 8; Cahan, "Werner Siemens," 259–60.

42. Griewank, *Staat und Wissenschaft im Deutschen Reich*, pp. 21–35; Ruske, "Reichs- und preussische Landesanstalten in Berlin," p. 21; Booms, *Die Deutschkonservative Partei*, pp. 69–75.

43. Cf. *Minerva*, which lists faculty members from the various institutions for each year.

44. See R. Steven Turner, "The Growth of Professorial Research," pp. 137–82, and his "The Prussian Universities and the Research Imperative."

45. For Berlin: Lenz, *Geschichte der Königlichen Friedrich-Wilhelms-Universität*; Berlin, Humboldt-Universität, *Forschen und Wirken*.

46. Busch, *Die Geschichte des Privatdozenten*, pp. 114–15; Rejewski, *Die Pflicht zur politischen Treue*, pp. 113–15; cf. Albisetti, *Secondary School Reform*, pp. 171–208.

47. Kaiser-Wilhelm-Gesellschaft zur Förderung, *Adolf von Harnack*, pp. 8–9 (speech by Prof. Hans Lietzmann); for Wilhelm's attitude to Harnack (1851–1930), see Wilhelm II, *Ereignisse und Gestalten*, p. 165.

48. Ruske, "Reichs- und preussische Landesanstalten in Berlin," pp. 24–25.

49. Manegold, *Universität, Technische Hochschule und Industrie*, pp. 82–83, 220, 283, 301; Sachse, *Friedrich Althoff*, pp. 307–9, 324; Jarausch, *Students, Society, and Politics in Imperial Germany*, pp. 107–9. Comparisons of university budget figures in *Minerva: Jahrbuch* 2 (1892/93) and 20 (1910/11), with enrollments in Prussia, Statistisches Landesamt, *Preussische Statistik*, 223:7, 236:17, 79, 90–99; Kaiser-Wilhelm-Institut für Landwirtschaft, *Jahresbericht* 1 (1907).

50. Germany, Reichstag, *Stenographische Berichte über die Verhandlungen*, 9. Legislaturperiode, V. Session 1897/98, I. Band, 25. Sitzung, Jan. 25, 1898, pp. 649–53; party affiliations in II. Anlageband, Drucksache Nr. 97, p. 996. On the Imperial Institute, see Ruske, "Reichs- und preussische Landesanstalten in Berlin," pp. 37–38; *Denkschrift über die Begründung und über die bisherige Thätigkeit der biologischen Abtheilung* (copy in U.S. Dept. of Agriculture Library); Aderhold, *Die Kaiserliche Biologische Anstalt*.

51. On Althoff (1837–1908), see Sachse, *Friedrich Althoff*, esp. pp. 73, 114–15, 176, 190, 234; and Brocke, "Hochschul- und Wissenschaftspolitik in Preussen," pp. 9–118.

52. Pres. Henry Pritchett, cited in Noble, *America By Design*, p. 137.

53. Friedrich Schmidt to Wilhelm von Siemens, May 14, 1911, Anlage 2, in SAA 4, Lk 110. The universities were Chicago, Columbia, Harvard, Johns Hopkins, Pennsylvania, Princeton, Yale, Cornell, California at Berkeley, Illinois at Urbana, Michigan at Ann Arbor, and Wisconsin at Madison; note that only the last four were mainly supported by public funds. Increases in expenditures from listings in *Minerva* 20–23 (1910/11–1913/14).

54. Kevles, *Physicists*, p. 79; Forman, Heilbron, and Weart, "Physics circa

1900," pp. 41–43, which notes the problem of comparing the standard of living in the two countries; Ben-David, *Scientist's Role*, pp. 141, 146.

55. Miller, *Dollars for Research*, pp. 132, 152, 164.

56. Carnegie Institution of Washington, *Year Book* 1 (1902): xiii–xiv; Corner, *A History of the Rockefeller Institute*; Reingold, "National Science Policy in a Private Foundation," pp. 313–41; Miller, *Dollars for Research*, pp. 132, 166–81; compare finances of Berlin or Leipzig universities in *Minerva: Jahrbuch* 10 (1900/1901): 68, 477.

57. Kevles, *Physicists*, p. 67; Lundgreen, "Measures for Objectivity," pp. 39–40, 47.

58. Dewar, "Presidential Address to the British Association," 2:764; "Protocoll über die Besprechung am 22. Dezember 1908, in der Lesegesellschaft zu Bonn," in SAK, Nr. 14063, no. 2. An obvious textual error, repeating "scientific life" instead of using "economic life," was corrected in a printed version of the speech.

59. Remarks of Emil Schroedter, representing the Verein Deutscher Eisenhüttenleute, "Protocoll," SAK, Nr. 14063, no. 7.

60. Siemens offer cited in Cahan, "Werner Siemens," 272.

61. Otto N. Witt, "Wechselwirkungen zwischen der chemischen Forschung und der chemischen Technik," p. 485.

62. Goldberger, *Land der unbegrenzten Möglichkeiten*, p. 12.

63. Remarks of Karl Goldschmidt in "Hauptversammlung des Vereins deutscher Chemiker in Mannheim," p. 1320.

64. Remarks of Otto Wenzel in "Protokoll der 29. Hauptversammlung," p. 534.

65. *50 Jahre KWG*, p. 119.

Chapter 2

1. Willstätter, *From My Life*, p. 113.

2. On Fischer (1852–1919), see Emil Fischer, *Aus meinem Leben*, an incomplete autobiography (to 1900), and Hoesch, *Emil Fischer*, a sketchy biography. See also Feldman, "A German Scientist," pp. 341–62.

3. Willstätter, *From My Life*, pp. 223–24; on the German Chemical Society, see Ruske, *100 Jahre Deutsche Chemische Gesellschaft*, esp. pp. 91–128; Lepsius, *Festschrift zur Feier des 50jährigen Bestehens*.

4. Meinel, "Reine und angewandte Chemie," esp. p. 40.

5. Cf. Foerster, "Walter Hempel," p. 141.

6. Willstätter, *From My Life*, p. 113.

7. Full names: Badische Anilin- & Soda-Fabrik in Ludwigshafen/Rhein, Farbenfabriken vorm. Bayer in Elberfeld, later also Leverkusen, Farbwerke vorm. Meister, Lucius & Brüning in Hoechst, near Frankfurt/Main, Leopold Cassella & Co., also near Frankfurt, and Aktien-Gesellschaft für Anilin-Fabrikation in Berlin. On the success of the German chemical industry and its cooperation with academic chemists: John J. Beer, *Emergence of the German Dye Industry*, pp. 24–25, 36–38, 45–46, 57–69, 118–20; L. F. Haber, *Chemical Industry during the Nineteenth Century*, pp. 80–84, 199–203; Hohenberg,

Chemicals in Western Europe, pp. 33–36, 81–82; Meyer-Thurow, "Industrialization of Invention," pp. 363–81. On German success in organic chemistry: Ihde, *Development of Modern Chemistry*, pp. 614–15; Hjelt, *Geschichte der organische Chemie*, pp. 531–37.

8. "Fünfundzwanzig Jahre unseres Vereinslebens," p. 406; Verein zur Wahrung der Interessen der chemischen Industrie, *Ausgewählte Kapitel*, p. 5.

9. Rassow, *Geschichte des Vereins Deutscher Chemiker*, pp. 2–5, 63–64; *Berichte D. C. G.* 20 (1887): 3427; 30 (1897): 3185; 40 (1907): 5029.

10. Ruske, *100 Jahre Deutsche Chemische Gesellschaft*, pp. 103–9, 122–26; Pinner, "Bericht," pp. iii–xv.

11. Fischer to Farbwerke Hoechst, Feb. 15, 1905, copy in EFP.

12. Fischer to Baeyer, June 13, 1898, in EFP; see also *Verhandlungen über Fragen des höheren Unterrichts*, pp. 13–15; Emil Fischer, *Aus meinem Leben*, pp. 77–78.

13. Emil Fischer, *Eröffnungs-Feier des neuen I. chemischen Instituts*, pp. 36–37 and 50 n. 16.

14. Johnson, "Academic Self-Regulation," pp. 249–56; Scholz, "Wechselbeziehungen."

15. An interesting recent account is Root-Bernstein, "The Ionists." On Wilhelm Ostwald (1853–1932), see among his extensive publications *Lebenslinien*, which must be used with caution, and his correspondence in *Aus dem wissenschaftlichen Briefwechsel*, of which a third volume, containing correspondence with Walther Nernst, is in preparation. The Ostwald Papers are themselves in the Akademie der Wissenschaften der DDR, Berlin. There is an extensive secondary literature, partially listed (up to 1975) in the Friedrich Wilhelm Ostwald entry (by Erwin N. Hiebert and Hans-Günter Körber), *Dictionary of Scientific Biography*, 15:455–69 (bibliography at 468–69), but still no full-length, scholarly biography.

16. Ostwald, *Lebenslinien*, 2:48; see Emil Fischer to Baeyer, May 10, 1902, in EFP.

17. Cited in Cohen, *Jacobus Henricus van't Hoff*, p. 283.

18. Ostwald, *Lebenslinien*, 2:51, 237; "Errichtung von Lehrstühlen und Laboratorien für Elektrochemie," p. 109; Ludwig F. Haber, *Chemical Industry, 1900–1930*, pp. 78–80; Manegold, *Universität, Technische Hochschule und Industrie*, pp. 124–27.

19. Ostwald, "Die wissenschaftliche Elektrochemie der Gegenwart," pp. 134–35.

20. Szabadvary, *History of Analytical Chemistry*, pp. 353–61; see Ostwald, *Die wissenschaftlichen Grundlagen der analytischen Chemie*.

21. See Ostwald, *Das physikalisch-chemische Institut*, pp. 5–8, 29–43.

22. Ostwald to van't Hoff, Nov. 13, 1900, in Ostwald, *Aus dem wissenschaftlichen Briefwechsel*, p. 297, and n. 1 on that page.

23. Ostwald, *Lebenslinien*, 2:236–51, 292–93; Johnson, "Academic Self-Regulation," pp. 250–52; Lepsius, *Festschrift zur Feier des 50jährigen Bestehens*, p. 178.

24. Ostwald, *Lebenslinien*, 2:283–84, 291, 3:9–16.

25. On Nernst (1864–1941) there is unfortunately very little; his books and

papers were destroyed during the Second World War, and there is still no adequate, full-length scholarly biography; the only book so far is Kurt Mendelssohn, *World of Walther Nernst*, which must be used with caution. Better is the Hermann Walther Nernst entry (by Erwin N. Hiebert) in the *Dictionary of Scientific Biography*, 15:432–53, with bibliography to 1973. Also Nernst, "Das Institut für physikalische chemie"; Manegold, *Universität, Technische Hochschule und Industrie*, pp. 124–27 and appendix listing members of the Göttingen Vereinigung.

26. Frank, *Einstein, His Life and Times*, p. 107; Mendelssohn, *World of Walther Nernst*, pp. 45–47.

27. Nernst, *Die Ziele der physikalischen Chemie*, pp. 7, 15–16.

28. Manegold, *Universität, Technische Hochschule und Industrie*, p. 294.

29. Mendelssohn, *World of Walther Nernst*, p. 47.

30. Suhling, "Walther Nernst und der 3. Hauptsatz," pp. 331–46.

31. Contrast Ostwald, *Lehrbuch der allgemeinen Chemie*, 2d ed., to Nernst, *Theoretische Chemie vom Standpunkte der Avogadroschen Regel und der Thermodynamik*; Merz, *A History of European Scientific Thought*, 2:185–86 n. 1.

32. Willstätter, *From My Life*, p. 118.

33. Richard Meyer, *Vorlesungen über die Geschichte der Chemie*, p. 435; Richter, *Lexikon der Kohlenstoffverbindungen*, 3d ed., p. 4709.

34. Nobelstiftelsen, *Nobel Lectures*, p. 35.

35. Johnson, "Academic Chemistry in Imperial Germany," pp. 507–9.

36. Brunck, "Entwickelungsgeschichte," pp. lxxi–lxxvi.

37. Duisberg to Fischer, Nov. 22, 1904, in EFP. On the mergers and their consequences, see John J. Beer, *Emergence of the German Dye Industry*, pp. 122–33; L. F. Haber, *Chemical Industry, 1900–1930*, pp. 124–34, and *Chemical Industry during the Nineteenth Century*, pp. 131–32, 177–80; on Duisberg (1861–1933) and his role, see Flechtner, *Carl Duisberg*, pp. 189–98. The latter, while based on the extensive collection of Duisberg's papers in the Bayer corporate archives in Leverkusen, is unfortunately not annotated. Duisberg, *Meine Lebenserinnerungen*, discusses the 1904 merger but unaccountably omits the following decade.

38. Cf. Riesser, *German Great Banks*, pp. 723–24.

39. "Protokoll der 29. Hauptversammlung," pp. 530–31.

40. Quoted in Flechtner, *Carl Duisberg*, p. 193.

41. Fischer to Duisberg, July 31, 1905, and to Merck, June–July 1905, in EFP; Johnson, "Academic, Proletarian, . . . Professional?"

42. Ihde, *Development of Modern Chemistry*, pp. 368–74, 382–84, 487–89.

43. Cohen, *Jacobus Henricus van't Hoff*, pp. 325–26, 341–42, 366, 375–76.

44. *Die chemische Industrie* 19 (1896): 401–2; Fischer to Baeyer, May 17, 1898; June 13, 1898; and Dec. 28, 1898, all in EFP; Emil Fischer, *Eröffnungs-Feier des neuen I. chemischen Instituts*, pp. 44–45.

45. L. F. Haber, *Chemical Industry, 1900–1930*, pp. 78–80.

46. Manegold, *Universität, Technische Hochschule und Industrie*, pp. 294–95.

47. Fischer to Geheimrat Schmidt, Prussian Kultusministerium, April 19, 1903, in EFP.

48. Fritz Haber, "Ueber Hochschulunterricht und elektrochemische

Technik in den Vereinigten Staaten," esp. pp. 294, 303; Fritz Haber entry (by Morris Goran) in *Dictionary of Scientific Biography*, 5:621; the only full-length biography of Haber (1868–1934) is Goran, *Story of Fritz Haber*.

49. On American chemistry, see Thackray et al., *Chemistry in America*, pp. 154–63; Servos, "Physical Chemistry in America," pp. 68–157, esp. 71–74, 102–6, 149–51.

50. Ostwald, *Lebenslinien*, 2:279–99; Welsch, "Bemerkungen," pp. 77–82.

51. Coates, "Haber Memorial Lecture," pp. 135–38; L. F. Haber, *Chemical Industry, 1900–1930*, pp. 84–97.

52. Szabadvary, *History of Analytical Chemistry*, p. 304; Duisberg to Geheimrat (Nernst?), Sept. 28, 1905, VCR-Z, no. c/2.

53. Fischer, *Eröffnungs-Feier des neuen I. chemischen Instituts*, pp. 42–45; Adolf Harnack, "Promemoria betreffend Ernennung von Adjuncten und Hilfsarbeitern bei der Königlichen Akademie der Wissenschaften" (unpublished ms.), July 16, 1898, pp. 7–11, in AHP, Sect. IV, Box 23, Gründung.

54. Comparisons of budget figures in *Minerva: Jahrbuch* 2 (1892/93) and 20 (1910/11), with enrollments in *Preussische Statistik*, 236:79, 90–99.

55. Emil Fischer, *Eröffnungs-Feier des neuen I. chemischen Instituts*, pp. 46–47.

56. Fischer to Baeyer, May 10, 1902, in EFP.

57. Fischer to Baeyer, July 26, 1901, and Fischer to Walther Löb June 27, 1903, both in EFP.

58. Hahn, *Vom Radiothor zur Uranspaltung*, p. 37.

59. See Emil Fischer, *Aus meinem Leben*, pp. 142, 148–49; Hoesch, *Emil Fischer*, p. 45. Also letters regarding overwork and his breakdown: Fischer to Beilstein, Jan. 28, 1903; to Kultusminister Konrad Studt, Feb. 28 and July 8, 1903; to Baeyer, May 17 and Dec. 18, 1903, and Feb. 14 and June 16, 1904; to H. Skraup, Nov. 2, 1904. On financial and patent matters, see Fischer's note dated Feb. 1, 1903, regarding his inheritance, and Fischer to Prussian Income Tax Commission, June 24, 1907, reporting approximately 400,000 marks in income for 1906, all in EFP.

60. Johnson, "Academic Chemistry in Imperial Germany," pp. 517–19.

61. *Minerva: Jahrbuch* 15 (1905/06), passim; Lexis, *Unterrichtswesen*, 4:pt. 1 passim; Johnson, "Academic Chemistry in Imperial Germany," p. 509, Table 3.

62. Emil Fischer, *Eröffnungs-Feier des neuen I. chemischen Instituts*, pp. 4–25; Prandtl, "Das chemische Laboratorium der bayerischen Akademie," pp. 81–97.

63. Emil Fischer, *Eröffnungs-Feier des neuen I. chemischen Instituts*, pp. 37–38.

64. Cohen, *Jacobus Henricus van't Hoff*, pp. 283, 307–8, 341–42, 354, 362, 366–67.

65. *Sitzungsberichte der Königlich preussischen Akademie der Wissenschaften zu Berlin*, Jahrgang 1890, zweiter Halbband (June–Dec.): 91–93.

66. Harnack, "Promemoria," in AHP, Sect. IV, Box 23, Gründung, pp. 7–16.

67. Harnack, "Königlich Preussische Akademie," p. 214.

68. Fischer to Althoff, Jan. 10, [1903], in EFP. Burchardt, "Wissenschaft und Wirtschaftswachstum," pp. 787–88.

69. *Landolt-Börnstein Physikalisch-chemische Tabellen*, pp. vi–vii.

70. Emil Fischer, Adolf Harnack, Walther Nernst, et al. to Wilhelm II, March 8, 1906, pp. 4–5, copy in AHP, Sect. IV, Box 23, Gründung.

71. Nernst, "Das Institut für physikalische Chemie," p. 636.

72. Günther Beer, *200 Jahre chemisches Laboratorium*, pp. 8–10; Johnson, "Academic Chemistry in Imperial Germany," p. 518.

73. Wilhelm Ostwald to Emil Fischer, Jan. 5, 1905, and Friedrich Althoff to Emil Fischer, Jan. 7, 1905, both in EFP.

74. Wilhelm Ostwald to Friedrich Althoff, Jan. 29, 1905, forwarded to Emil Fischer, Jan. 30, 1905, in EFP.

75. Ostwald to Arrhenius, Jan. 14, 1901, in *Aus dem wissenschaftlichen Briefwechsel*, 2:162–63; Ostwald, *Lebenslinien*, 2:297–98, 444–45.

76. Ostwald to Arrhenius, April 10, 1905, in *Aus dem wissenschaftlichen Briefwechsel*, 2:184; Brocke, "Der deutsch-amerikanische Professorenaustausch," pp. 140–41.

77. T. W. Richards, "Minority Report of Advisory Committee on Chemistry," pp. 85–86; H. Landolt et al., "Bericht des Internationalen Atomgewichts-Ausschusses, 1906," pp. 13–14; Fischer to Richards, Mar. 30 and June 19, 1905, and April 29, 1906, in EFP; Fischer, *Aus meinem Leben*, p. 201. On Richards and his Harvard laboratory, see Ihde, *Development of Modern Chemistry*, pp. 287–88; Tilden, *Chemical Discovery and Invention*, pp. 32–37.

78. The colleges did promote innovative research by 1914; see Johnson, "Hierarchy and Creativity in Chemistry, 1871–1914," pp. 217–22.

79. See Chapter 1.

80. Ostwald, "Für die chemische Reichsanstalt," p. 647 (emphasis in original).

Chapter 3

1. *Vorläufiger Entwurf*, p. 3; copy in HA VCR and in VCR-1.

2. Bose, "Die chemisch-technische Reichsanstalt," pp. 73–74; Fischer to Althoff, Feb. 2, 1900, cited in Burchardt, "Wissenschaft und Wirtschaftswachstum," p. 789; Ostwald, *Die chemische Reichsanstalt*, p. 3.

3. Fay, *Origins of the World War*, 1:190–91.

4. Verein zur Wahrung der Interessen, *Ausgewählte Kapitel*, p. 53; L. F. Haber, *Chemical Industry during the Nineteenth Century*, p. 177; Duisberg's remarks in the meeting of Oct. 14, 1905, in *Vorschläge betreffend die Begründung einer chemischen Reichsanstalt*, 1st ed. (henceforth *Vorschläge-1*), p. 9.

5. Hoesch, *Emil Fischer*, p. 143; Krebs, *Otto Warburg*, pp. 77–80.

6. "Technische Tagesordnung," p. 120.

7. Walther Nernst to Fischer and Ostwald, Sept. 8, 1905, and Nernst to Fischer, Sept. 21, 1905, in EFP. Nernst to Ostwald, July 21, 1905, in Archiv der Akademie des Wissenschaften der DDR, Nr. 95, no. 79. Ostwald revised his version and published it as Ostwald, *Die chemische Reichsanstalt*.

8. Cf. "Technische Tagesordnung," pp. 116–17; *Vorschläge betreffend die Begründung einer chemischen Reichsanstalt*, 2d ed., 2:21–22 (henceforth:

Vorschläge-2); copy in U.S. National Bureau of Standards and BA.
9. *Vorläufiger Entwurf*, pp. 3–6.
10. Ibid., pp. 3–4.
11. Ibid., pp. 4–6.
12. Ibid., pp. 5–7.
13. Ibid., pp. 7–8; Ostwald's preface to *Zeitschrift für physikalische Chemie* 1 (1887); Nernst and Schönflies, *Einführung in die mathematische Behandlung der Naturwissenschaften*.
14. Cf. Lockemann, *Ernst Beckmann*. Fischer to Berlin University Philosophical Faculty, April 19, 1903, and to Baeyer, May 10, 1902, and Sept. 28, 1906, all in EFP.
15. Cahan, "Werner Siemens"; *Vorläufiger Entwurf*, pp. 7–8.
16. Cf. Verein zur Wahrung der Interessen, *Ausgewählte Kapitel*, p. 3.
17. Fischer to Witt, Sept. 27, 1905, in EFP; list from *Vorschläge-1*, pp. 4–5. On Witt, see Noelting, "Otto Nikolaus Witt," pp. 1751–1832; Otto N. Witt, *Das neue technisch-chemische Institut*, pp. 10–16.
18. Kaznelson, *Juden im deutschen Kulturbereich*, pp. 88–89, 429–30, 435, 792; Willstätter, *From My Life*, pp. 114–15, and "Franz Oppenheim," p. 136; Partridge and Schierz, "Otto Wallach," pp. 106–8.
19. Willstätter, *From My Life*, pp. 277–78; Carl Pfeiffer, "Carl Engler," excerpt from *Die Technische Hochschule Fredriciana Karlsruhe* (1950), pp. 40–45, copy in Carl Engler File, BASF Archive; Fischer to Witt, Sept. 27, 1905, in EFP.
20. "Max Delbrück," [obituary], pp. 47–62; entries under Delbrück family in *Neue Deutsche Biographie*.
21. Hofmann, "Georg Merck," pp. 1582–83.
22. *Zeits. angew. Chem.* 26 (1913), Aufsatzteil: 756–57.
23. Fischer to Witt, Sept. 27, 1905, in EFP.
24. Duisberg to Geheimrat (Nernst?), Sept. 28, 1905, VCR-Z, p. 2.
25. Printed transcript is in *Vorschläge-1*, pp. 4–17, and in *Vorschläge-2*, 1:4–17. Here see pp. 6–7 in either edition.
26. Martius's previous objections cited in Nernst to Fischer, Oct. 12, 1905, in EFP.
27. *Vorschläge-1*, pp. 8–13; on the Social Democrats and science, see Pfetsch, "Scientific Organisation and Science Policy," pp. 563, 570.
28. *Vorschläge-1*, pp. 15–16, Duisberg's notes in BA 46/6, VCR/B, no. 8.
29. *Vorschläge-1*, p. 16.
30. Fischer to Nernst, Nov. 4, 1905, in EFP; on Thiel, see "Hugo Thiel" [obituary], p. 706.
31. Nernst to Fischer, Nov. 21, 1905, and to Select Committee, Dec. 7, 1905, in EFP; no complete list of the organizations to which memoranda were mailed is available, but there is an extensive collection of responses in *Vorschläge-2* and VCR-Z.
32. Transcript of January 15 meeting in *Vorschläge-2*, 1:18–23; Emil Fischer, *Aus meinem Leben*, p. 82; Fischer to Ehrensberger, Jan. 10, 1906, in EFP.
33. Fischer to Berthold Rassow (editor, *Zeits. angew. Chem.*), Jan. 12 and Jan. 19, 1906, in EFP.

34. *Vorschläge-2*, 1:32. Fischer to Lexis, Feb. 2, 1906; Nernst to Fischer, Feb. 4; Lexis to Althoff, Feb. 6; Lexis to Fischer, Feb. 5; Althoff to Fischer, Feb. 8; Fischer to Althoff, Feb. 12; all in EFP. I thank Dr. Bernhard vom Brocke for calling my attention to this correspondence.

35. Letters from twenty-six groups in *Vorschläge-2*, 1:47–63, 2:4–13; Emil Schrödter (Verein deutscher Eisenhüttenleute) to Nernst, Jan. 23, 1906, in VCR-Z; and excerpt from the minutes of the board of the Verein Deutscher Chemiker, Jan. 13, 1906, in BA 46/6, VCR/B, no. 12.

36. *Vorschläge-1*, pp. 17, 22.

37. *Vorschläge-2*, 2:4, 6.

38. Manegold, *Universität, Technische Hochschule und Industrie*, pp. 219–20.

39. Wohlgemuth, "Zur Begründung einer chemischen Reichsanstalt," p. 275.

40. *Vorschläge-2*, 2:19–22. The following discussion is taken from the printed transcripts in *Vorschläge-2*, 2:19–78, except for those of Duisberg's remarks that were available in the original stenographic version, BA 46/6, VCR/B, nos. 28–41; list of Imperial expenditures for science in VCR-B.

41. *Vorschläge-2*, 2:28–47.

42. BA 46/6, VCR/B, no. 31; far more negatively phrased here than in printed version, *Vorschläge-2*, 2:38.

43. *Vorschläge-2*, 2:40, 43, 30–31; BA 46/6, VCR/B, nos. 34, 40.

44. *Vorschläge-2*, 2:33; Ostwald to Beckmann, Jan. 1906, cited in Beckmann to "Reichsanstalt Komitee," Jan. 22, 1906, VCR-Z.

45. *Vorschläge-2*, 2:45–46.

46. Ibid., 61–63, 70–71.

47. Ibid., 67–69.

48. Ibid., 71–73.

49. Ibid., 74–76; Althoff to Fischer, Feb. 8, 1906, in EFP.

50. *Vorschläge-2*, 2:77.

51. "Kleines Feuilleton: Der Trompetenstoss der deutschen Chemie," clipping in VCR-1, p. 18a.

Chapter 4

1. Emil Warburg, "Die Physikalisch-Technische Reichsanstalt," p. 26.

2. Cahan, "Werner Siemens," p. 282; Cahan, *Institute for an Empire*, p. 177; Forman, Heilbron, and Weart, "Physics circa 1900," pp. 61–64, with estimates from 1903 for Jena and Munich.

3. Fischer to Lepsius, Feb. 13 and Feb. 18, 1906, in EFP; Warburg's comments on Oct. 14, 1905, in *Vorschläge-1*, p. 12.

4. Warburg, "Die Physikalisch-Technische Reichsanstalt," pp. 8, 13–24, 26.

5. Cahan, *Institute for an Empire*, pp. 81, 168–77, 204–8, 215–23, 240 n. 62, 243 n. 59.

6. "Geschäftsordnung für die Physikalisch-Technische Reichsanstalt," July 26, 1888, copy in SAA 61, vol. 2, no. 69; Cahan, *Institute for an Empire*, pp. 80–81, 132–36.

7. Inferred from the rather bland published accounts in L. F. Haber, *Chemi-*

cal Industry during the Nineteenth Century, pp. 176–80; J. J. Beer, *Emergence of the Geman Dye Industry,* pp. 124–33.

8. "Fünfundzwanzig Jahre unseres Vereinslebens," pp. 413–15; C. H. Wichelhaus, "Carl Alexander von Martius," pp. 72–75; entry under "Martius" in *Allgemeine Deutsche Biographie.*

9. "Protokoll der 34. Hauptversammlung: Gewerblich-technische Reichsbehörde," pp. 1436–38.

10. Martius, *Die Errichtung einer gewerblich-technischen Reichsbehörde,* p. 3; copy in HA VCR.

11. Personal recollection of Felix Gilbert in conversation with author, 1978.

12. Emil Fischer to Ludwig Mond, June 7, 1906, VCR-B. I have not yet been able to determine the exact nature of this relationship.

13. Martius, "Eine chemische Reichsanstalt?," pp. 135–39.

14. "Die chemische Reichsanstalt," p. 253.

15. Fischer to "Freund," Mar. 21, 1906, in EFP; Martens to Martius, Mar. 22, 1906, BAM C.1, no. 72; Nernst to Ostwald, Mar. 21, 1906, copy in EFP.

16. Ostwald, "Die chemische Reichsanstalt," pp. 1025–27; "Technische Tagesordnung," pp. 118–19, 121–23.

17. Gans to Hoechst directors, Nov. 19, 1906, in HA VCR; Cassella Farbwerke Mainkur A. G., *Ein farbiges Jahrhundert,* pp. 56–58, is sketchy.

18. Gans, "Gegen die chemische Reichsanstalt!," pp. 589–93.

19. Gans to Hoechst directors, Nov. 19, 1906, in HA VCR.

20. Ostwald, "Für die chemische Reichsanstalt," p. 645 (emphasis in the original).

21. *Das Institut für Gärungsgewerbe und Stärkefabrikation;* Stutzer, "Zur Begründung einer chemischen Reichsanstalt," p. 420.

22. Stutzer, "Zur Begründung einer chemischen Reichanstalt," p. 420.

23. "Gründung einer chemischen Reichsanstalt," pp. 1495–98.

24. *Centralblatt für Zuckerindustrie* 14 (1906): 149, cited in "Die chemische Reichsanstalt," p. 254; letter from Verein der Deutschen Zucker-Industrie, Feb. 12, 1906, in *Vorschläge,* 2d ed., 2:6.

25. Verein zur Wahrung der Interessen, *Ausgewählte Kapitel,* pp. 376–94.

26. Annual report by Wenzel in *Die chemische Industrie* 30 (1907): 476; J. J. Beer, *Emergence of the German Dye Industry,* p. 130; L. F. Haber, *Chemical Industry, 1900–1930,* p. 126; Tipton, *Regional Variations,* pp. 127–28.

27. Stinnes to Fischer, May 6, 1907, VCR-B.

28. Holle to Posadowsky, April 25, 1907, forwarded with a copy of the reply, from Posadowsky to Fischer, May 4, 1907, VCR-B; Ehrensberger to Martens, Dec. 13, 1905, BAM C.1, no. 8.

29. "Technische Tagesordnung," p. 120.

30. Cahan, *Institute for an Empire,* pp. 188–93.

31. BAM C.1, nos. 27–33.

32. *Vorläufiger Entwurf,* pp. 4–5.

33. "Frankfurter Bezirksverein," (minutes of meeting, Jan. 16, 1907), pp. 2–3, proof copy of report in BA 46/6, VCR/B, no. 46 (4); published in *Zeits. angew. Chem.* 20 (1907): 603. For Keppeler's academic position see *Minerva: Jahrbuch,* 15 (1905/6): 300.

34. Correspondence between Duisberg, Delbrück (as vice-chairman of the Association), and Rassow (editor, *Zeits. angew. Chem.*), in BA 46/6, VCR/B, nos. 49–58, 62–63.

35. Ostwald, "Für die chemische Reichsanstalt," pp. 645–46 (emphasis in original).

36. President's Report in: Carnegie Institution of Washington, *Year Book* 13 (1914): 33; Kevles, *Physicists*, pp. 82–84.

37. "Technische Tagesordnung," pp. 116, 122.

38. See Sachse, *Friedrich Althoff*, pp. 72–74, 277.

39. Ruske, "Reichs- und preussische Landesanstalten in Berlin," pp. 21–22; Ruske, *100 Jahre Materialprüfung in Berlin*. See also "Adolf Martens" [obituary], pp. 69–71.

40. BAM C.1, no. 5.

41. Martens to Fischer, Oct. 24, 1905, BAM C.1, nos. 6–7.

42. BAM C.1, nos. 10–28 (first draft), 29–36 (second draft), and Ehrensberger to Martens, Dec. 13, 1905, no. 8.

43. BAM C.1, nos. 33, 36. The specific titles are meaningless; Martens was only trying to illustrate the difference in status suggested by a "president" as opposed to a "professor," parallel to the differences between an Imperial chancellor (first class) and an ordinary *Regierungsrat* (government councillor), i.e., a lower-ranking official.

44. Martens to Ehrensberger, Dec. 18, 1905, no. 9; to Schmidtmann (Kgl. Versuchs- u. Prüfungsanstalt f. Wasserversorgung u. Abwässerbeseitigung), Dec. 20, 1905, nos. 44–45; to Brunck, Jan. 20 and Jan. 30, 1906, nos. 47, 49–50; to Naumann (Kultusministerium), Dec. 21, 1905, no. 46; Frank (Deutsche Acetylen-Gesellschaft) to Martens, Feb. 29, 1906, no. 61; Schmidtmann to Martens, Jan. 25, 1906, no. 60; Brunck to Martens, Jan. 27, and Feb. 9, 1906, nos. 49 and 51; Ehrensberger to Martens, Jan. 27, 1906, no. 48; Martens to Kultusminister, Jan. 26, 1906, nos. 57–59; all in BAM C.1.

45. Corrected copy of *Vorschläge-2*, 1:38–39 in BAM C.1, no. 113, pp. 38–39.

46. "Althoffs Pläne für Dahlem," p. 6, typescript in AHP, Sect. IV, Box 22, Aufteilung; see also Burchardt, *Wissenschaftspolitik*, pp. 17–21; Sachse, *Friedrich Althoff*, pp. 281–83.

47. Fischer to Nernst, Sept. 14, 1906, and to Baeyer, Sept. 18, 1906, in EFP; Lewald to Böttinger, April 8, 1907, VCR-B.

48. P.-C. Witt, *Finanzpolitik*, pp. 63–74, 80–83, 377, 380; Kehr, *Battleship Building*, pp. 212–19, 328–34; Eley, *Reshaping the German Right*, pp. 94–98, 239–42, 316–34, 349–52.

49. P.-C. Witt, *Finanzpolitik*, p. 380–81.

50. Fischer to Baeyer, Jan. 2, 1899 [misdated 1898], in EFP; Wendel, *Kaiser-Wilhelm-Gesellschaft*, p. 57.

51. Ruske, "Reichs- und preussische Landesanstalten in Berlin," p. 23; Fischer to Ehrensberger, May 8, 1911, in EFP; Gummert, "Entwicklung neuer technischer Methoden," pp. 113–32.

52. Ritter, *Schlieffen Plan*, pp. 47, 70–71, 122, 128.

53. Ritter, *Sword and the Scepter*, 2:152.

54. P.-C. Witt, *Finanzpolitik*, pp. 94–132, 377.
55. Hoffmann, *Wachstum*, p. 826 (value in prices of 1900); Grabower, *Die finanzielle Entwicklung der Aktiengesellschaften*, p. 18n.
56. Cf. Lundgreen, "Measures for Objectivity," pp. 6–7, 94–98.
57. Fischer to Bülow, March 3, 1906, in EFP.
58. Select Committee to Bülow, to Posadowsky, and to Stengel, three letters dated May 12, 1906, in EFP and printed in minutes of Select Committee meeting March 2, 1907, VCR-P; Fischer to Althoff, May 28, 1906, in EFP.
59. Imperial Institute Committee to Stengel, June 23, 1906, and Fischer to Böttinger, June 29, 1906, in EFP.
60. Fischer to Mond, June 30, 1906, in EFP; minutes of Select Committee meeting March 2, 1907, p. 5, in VCR-P.
61. Speech of April 13, 1907, cited in Martius, *Die Errichtung einer gewerblich-technischen Reichsbehörde*, p. 12.
62. Minutes, Select Committee, March 2, 1907, pp. 5–8, VCR-P; this is not the stenographic record of Lewald's remarks but rather an "official" version that he sent to the *Zeits. angew. Chem.* 30 (1907): 1477–78.
63. *Vorschläge-2*, 2:45; see Chapter 3.
64. Ostwald, "Für die chemische Reichsanstalt," p. 647.
65. Delbrück to Duisberg, March 7, 1907, BA 46/6, VCR/B, after no. 46.

Chapter 5

1. E. Fischer and Beckmann, *Das Kaiser-Wilhelm-Institut für Chemie*, p. 9.
2. Fischer to Hugo Münsterberg, Jan. 6, 1911, in EFP.
3. See Fischer to Stroof, July 6, 1911, in VCR-B; "Bemerkungen zur Rechtsform der Chemischen Institute," undated, AHP, Sect. IV, Box 24, KWICh.
4. Duisberg to Fischer, May 16, 1908, in BA 46/6, VCR/B (after mid-1907, items in this volume are not numbered); Gutsche, "Probleme des Verhältnisses zwischen Monopolkapital und Staat," p. 45.
5. Compare Heise, "Zur Rolle der staatlichen Forschungspolitik," pp. 26–34.
6. Carnegie, *Gospel of Wealth*, pp. 1, 24–41.
7. Veblen, *Theory of the Leisure Class*, pp. 381–94.
8. Sombart cited by Ben-David, *Scientist's Role*, p. 135 n. 48; Weber, "Capitalism and Rural Society in Germany," p. 383.
9. Burchardt, *Wissenschaftspolitik*, pp. 79–80; Mosse, *Jews in the German Economy*, p. 4.
10. See Busch, *Geschichte des Privatdozenten*, pp. 148–62; Hamburger, *Juden im öffentlichen Leben Deutschlands*, p. 71; Willstätter, *From My Life*, p. 83.
11. Schorsch, *Jewish Reactions to German Anti-Semitism*, pp. 116–48; Wertheimer, *Unwelcome Strangers*, esp. pp. 143–49, 157–61, 175, 181; and Aschheim, *Brothers and Strangers*, pp. 57, 79.
12. Hamburger, *Juden im öffentlichen Leben Deutschlands*, pp. 95–96.
13. Burchardt, *Wissenschaftspolitik*, pp. 79–80; Kluke, *Stiftungsuniversität*

Frankfurt am Main, p. 104; Cecil, "Wilhelm II. und die Juden," pp. 313–47.

14. Mosse, "Die Juden in Wirtschaft und Gesellschaft," pp. 77–79; Birnbaum, "Die jüdische Bevölkerung in Preussen," pp. 117, 124–26.

15. Nernst to Fischer, Feb. 19, 1906, in EFP; on Friedländer, who was indeed later ennobled (but for other reasons) as Fritz von Friedländer-Fuld, see Ress, *Geschichte der Kokereitechnik*, pp. 255–56, and Mosse, *Jews in the German Economy*, pp. 151–52, 181.

16. Fischer to Oppenheim, Sept. 16, 1906, in EFP.

17. Walther Nernst, "Vertrauliche Aktennotiz: Eine Unterredung . . . mit Herrn Ludwig Mond . . . (Anfang Mai) betreffend," in VCR-B; Ostwald, *Lebenslinien*, 3:265–66.

18. Fischer to Ernest Solvay, June 24, 1908, and Solvay to Fischer, July 4, 1908, in Archives de la Section A, Solvay et Cie, Brussels, (copies furnished by Solvay et Cie); Fischer to Duisberg, Aug. 21, 1914, in EFP.

19. Duisberg's notes in BA 46/6, VCR/B, no. 45; draft of funding committee appeal to members of the chemical industry interest group, forwarded March 13, 1907, from Verein zur Wahrung to von Brüning, in HA VCR.

20. *Chemische Industrie* 29 (Oct. 15, 1906): 542–44; minutes of funding committee meeting, Mar. 2, 1907, in HA VCR.

21. Fischer to Ehrensberger, Oct. 27, 1906, in EFP.

22. Fischer to Nernst, Oct. 24, 1906, in EFP; information on Leo Gans (1843–1935) and Arthur von Weinberg (1860–1943) obtained from files in Stadtarchiv Frankfurt/Main: clippings from *Frankfurter Adressbuch*, 1966, pp. 21–22 and the *Frankfurter Jüdisches Gemeindeblatt*, 1968, Nr. 14, p. 9 (Sammlungen S2 Personen, Nr. 351-Gans, Nr. 789-Weinberg); and Mosse, *Jews in the German Economy*, pp. 179–80, 183, 187.

23. Fischer to Ehrensberger, Oct. 27, 1906, in EFP.

24. Arthur von Weinberg to Häuser, Jan. 25, 1907, on display, HA Museum; Greiling, *Im Banne der Medizin*, pp. 129–30, 152–53, 160. Although the latter work contains no footnotes or bibliography, the author told me it was based upon documents in the Paul-Ehrlich-Institut, Frankfurt/Main.

25. Gustav von Brüning to Gans, Nov. 27, 1906; Hoechst Directors to Oppenheim and von Brüning to Oppenheim, Nov. 29, 1906, HA VCR.

26. Gans to Fischer, Dec. 20, 1906, VCR-B.

27. Draft circular forwarded to von Brüning by Verein zur Wahrung, Mar. 13, 1907, HA VCR.

28. *Chemische Industrie* 30 (1907): 492–94; Duisberg's remarks, suppressed from the printed version, were cited by Leo Gans, "Bemerkung zu der Debatte," pp. 579–80.

29. Minutes, Select Committee, March 2, 1907, pp. 5–8, VCR-P.

30. Cited in Martius, *Die Errichtung*, p. 12.

31. Duisberg to Max Delbrück, Mar. 9, 1907, BA 46/6, VCR/B, no. 48.

32. Fischer to Ehrensberger, Dec. 14, 1906; Nernst to Fischer, Sept. 8, 1906; and Fischer to Nernst, Sept. 5/6, 1906, in EFP.

33. Verein zur förderung der bergbaulichen Interessen im Oberbergamtsbezirk Dortmund to Fischer, May 31, 1907, VCR-Z; E. Fischer,

"Die Aufgaben des Kaiser-Wilhelm-Institute für Kohlenforschung," pp. 1898–1903.

34. Max Delbrück to Fischer, June 11, 1907, VCR-B; Delbrück to Nernst, June 11, 1907, VCR-Z.

35. Delbrück to Duisberg, March 7, 1907, BA 46/6, VCR/B, following no. 46.

36. Delbrück to Duisberg, April 26, 1907, BA 46/6, VCR/B, no. 67 (7).

37. Fischer to Ostwald, Aug. 17, 1907, and Fischer to Althoff, Nov. 16, 1907, in EFP; Fischer to Duisberg, Dec. 10, 1907, BA 46/6, VCR/B.

38. Wendel, *Kaiser-Wilhelm-Gesellschaft*, pp. 277–78.

39. Stengel to Bethmann-Hollweg, Dec. 17, 1907; see also Fischer to Lewald, Oct. 25, 1907, and Bethmann-Hollweg to Stengel, Nov. 28, 1907; all reprinted in Wendel, *Kaiser-Wilhelm-Gesellschaft*, pp. 265, 278–79.

40. Fischer to Duisberg, Dec. 10, 1907, and Duisberg to Fischer, Dec. 12, 1907, BA 46/6, VCR/B.

41. "Leitsätze betreffend die Beteiligung der Industrie an der Errichtung und Verwaltung der geplanten Chemischen Reichsanstalt," appended to letter of Delbrück to Fischer, June 11, 1907, VCR-B; Delbrück to Duisberg, June 19, 1907, and Delbrück to Duisberg, Dec. 19, 1907, BA 46/6, VCR/B.

42. Duisberg to Delbrück, Dec. 21, 1907, and Duisberg to Fischer, Dec. 21, 1907, both in BA 46/6, VCR/B.

43. Ostwald to Nernst, Jan. 7, 1907, VCR-B; Ostwald, *Lebenslinien*, 3:265–72.

44. E. A. Merck to Nernst, Jan. 16, 1908, VCR-B; Minutes, Select Committee, Jan. 18, 1908, HA VCR.

45. Fischer to Dörmer, Jan. 26, 1908, BA 46/6, VCR/B; Doermer to Fischer, Jan. 28, 1908, VCR-B and BA 46/6, VCR/B; Fischer to Doermer, Feb. 1, 1908, BA 46/6, VCR/B; Fischer and Nernst to Members of the General Committee, Feb. 20, 1908, HA VCR.

46. "Leitsätze," June 11, 1907; R. Oppenheim to Franz Oppenheim, Feb. 7, 1908; and draft statutes; all in VCR-B.

47. Von Brunck to Duisberg, Feb. 24, 1908, with enclosed Geschäftsführer letter, Feb. 24, 1908, BA 46/6.

48. Fischer to von Brüning, Feb. 27, 1908, HA VCR.

49. Fischer to Duisberg, Mar. 2, 1908, BA 46/6, VCR/B.

50. Fischer to Duisberg, Mar. 8, 1908, BA 46/6, VCR/B.

51. Minutes, Wider [General] Committee, Mar. 7, 1908, VCR-P.

52. Draft of von Brüning to Fischer, Mar. 5, 1908, HA VCR.

53. Beckmann to Kollege [Fischer?], June 15, 1908, VCR-B.

54. On Harries (1866–1923), see Richard Willstätter, "Carl Dietrich Harries Lebensbeschreibung," pp. 123–57.

55. Fischer to Brüning, Feb. 27, 1908, HA VCR.

56. Martens to Ressortminister, Jan. 22, 1908, BAM C.1, nos. 104–6.

57. C. A. von Martius to Fischer, Mar. 9, 1908, VCR-B.

58. Lewald to Nernst, April 3, 1908, VCR-B.

59. Fischer to Duisberg, Feb. 17, 1908, BA 46/6, VCR/B.

60. Nernst, "Die Begründung einer chemischen Reichsanstalt," VCR-1, no. 18.

61. *Zur Begründung einer Chemischen Reichsanstalt*, p. 2. Also in Wendel, *Kaiser-Wilhelm-Gesellschaft*, pp. 271–77.

62. *Zur Begründung einer Chemischen Reichanstalt*, pp. 3, 9–10.

63. Fischer to Richards, Apr. 25 and Aug. 18, 1909, in EFP.

64. Mond to Fischer, June 1, 1908, VCR-G, no. 29; further correspondence in July, no. 30.

65. Fischer to Solvay, June 24, 1908, and Solvay to Fischer, July 4, 1908, Archives de la Section A, Solvay et Cie, Brussels (original of latter is in VCR-B); Fischer to Solvay, Jan. 12, 1909, in EFP.

66. Duisberg to Fischer, May 16, 1908, BA 46/6, VCR/B; "Fonds der Deutschen Chemischen Gesellschaft für chemische Sammel-Literatur," p. 3639.

67. Duisberg to Beckmann, Mar. 30, 1908; E. Beckmann, "Erläuterungen zu den generellen Bauplänen für die Chemische Reichsanstalt," no date, pp. 13–14, and attached plans, dated June 25, 1908, and Nov. 4, 1908, BA 46/6, VCR/B and HA VCR; Johnson, "Academic Chemistry in Imperial Germany," pp. 502, 515.

68. Fischer to Delbrück, Oct. 22, 1908, VCR-B.

69. Minutes, VCR Vorstandsrat, Oct. 24, 1908, p. 304, and VCR Ordentliche Mitgliederversammlung, Oct. 24, 1908, pp. 4–7, both in VCR-P.

70. Vorstand des Vereins "Chemische Reichsanstalt" to Bethmann-Hollweg, Dec. 22, 1908, reprinted in Wendel, *Kaiser-Wilhelm-Gesellschaft*, pp. 267–71; Wendel's commentary, pp. 66–67.

71. Sydow to Bethmann-Hollweg, Feb. 1907, cited in Wendel, *Kaiser-Wilhelm-Gesellschaft*, p. 71; Bethmann-Hollweg to Sydow, Jan. 30, 1909, excerpted in Wendel, *Kaiser-Wilhelm-Gesellschaft*, pp. 279–80.

72. Extensive correspondence from November 1908 in EFP; Fischer to Duisberg, Nov. 11, 1909, BA 46/6, VCR/B.

73. Fischer to Max Delbrück, Sept. 15, 1909, in EFP.

74. Minutes, VCR Vorstandsrat, Oct. 16, 1909, p. 3, in VCR-P.

75. Fischer to Duisberg, Nov. 11, 1909, BA 46/6, VCR/B.

76. Minutes, VCR Vorstandsrat, Oct. 16, 1909, p. 4, in VCR-P.

77. Minutes, Building Committee, Oct. 18, 1909, VCR-1, nos. 94–99. Guth to Geheimrat, Nov. 14, 1909, VCR-B.

78. Max Delbrück to Fischer, Dec. 16, 1909, VCR-1, no. 107, and accompanying draft contract, nos. 108–10.

79. Naumann to Geheimrat, Nov. 22, 1909, VCR-B; Minutes, VCR Vorstand, Nov. 15, 1909, VCR-1, nos. 100–101; VCR Vorstand to Vorstandsrat, Nov. 27, 1909, and replies, Dec. 1909, in VCR-B.

80. P. Reiner (G. von Siegle Estate) to H. von Brunck, Oct. 20, 1909; Fischer to Gustav von Müller, to Eduard von Pfeiffer, and to Alfred von Kaulla, all dated Oct. 23, 1909; all in VCR-B.

81. Fischer to H. von Brunck, Dec. 24, 1909, VCR-B; and Fischer to Nernst, Jan. 7, 1910, VCR-B. Duisberg to Fischer, Dec. 13, 1909, BA 46/6, VCR/B.

82. Oppenheim to Fischer, Oct. 22, 1909, in EFP. Duisberg to Fischer, Dec. 13, 1909, BA 46/6, VCR/B.

83. Willstätter, *From My Life*, pp. 83–85, 166, 183, 199–202; Fischer to Lunge, June 22, 1905, in EFP.
84. See Chapter 1.

Chapter 6

1. Fischer to Kultusminister von Studt, May [?], 1907, in EFP; Nernst to Althoff, April 1, 1908, cited in Burchardt, *Wissenschaftspolitik*, p. 27 (see also p. 23); "Althoff's Pläne für Dahlem" (no date), p. 1, in AHP, Sect. IV, Box 22, Aufteilung.
2. Fritz Fischer, *War of Illusions*, pp. 60–62.
3. Reichschancellery to "Euer Hochwohlgeboren," June 19, 1908; Civil Cabinet to Staatsministerium, March 24, 1909; "Votum des Ministers für Landwirtschaft, Domänen und Forsten und des Finanzministers dem Königlichen Staatsministerium vorzulegen," July 9, 1909; Immediatbericht to the Kaiser, May 28, 1910; Civil Cabinet to Staatsministerium, June 11, 1910; all in AHP, Sect. IV, Box 22, Aufteilung; Burchardt, *Wissenschaftspolitik*, pp. 28–29.
4. Schmidt-Ott, "Anfänge der Kaiser-Wilhelm-Gesellschaft," *50 Jahre KWG*, pp. 53–55 (typed draft is in GSA-PK, Rep 92 (Schmidt-Ott), vol. 13. The version in *50 Jahre KWG* is slightly abridged. Schmidt to Harnack, July 13, 1909, AHP, Sect. V, Box 41, Schmidt-Ott Letters, nos. 14–15; Burchardt, *Wissenschaftspolitik*, pp. 18–22. Note that Schmidt later changed his name to Schmidt-Ott.
5. Bülow, *Memoirs of Prince von Bülow*, 2:318, 3:105–7.
6. Althoff to Harnack, April 21, 1908, AHP, Sect. V, Box 26, Friedrich Althoff Letters, no. 63; "Althoffs Pläne für Dahlem," pp. 24–25.
7. Fischer to Schmidt, June 8, 1909, EFP; Schmidt-Ott, "Anfänge der Kaiser-Wilhelm-Gesellschaft," p. 55; "Kaiser-Wilhelm-Institut für Naturforschung," reprinted in *50 Jahre KWG*, pp. 71–79. Copy forwarded to Harnack by Krüss, July 19, 1909, AHP, Sect. V, Box 35, Hugo A. Krüss Letters, no. 1.
8. "Krüss, Hugo Andr.," *Wer Ist's*, 10th ed.; on Gerhard Krüss, see Emil Fischer, *Aus meinem Leben*, p. 81, and his obituary written by Fischer.
9. *50 Jahre KWG*, p. 77–79.
10. Adolf Harnack, "Carnegies Schrift über die Pflicht der Reichen," (1903), and "Die Nachlaßsteuer vom sozial ethischen Gesichtspunkt" (1909), in his *Aus Wissenschaft und Leben*, 1:67–171 and 172–81; Harnack's memorandum to the Kaiser, Nov. 21, 1909, in *50 Jahre KWG*, pp. 80–94, esp. p. 91.
11. Valentini to Harnack, Dec. 10, 1909, *50 Jahre KWG*, p. 94.
12. *50 Jahre KWG*, p. 90; Minutes, VCR Vorstand, Nov. 15, 1909, VCR-1, no. 100.
13. Minutes, VCR Vorstand, Jan. 12, 1910, VCR-1, nos. 115–16.
14. Bethmann-Hollweg to Trott zu Solz, Dec. 19, 1909, copy in GSA-PK, Rep 92, (Schmidt-Ott), vol. 13.
15. Friedrich Schmidt and Theodor Lewald, "Aufzeichnung betreffend die Harnacksche Denkschrift wegen Gründung naturwissenschaftlicher

Forschungsinstitute," in *50 Jahre KWG*, pp. 96–102; complete version in MPG, I A 1, vol. 1, nos. 19–31.

16. Harnack Memorandum and "Aufzeichnung betreffend die Harnacksche Denkschrift wegen Gründung naturwissenschaftlicher Forschungsinstitute," in *50 Jahre KWG*, pp. 90–91 and 96–97, 99; MPG, I A 1, vol. 1, nos. 24–25. Harnack to the Kaiser, Nov. 20, 1911, reprinted in *50 Jahre KWG*, pp. 141–45, esp. p. 142.

17. Harnack to Trott zu Solz, Jan. 22, 1910, in *50 Jahre KWG*, p. 95.

18. "Aufzeichnung betreffend die Harnacksche Denkschrift wegen Gründung naturwissenschaftlicher Forschungsinstitute," MPG, I A 1, vol. 1, nos. 27, 29.

19. *50 Jahre KWG*, p. 91.

20. "Aufzeichnung betreffend die Harnacksche Denkschrift wegen Gründung naturwissenschaftlicher Forschungsinstitute," MPG, I A 1, vol. 1, nos. 28–30.

21. Ibid., no. 27; *50 Jahre KWG*, p. 102.

22. No minutes appear to exist; see Harnack to the Kaiser, Nov. 20, 1911, in *50 Jahre KWG*, pp. 141–45; Burchardt, *Wissenschaftspolitik*, p. 37 n. 83, and pp. 43–44.

23. Minutes, VCR Vorstandsrat, Mar. 5, 1910, pp. 2–3, VCR-P.

24. Ibid., p. 4; *50 Jahre KWG*, p. 87.

25. Bethmann-Hollweg to the Kaiser, April 7, 1910, in *50 Jahre KWG*, p. 103. This is an excerpt from the full report, a copy of the draft of which is in GSA-PK, Rep 92 (Schmidt-Ott), vol. 14.

26. Valentini to Bethmann-Hollweg, April 13, 1910, and "Aufzeichnung über eine Besprechung. . . ," May 6, 1910 in *50 Jahre KWG*, pp. 106–7 (slightly abridged; complete text is in MPG, I A 1, vol. 1, nos. 33–36) Burchardt, *Wissenschaftspolitik*, p. 83.

27. Fischer to Baeyer, April 21, 1910; see also his letters to Harries, April 8, 1910, and to Brunck, June 23, 1910, all in EFP.

28. List of potential invitees in "Aufzeichnung über eine Besprechung . . . ," in *50 Jahre KWG*, p. 108; Lewald to von Guenther, May 9, 1910, GSA-PK, Rep 90, no. 30; see Burchardt, *Wissenschaftspolitik*, pp. 38–41.

29. Burchardt, *Wissenschaftspolitik*, p. 40 n. 95. For competing interests in Frankfurt, see Kluke, *Stiftungsuniversität Frankfurt am Main*, pp. 23–65.

30. Adolf Harnack, "Gedanken über eine neue Art der Wissenschaftsförderung," May 21, 1910, pp. 11–12, copy in MPG, I A 1, vol. 1, no. 32.

31. "Aufzeichnung über eine Besprechung . . . ," in *50 Jahre KWG*, p. 108; Burchardt, *Wissenschaftspolitik*, pp. 78–79.

32. Burchardt, *Wissenschaftspolitik*, p. 38.

33. Wilhelm von Siemens to Geheimrat [Lewald], May 19, 1910, SAA 4, Lk 110; Burchardt, *Wissenschaftspolitik*, p. 38; Walther Rathenau, "Promemoria betreffend die Begründung einer Königlichen Preussischen Gesellschaft," Mar. 14, 1910, in AHP, Sect. IV, Box 23, Gründung; also in Rathenau, *Zur Kritik der Zeit*, pp. 244–55; Hugenberg to Krupp von Bohlen und Halbach

(henceforth KBH), May 21, 1910, KA IV-E-244, KBH to Oscar Vogt, June 9, 1910, KA, IV-E-264.

34. Harnack, "Gedanken," p. 10.

35. Cited in Craig, *Politics of the Prussian Army*, p. 237.

36. Wendel, *Kaiser-Wilhelm-Gesellschaft*, pp. 54–56.

37. Fritz Fischer, *War of Illusions*, p. 107; Eley, *Reshaping the German Right*, p. 366.

38. Adolf Harnack, "Die Kaiser-Wilhelm-Gesellschaft am Schluss ihres ersten Jahres," cols. 4–6, cited in Wendel, *Kaiser-Wilhelm-Gesellschaft*, pp. 101–2.

39. On Rathenau, see Burchardt, *Wissenschaftspolitik*, p. 39; Harnack to Schmidt, Mar. 17, 1910, copy in GSA-PK, Rep 92, vol. 14. On the Krupps: Valentini to KBH, May 19, 1910, KA IV-E-87, Stiftung. "Entwurf" to Valentini, undated, marked "nicht ausgef."; "Notiz," by KBH although unsigned, dated Kiel, June 27, 1910, KA IV-E-87, Stiftung.

40. Siemens, "Zur Frage der Gründung neuer wissenschaftlichen Forschungsinstitute," later published in *Elektrotechnische Zeitschrift*; a draft copy in SAA 4, Lk 110, was sent to F. Meissner on Feb. 24, 1911.

41. Runderlass of Prussian Minister-Präsident (Bethmann-Hollweg, but drafted by Guenther with corrections by Krüss and others) to Oberpräsidenten of Prussian provinces, draft copy, June 1910, in GSA-PK, Rep 92 (Schmidt-Ott), vol. 12; also in MPG, I A 1, vol. 1, pp. 37–41; Burchardt, *Wissenschaftspolitik*, p. 40 n. 94; KWG statutes in *50 Jahre KWG*, pp. 126–31.

42. List in Burchardt, *Wissenschaftspolitik*, pp. 155–58.

43. Krüss to Schmidt, June 2, 1910 (see also May 31, 1910), GSA-PK, Rep 92 (Schmidt-Ott), vol. 12. Runderlass to Oberpräsidenten, June 1910, MPG, I A 1, vol. 1, nos. 37–38.

44. Krüss to Schmidt, May 31, 1910; minutes of meeting with Delbrück and other businessmen, June 18, 1910, in Krüss's handwriting, GSA-PK, Rep 92 (Schmidt-Ott), vol. 12.

45. Valentini to Schmidt, June 20, 1910, GSA-PK, Rep 92 (Schmidt-Ott), vol. 12.

46. Reprinted in *50 Jahre KWG*, pp. 113–16.

47. Burchardt, *Wissenschaftspolitik*, pp. 79–80.

48. "Anfänge der Kaiser-Wilhelm-Gesellschaft," typescript in GSA-PK, Rep 92 (Schmidt-Ott), vol. 13; the relevant passage was left out of the printed version in *50 Jahre KWG*.

49. Wiesbaden Regierungspräsident (Wilhelm von Meister) to the Oberpräsident of Hessen-Nassau, Aug. 27, 1910, GSA-PK, Rep 90, no. 102, pp. 3–4. Harnack on Loeb in *50 Jahre KWG*, p. 87. Loeb's motivations involved both of these considerations; see Pauly, *Controlling Life*, pp. 28–29, 41, 55–56, 60.

50. Schmidt-Ott, "Anfänge," typescript in GSA-PK, Rep 92 (Schmidt-Ott), vol. 13; Burchardt, *Wissenschaftspolitik*, pp. 57, 100, 55; and preliminary lists in GSA-PK, Rep 90, nos. 114, 123–30.

51. Burchardt, *Wissenschaftspolitik*, p. 82.

52. Ibid., pp. 80–81; GSA-PK, Rep 90, nos. 114, 123–31.

53. "Nachtrag," GSA-PK, Rep 90, nos. 140–41; Harnack's request to Henckel detailed in Krüss to Schmidt, May 31, 1910, GSA-PK, Rep 92 (Schmidt-Ott), vol. 12; rankings of wealth given in Burchardt, *Wissenschafts-politik*, p. 82 n. 227.

54. GSA-PK, Rep 90, no. 127.

55. On Thyssen and Speyer, see Burchardt, *Wissenschaftspolitik*, pp. 62–63, 82; Meister to Schmidt, Aug. 20, 1910, GSA-PK, Rep 92 (Schmidt-Ott), vol. 12.

56. On the Krupps, see the correspondence between KBH and Oskar Vogt in KA IV-E-264, esp. KBH to Vogt, June 9, 1910; Graham, "Science and Values," pp. 1135–36. For other donors interested in racial and other biological issues, see Ernst Paul Lehmann to Oberpräsident of Brandenburg, Oct. 30, 1910, GSA-PK, Rep 90, nos. 144–45; and Burchardt, *Wissenschaftspolitik*, p. 110.

57. Kirdorf to "Excellenz" (Oberpräsident of the Rheinprovinz), Aug. 3, 1910, SAK, Nr. 14065, nos. 17–20.

58. Oberpräsident, Magdeburg (Prussian Saxony) to Bethmann-Hollweg, Sept. 5, 1910, GSA-PK, Rep 90, nos. 70–71.

59. Burchardt, *Wissenschaftspolitik*, p. 78.

60. Cf. GSA-PK, Rep 90, no. 127; Burchardt, *Wissenschaftspolitik*, pp. 156, 80.

61. Duisberg to Franz Kruse (Regierungspräsident, Düsseldorf), Dec. 23, 1910, HD, Nr. 1324, nos. 124–26.

62. Amounts contributed are listed in Burchardt, *Wissenschaftspolitik*, pp. 155–58. Arguments against research institutes can be found in Meister (Wiesbaden) to Oberpräsident of Hessen-Nassau, Aug. 27, 1910, GSA-PK, Rep 90, no. 102, p. 4, and no. 105.

63. Amounts in Burchardt, *Wissenschaftspolitik*, pp. 155–58.

64. Fischer to Brunck, Dec. 4, 1910, and to Schmidt, Dec. 10, 1910, in EFP. Note that Fritz von Friedländer-Fuld is the same Fritz Friedländer, now enno-bled, whom the chemists had approached earlier for a contribution to the Imperial Institute.

65. Amounts are listed in Burchardt, *Wissenschaftspolitik*, pp. 155–58; Fi-scher to Ladenburg, Oct. 29, 1910, in EFP.

66. Burchardt, *Wissenschaftspolitik*, pp. 43–45, 98–99; on Koppel, see Mosse, *Jews in the German Economy*, pp. 182, 208.

67. Friedrich Schmidt-Ott to Dr. Otto Benecke, Feb. 14, 1954, copy in GSA-PK, Rep 92 (Schmidt-Ott), vol. 13.

68. Burchardt, *Wissenschaftspolitik*, pp. 43–45.

69. Fischer to Duisberg, Oct. 15, 1910, and to Baeyer, Oct. 17, 1910, both in EFP.

70. Kaiser's speech, in *50 Jahre KWG*, pp. 113–16, quotation on p. 114; drafts in MPG, I A 1, vol. 1, no. 41b; AHP, Sect. IV, Box 22, Jubiläum; and GSA-PK, Rep 92 (Schmidt-Ott), vol. 12. Harnack to the Kaiser, Nov. 20, 1911,

in *50 Jahre KWG*, pp. 141–45; Burchardt, *Wissenschaftspolitik*, pp. 46–47, 89–93.
71. See Dr. von Simson, "Die Kaiser-Wilhelm-Gesellschaft," pp. 79–84.

Chapter 7

1. Nernst to Fischer, Jan. 8, 1910, EFP.
2. Johnson, "Chemical Reichsanstalt Association," pp. 460–554 and 609–49, provides a more detailed narrative of the creation of the first Kaiser Wilhelm Institutes for chemistry.
3. Minutes, VCR Directorate, Jan. 12, 1910, VCR-1, nos. 115–16; Fischer to Schmidt, Jan. 13, 1910, VCR-B.
4. Fischer to Geh. Oberfinanzrat Dulheuer, Jan. 26, 1910, in EFP.
5. Burchardt, *Wissenschaftspolitik*, p. 45.
6. Goran, *Story of Fritz Haber*, p. 38; Coates, "Haber Memorial Lecture," p. 136; Mendelssohn, *World of Walther Nernst*, pp. 85–87.
7. Schmidt-Ott, *Erlebtes und Erstrebtes*, p. 122; see also Crawford and Heilbron, "Die Kaiser Wilhelm-Institute."
8. Fischer to Duisberg, Oct. 15, 1910, in EFP.
9. Fischer to Brunck, Nov. 19, 1910, and to Schmidt, Dec. 11, 1910, in EFP.
10. Minutes, Vorstandsrat, p. 6; General Meeting, VCR, Nov. 26, 1910, pp. 5–6, in VCR-P; *50 Jahre KWG*, p. 134 n. 1; Fischer to Schmidt, Jan. 13, 1911, GSA-PK, Rep 92 (Schmidt-Ott), vol. 12.
11. Cf. lists in *50 Jahre KWG*, pp. 122 and 134 n. 1.
12. Burchardt, *Wissenschaftspolitik*, p. 99 n. 282.
13. "Protokoll über die erste Sitzung des Senats . . . ," Jan. 23, 1911, MPG, I A 1, vol. 1, nos. 166–68.
14. See especially Harnack to Trott zu Solz, Jan. 22, 1910, in *50 Jahre KWG*, p. 95; Harnack to Schmidt, Oct. 9, 1910, in ibid., pp. 110–11; Harnack to Schmidt, July 21, July 28, and Oct. 24, 1911, copies of all in GSA-PK, Rep 92 (Schmidt-Ott), vol. 12.
15. Harnack to Schmidt, May 10 and Oct. 24, 1911, and April 23, 1912, copies of all in GSA-PK, Rep 92 (Schmidt-Ott), vol. 12; Fischer to Harnack, Oct. 12, 1912, AHP, Sect. V, Box 31, Emil Fischer, nos. 3–4.
16. Harnack to Schmidt, Jan. 28 and Mar. 18, 1913, GSA-PK, Rep 92 (Schmidt-Ott), vol. 12.
17. KBH to Harnack, Mar. 13, 1913, KA, IV-E-245.
18. Emil Fischer, "Neuere Erfolge und Probleme," pp. 757–71.
19. Ibid., p. 757. He checked with Max Planck before publishing this assertion; see Fischer to Planck, Jan. 21, 1911, in EFP.
20. Emil Fischer, "Neuere Erfolge und Probleme," pp. 758–59; Fischer to Harnack, Nov. 14, 1910, in EFP.
21. Emil Fischer, "Neuere Erfolge und Probleme," p. 760; Fischer to Böttinger, July 22 and 25, 1910, both in EFP.
22. Emil Fischer, "Neuere Erfolge und Probleme," pp. 760–61.
23. Fischer to Prof. O. Wiener, Leipzig, Jan. 13, 1911, in EFP.
24. Fischer to Haber, Mar. 15, 1911, in EFP.

25. Fischer to Nikodem Caro (one of the developers of the cyanamid process of nitrogen fixation), Jan. 14, 1911, in EFP.

26. Emil Fischer, "Neuere Erfolge und Probleme," p. 762.

27. Ibid., pp. 763–64.

28. Ibid., pp. 764–70.

29. Fischer to E. Erdmann, Halle, Feb. 20, 1912, and later letters, in EFP.

30. Duisberg to Fischer, Nov. 23, 1910, copy in BA 46/6, VCR-V; Fischer to Kolonialwirtschaftliches Komitee E. V. zu Händen des Vorsitzenden Herrn Sumpf, Berlin, Nov. 6, 1909, in EFP.

31. Emil Fischer, "Neuere Erfolge und Probleme," p. 771.

32. Fischer to Ramsay, Oct. 31, 1911, EFP.

33. Wendel, *Kaiser-Wilhelm-Gesellschaft*, pp. 161–62; Burchardt, *Wissenschaftspolitik*, pp. 45, 100.

34. Rasch, *Vorgeschichte und Gründung*, pp. 17–26 (no minutes appear to have survived of either meeting, which took place November 18 and 27, 1911); "Errichtung eines grossen biologischen Instituts mit 3 Abteilungen," in letter of Prof. Otto Lubarsch to Karl Goldschmidt, Aug. 3, 1911, in TGA, Nr. 16.

35. Emil Fischer, "Die Aufgaben des Kaiser-Wilhelm-Instituts für Kohlenforschung," p. 1900; Rasch, *Vorgeschichte und Gründung*, pp. 27–28, 133–38, 144–55, 171–83 (with texts of relevant documents including Fischer, "Aufgaben").

36. Franz Fischer, *Leben und Forschung*, pp. 30–31; Emil Fischer, "Neuere Erfolge und Probleme," p. 763; cf. Rasch, *Vorgeschichte und Gründung*, pp. 66–67.

37. Fischer to Frank, June 26, 1912, and to Bunte, June 30, 1912, in EFP; Emil Fischer, "Die Aufgaben des Kaiser-Wilhelm-Instituts für Kohlenforschung," p. 1903.

38. Franz Fischer, "Chemie und Kohle," p. 4 (reprint in TGA, Nr. 16); Emil Fischer, "Die Aufgaben des Kaiser-Wilhelm-Instituts für Kohlenforschung," p. 1901.

39. Emil Fischer, "Die Aufgaben des Kaiser-Wilhelm-Instituts für Kohlenforschung," p. 1901–3.

40. Ibid., p. 1902. Franz Fischer, "Ziele und Ergebnisse der Kohlenforschung," p. 8 (reprint in TGA, Nr. 16).

41. Fischer to Duisberg, Aug. 3, 1912, in EFP.

42. Emil Fischer, "Die Aufgaben des Kaiser-Wilhelm-Instituts für Kohlenforschung," pp. 1898–99, 1900, 1902; "Das Kaiser-Wilhelm-Institut für Kohlenforschung," p. 1897.

43. Fischer to Duisberg, Aug. 3, 1912, in EFP; Rasch, *Vorgeschichte und Gründung*, pp. 49–51, 156–70 (the latter pages include the text of minutes).

44. Information from the Bayer Archive; cf. Fischer to Baeyer, March 1, 1913, in EFP.

45. Cf. MPG, II 10/2; on military efforts to promote the mechanical side of aviation and automobiles, see Morrow, *Building German Airpower*, pp. 52–71, and Schröter, *Krieg-Staat-Monopol*, p. 30.

46. Fischer to Richards, Jan. 20, 1913, in EFP.

NOTES TO PAGES 131–36 | 235

47. Schmidt-Ott, "Anfänge der KWG," in *50 Jahre KWG*, p. 55.

48. Burchardt, *Wissenschaftspolitik*, pp. 116–18; correspondence in KA IV-E-264. Fischer to Abderhalden, Dec. 27, 1913, and to Krüss, Jan. 1, 1914; Abderhalden to Fischer, Dec. 30, 1915; all in EFP.

49. Twenty-seven printed replies to the survey are in AHP, Sect. IV, Box 24, Biologische Forschungsinstitute; the minutes of the conference (January 3, 1912) were printed separately as *Zur Errichtung biologischer Forschungsinstitute* (copy in MPG, II 4, vol. 3, p. 2). A detailed analysis is in the Ph.D. dissertation currently being completed by Natasha X. Jacobs, Indiana University.

50. Emil Fischer, "Die Kaiser-Wilhelm-Institute und der Zusammenhang von organischer Chemie und Biologie," p. 808.

51. "Vorbesprechung," Mar. 16, 1911, Anlage E to Minutes, Senat KWG, Mar. 18, 1911; and Minutes, Verwaltungsausschuss KWG, Mar. 16, 1911, both in AHP, Sect. IV, Box 23, Protokolle; Minutes, Vorstand and Building Committee, VCR, April 3, 1911, in VCR-1, p. 169.

52. Fischer to Duisberg, Jan. 30, 1911, and Duisberg to Fischer, Feb. 4, 1911, BA 46/6, VCR-V.

53. The phrase cited is in "Bemerkungen zur Rechtsform der chemischen Institute," undated, AHP, Sect. IV, Box 24, KWICh. See also "Vorbesprechung," Mar. 16, 1911, Anlage E to Minutes, Senat KWG, Mar. 18, 1911; and Minutes, Verwaltungsausschuss KWG, Mar. 16, 1911, both in AHP, Sect. IV, Box 23, Protokolle.

54. Finance Minister Lentze to Harnack, May 11, 1911, copy in AHP, Sect. IV, Box 24, KWICh.

55. Fischer to von Böttinger, Oct. 7, 1911, in EFP.

56. Inference from typed agenda for Verwaltungsausschuss KWG, Nov. 11, 1911, pp. 1–3, referring to correspondence (copies not available) on the issue of "Kapitaldeckung"; AHP, Sect. IV, Box 23, Protokolle. See also Burchardt, *Wissenschaftspolitik*, pp. 89–90.

57. Paragraph 21 of printed contract attached to Minutes, Senat KWG, Nov. 18, 1911, AHP, Sect. IV, Box 23, Protokolle.

58. Lentze to Verwaltungsausschuss KWG, Nov. 8, 1911, reprinted in *50 Jahre KWG*, p. 136.

59. Verwaltungsausschuss KWG to Lentze, Nov. 20, 1911; Harnack to the Kaiser, Nov. 20, 1911, *50 Jahre KWG*, pp. 140–45.

60. Cf. "Aufzeichnung über die Bereitstellung von Staatsstellen," MPG, I A 14, no. 42; and "Aufzeichnung über den Anteil von Preussen und vom Reich an der Gründung der Kaiser-Wilhelm-Gesellschaft zur Förderung der Wissenschaften," Aug. 23, 1929, in ibid., nos. 33–35.

61. Final version: VCR-2, nos. 50–62; also printed in "Mitteilungen für die Mitglieder . . . ," no. 3, April 1912, pp. 18–24 (following p. 2 of the regular Mitteilungen, which are separately paginated), copy in SAA 4, Lk 110.

62. Cf. Minutes, Vorstandsrat VCR, Oct. 26, 1912, pp. 1, 7, in VCR-P.

63. Minutes, Verwaltungsausschuss KWG, May 18, 1911, AHP, Sect. IV, Box 23, Protokolle; Wendel, *Kaiser-Wilhelm-Gesellschaft*, pp. 51–52, 327–28.

64. Rasch, *Vorgeschichte und Gründung*, pp. 79–86.

65. Harnack to Schmidt, July 28, 1912, GSA-PK, Rep 92 (Schmidt-Ott), vol.

12; Kruse to Oberpräsident von Rheinbaben, Nov. 2, 1912, SAK, Nr. 15622, nos. 13–15; contract between KWG and City of Mülheim/Ruhr (Berlin and Mülheim), March 4 and Feb. 17, 1913; Anlage to minutes, Senat KWG, Mar. 4, 1913, in AHP, Sect. IV, Box 23, Protokolle; Mülheim's copy reproduced in Rasch, *Vorgeschichte und Gründung*, pp. 206–7; see also 137.

66. Minutes, Vorstandsrat VCR, Nov. 26, p. 6.

67. Fischer to Willstätter, Dec. 1, 1910, in EFP.

68. Decree appointing Harnack and Ihne to Dahlem Commission, Dec. 5, 1910, copy in AHP, Sect. IV, Box 22, Aufteilung; on Ihne see Wilhelm II, *Ereignisse und Gestalten*, pp. 36, 144, 167–68.

69. Fischer to Geh. Oberbaurat Thür (Guth's superior), Dec. 6, 1910, in EFP.

70. Fischer to Nernst and to Beckmann, Dec. 10, 1910 in EFP.

71. Haber's letter of resignation to his institute, Oct. 1, 1933, *50 Jahre KWG*, p. 191.

72. Minutes, Vorstand and building committee, VCR, Feb. 18 and March 15, 1911, in VCR-1, pp. 158, 167–68. Minutes, Verwaltungsausschuss KWG, Feb. 21, 1911, in AHP, Sect. IV, Box 23, Protokolle. Description of March meeting: Franz Oppenheim to Carl Duisberg, Mar. 17, 1911, BA 46/6, VCR-V.

73. Duisberg to Oppenheim, Mar. 18, 1911, BA 46/6, VCR-V.

74. E. Beckmann, "Erläuterungen zu den generellen Bauplänen für die Chemische Reichsanstalt," no date, pp. 1, 11; attached plan no. 8; copies in BA 46/6, VCR/B and HA VCR. Beckmann and Fischer, *Kaiser-Wilhelm-Institut*, pp. 12, 23.

75. Beckmann, "Bemerkungen zu den generellen Bauplänen des Kaiser Wilhelm Instituts für Chemie," undated (ca. Feb. 1911), pp. 3, 8, in HA VCR.

76. Oppenheim to Duisberg, Mar. 17, 1911, BA 46/6, VCR-V.

77. Nernst to Kollege (Duisberg), Mar. 20, 1911, BA 46/6, VCR-V.

78. Duisberg to Nernst, Mar. 22, 1911, BA 46/6, VCR-V.

79. Brüning to Schmidt, Apr. 2, 1911, GSA-PK, Rep 92 (Schmidt-Ott), vol. 12.

80. Schmidt to Herr Doktor (Brüning), Apr. 11, 1911, in ibid.

81. Beckmann to Brüning, Mar. 25 and Mar. 30, 1911, and Brüning to Beckmann, Apr. 3, 1911, HA VCR; Beckmann to Duisberg, Mar. 29, 1911, BA 46/6, VCR-V.

82. Willstätter, *From My Life*, p. 214.

83. Ibid., p. 218.

84. Noted by Rhodes, *Making of the Atomic Bomb*, p. 79.

85. Nernst to Fischer, Apr. 8, 1911, in EFP.

86. Nernst to Fischer, Apr. 21, 1911, in ibid.

87. Fischer to Harnack, May 2, 1911, VCR-1, nos. 173–74. Minutes, Vorstandsrat VCR, May 1, pp. 1–2, in VCR-P; Stroof to Fischer, July 5, 1911, in VCR-B.

88. II. Sitzung, Verwaltungsrat des Kaiser-Wilhelm-Instituts für Chemie (henceforth: Verwaltungsrat KWICh), Mar. 2, 1912, p. 5; V. Sitzung, Verwaltungsrat KWICh, Oct. 29, 1913, pp. 2–3, 67; VI. Sitzung, Verwaltungsrat KWICh, Mar. 14, 1914, p. 3–6, all in BA, Nr. 142, Sitzungen; Minutes,

Verwaltungsausschuss KWICh, July 2, 1912, p. 1, in HA KWICh, 1912–42.

89. Burchardt, *Wissenschaftspolitik*, p. 100.

90. Wendel, *Kaiser-Wilhelm-Gesellschaft*, pp. 327–28.

91. Speech reprinted in *50 Jahre KWG*, p. 153.

92. Burchardt, *Wissenschaftspolitik*, p. 100; *50 Jahre KWG*, p. 154; cf. also Willstätter, *From My Life*, p. 219.

93. *50 Jahre KWG*, p. 150.

94. Hoesch, *Emil Fischer*, p. 149; on the French reaction, see Paul, "Die Entwicklung der Forschungsförderung im modernen Frankreich."

95. Fischer to E. Arnhold, Feb. 2, 1913, in EFP.

96. Rasch, *Vorgeschichte und Gründung*, p. 89.

97. Fischer, "Die Aufgaben des Kaiser-Wilhelm-Instituts für Kohlenforschung," p. 1902; "Denkschrift, betreffend die Errichtung eines Kaiser-Wilhelm-Instituts für Kohlenforschung in Mülheim an der Ruhr," Berlin, Sept. 3, 1912, p. 1, in Anlage to minutes, Verwaltungsausschuss KWG, Sept. 19, 1912, AHP, Sect. IV, Box 23, Protokolle.

98. E. Fischer to Kruse, Sept. 30, 1912, in EFP.

99. Emil Fischer, "Tischrede bei der Einweihung des Instituts für Kohlenforschung," pp. 823–26; cf. Rasch, *Vorgeschichte und Gründung*, illustration on pp. 56, 73, 78, 91, 95, and cover.

100. Minutes, Vorstandsrat VCR, May 1, 1911, p. 5, in VCR-P.

101. Minutes, Vorstandsrat VCR, July 12, 1911, VCR-1, nos. 24–25.

102. Nernst to Fischer, Apr. 8, 1911, in EFP.

103. Minutes, Vorstandsrat VCR, May 1, 1911, p. 5, in VCR-P; Minutes, Senat KWG, June 23, 1911, Anlage A (notarized election protocol for "Gesellschaft 'Kaiser-Wilhelm-Institut für Chemie' "), in AHP, Sect. IV, Box 23, Protokolle. "Protokoll über die konstituierende Versammlung und I. Sitzung des Verwaltungsausschusses des Kaiser Wilhelm Instituts für Chemie . . . ," Aug. 2, 1911, HA VCR.

104. Copy of draft contract, Feb. 1, 1911; Brunck to "Exzellenz" (Fischer), Feb. 2, 1911, VCR-1, nos. 150–51, 152–53. Fischer to Harnack, Mar. 5, 1911, in EFP.

105. Minutes, Verwaltungsausschuss KWG, May 18, 1911, in AHP, Sect. IV, Box 23, Protokolle; minutes, Extraordinary General Meeting, VCR, July 10, 1911, p. 2, in VCR-P.

106. Burchardt, *Wissenschaftspolitik*, p. 100 n. 289.

107. Minutes, Extraordinary General Meeting, VCR, July 10, 1911, p. 2, in VCR-P.

108. Minutes, Extraordinary General Meeting, VCR, pp. 1–2, in VCR-P; Minutes, Erste konstituierende Versammlung des Verwaltungsrates des KWICh, Oct. 28, 1911, p. 1, copy from BA, Nr. 142, Sitzungen; also in HA KWICh, 1912–42.

109. Minutes, KWICh, II. Sitzung des Verwaltungsrates, Mar. 2, 1912, p. 1, copy from BA, Nr. 142, Sitzungen; Brüning to Emil Fischer, Dec. 13 and Dec. 15, 1911, HA VCR.

110. Minutes, Vorstandsrat VCR, Dec. 16, 1911, pp. 1–2, in VCR-P.

111. Minutes, Extraordinary Membership Meeting VCR, Mar. 8, 1913), pp.

1–5; changes listed pp. 5–9, in HA VCR-V. Cf. Martius to Fischer, Mar. 9, 1908, VCR-B: "Deutscher Verein zur Förderung wissenschaftlich-chemischer Forschung" (German Association for the Advancement of Scientific Research in Chemistry).

112. Farbwerke Hoechst to Vorstand VCR, Feb. 18, 1913, VCR-2, no. 148. R. Pschorr to Herbert von Meister, Feb. 21, 1913 and Meister to Pschorr, Feb. 24, 1913, VCR-2, nos. 149–51, 152–53. Copies of nos. 149–54 are also in HA 71 VCR-V. Minutes, Senat KWG, March 4 and June 17, 1913, in AHP, Sect. IV, Box 24, Sammlung, pp. 35–37, 41–43.

113. H. von Meister to Arthur von Weinberg, Nov. 17, 1913, HA 71 VCR-V.

114. "Vertrag über die Errichtung des Kaiser-Wilhelm-Instituts für Chemie," Dec. 23, 1911, paragraphs 9, 10, and 14, printed in "Mitteilungen an die Mitgleider . . . ," Nr. 3, April 1912, in pp. 18–24 of senate minutes; mimeographed version in VCR-2, nos. 50–62.

115. Wallach to Duisberg, Oct. 5, 1926, BA unnumbered, KWG KWICh, Wahl des Direktors.

116. Minutes and typed agenda, Verwaltungsausschuss KWG, Nov. 18, 1911, AHP, Sect. IV, Box 23, Protokolle.

117. Lists of grantees (without amounts) in printed minutes of KWG senate, March 4 and March 21, 1914, available in SAA 4, Lk 111, or in AHP, Sect. IV, Box 24, Sammlung, pp. 35–37 and 49–51. A brief discussion of the program and grantees is in Johnson, "Chemical Reichsanstalt Association," pp. 492–98. More detailed information regarding the operation of the scientific advisory council, including applications for grants, is in the following original documents of the council, available in BA: Wissenschaftlicher Beirat des KWICh, vol. 1 (Nov. 1912–1918), Hauptakten, vol. 2, Wissenschaftlicher Beirat [undated], and Spendenbewerbungen. See also BA, Nr. 144, Leo-Gans-Stiftung.

118. Minutes, Verwaltungsausschuss KWG, July 2, 1912, p. 5, AHP, Sect. IV, Box 23, Protokolle; Friedrich Schmidt to Harnack, July 26, 1912, AHP, Sect. V, Box 41, Friedrich Schmidt-Ott, nos. 50–51.

119. Burchardt, *Wissenschaftspolitik*, pp. 104–5. Minutes, Senat KWG, Sept. 19, 1912, AHP, Sect. IV, Box 24, Sammlung, pp. 26–27. Draft petition, undated, unsigned, October (?) 1912, in EFP; cf. Valentini to Harnack, Jan. 1, 1913, AHP, Sect. V, Box 44, Rudolf v. Valentini, pp. 7–8.

120. Cf. "Denkschrift," Sept. 3, 1912, p. 3, cited in n. 97 above.

121. Both cited, Burchardt, *Wissenschaftspolitik*, p. 106 (citation from Committee minutes here given at slightly greater length; see "Gründungsversammlung des Ausschusses des Kaiser-Wilhelm-Instituts für Kohlenforschung in Mülheim/Ruhr," Oct. 28, 1912, SAK, Nr. 15622, no. 27).

122. Draft statutes KWIKf, July 25, 1912, AHP, Sect. IV, Box 24, KWIKf.

123. "Gründungsversammlung," Oct. 28, 1912, SAK, Nr. 15622, p. 28.

124. Contract with Franz Fischer, signed by Kruse, Nov. 22, 1912, and by F. Fischer, Nov. 27, 1912, copy in AHP, Sect. IV, Box 24, KWIKf. E. Fischer to Kruse, Sept. 30, 1912, in EFP.

125. Text of institute's statutes in Rasch, *Vorgeschichte und Gründung*, pp. 190–99. Cf. pp. 67, 90, and 111 n. 237.

126. "Kaiser-Wilhelm-Institut für Naturforschung," in *50 Jahre KWG*, p. 75; similar phrases used in Harnack's memorandum to the Kaiser of Nov. 21, 1909, in ibid., p. 83.

127. Emil Fischer, *Eröffnungs-Feier des neuen I. chemischen Instituts*, pp. 46–47.

128. Emil Fischer, "Die Aufgaben des Kaiser-Wilhelm-Instituts für Kohlenforschung," p. 1900.

129. Willstätter, *From My Life*, pp. 212, 220.

130. *50 Jahre KWG*, p. 151.

131. "Geschäftsordnung für die Physikalisch-Technische Reichsanstalt," July 26, 1888, paragraph 37; copy in SAA 61, Lc 973, vol. 2. Cahan, *Institute for an Empire*, p. 81.

132. Prussian Education Minister to Finance Minister, Aug. 21, 1911, and Haber to Schmidt, Dec. 22, 1913, excerpts in Wendel, *Kaiser-Wilhelm-Gesellschaft*, pp. 327–29.

133. Brunck to Exzellenz (Fischer), Feb. 2, 1911, VCR-1, nos. 152–53; Brüning to Beckmann, Apr. 3, 1911, HA VCR.

134. Erste konstituierende Versammlung des Vorstandsrat des KWICh, Oct. 28, 1911, pp. 7–8, copy in BA, Nr. 142, Sitzungen.

135. Copies of notarized contracts between KWICh and Willstätter, Berlin, Jan. 15, 1912, and Zurich, Jan. 18, 1912, and Beckmann, Berlin, Jan. 15, 1912, and Leipzig, Jan. 18, 1912, both in VCR-2, nos. 66–68 and 63–64. Willstätter, *From My Life*, p. 214.

136. Rasch, *Vorgeschichte und Gründung*, p. 69.

137. Emil Fischer, "Die Aufgaben des Kaiser-Wilhelm-Instituts für Kohlenforschung," p. 1899.

138. "Satzung des Kaiser-Wilhelm-Instituts für Kohlenforschung," text in Rasch, *Vorgeschichte und Gründung*, pp. 184–99, citation at 197; for patents, see pp. 70–74.

139. E. Fischer, "Tischrede bei der Einweihung des Instituts für Kohlenforschung," pp. 824, 826; Siemens memorandum to Boetticher, Mar. 20, 1884, copy in SAA 61, Lc 973, vol. 1, no. 24a; Franz Fischer, "Ziele und Ergebnisse der Kohlenforschung," pp. 1, 4; Franz Fischer and Tropsch, "Die Erdölsynthese bei gewöhnlichem Druck," pp. 1, 8.

Chapter 8

1. Wilamowitz-Moellendorf, *My Recollections*, p. 374.

2. *50 Jahre KWG*, pp. 154–55; Willstätter, *From My Life*, pp. 218–19.

3. Harnack to Friedrich Schmidt, Oct. 24, 1911, GSA-PK, Rep 92 (Schmidt-Ott), vol. 12.

4. Harnack to Schmidt, July 21, 1911, in ibid.

5. Wilamowitz-Moellendorf, *My Recollections*, p. 304 n. 1.

6. Ibid., pp. 385–86 (excerpts from his speech at the Berlin University jubilee, 1910); also p. 303.

7. Speech by Social-Democratic deputy Ströbel in Prussian diet, Jan. 16, 1911, excerpted in Wendel, *Kaiser-Wilhelm-Gesellschaft*, pp. 141, 323–24.

8. Harnack to Hochverehrter Herr Kollege [Hermann Diels, permanent secretary of the academy (see Wendel, *Kaiser-Wilhelm-Gesellschaft*, p. 133)] (Vertraulich und Sekret), Oct. 28, 1912, AHP, Sect. IV, Box 23, Gründung der KWG (this letter was at one time in the Walther-Rathenau-Archiv; see attached note in the file).

9. Friedrich Schmidt to Harnack, July 13, 1909, AHP, Sect. V, Box 41, Friedrich Schmidt-Ott, nos. 14–15.

10. Wilhelm II, Erlass, June 6, 1911; Schmidt to Berlin Academy, June 20, 1911, both reprinted in Wendel, *Kaiser-Wilhelm-Gesellschaft*, pp. 312–13.

11. Excerpt from minutes, phys.-math. Klasse, July 20, 1911; reprinted in Wendel, *Kaiser-Wilhelm-Gesellschaft*, pp. 314–15.

12. Harnack to Friedrich Schmidt, July 21, 1911, GSA-PK, Rep 92 (Schmidt-Ott), vol. 12; Schmidt-Ott, "Anfänge der KWG," *50 Jahre KWG*, pp. 62–63; excerpt from minutes, phil.-hist. Klasse, July 20, 1911, reprinted in Wendel, *Kaiser-Wilhelm-Gesellschaft*, pp. 315–16.

13. Harnack to Schmidt, July 28, 1911, GSA-PK, Rep 92 (Schmidt-Ott), vol. 12; Berlin Academy to Prussian Minister of Education, July 27, 1911, reprinted in Wendel, *Kaiser-Wilhelm-Gesellschaft*, pp. 316–17.

14. Schmidt-Ott, "Anfänge der KWG," *50 Jahre KWG*, p. 63; cf. Schmidt to Harnack, July 23, 1911, AHP, Sect. V, Box 41, Friedrich Schmidt-Ott, nos. 36–37; minutes of meeting in Prussian Ministry of Education, Nov. 25, 1911, reprinted in Wendel, *Kaiser-Wilhelm-Gesellschaft*, pp. 318–21.

15. Cf. reactions of Professors Penck, Waldeyer, and Bumm, interviewed by the B[erliner]. Z[eitung]. am Mittag, Oct. 12, 1910, 1–3, clipping in AHP, Sect. IV, Box 22, Jubiläum.

16. Kraepelin, "Forschungsinstitute und Hochschulen" (speech to the Ortsgruppe München of the Deutscher Hochschullehrertag), p. 607. Tietze, "Bemerkungen zur Frage der freien Forschungsinstitute," pp. 60–74, with references to discussions at the Dresden Hoschschullehrerkonferenz, October 12, 1911 (with Karl Lamprecht in opposition to the KWG); reported by the *Neue Freie Presse* (Vienna), Oct. 14, 1911, p. 11; criticisms of the Kaiser's speech by Lamprecht in *Die Woche*, Oct. 22, 1910, p. 1809 (cited, pp. 61–62); copies in MPG, I A 1, vol. 1, nos. 181 (Kraepelin) and 184 (Tietze).

17. Ostwald, "Die Universitäten der Zukunft und die Zukunft der Universitäten," pp. 429–43.

18. Ernst Beckmann (Leipzig), Fritz Haber (Karlsruhe), Richard Willstätter (Zurich), and Theodor Boveri (Würzburg; Boveri was first choice for the biological institute, though he later declined).

19. Ernst Beckmann to Emil Fischer, July 27, 1911, with copy of Beckmann to Krüss, July 27, 1911, in EFP.

20. Remarks reported by Dr. von Savigny in Haus der Abgeordneten, *Stenographische Berichte*, 50. Sitzung, Mar. 16, 1911, Sp. 4168; copy in GSA-PK, Rep 84a, nos. 19–20 (emphasis in original).

21. Remarks of Schmedding in ibid., Sp. 4172.

22. Remarks of Trott zu Solz in ibid., Sp. 4195–96.

23. Schmidt to Harnack, Feb. 7, 1911, AHP, Sect. V, Box 41, Friedrich Schmidt-Ott, nos. 29–32.

24. Willstätter, *From My Life*, p. 225.
25. On the "Göttingen clique," see Meinecke, *Autobiographische Schriften*, p. 249.
26. Willstätter, *From My Life*, pp. 214, 226. Cf. Prussia, Statistisches Landesamt, *Preussische Statistik*, 236:98–99; *Minerva: Jahrbuch der gelehrten Welt* 10 (1900/01), 15 (1905/06), 20 (1910/11), 23 (1913/14), passim (colleges of technology).
27. Fischer to ter Meer (of Weiler-ter Meer), Oct. 1, 1913, in EFP.
28. Boveri, memorandum on a biological institute, Sept. 25, 1912, pp. 9–10, copy in AHP, Sect. IV, Box 24, Inst. Boveri.
29. Boveri to Schmidt, Nov. 4, 1912, copy in ibid.
30. Fischer to Boveri, Feb. 3, 1913, in EFP.
31. Nernst to Fischer, Feb. 26, 1913, in ibid.
32. Boveri to Schmidt, May 3, 1913, in KA IV-E-272.
33. Fritz Baltzer, *Theodor Boveri*, pp. 20–21; W. Wien's recollections, cited in Wendel, *Kaiser-Wilhelm-Gesellschaft*, p. 337.
34. "Aufzeichnung über die Bereitstellung von Staatsstellen" (n.d., probably 1929), MPG, I A 14.
35. Harnack to Trott zu Solz, Aug. 12, 1912, MPG, II/9, vol. 1, nos. 36–38; Trott zu Solz to Harnack, Nov. 23, 1912, no. 73, in ibid.
36. Willstätter, *From My Life*, p. 214.
37. On Neuberg as an example, see his contract (Aug. 16, 1913), in MPG, II/9, vol. 1, nos. 160–61; Wassermann to Harnack, Apr. 22, 1913, nos. 124–25, in ibid.
38. Willstätter, *From My Life*, p. 222.
39. See Busch, *Geschichte des Privatdozenten*, pp. 160–61; also Fischer to Baeyer, Aug. 4, 1913, in EFP. A comparison with foreign universities is not implied here.
40. See Kaznelson, *Juden im deutschen Kulturbereich*, pp. 459 and 454 for Richard Goldschmidt and Otto Warburg.
41. Wendel, *Kaiser-Wilhelm-Gesellschaft*, pp. 201, 223, 358–59; letter drafted by Emil Fischer and sent by Carl Duisberg to members, Verwaltungsrat KWICh, Apr. 1, 1914, with other correspondence on this subject in BA, Nr. 142, Rundschreiben.
42. See excerpt from Reichstag debates (ca. 1930) in GSA-PK, Rep 90.
43. Kluke, *Stiftungsuniversität Frankfurt am Main*, p. 66 (citing *Kreuzzeitung* on "Jewish-democratic spirit" in Frankfurt), pp. 89–90, 121–22.
44. Beckmann to Fischer, June 16, 1911, VCR-B.
45. See Lockemann, *Ernst Beckmann*, pp. 12–13, 17–20, 15; Goran, *Story of Fritz Haber*, pp. 8–12, 38–41. Goran gives the false impression that Haber converted during the early 1900s, when in fact he had converted a decade earlier, at the very beginning of his academic career; see Johannes Jaenicke to Kurt Zierold, Mar. 16, 1966, in Bundesarchiv R73, Nr. 74.
46. See letters written during 1911 from Haber to Willstätter in the Haber-Wilstätter Correspondence, esp. nos. 4–11.
47. Willstätter, *From My Life*, pp. 222–23.
48. Harnack to Staatsminister (Richter?), Mar. 20, 1929, MPG, I A 14, vol.

1, nos. 20–21; Kohler, *From Medical Chemistry to Biochemistry*, pp. 38–39.

49. Fischer to Trott zu Solz, Nov. [?], 1911, in EFP.

50. Willstätter, *From My Life*, p. 215.

51. IV. Sitzung, Verwaltungsrat KWICh, Mar. 8, 1913, p. 7, in BA, Nr. 142, Sitzungen.

52. Pschorr to Meister, May 2, 1913, HA VCR-V; VI. Sitzung, Verwaltungsrat KWICh, Mar. 14, 1914, p. 4, in BA, Nr. 142, Sitzungen.

53. VIII. Sitzung, Verwaltungsrat KWICh, Mar. 26, 1915, p. 3, in BA, Nr. 142, Sitzungen.

54. Quoted in Willstätter, *From My Life*, p. 83. Regarding tax, see Wendel, *Kaiser-Wilhelm-Gesellschaft*, p. 159, 327–28.

55. Fischer to Beckmann, Oct. 21, 1911, in EFP.

56. "Unterredung zwischen den Herren E. Beckmann und E. Fischer am 26. Oktober 1911," typed summary, Oct. 26, 1911, VCR-2, no. 37; also in minutes, I. konst. Versammlung, Verwaltungsrat KWICh, Oct. 28, 1911, p. 4, in BA, Nr. 142, Sitzungen; Nernst to Fischer, Oct. 27, 1911, in EFP.

57. Draft budget in II. Sitzung, Verwaltungsrat KWICh, Mar. 2, 1912, pp. 2–3, in BA, Nr. 142, Sitzungen; Minutes, Verwaltungsausschuss KWICh, Oct. 24, 1912, in HA KWICh, 1912–42.

58. Cf. "Haushaltungsplan für das Jahr 1913/14," in IV. Sitzung, Verwaltungsrat KWICh, Mar. 8, 1913, p. 6, in BA, Nr. 142, Sitzungen.

59. I. konst. Versammlung, Verwaltungsrat KWICh, Oct. 28, 1911, p. 6 and footnote, in ibid.

60. Until recently, the only full-length biography of Meitner (1878–1968) was Deborah Crawford, *Lise Meitner*. This is being superseded by several recent publications that are unfortunately appearing too late for systematic use here: Patricia Rife, "Lise Meitner," about to be published in book form, and a study by Ruth Sime. See also Krafft, *Im Schatten der Sensation*, pp. 165–88.

61. Minutes, General Meeting, VFCF, Oct. 29, 1913, p. 5, in HA VCR-V.

62. Erste konstituierende Versammlung des Verwaltungsrates des KWICh, pp. 4–6, in BA, Nr. 142, Sitzungen.

63. Willstätter, *From My Life*, p. 214.

64. Lockemann, *Ernst Beckmann*, p. 44; Willstätter, *From My Life*, pp. 220–21.

65. Willstätter, *From My Life*, pp. 83, 214, 220. These titles, meaning "privy councillor" and "privy court councillor" respectively, were generally awarded to honor distinguished scholars.

66. Fischer to Ehrlich, Jan. 14, 1912, in EFP.

67. Willstätter, *From My Life*, p. 212.

68. IV. Sitzung, Verwaltungsrat KWICh, Mar. 8, 1913, p. 5, in BA, Nr. 142, Sitzungen; Beckmann "Die Tätigkeit des Kaiser-Wilhelm Instituts für Chemie," p. 305.

69. Willstätter, *From My Life*, p. 215.

70. IV. Sitzung, Verwaltungsrat KWICh, Mar. 8, 1913, p. 5, in BA, Nr. 142, Sitzungen.

71. VI. Sitzung, Verwaltungsrat KWICh, Mar. 14, 1914, p. 2, in ibid.

72. Willstätter, *From My Life*, pp. 214–15, 237–38.

73. VI. Sitzung, Verwaltungsrat KWICh, Mar. 14, 1914, p. 4, in BA, Nr. 142, Sitzungen.

74. Accounts are in V. Sitzung, Verwaltungsrat KWICh, Oct. 29, 1913, pp. 6–7 (for year ending Mar. 31, 1913), and in VII. Sitzung, Dec. 11, 1914, pp. 4–5 (year ending Mar. 31, 1914), all in BA, Nr. 142, Sitzungen. Fischer to Franz Oppenheim, Jan. 2, 1912 (sic—should be 1913), in EFP.

75. Delbrück to Duisberg, Mar. 16, 1914, copy in BA, Nr. 142, Sitzungen.

76. Duisberg to Delbrück, Mar. 18, 1914, copy in ibid.

77. VI. Sitzung, Verwaltungsrat KWICh, Mar. 14, 1914, p. 2, in ibid.; Minutes, Membership Meeting, VFCF, Oct. 29, 1913, p. 5, in HA VCR-V.

78. Fischer to Duisberg, May 20, 1914, BA 46/6, VCR-V.

79. Fischer to Stock, June 22, 1914, in EFP.

80. Emil Fischer, Aus meinem Leben, pp. 193–94.

81. See IX. Sitzung, Verwaltungsrat KWICh, Aug. 7, 1915, pp. 1–3, in BA, Nr. 142, Sitzungen.

82. VIII. Sitzung, Verwaltungsrat KWICh, Mar. 26, 1915, pp. 1–3; X. Sitzung, Mar. 11, 1916, pp. 6–7 (account for year ending Mar. 31, 1915), both in ibid.

83. Willstätter, From My Life, p. 229.

84. Hahn, Vom Radiothor zur Uranspaltung, pp. 57–63, 69–70; Krafft, Im Schatten der Sensation, pp. 168–69, 213–15.

85. Willstätter, From My Life, pp. 216–17, 308–13.

86. Fischer to T. W. Richards, Dec. 23, 1911, in EFP.

87. Fischer to T. W. Richards, Jan. 20, 1913, in ibid.

Chapter 9

1. Willstätter, From My Life, p. 241.

2. Fischer to Gerhard Schmits, Aug. 18, 1914, and to Lt. Dr. Pfähler, Nov. 14, 1914, in EFP. Cf. Schröter, Krieg-Staat-Monopol, p. 41.

3. Fischer to Schmits, Aug. 18, 1914, in EFP. Cf. Fritz Fischer, War of Illusions, pp. 381, 388, 397–403, 469–70.

4. Cf. Fischer to W. Wislicenus, Oct. 14, 1914, in EFP.

5. Fischer to A. Guye (Geneva), Dec. 1, 1914, in ibid.

6. Fischer to Liebermann, Sept. 16, 1914; and to Carl Engler, Oct. 1, 1914; to Arnold Berliner, Oct. 8, 1914; to E. von Meyer, Mar. 31, 1915; to Herr Kollege, July 13, 1915; all in ibid.

7. Herneck, Abenteuer der Erkenntnis, pp. 141–42; Brocke, "Wissenschaft und Militarismus," p. 674.

8. Fischer to Eduard Hjelt, July 2, 1915, in EFP.

9. Herneck, Abenteuer der Erkenntnis, pp. 195–99.

10. Ostwald, Denkschrift über die Gründung eines internationalen Instituts für Chemie, p. 15; Berichte D. C. G. 46 (1913): 3909. Cf. also Jagdish Mehra, The Solvay Conferences on Physics.

11. Harnack to Valentini, Oct. 30, 1917, AHP, Sect. V, Box 44, Valentini, no. 35; Herneck, Abenteuer der Erkenntnis, p. 198.

12. Fischer to Klason, Jan. 10, 1915, in EFP, which also contain similar let-

244 | NOTES TO PAGES 182–85

ters to colleagues in such nations as Rumania and the U.S.

13. On Wilamowitz and the manifesto in general, see Brocke, "Wissenschaft und Militarismus." On Fischer, see Herneck, *Abenteuer der Erkenntnis*, p. 141; Ruske, *100 Jahre Deutsche Chemische Gesellschaft*, p. 129.

14. Willstätter, *From My Life*, p. 241.

15. Official English text in Lutz, *Fall of the German Empire*, pp. 74–75; list of signers, pp. 75–78.

16. Fischer to Ostwald, Oct. 8, 1914; to Ludwig Fulda, Oct. 15, 1914; to Duisberg, Oct. 22, 1914, all in EFP.

17. E.g., in the U.S.; see Fischer to W. A. Noyes, Dec. 6, 1914; to L. Kahlenberg, Nov. 24, 1914; both in EFP.

18. *From My Life*, p. 240. Cf. Kevles, *The Physicists*, pp. 141–42.

19. Clark, *Einstein*, pp. 228–30.

20. Duisberg to Fischer, Aug. 12, 1914, in EFP. The overall problem is well discussed in Feldman, "A German Scientist," pp. 349–53.

21. Fischer to Duisberg, Aug. 21, 1914, in EFP; Fritz Fischer, *Germany's Aims in the First World War*, pp. 98–119, 247–56, esp. 248–51.

22. Fischer to Baeyer, Nov. 10, 1914; to Robert Pschorr, Nov. 29, 1914; and to Pfähler, Nov. 12, 1914; all in EFP.

23. Fischer to Kahlenberg, Nov. 24, 1914, in ibid.

24. Willstätter, *From My Life*, p. 243.

25. Haber to Euer Exzellenz (Valentini?), Sept. 18, 1917, pp. 1–2; copy in KA IV-E-295.

26. Excerpt from minutes, Verein Deutscher Chemiker directorate, forwarded by Duisberg to V.D.C. headquarters in Leipzig, Sept. 24, 1915; copy in BA 46/6, VCR-V.

27. Willstätter, *From My Life*, pp. 243, 264–65, 279; Willstätter, "Carl Dietrich Harries Lebensbeschreibung," p. 139.

28. Fischer to Pschorr, Nov. 29, 1914, in EFP.

29. "Beratung wegen der aus Anlass des Krieges erforderlichen Anordnungen," Aug. 12, 1914, MPG, II/9, vol. 2, nos. 28–30.

30. Schröter, *Krieg-Staat-Monopol*, pp. 37, 43, 51, 57.

31. L. C. F. Turner, *Origins of the First World War*, p. 62; Hale, *The Great Illusion*, p. 68.

32. Cf. Schröter, *Krieg-Staat-Monopol*, p. 55; L. F. Haber, *Chemical Industry, 1900–1930*, pp. 184–218. Cf. Fischer to Kempner (Chairman, Potash Syndicate), Aug. 20, 1914, in EFP. J. J. Beer, *Emergence of the German Dye Industry*, p. 135.

33. See the discussion in Chapter 7.

34. See Lefebure, *The Riddle of the Rhine*, p. 187; Haber, *Chemical Industry, 1900–1930*, pp. 198–99, 202–3; Burchardt, *Friedenswirtschaft und Kriegsvorsorge*, pp. 171–72. Cf. the sections regarding the chemical industry in "Denkschrift betreffend wirtschaftliche Mobilmachung," Berlin, Ende August 1913, in ZSA-P, Altes Reichskanzlei, Nr. 1268, vol. 4, nos. 37-42, 59, 86–87. This appears to typify the limitations of the bureaucracy's thinking on the issue.

35. Cited in Willstätter, *From My Life*, p. 178.

36. Haber to Euer Exzellenz, Sept. 18, 1917, p. 12; to which contrast Lefebure, *The Riddle of the Rhine*, p. 49.

37. Schröter, *Krieg-Staat-Monopol*, pp. 77–78; Rasch, "Coal Liquefaction."

38. Fischer to Kruse, Sept. 16, 1914, in EFP.

39. Burchardt, *Wissenschaftspolitik*, p. 108.

40. E. Fischer to F. Fischer, Nov. 14, 1914, and to Gewerkschaft deutscher Kaiser, Nov. 23, 1914, both in EFP.

41. E. Fischer to F. Fischer, Nov. 29, 1914; to Ramm (?), Nov. 19, 1914; and to Gewerkschaft deutscher Kaiser, Nov. 29, 1914; all in ibid.

42. 1. Tätigkeitsbericht of KWIKf (1916), cited by Burchardt, *Wissenschaftspolitik*, p. 108; E. Fischer to Trott zu Solz, Apr. 10, 1915, and to F. Fischer, Aug. 8, 1915, both in EFP. See also Franz Fischer to Reichsamt des Innern, June 29, 1915, in ZSA-P, Reichsministerium des Innern, Nr. 18775, no. 55, and his reports, nos. 56–58, 78, 81.

43. A copy of details provided by Fischer in his speech of Sept. 22, 1914, is in BA, Nr. 145, KWG-KWIKf, Allgemeines. On the Oct. 1 report (no copy available) see Haber, *Chemical Industry, 1900–1930*, p. 200, and pp. 198–204 for general issues. See also Willstätter, *From My Life*, p. 279; *Frankfürter Zeitung*, Nov. 23, 1919, cited by Lefebure, *The Riddle of the Rhine*, p. 269.

44. Notes of telephonic conversations between Duisberg and the BASF, Ludwigshafen, Sept. 23, 1914, BA, Nr. 145, KWG-KWIKf, Allgemeines.

45. All in EFP, Oct. 1914 ff.

46. Fischer to Haber, Dec. 17, 1914, in ibid.

47. Schröter, *Krieg-Staat-Monopol*, pp. 78, 104, 144; Emil Fischer to Kriegschemikalien A.G., Oct. 4, 1914.

48. Adolf von Harnack, *An der Schwelle des dritten Kriegsjahres*, cited by Feldman, "A German Scientist," p. 354. Cf. Fischer to Carl Engler, Apr. 1, 1915, and to Holl, Aug. 9, 1917, both in EFP. Emil Fischer to Harnack, Aug. 16, 1918, AHP, Sect. V, Box 31, Fischer, nos. 10–12; Wilhelm v. Siemens to Harnack, Feb. 7 and Feb. 13, 1917, AHP, Sect. V, Box 42, Siemens, Wilhelm v., nos. 1–2, 3–4; extensive correspondence between Krupp von Bohlen and other businessmen, 1916, in KA IV-E-246.

49. Haber to Herr Direktor [Koppel?], Mar. 2, 1916, in SAM, Rep 92 (Schmidt-Ott), B XIII, vol. 4, nos. 33–35, and subsequent documents, 1916–17, nos. 36–81. L. F. Haber, *Chemical Industry, 1900–1930*, p. 223; Fischer to Kriegs-Rohstoff-Abteilung, July 2, 1917, and to Mitglieder des Fachausschusses I der KWKW, Dec. 3, 1917, in EFP. See also Duisberg, "Emil Fischer und die Industrie," p. 151; also Arthur v. Weinberg, "Emil Fischers Tätigkeit während des Krieges," pp. 868–73.

50. Fischer to Kriegs-Ersatz- und Arbeits-Department, Dec. 11, 1917, in EFP; Lockemann, *Ernst Beckmann*, p. 48.

51. Willstätter, *From My Life*, p. 236; cf. also TGA technical archive, Willstätter File.

52. Willstätter, "Carl Dietrich Harries Lebensbeschreibung," p. 141, Lefebure, *The Riddle of the Rhine*, p. 132.

53. Karl Goldschmidt, "Wirtschaftliche Entwicklung des

Berginverfahrens," unpubl. ms. (ca. 1920), pp. 2–5, in TGA, Lit.-Abtlg., Bergius File; Stranges, "Friedrich Bergius," pp. 659–60.

54. Minutes for 1916 ff. in KA IV-E-304; "Jahresbericht April 1921–Oktober 1922," pp. 5–7, copy in AHP, Sect. IV, Box 23, Gründung; also surviving files of the relevant institutes in MPG.

55. The best general work is L. F. Haber, *Poisonous Cloud*, esp. chaps. 6–7, using official archives but not German corporate archives or the Emil Fischer Papers; L. F. Haber is fairly objective on his father Fritz's role, for which see also Willstätter, *From My Life*, pp. 243, 264–66, 279–80.

56. Falkenhayn, *General Headquarters, 1914–1916*, p. 47.

57. Trumpener, "Road to Ypres," pp. 463–64.

58. Haber to Euer Exzellenz, Sept. 18, 1917, p. 1, copy in KA IV-E-295; Duisberg to Krupp von Bohlen, Nov. 14 and Dec. 18, 1914), KA IV-E-498; Trumpener, "Road to Ypres," pp. 464–65; L. F. Haber, *Poisonous Cloud*, pp. 20–25.

59. Krupp to Duisberg, Dec. 15, 1914, and Duisberg to Krupp, Dec. 18, 1914, KA IV-E-498; Fischer to Duisberg, Dec. 10, 1914, and Duisberg to Fischer, Dec. 23, 1914, both in EFP; L. F. Haber, *Poisonous Cloud*, pp. 25–28.

60. Fischer to Duisberg, Mar. 7, 1915, and Duisberg to Fischer, Mar. 4 and Mar. 9, 1915, all in EFP; on the Kaiser's role see Willstätter, *From My Life*, p. 243; Trumpener, "Road to Ypres," pp. 468–71.

61. L. F. Haber, *Poisonous Cloud*, pp. 27–36; Trumpener, "Road to Ypres," pp. 471–78.

62. L. F. Haber, *Poisonous Cloud*, pp. 52–57.

63. War Ministry to Education Ministry, Feb. 13, 1917; Haber to Euer Exzellenz, Sept. 18, 1917, pp. 2, 7–10, giving the outlines of the Dahlem research organization and naming Haber's principal subordinates; both in KA IV-E-295.

64. L. F. Haber, *Poisonous Cloud*, pp. 129–30, 139–41; Jaenicke to Zierold, Mar. 16, 1966, in Bundesarchiv R73, Nr. 74.

65. Ibid., pp. 153 and 110; Willstätter, *From My Life*, pp. 250–53.

66. On difficulties of research, see L. F. Haber, *Poisonous Cloud*, pp. 43–45, 107–15; on Haber and organic chemistry, see Willstätter, *From My Life*, pp. 257–58; on Haber formula and arsenic reserves, see Julius Meyer, *Gaskampf*, pp. 109–17.

67. Lefebure, *The Riddle of the Rhine*, p. 145.

68. Willstätter, *From My Life*, p. 266; L. F. Haber, *Poisonous Cloud*, pp. 157–59, 277–78; Duisberg to Fischer, Dec. 23, 1914, in EFP.

69. Feldman, "A German Scientist," pp. 354–61; L. F. Haber, *Chemical Industry, 1900–1930*, pp. 279–83; Schröter, *Krieg-Staat-Monopol*, p. 148; Duisberg to Fischer, Mar. 4, 1919, in EFP.

70. Harnack memorandum, 1910 ed., p. 10; in MPG, I A 1, vol. 1, p. 32.

71. KWG, *3.–5. Jahresbericht*, pp. 3–5; copy in AHP, Sect. IV, Box 23, Gründung. Emphasis in original.

72. Valentini to Harnack, Sept. 5, 1916, AHP, Sect. V, Box 44, Valentini, nos. 27–28; Fischer to Trott zu Solz, Aug. 11, 1915, EFP.

73. Haber to Euer Exzellenz, Sept. 18, 1917, p. 12, in KA IV-E-295. Koppel's statement of purpose in funding the Kaiser Wilhelm Foundation, Nov. 13, 1916, in SAM, Rep 92 (Schmidt-Ott), B XIII, vol. 4, nos. 52–55.

74. War Ministry to Education Ministry, Feb. 13, 1917, and Haber to Euer Exzellenz, Sept. 18, 1917, pp. 5–7, 12, both in KA IV-E-295.

75. Minutes of Verwaltungsausschuss and Senat der KWG, Oct. 24, 1918, pp. 2 and 3–4 respectively; copies in KA IV-E-304.

76. Fischer to Margarete Oppenheim, Dec. 14, 1917; see also Fischer to Wilhelm von Leube, May 11, 1917, both in EFP.

77. Remarks of Karl Liebknecht in Haus der Abgeordneten, *Stenographische Berichte*, 50. Sitzung (Mar. 16, 1911), Sp. 4214 (emphasis in original); copy in GSA-PK, Rep 84a.

78. Fischer to Leo Arons, Nov. 13, 1918, in EFP.

79. Willstätter, *From My Life*, p. 225, says he took cyanide, but this is not mentioned in Hoesch, *Emil Fischer*, pp. 197–98.

80. On Ostwald, see Herneck, *Abenteuer der Erkenntnis*, pp. 199–213; on Nernst, see Mendelssohn, *World of Walther Nernst*, pp. 137–38, 146–47, 151–52, 157–61.

81. Ruske, *100 Jahre Materialprüfung*, pp. 277–329.

82. Lockemann, *Ernst Beckmann*, pp. 48–50; Duisberg to Beckmann, Feb. 27, 1920, in BA, Nr. 151.

83. Nachmansohn, *German-Jewish Pioneers*, pp. 180–89.

84. Cf. Duisberg to Harnack, Mar. 15, 1920, in BA, Nr. 148.

85. Glum, *Zwischen Wissenschaft, Wirtschaft und Politik*, p. 449. Jander to Vahlen, Sept. 25, 1933, in SAM, Rep 76 Vc, Nr. 108, vol. 4, nos. 2–5.

86. Nachmansohn, *German-Jewish Pioneers*, p. 222; cf. Willstätter, *From My Life*, pp. 333–34, 359–70, 377–89, 424–37.

87. Krafft, *Im Schatten der Sensation*, pp. 86–93, 259–302; Rhodes, *Making of the Atomic Bomb*, pp. 251–64.

Conclusion

1. Burchardt, *Wissenschaftspolitik*, p. 144.

2. Fischer to Baeyer, Aug. 14, 1913, and Jan. 13, 1915, in EFP.

3. Cf. Ben-David, *Scientist's Role*, p. 135.

4. Willstätter, *From My Life*, p. 241.

5. Rhodes, *Making of the Atomic Bomb*, p. 788.

Bibliography

Archival Sources

In the following I will indicate the collections of documents that proved most useful, as well as those which, for various reasons, I could not use.

GOVERNMENT DOCUMENTS AND PAPERS OF KEY OFFICIALS

Imperial Government

Zentrales Staatsarchiv der DDR, Potsdam.

This contains the bulk of the relevant surviving official documents of the Imperial government and the successor government of the Weimar Republic. I have not cited these documents extensively; because scholars of the German Democratic Republic were using them at the time of my initial research, I was unable to examine them (or the former Prussian documents in the Staatsarchiv Merseburg) until summer 1989. My notes thus reflect my dependence, for tracing developments within the bureaucracy, on the well-documented works of Günter Wendel and Lothar Burchardt on the Kaiser-Wilhelm-Gesellschaft. I have verified their accuracy by examining the following primary documents, parts of which I also cite.

Altes Reichskanzlei

Nr. 1267/2. Vorbereitungen für den Kriegsfall, vol. 2, Jan. 1900–Nov. 1911.

Nr. 1267/3. Vorbereitungen für den Kriegsfall, vol. 3, 1912–13.

Nr. 1268. Vorbereitungen für den Kreigsfall, vol. 4, 1913–Oct. 1914. Reichsamt/Reichsministerium des Innern

Nr. 5549/2. Chemisch-technische Reichsanstalt, May 1919–Feb. 1922.

Nr. 5557. Errichtung einer chemischen Reichsanstalt, vol. 2, June 1907–Nov. 1911. [Vol. 1 appears to be missing.]

Nr. 8970/1. Kaiser-Wilhelm-Gesellschaft, vol. 1, 1910–16.

Nr. 8970/2. Kaiser-Wilhelm-Gesellschaft, vol. 2, 1917–21.

Nr. 18775. Schwefelsäurbeschaffung, Dec. 1914–Jan. 1916.

249

Bundesarchiv, Koblenz.

The bulk of the materials in this archive pertains to the national government and its scientific institutions after 1918 (especially after 1933); although it does contain earlier internal files of the Kaiserliches Gesundheitsamt and the Biologische Reichanstalt, I found these to be of peripheral interest to the present work and have not cited them here. The following file does, however, contain useful insights.

R73 (Notgemeinschaft), Nr. 74. Dokumentation über . . . Fritz Haber. 1929–[66].

Prussian Government

Geheimes Staatsarchiv Preussischer Kulturbesitz, West Berlin–Dahlem.

This was once the Prussian state archive. Most of the official documents were moved to Merseburg, but the following relevant files remain.

Rep 84a (Kgl. Justizminsterium), Nr. 5283. Kaiser-Wilhelm-Gesellschaft z. F. d. W. und deren Institute, 1910–34.

Rep 90 (Kgl. Staatsministerium), Nr. 1786, vol. 1. Kaiser-Wilhelm-Gesellschaft z. F. d. W., 1909–36.

Rep 92 (Schmidt-Ott). The Friedrich Schmidt-Ott Papers [partial collection; others are in Merseburg]; the most useful files are:

Vol. 12. Gründung und Organisation der Kaiser-Wilhelm-Gesellschaft, 1919–39. [Some of the letters in this and the next two volumes are typed copies of originals located elsewhere in the papers.]

Vol. 13. Material zur Geschichte der Kaiser-Wilhelm-Gesellschaft.

Vol. 14. Die Harnack-Denkschrift und ihre Bedeutung für die Kaiser-Wilhelm-Gesellschaft, 1909–10.

Staatsarchiv Merseburg, DDR

This contains most of the surviving documents of the former Prussian government, particularly those of the ministry of education (in Rep 76). I have not cited them extensively for the same reason I have not frequently cited documents in Potsdam, but I have checked and make occasional reference to the following documents.

Rep 76 Vb. (Technische Hochschulen), Sekt. 1. Tit. X.

Nr. 5. Die chemisch-technische Reichanstalt, 1900–11.

Rep 76 Vc. (Wissenschaftssachen), Sekt. 2, Tit. XIII, Litt. A.

Nr. 108. Das Kaiser-Wilhelm-Institut für physikalische Chemie in Dahlem, vols. 1, 1910–12; 2, 1913–18; and 4, 1933–34. [Vol. 3 is missing.]

Rep 92 (Althoff). The Friedrich Althoff Papers.

AI, Nr. 214. Chemische Reichsanstalt [1905–8].

Rep 92 (Schmidt-Ott). The Friedrich Schmidt-Ott Papers. [Partial collection; others are in West Berlin–Dahlem.]

B XIII. Stifter und Stiftung, Nr. 4. Koppel Stiftung; Kaiser-Wilhelm-Stiftung für Kriegstechnische Wissenschaften, 1916–17.

Former Prussian State Scientific Institutions

Bundesanstalt für Materialprüfung, Berlin-Lichterfelde West.
C.1. Chemische Reichsanstalt, 1905–8.

Former Provincial and District Archives

Hauptstaatsarchiv Düsseldorf, G 21/2 (Regierung Düsseldorf Präsidialbüro).
Nr. 1323 (previously numbered Fach 49, Nr. 43). Die Rheinische Gesellschaft
    für wissenschaftliche Forschung in Bonn, 1909–[15].
Nr. 1324 (previously numbered Fach 49, Nr. 44). Die Kaiser-Wilhelm-Gesell-
    schaft zur Förderung der Wissenschaften in Berlin, vol. 1, 1910–25.

Staatsarchiv Koblenz, Titel 403 (Oberpräsidium der Rheinprovinz).
Nr. 14063. Die Gründung einer Rheinischen Akademie der Wissenschaften zu
    Bonn und der "Rheinischen Gesellschaft für wissenschaftliche Forsch-
    ung" in Bonn, 1909–12.
Nr. 14065. Das wiss. Forschungsinstitut in Berlin: Kaiser-Wilhelm-Gesell-
    schaft zur Förderung der Wissenschaften, 1910–13.
Nr. 15622. Kaiser-Wilhelm-Institut für Kohlenforschung in Mülheim/Ruhr,
    1912–14.

Municipal Archives

Stadtarchiv Frankfurt/Main.
Sammlungen S2 Personen [clipping files].
Nr. 351. Gans, Leo.
Nr. 789. Weinberg, Arthur Bernhard von.

PAPERS OF LEADING SCHOLARS AND SCIENTISTS

Adolf von Harnack Papers (Nachlass Harnack, Handschriftenabteilung),
Deutsche Staatsbibliothek, Berlin-DDR.
Sect. IV. Amtliche Tätigkeit.
    Box 22   Aufteilung der Domäne Dahlem, 1910.
                    Jubiläum der Universität Berlin, 1910.
    Box 23   Gründung der Kaiser-Wilhelm-Gesellschaft.
                    Protokolle, [1911–13].
    Box 24   Biologische Forschungsintitute-Gutachten, [1911].
                    Inst. f. Entwicklungs- und Vererbungsforschung
                    Boveri, 1912.
                    Kaiser-Wilhelm-Institut für Chemie, 1911.
                    Kaiser-Wilhelm-Institut für Kohlenforschung, 1912.
                    Sammlung der Senats-Protokolle, [1911–16].
                    Sect. V. Briefe.
    Boxes 26–45 Correspondence with various individuals, filed
                    alphabetically.

Emil Fischer Papers, Bancroft Library, University of California, Berkeley. These papers illuminate Fischer's activities from 1902, when he began saving carbon copies of his outgoing typewritten letters. Few of his earlier letters are preserved, except for his correspondence with Adolf von Baeyer, which was also transcribed some time after Fischer's death. The papers also have many letters from other chemists and businessmen to Fischer, including correspondence with Wilhelm Ostwald, Walther Nernst, Ernst Beckmann, and Carl Duisberg, but relatively few documents of institutes or organizations.

Haber-Willstätter Correspondence, Leo Baeck Institute, New York, New York. This is filed under AR-C.A.79, 182 No. 15, and contains photocopied letters (mostly personal matters) from Fritz Haber to Richard Willstätter, 1910–34.

Wilhelm Ostwald Papers, Akademie-Archiv, Akademie der Wissenschaften der DDR, Berlin-DDR. This collection contains letters to Ostwald from Nernst (whose own papers were apparently destroyed during the Second World War), filed under Nr. 95, Nernst, W. Ostwald's copybooks contain letters to Nernst for 1890–1901 and 1907–8 only. The letters are being edited for eventual publication, but the archivist and editors were kind enough to permit me to examine them in the summer of 1989.

Documents of Organizations

The Archiv zur Geschichte der Max-Planck-Gesellschaft, West Berlin–Dahlem (formerly in Munich), contains surviving documents of the Kaiser Wilhelm Society and a growing collection of papers of scientists associated with the society. The society's files, originally catalogued under the heading Kaiser-Wilhelm-Gesellschaft zur Förderung der Wissenschaften e. V., Alte Akten, have many gaps due to wartime damage to the society's offices in Berlin, so that all the volumes on the prewar development of the chemical institutes are missing; others I found useful include:
I A 1. Gründung d. Kaiser-Wilhelm-Gesellschaft z. F. d. W., vol. 1, 1911-18, and vol. 2, 1918–21.
I A 14. Verhältnis der KWG zur Preuss. Unterrichtsverwaltung und zum Reich, vol. 1, [1920, 1927–40].
I D 1. Finanzielle Sicherstellung der KWG und ihrer Institute, vol. 1, 1920–22.
II 4. Biologische Institute im allgemeinen, vol. 1, [1910–]11, and vol. 3, 1912–14. [Vol. 2 is missing.]
II 9. Errichtung eines Kaiser-Wilhelm-Instituts für experimentelle Therapie, vol. 1, 1912–13, and vol. 2, 1913–19.
II 10/2. Errichtung eines Kaiser-Wilhelm-Instituts für Aerodynamik und Hydrodynamik in Göttingen, vol. 1, 1911–16.

Verein Chemische Reichsanstalt (Imperial Chemical Institute Association). The original documents of this association and its predecessor committees as well as successor associations, in addition to some key documents of the Kaiser Wilhelm Institute for Chemistry and its administrative agencies, are located in the Werksarchiv der Farbenfabriken Bayer AG, Leverkusen; they provide a detailed view of the institutional efforts of the chemists. The most significant are:

Kaiser-Wilhelm-Institut f. Chemie. Briefe, 1911–15.

Verein Chemische Reichsanstalt e. V., vol. 1, [1905–13], and vol. 2, [June 1911–March 1913].

> Briefe, [1905–11].

> Gesuche um Beitritt als Mitglied, [1908, 1911].

> [Protokolle (printed minutes of meetings)], [1907–13].

> Zustimmende Äusserungen für die Gründung einer Chemischen Reichsanstalt, [1900, 1905–7].

Verein zur Förderung Chemische Forschung e. V. [printed minutes of annual meetings], [1913–19].

Wissenschaftlicher Beirat des Kaiser Wilhelm Institut für Chemie.

> Vol. 1, Nov. 1912–18.

> Hauptakten, vol. 2, Mar. 1919–Aug. 1923.

> [Undated. A small binder containing printed statutes, bylaws, etc.]

> Spendenbewerbungen, 1913. [A large manila envelope with the seal of the Kaiser-Wilhelm-Gesellschaft, containing applications for Gans grants.]

CORPORATE ARCHIVES

Werksarchiv der Farbenfabriken Bayer AG, Leverkusen, also contains the Carl Duisberg Papers, which provide an excellent view from the perspective of one of the businessmen most actively involved in the establishment of the Kaiser Wilhelm Institutes. Unfortunately, few relevant papers of Duisberg's colleague, Henry von Böttinger, have been preserved. The most useful of the Duisberg files, which also contain many relevant printed documents, are the following, under Titel 46 (Wissenschaft "Verbände, Vereine, etc."):

Nr. 46/6: Verein Chemische Reichsanstalt, Begründung einer chemischen Reichsanstalt, 1905–[1910].

> Verein zur Förderung chem. Forschung, ehemals Verein Chemische Reichsanstalt, 1908–[1920].

Nr. 141 (old 87). Kaiser-Wilhelm-Gesellschaft. Kaiser-Wilhelm-Institut für Chemie. Werwaltungsausschuss, Allgemeines, [1911–23].

Nr. 142 (old 88). Kaiser-Wilhelm-Gesellschaft. Kaiser-Wilhelm-Institut für Chemie.

> Verwaltungsrat, Rundschreiben, [1914–22].

> Verwaltungsrat, Sitzungen, vol. 1, 1911–17.

Nr. 144 (old 90). Kaiser-Wilhelm-Gesellschaft. Kaiser-Wilhelm-Institut für Chemie.

> Baupläne u. a. des Kaiser-Wilhelm-Instituts für Chemie und darauf bezughabende Korrespondenz.

Leo-Gans-Stiftung, 1912–22.
Nr. 145 (old 91). Kaiser-Wilhelm-Gesellschaft. Kaiser-Wilhelm-Institut für Kohlenforschung.
Allgemeines, [1912–34].
Wahl zum Mitglied des Wissenschaftl. Beirats des Kaiser-Wilhelm-Instituts für Kohlenforschung in Mülheim-Ruhr, [1912].
Nr. 148 (old 94). Kaiser-Wilhelm-Gesellschaft. Besetzung der Emil-Fischer-Professur an der Berliner Universität, Feb.–Aug. 1920.
Unnumbered Documents.
Kaiser-Wilhelm-Institut für Chemie: Wahl des Direktors, [1926–28].

I had less success with the archives of Bayer's principal allies in the Triple Alliance, the BASF, and Agfa. The Unternehmensarchiv der BASF AG, Mannheim, does have files for leaders of the firm, most of which contain little more than reprints of obituary notices, but no relevant original correspondence or documents, which apparently disappeared during the Second World War or were not made available to me. The surviving archive of the former Agfa corporation, which is now owned by the German Democratic Republic, was not accessible to me during my research for this book.

Firmenarchiv der Farbwerke Hoechst AG, Frankfurt/Main-Hoechst, contains materials that document the attitudes of the Triple Alliance's principal rivals, including some correspondence with the leaders of the Cassella firm, whose archive was also destroyed during the Second World War. Files under Titel 71 (Wissenschaftliche Gesellschaften):

Kaiser-Wilhelm-Institut für Chemie. In two unnumbered parts, dated 1900–1912 and 1912–42.
Kaiser-Wilhelm-Institut für Kohlenforschung. In two unnumbered parts, the first undated and the second dated 1912–26.
Verein Chemische Reichsanstalt, 1905–12; Verein z. Förderung Chem. Forschung. A single volume with two sections.

Historiches Archiv der Fried. Krupp GmbH, Villa Hügel, Essen-Bredeney, has valuable materials on the administration of the Kaiser Wilhelm Society and on the Krupp family's interest in biological research. I could not locate papers of Emil Ehrensberger regarding the Verein Chemische Reichsanstalt or Kaiser-Wilhelm-Institut für Chemie. The most useful sources were filed under Privatbüro [Gustav] Krupp von Bohlen und Halbach:

IV-E-87. Akta betreffend Stiftung, anlässlich der Jahrhundertfeier der Universität Berlin, 1909–19 [sic; 1909–10].
Akta betreffend Vereinsangelegenheiten.
IV-E-244. Kaiser-Wilhelm-Gesellschaft, Allgemeines, vol. 1, 1910–12.
IV-E-245. Kaiser-Wilhelm-Gesellschaft, Allgemeines, vol. 2, 1912–16.
IV-E-246. Kaiser-Wilhelm-Gesellschaft, Allgemeines, vol. 3, 1916–18.
IV-E-264. Kaiser-Wilhelm-Institut für Physiologie und Hirnforschung, vol. 1, Jan. 1910–Dec. 1917.
IV-E-272. Kaiser-Wilhelm-Institut für Biologie, [1906–12].

IV-E-295. Kaiser-Wilhelm-Institut für angewandte physikalische Chemie u. Biochemie, Feb. 1917–Apr. 1935. [This is filed under "Biochemie u. Tabakforschung" but is chiefly on physical chemistry and gas research.]

IV-E-298. Kaiser-Wilhelm-Gesellschaft, Finanzielles, Dec. 1912–Apr. 17, 1932.

IV-E-304. Kaiser-Wilhelm-Gesellschaft, Verhandlungs-Protokolle über die Sitzungen des Senats u. des Verwaltungsausschusses, Feb. 1911–Nov. 1920.

Correspondence
IV-E-60. Adolf von Harnack [and family], 1911–39.
IV-E-498. Geh. Rat Dr. Carl Duisberg, vol. 1, 1913–29.

Solvay et Cie, Brussels. The Archives de la Section A furnished me with copies of Ernest Solvay's 1908 correspondence with Emil Fischer.

Chemische Fabrik Th. Goldschmidt AG, Essen. The Literatur-Abteilung (literature archive) contains the following useful documents.
Nr. 16 (old 69). Kaiser-Wilhelm-Institut für Kohlenforschung, Mülheim-Ruhr, [1911–50].
Friedrich Bergius File
Th. Goldschmidt's separate technical archive contains records of its cooperative work with Richard Willstätter on the production of sugar from wood (Willstätter file).

Werner-von-Siemens-Institut für Geschichte des Hauses Siemens, Munich.
SAA 4 (Wilhelm von Siemens)
Lk 110. Kaiser-Wilhelm-Gesellschaft Schriftwechsel, 1910–13.
Lk 111. Kaiser-Wilhelm-Gesellschaft Schriftwechsel, 1913–16.
Lk 112. Kaiser-Wilhelm-Gesellschaft Schriftwechsel, 1917–19.
SAA 61
Lc 973. Physikalisch-Technische Reichsanstalt, vols. 1–4, [1873–1968].

Published Sources and Dissertations

Aderhold, Rudolf. *Die Kaiserliche Biologische Anstalt für Land- und Forstwirtschaft in Dahlem.* Heft 1 of *Mitteilungen aus der Kaiserlichen Biologischen Anstalt für Land- und Forstwirtschaft.* Berlin-Dahlem, 1906.
"Adolf Frank." [Obituary.] *Berichte der Deutschen Chemischen Gesellschaft* 49 (1916): 1533–34.
"Adolf Martens." [Obituary.] *Deutsches biographisches Jahrbuch, Überleitungsband 1 (1914–1916),* pp. 69–71. Berlin, Leipzig, and Stuttgart, 1925.
Albisetti, James C. *Secondary School Reform in Imperial Germany.* Princeton, N.J., 1983.
Allgemeine deutsche Biographie. 2d ed. 56 vols. Berlin, 1967–71.
Alter, Peter. *Wissenschaft, Staat, Mäzene: Anfänge moderner Wissenschaftspolitik in Grossbritannien 1850–1920.* Stuttgart, 1982.
Aschheim, Stephen. *Brothers and Strangers: The East European Jews in German*

and German Jewish Consciousness 1800–1923. Madison, Wis., 1982.

Baltzer, Fritz. *Theodor Boveri: Life and Work of a Great Biologist 1862–1915*. Translated by Dorothea Rudnick. Berkeley, Calif., 1967.

Baumgart, Peter, ed. *Bildungspolitik in Preussen zur Zeit des Kaiserreichs*. Stuttgart, 1980.

Beckmann, Ernst. "Die Tätigkeit des Kaiser-Wilhelm-Instituts für Chemie von 1912 bis 1921." *Die Naturwissenschaften* 9 (1921): 305–8.

Beer, Günther. *200 Jahre chemisches Laboratorium an der Georg-August-Universität Göttingen 1783–1983: Vorarbeiten zur Geschichte der Chemie in Göttingen*. Vol. 1: *Die Lehrenden*. Privately printed. Göttingen, 1983.

Beer, John Joseph. *The Emergence of the German Dye Industry*. Urbana, Ill., 1959.

Ben-David, Joseph. *The Scientist's Role in Society: A Comparative Study*. Englewood Cliffs, N.J., 1971.

Berlin, Humboldt-Universität. *Forschung und Wirken: Festschrift zur 150-Jahr-Feier der Humboldt-Universität zu Berlin*. 2 vols. Berlin, 1960.

Bernhard, Carl Gustaf, Elisabeth Crawford, and Per Sorbom, eds. *Science, Technology and Society in the Time of Alfred Nobel: Nobel Symposium, Held at Bjorkborn, Karlskoga, Sweden, 17–22 August 1981*. Oxford, 1982.

Beyerchen, Alan. "On the Stimulation of Excellence in Wilhelmian Science." In *Another Germany: A Reconsideration of the Imperial Era*, edited by Joachim Remak and Jack Dukes, pp. 139–68. Boulder, Colo., 1987.

Birnbaum, Max P. "Die jüdische Bevölkerung in Preussen: Verteilung und wirtschaftliche Struktur im Jahre 1931." In *Gegenwart im Rückblick: Festgabe für die Jüdische Gemeinde zu Berlin 25 Jahre nach dem Neubeginn*, edited by Herbert A. Strauss and Kurt R. Grossman, pp. 113–29. Heidelberg, 1970.

Black, Cyril E., et al. *The Modernization of Japan and Russia: A Comparative Study*. New York, 1975.

Booms, Hans. *Die Deutschkonservative Partei: Preussischer Charakter, Reichsauffassung, Nationalbegriff*. Düsseldorf, 1954.

Bose, Emil. "Die chemisch-technische Reichsanstalt, ein wichtiges Erfordniss für die Weiterentwicklung von Wissenschaft und Technik." *Chemiker-Zeitung* 24 (Jan. 31, 1900): 73–74.

Brocke, Bernhard vom. "Der deutsch-amerikanische Professorenaustausch: Preussische Wissenschaftspolitik, internationale Wissenschaftsbeziehungen und die Anfänge einer deutschen auswärtigen Kulturpolitik vor dem Ersten Weltkrieg." *Zeitschrift für Kulturaustausch* 31 (1981), *Sonderdruck: Interne Faktoren auswärtiger Kulturpolitik im 19. und 20. Jahrhundert*. 2. Teil:128–82.

———. "Hochschul- und Wissenschaftspolitik in Preussen und im Deutschen Kaiserreich 1882–1907: Das 'System Althoff.'" In *Bildungspolitik in Preussen zur Zeit des Kaiserreichs*, edited by Peter Baumgart, pp. 9–118. Stuttgart, 1980.

———. "Wissenschaft und Militarismus." In *Wilamowitz nach 50 Jahren*, edited by William M. Calder III, Hellmut Flashar, Theodor Lindken, pp. 649–719. Darmstadt, 1985.

Brunck, Heinrich. "Die Entwickelungsgeschichte der Indigo-Fabrication." *Berichte der Deutschen Chemischen Gesellschaft* 33 (1900), *Sonderheft*, lxxi–lxxvi.

Bülow, Bernhard H. M. K. Fürst von. *Denkwürdigkeiten*. 4 vols. Berlin, 1930–31.

———. *The Memoirs of Prince von Bülow*. Translated by F. A. Voigt. Vol. 1, *From Secretary of State to Imperial Chancellor, 1897–1903*. Vol. 2, *From the Morocco Crisis to Resignation, 1903–1909*. Vol. 3, *The World War and Germany's Collapse, 1909–1919*. Vol. 4, *Early Years and Diplomatic Service, 1849–1897*. Boston, 1931–32.

Burchardt, Lothar. *Friedenswirtschaft und Kriegsvorsorge: Deutschlands wirtschaftliche Rüstungsbestrebungen vor 1914*. Boppard, 1966.

———. "Wissenschaft und Wirtschaftswachstum: Industrielle Einflussnahmen auf die Wissenschaftspolitik im wilhelminischen Deutschland." In *Soziale Bewegung und politische Verfassung: Beiträge zur Geschichte der modernen Welt*, edited by Ulrich Engelhardt, pp. 770–97. Stuttgart, 1976.

———. *Wissenschaftspolitik im Wilhelminischen Deutschland: Vorgeschichte, Gründung und Aufbau der Kaiser-Wilhelm-Gesellschaft zur Förderung der Wissenschaften*. Göttingen, 1975.

Busch, Alexander. *Die Geschichte des Privatdozenten: Eine soziologische Studie zur grossbetrieblichen Entwicklung der deutschen Universitäten*. Stuttgart, 1959.

Bush, Vannevar. *Science—The Endless Frontier: A Report to the President*. Washington, D.C., 1945.

Cahan, David. *An Institute for an Empire: The Physikalisch-Technische Reichsanstalt, 1871–1918*. Cambridge, 1989.

———. "Werner Siemens and the Origin of the Physikalisch-Technische Reichsanstalt, 1872–1887." *Historical Studies in the Physical Sciences* 12 (2) (1982): 253–83.

Calder, William M. III, Hellmut Flashar, and Theodor Lindken, eds. *Wilamowitz nach 50 Jahren*. Darmstadt, 1985.

Carnegie, Andrew. *The Gospel of Wealth*. New York, 1900.

Carnegie Institution of Washington. *Year Book* 1 (1902).

Caro, Heinrich. "Uber die Entwicklung der Teerfarbenindustrie." *Berichte der Deutschen Chemischen Gesellschaft* 25 (1892): 955–1105.

Cassella Farbwerke Mainkur Aktiengesellschaft. *Ein farbiges Jahrhundert: Cassella*. Munich, 1970.

Cecil, Lamar. "Wilhelm II. und die Juden." In *Juden im Wilhelmischen Deutschland, 1890–1914*, edited by Werner E. Mosse, pp. 313–47. Tübingen, 1976.

"Die chemische Reichsanstalt." *Chemische Zeitschrift* 5 (1906): 254.

Churchill, Winston. *The World Crisis*. 1 vol. ed. New York, 1931.

Clark, Ronald W. *Einstein: The Life and Times*. New York, 1972.

Clarke, F. W., K. Seubert, H. Moissan, and T. E. Thorpe. "Bericht des Internationalen Atomgewichts-Ausschusses, 1906." *Berichte der Deutschen Chemischen Gesellschaft* 39 (1906): 6–14.

Coates, J. E. "The Haber Memorial Lecture." *Memorial Lectures Delivered before the Chemical Society* 4 (1933–42): 127–57.

Cohen, Ernst. *Jacobus Henricus van't Hoff: Sein Leben und Wirken*. Leipzig, 1912.

Corner, G. W. *A History of the Rockefeller Institute, 1901–1953: Origins and Growth*. New York, 1964.

Craig, Gordon A. *The Politics of the Prussian Army, 1640–1945*. New York, 1965.

Crawford, Deborah. *Lise Meitner: Atomic Pioneer.* New York, 1969.

Crawford, Elisabeth, and John L. Heilbron. "Die Kaiser Wilhelm-Institute für Grundlagenforschung und die Nobelinstitution." In *Forschung im Spannungsfeld von Politik und Gesellschaft: Aus Anlass des 75jährigen Bestehens der Kaiser-Wilhelm/Max-Planck Gesellschaft (1911–1986),* edited by Rudolf Vierhaus and Bernhard vom Brocke. Stuttgart, 1989.

Dahrendorf, Ralf. *Society and Democracy in Germany.* Munich, 1965. Translated by Ralf Dahrendorf from *Gesellschaft und Demokratie in Deutschland.* New York, 1967.

Denkschrift über die Begründung und über die bisherige Thätigkeit der biologischen Abtheilung für Land- und Fortswirtschaft am Kaiserlichen Gesundheitsamt. N.p., 1901.

Dewar, Sir James. "Presidential Address to the British Association (1902)." In *Collected Papers of Sir James Dewar,* edited by Lady Dewar. 2 vols. 2:753–800. Cambridge, 1927.

Dictionary of Scientific Biography. Charles C. Gillispie, editor in chief. 15 vols. New York, 1970–78.

Duisberg, Carl. "Emil Fischer und die Industrie." *Berichte der Deutschen Chemischen Gesellschaft* 52 (1919): 149–64.

———. *Meine Lebenserinnerungen.* Leipzig, 1933.

Dupree, A. Hunter. "Nationalism and Science—Sir Joseph Banks and the Wars with France." In *A Festschrift for Frederick B. Artz,* edited by David H. Pinkney and Theodore Ropp, pp. 37–51. Durham, N.C., 1964.

Eley, Geoff. *Reshaping the German Right: Radical Nationalism and Political Change after Bismarck.* New Haven and London, 1980.

Engelhardt, Ulrich, ed. *Soziale Bewegung und politische Verfassung: Beiträge zur Geschichte der modernen Welt.* Stuttgart, 1976.

"Errichtung von Lehrstühlen und Laboratorien für Elektrochemie." *Die chemische Industrie* 18 (1895): 109.

Falkenhayn, Erich von. *General Headquarters, 1914–1916 and Its Critical Decisions.* London, n.d. [1920?]. Translation of *Die oberste Heeresleitung, 1914–1916.* Berlin, 1920.

Fay, Sidney B. *The Origins of the World War.* 2 vols. 2d ed. Reprint. New York, 1966.

Feldman, Gerald D. "A German Scientist between Illusion and Reality: Emil Fischer, 1909–1919." In *Deutschland in der Weltpolitik des 19. und 20. Jahrhunderts: Fritz Fischer zum 65. Geburtstag,* edited by Immanuel Geiss and Bernd-Jürgen Wendt, pp. 341–62. Düsseldorf, 1973.

Fischer, Emil. "Die Aufgaben des Kaiser-Wilhelm-Instituts für Kohlenforschung." *Stahl und Eisen* 32 (1912): 1898–1903.

———. *Aus meinem Leben.* Berlin, 1922.

———. *Eröffnungs-Feier des neuen I. chemischen Instituts der Universität Berlin, am 14. Juli 1900.* Berlin, 1900.

———. "Die Kaiser-Wilhelm-Institute und der Zusammenhang von organischer Chemie und Biologie." In *Untersuchungen aus verschiedenen Gebieten,* edited by Max Bergmann, pp. 797–809. Berlin, 1924.

———. "Neuere Erfolge und Probleme der Chemie." *Internationale Wochen-*

schrift für Wissenschaft, Kunst und Technik 5 (Feb. 5, 1911): cols. 1–20. Reprinted in *Untersuchungen aus verschiedenen Gebieten: Vorträge und Abhandlungen allgemeinen Inhalts,* edited by Max Bergmann, pp. 757–71. Berlin, 1924.

————. Obituary of Gerhard Krüss. *Berichte der Deutschen Chemischen Gesellschaft* 28 (1895): 177–79.

————. "Tischrede bei der Einweihung des Instituts für Kohlenforschung." In *Untersuchungen aus verschiedenen Gebieten: Vorträge und Abhandlungen allgemeinen Inhalts,* edited by Max Bergmann, pp. 823–26. Berlin, 1924.

————. *Untersuchungen aus verschiedenen Gebieten: Vorträge und Abhandlungen allgemeinen Inhalts,* edited by Max Bergmann. Berlin, 1924.

Fischer, Emil, and Ernst Beckmann. *Das Kaiser-Wilhelm-Institut für Chemie, Berlin-Dahlem.* Braunschweig, 1913.

Fischer, Franz. "Chemie und Kohle." *Brennstoff-Chemie* 8, no. 14 (1927). Reprint.

————. *Leben und Forschung: Erinnerungen aufgezeichnet in den Jahren 1944 bis 1946.* Mülheim/Ruhr, 1957.

————. "Ziele und Ergebnisse der Kohlenforschung." *Brennstoff-Chemie* 2, no. 15 (1921). Reprint.

Fischer, Franz, and Hans Tropsch. "Die Erdölsynthese bei gewöhnlichem Druck aus den Vergasungsprodukten der Kohlen." *Brennstoff-Chemie* 7, no. 7 (1926). Reprint.

Fischer, Fritz. *Griff nach der Weltmacht.* Düsseldorf, 1961. Translated and abridged by Marian Jackson as *Germany's Aims in the First World War.* New York, 1967.

————. *War of Illusions: German Policies from 1911 to 1914.* New York, 1975. Translated by Marian Jackson from *Krieg der Illusionen: Die deutsche Politik von 1911 bis 1914.* Düsseldorf, 1969.

Flechtner, Hans-Joachim. *Carl Duisberg: Von Chemiker zum Wirtschaftsführer.* Düsseldorf, 1959.

Foerster, F. "Walter Hempel." *Berichte der Deutschen Chemischen Gesellschaft* 53 (1920): 123–43.

"Fonds der Deutschen Chemischen Gesellschaft für chemische Sammel-Literatur." *Berichte der Deutschen Chemischen Gesellschaft* 43 (1910): 3639.

Forman, Paul, John L. Heilbron, and Spencer Weart. "Physics circa 1900: Personnel, Funding, and Productivity of the Academic Establishments." *Historical Studies in the Physical Sciences* 5 (1975): 1–185 [entire volume].

Frank, Philipp. *Einstein, His Life and Times.* New York, 1947.

"Frankfurter Bezirksverein." *Zeitschrift für angewandte Chemie* 20 (1907): 603. (Gustav Keppeler, "Zur Gründung einer chemischen Reichsanstalt.")

Fried, A. H., H. La Fontaine, and P. Otlet, eds. *Annuaire de la vie internationale.* Brussels, 1908–9, 1910–11.

"Fünfundzwanzig Jahre unseres Vereinslebens." *Die chemische Industrie* 25 (1902): 405–17.

Gans, Leo. "Bemerkung zu der Debatte über die chemische Reichsanstalt in der Hauptversammlung in Lübeck." *Die chemische Industrie* 30 (1907): 597–80.

──────. "Chemische Reichsanstalt oder chemische Reichsfonds?" *Die chemische Industrie* 30 (1907): 29–30.

──────. "Gegen die chemische Reichsanstalt!" *Die chemische Industrie* 29 (1906): 589–93.

Generalverwaltung der Max-Planck-Gesellschaft zur Förderung der Wissenschaften. *50 Jahre Kaiser-Wilhelm-Gesellschaft und Max-Planck-Gesellschaft zur Förderung der Wissenschaften, 1911–1961: Beiträge und Dokumente.* Göttingen, 1961.

Germany. Reichstag. *Stenographische Berichte über die Verhandlungen.* Berlin, 1871–1918.

──────. Statistisches Reichsamt. *Statistik des Deutschen Reichs.* N.s., vol. 221. *Zusammenfassende Übersichten für die gewerbliche Betriebszählung von 1907.* Berlin, 1914.

Gerschenkron, Alexander. *Bread and Democracy in Germany.* New York, 1966.

Gillis, John R. "Aristocracy and Bureaucracy in Nineteenth-Century Prussia." *Past and Present* 41 (Dec. 1968): 105–29.

Glum, Friedrich. *Zwischen Wissenschaft, Wirtschaft und Politik: Erlebtes und Erdachtes in vier Reichen.* Bonn, 1964.

Goldberger, Ludwig Max. *Das Land der unbegrenzten Möglichkeiten: Beobachtungen über das Wirtschaftsleben der Vereinigten Staaten von Amerika.* Berlin, 1903.

Goran, Morris. *The Story of Fritz Haber.* Norman, Okla., 1967.

Grabower, Rolf. *Die finanzielle Entwicklung der Aktiengesellschaften der deutschen chemischen Industrie und Ihre Beziehungen zur Bankwelt.* Partially printed dissertation. Berlin, 1910.

Graham, Loren R. "Science and Values: The Eugenics Movement in Germany and Russia in the 1920s." *American Historical Review* 82 (1977): 1133–64.

Greiling, Walter. *Im Banne der Medizin: Paul Ehrlich, Leben und Werk.* Düsseldorf, 1954.

Griewank, Karl. *Staat und Wissenschaft im Deutschen Reich: Zur Geschichte und Organisation der Wissenschaftspflege in Deutschland.* Freiburg i. Br., 1927.

"Gründung einer chemischen Reichsanstalt." *Zeitschrift für angewandte Chemie* 19 (1906): 1495–98.

Gummert, Heinz. "Entwicklung neuer technischen Methoden unter Anwendung wissenschaftlicher Erkenntnisse im Bereich der deutschen Schwerindustrie, gezeigt am Beispiel der Firma Krupp, Essen." In *Geschichte der Naturwissenschaften und der Technik im 19. Jahrhundert: 6. Gespräch der Georg-Agricola-Gesellschaft*, a special issue of *Technikgeschichte in Einzeldarstellungen* 16 (1970): 113–32.

Gutsche, Willibald, "Probleme des Verhältnisses zwischen Monopolkapital und Staat in Deutschland vom Ende des 19. Jahrhunderts bis zum Vorabend des Weltkrieges." In *Studien zum deutschen Imperialismus*, edited by Fritz Klein, pp. 33–84. Berlin, 1976.

Haber, Fritz. *Fünf Vorträge aus den Jahren 1920–1923.* Berlin, 1924.

──────. "Ueber Hochschulunterricht und elektrochemische Technik in den Vereinigten Staaten." *Zeitschrift für Elektrochemie* 9 (1903): 291–303, 347–70, 379–406.

Haber, Lutz F. *The Chemical Industry during the Nineteenth Century*. Oxford, 1958.

————. *The Chemical Industry, 1900–1930: International Growth and Technological Change*. Oxford, 1971.

————. *The Poisonous Cloud: Chemical Warfare in the First World War*. New York, 1986.

Hahn, Otto. *Vom Radiothor zur Uranspaltung: Eine wissenschaftliche Selbstbiographie*. Braunschweig, 1962.

Hale, Oron J. *The Great Illusion, 1900–1914*. New York, 1971.

Hamburger, Ernest. *Juden im öffentlichen Leben Deutschlands: Regierungsmitglieder, Beamte und Parlamentarier in der monarchischen Zeit, 1848–1918*. Tübingen, 1968.

Hanslian, Rudolf, ed. *Der chemische Krieg*. Berlin, 1927. 3d ed., Berlin, 1937.

Harnack, Adolf von. *An der Schwelle des dritten Kriegsjahres*. Berlin, 1916.

————. *Aus Wissenschaft und Leben*. 2 vols. Giessen, 1911.

————. "Die Kaiser-Wilhelm-Gesellschaft am Schluss ihres ersten Jahres." *Internationale Wochenschrift für Wissenschaft, Kunst und Technik* 6 (Feb. 1912): cols. 1–14.

————. "Die Königlich Preussische Akademie der Wissenschaften." In *Reden und Aufsätze*. 2 vols. 2:191–215. Giessen, 1904.

"Hauptversammlung des Vereins deutscher Chemiker in Mannheim. II. Antrag des Bezirksvereins Rheinland-Westfalen: Studium der Ausländer an deutschen Hochschulen." *Zeitschrift für angewandte chemie* 17 (1904): 1318–28.

Heise, K.-H. "Zur Rolle der staatlichen Forschungspolitik im Prozess der Kapitalverwertung." In Vadim Nikolajew, *Forschung und Entwicklung im Imperialismus*, pp. 26–34. Berlin-DDR, 1972.

Herneck, Friedrich. *Abenteuer der Erkenntnis: Fünf Naturforscher aus drei Epochen*. Berlin-DDR, 1973.

Herwig, Holger. *The German Naval Officer Corps: A Social and Political History*. Oxford, 1973.

Hjelt, Edvard. *Geschichte der organische Chemie*. Braunschweig, 1916.

Hoesch, Kurt. *Emil Fischer: Sein Leben und sein Werk*. Berlin, 1921.

Hoffmann, Walther G. *Das Wachstum der deutschen Wirtschaft seit der Mitte des 19. Jahrhunderts*. Berlin, Heidelberg, and New York, 1965.

Hofmann, August Wilhelm (von). "Georg Merck." *Berichte der Deutschen Chemischen Gesellschaft* 6 (1873): 1582–83.

Hohenberg, Paul M. *Chemicals in Western Europe, 1850–1914: An Economic Study of Technical Change*. Chicago, 1967.

"Hugo Thiel." [Obituary.] *Deutsches biographisches Jahrbuch, Überleitungsband 2 (1917–20)*, pp. 706. Berlin, Leipzig, and Stuttgart, 1928.

Ihde, Aaron J. *The Development of Modern Chemistry*. New York, 1964.

Das Institut für Gärungsgewerbe und Stärkefabrikation: Sonderabdruck aus der Festschrift zur Feier des 25 jährigen Bestehens der Königl. Landwirtschaftlichen Hochschule in Berlin. Berlin, 1906.

Jarausch, Konrad H. *Students, Society, and Politics in Imperial Germany: The Rise of Academic Illiberalism*. Princeton, N.J., 1982.

————., ed. *The Transformation of Higher Learning, 1860–1930.* Stutttgart, 1983.

Jarausch, Konrad H., and Geoffrey Cocks, eds. *German Professions, 1800–1950.* Oxford, 1990.

Johnson, Jeffrey A. "Academic Chemistry in Imperial Germany." *Isis* 76 (1985): 500–524.

————. "Academic Self-Regulation and the Chemical Profession in Imperial Germany." *Minerva* 23 (1985): 241–71.

————. "Academic, Proletarian, . . . Professional? Shaping Professionalization for German Industrial Chemists, 1887–1920." In *German Professions, 1800–1950,* edited by Konrad H. Jarausch and Geoffrey Cocks. Oxford, 1990.

————. "The Chemical Reichsanstalt Association: Big Science in Imperial Germany." Ph.D. diss., Princeton University, 1980.

————. "Hierarchy and Creativity in Chemistry, 1871–1914." *Osiris* n.s. 5 (1989): 214–40.

Kaiser-Wilhelm-Gesellschaft zur Förderung der Wissenschaften. *Adolf von Harnack zum Gedächtnis.* Berlin, 1930.

————. *3.–5. Jahresbericht.* Berlin, 1916.

"Das Kaiser-Wilhelm-Institut für Kohlenforschung zu Mülheim (Ruhr)." *Stahl und Eisen* 32 (1912): 1897.

Kaiser-Wilhelm-Institut für Landwirtschaft, Bromberg, Prussia. *Jahresbericht* 1 (1907).

Kaznelson, Siegmund. *Juden im deutschen Kulturbereich: Ein Sammelwerk.* 2d ed., Berlin, 1962.

Kehr, Eckart. *Battleship Building and Party Politics in Germany, 1894–1901: A Cross-Section of the Political, Social, and Ideological Preconditions of German Imperialism.* Edited, translated, with an introduction by Pauline R. Anderson and Eugene N. Anderson. Chicago and London, 1973.

Keppeler, Gustav. "Zur Gründung einer chemischen Reichsanstalt." (See "Frankfurter Bezirksverein.")

Kevles, Daniel J. *The Physicists: The History of a Scientific Community in Modern America.* New York, 1978.

Kitchin, Martin. *The German Officer Corps, 1890–1914.* Oxford, 1968.

"Kleines Feuilleton: Der Trompetenstoss der deutschen Chemie." *Danziger Zeitung,* March 13, 1906.

Kluke, Paul. *Die Stiftungsuniversität Frankfurt am Main, 1914–1932.* Frankfurt/Main, 1972.

Kocka, Jürgen. "Organisierter Kapitalismus oder Staatsmonopolistischer Kapitalismus? Begriffliche Vorbemerkungen." In *Organisierter Kapitalismus,* edited by Heinrich A. Winkler, pp. 19–35. Göttingen, 1974.

Kohler, Robert. *From Medical Chemistry to Biochemistry: The Making of a Biomedical Discipline.* Cambridge, 1982.

Kraepelin, Emil. "Forschungsinstitute und Hochschulen." *Süddeutsche Monatshefte* 8 (1911): 597–607.

Krafft, Fritz. *Im Schatten der Sensation: Leben und Wirken von Fritz Strassmann.* Weinheim and Deerfield Beach, Fla., 1981.

Krebs, Hans. *Otto Warburg: Cell Physiologist, Biochemist, and Eccentric.* Oxford, 1981.

Kuhn, Thomas S. *The Structure of Scientific Revolutions.* 2d ed. Chicago, 1970.

Landes, David S. *The Unbound Prometheus: Technological Change and Industrial Development in Western Europe from 1750 to the Present.* Cambridge, 1969.

Landolt, Hans, and Richard Börnstein. *Physikalisch-Chemische Tabellen.* 1st ed., Berlin, 1883; 2d ed., Berlin, 1894.

Landolt-Börnstein Physikalisch-Chemische Tabellen. 3d ed. Edited by Richard Börnstein and Wilhelm Meyerhoffer. Berlin, 1905.

Lefebure, Victor. *The Riddle of the Rhine: Chemical Strategy in Peace and War.* New York, 1923.

Lenz, Max. *Geschichte der Königlichen Friedrich-Wilhelms-Universität zu Berlin.* 4 vols. Halle, 1910–18.

Lepsius, Bernhard. *Deutschlands chemische Industrie, 1888–1913.* Berlin, 1914.

——————. *Festschrift zur Feier des 50jährigen Bestehens der Deutschen Chemischen Gesellschaft und des 100. Geburtstages ihres Begründers August Wilhelm von Hofmann.* Berlin, 1918.

Lexis, Wilhelm Hector. *A General View of the History and Organisation of Public Education in the German Empire.* Berlin, 1904.

——————, ed. *Das Unterrichtswesen im Deutschen Reich: Aus Anlass der Weltausstellung in St. Louis.* Vol. 1, *Die Universitäten im Deutschen Reich.* Vol. 4, *Das Technische Unterrichtswesen.* Part 1, *Die Technischen Hochschulen im Deutschen Reich.* Berlin, 1904.

Lockemann, Georg. *Ernst Beckmann (1853–1923): Sein Leben und Wirken.* Berlin, 1927.

Lundgreen, Peter. "Measures for Objectivity in the Public Interest. The Role of Scientific Expertise in the Politics of Technical Regulation: Germany and the U.S., 1865–1916." In *Standardization–Testing–Regulation: Studies in the History of the Science-Based Regulatory State (Germany and the U.S.A., 19th and 20th centuries),* Separately paginated. Report Wissenschaftsforschung, no. 29. Bielefeld, March 1985.

Lutz, Ralph H. *Fall of the German Empire, 1914–1918.* Reprint. New York, 1969.

McClelland, Charles E. *State, Society, and University in Germany, 1700–1914.* Cambridge, 1980.

McNeill, William H. *The Pursuit of Power: Technology, Armed Force, and Society since A.D. 1000.* Chicago, 1982.

Manegold, Karl-Heinz. *Universität, Technische Hochschule und Industrie: Ein Beitrag zur Emanzipation der Technik im 19. Jahrhundert unter besonderer Berücksichtigung der Bestrebungen Felix Kleins.* Berlin, 1970.

Martius, Carl Alexander von. "Eine chemische Reichsanstalt?" *Die chemische Industrie* 29 (1906): 135–39.

——————. *Die Errichtung einer gewerblich-technischen Reichsbehörde und einer chemischen Reichsanstalt.* Privately printed, Berlin, [1907?].

"Max Delbrück." [Obituary.] *Berichte der Deutschen Chemischen Gesellschaft* 53 (1919): 47–62.

Mehra, Jagdish. *The Solvay Conferences on Physics: Aspects of the Development of Physics since 1911.* Dordrecht, 1975.

Meinecke, Friedrich. *Autobiographische Schriften*. Stuttgart, 1969.

Meinel, Christoph. "Reine und angewandte Chemie: Die Entstehung einer neuen Wissenschaftskonzeption in der Chemie der Aufklärung." *Berichte zur Wissenschaftsgeschichte* 8 (1985): 25–45.

Memorial Lectures Delivered before the Chemical Society [of London]. Vol. 1, *1893–1900*. London, 1901. Vol. 2, *1901–1913*. London, 1914. Vol. 3, *1914–1932*. London, 1933. Vol. 4, *1933–1942*. London, 1951.

Mendelssohn, Kurt. *The World of Walther Nernst: The Rise and Fall of German Science*. London, 1973.

Merz, John Theodore. *A History of European Scientific Thought in the Nineteenth Century*. 2 vols. 1904–12. Reprint. New York, 1956.

Meyer, Ernst von, ed. *Chemie*. Leipzig and Berlin, 1913. Teil 3, Abt. 3, Bd. 2 of *Die Kultur der Gegenwart: Ihre Entwicklung und ihre Ziele*, edited by Paul Hinneberg. Leipzig and Berlin, 1908–[14].

Meyer, Julius. *Der Gaskampf und die chemischen Kampfstoffe*. Leipzig, 1926.

Meyer, Richard. *Vorlesungen über die Geschichte der Chemie*. Leipzig, 1922.

Meyer-Thurow, Georg. "The Industrialization of Invention: A Case-Study from the German Chemical Industry." *Isis* 73 (1982): 363–81.

Miller, Howard S. *Dollars for Research: Science and Its Patrons in Nineteenth-Century America*. Seattle, Wash., 1970.

Minerva: Jahrbuch der gelehrten Welt. Strassburg, 1892–.

Moore, Barrington, Jr. *Social Origins of Dictatorship and Democracy: Lord and Peasant in the Making of the Modern World*. Boston, 1966.

Morrow, John Howard, Jr. *Building German Airpower, 1909–1914*. Knoxville, Tenn., 1976.

Mosse, Werner E. "Die Juden in Wirtschaft und Gesellschaft." In *Juden im Wilhelminischen Deutschland, 1890–1914*, edited by Werner E. Mosse, pp. 57–113. Tübingen, 1976.

———. *Jews in the German Economy: The German-Jewish Economic Elite, 1820–1935*. Oxford, 1987.

Nachmansohn, David. *German-Jewish Pioneers in Science, 1900–1933*. New York, 1979.

Nernst, Walther. "Die Begründung einer chemischen Reichsanstalt." *Berliner Tageblatt*, March 28, 1908.

———. "Das Institut für physikalische Chemie und besonders Elektrochemie an der Universität Göttingen." *Zeitschrift für Elektrochemie* 3 (1896): 629–36.

———. *Theoretische Chemie vom Standpunkte der Avogadroschen Regel und der Thermodynamik*. Göttingen, 1893. 5th English edition translated by L. W. Codd as *Theoretical Chemistry from the Standpoint of Avogadro's Rule and Thermodynamics*. London, 1923.

———. *Die Ziele der physikalischen Chemie*. Göttingen, 1896.

Nernst, Walther, and A. Schöflies. *Einführung in die mathematische Behandlung der Naturwissenschaften*. Munich, 1895.

Neue Deutsche Biographie. Berlin, 1953–.

Nikolajew, Vadim. *Forschung und Entwicklung im Imperialismus*. Berlin-DDR, 1972.

Nobelstiftelsen [Nobel Foundation], Stockholm. *Nobel Lectures, Including Pre-*

sentation Speeches and Laureates' Biographies: Chemistry, 1901–1921. Amsterdam, London, and New York, 1966.

Noble, David F. *America by Design: Science, Technology, and the Rise of Corporate Capitalism.* New York, 1977.

Noelting, Emilio. "Otto Nikolaus Witt 1853–1915." *Berichte der Deutschen Chemischen Gesellschaft* 49 (1916): 1751–1832.

Oleson, Alexandra, and John Voss, eds. *The Organization of Knowledge in Modern America, 1860–1920.* Baltimore, Md., 1979.

Ostwald, Wilhelm. *Abhandlungen und Vorträge Allgemeinen Inhalts (1887–1903).* Leipzig, 1904.

_____. *Aus dem wissenschaftlichen Briefwechsel Wilhelm Ostwalds.* Edited by Hans-Günther Körber. 2 vols. Berlin, 1961–69.

_____. *Die Chemische Reichsanstalt.* Leipzig, 1906.

_____. "Die chemische Reichsanstalt." *Zeitschrift für angewandte Chemie* 19 (1906): 1025–27.

_____. *Denkschrift über die Gründung eines internationalen Instituts für Chemie.* Leipzig, 1912.

_____. Für die chemische Reichsanstalt." *Die chemische Industrie* 29 (1906): 645–47.

_____. *Lebenslinien: Eine Selbstbiographie.* 3 vols. Berlin, 1926–27.

_____. *Lehrbuch der allgemeinen Chemie.* 2 vols. Leipzig, 1885–87. 2d ed. Leipzig, 1891–1902.

_____. *Das physikalisch-chemische Institut der Universität Leipzig und die Feier seiner Eröffnung am 3. Januar 1898.* Leipzig, 1898.

_____. "Die Universitäten der Zukunft und die Zukunft der Universitäten." In his *Der energetische Imperativ,* pp. 429–43. Leipzig, 1912.

_____. *Die wissenschaftlichen Grundlagen der analytischen Chemie.* Leipzig, 1894.

_____. "Die wissenschaftlische Elektrochemie der Gegenwart und die technische der Zukunft." In his *Abhandlungen und Vorträge Allgemeinen Inhalts,* pp. 133–60. Leipzig, 1904.

Partridge, William S., and Ernest R. Schierz, "Otto Wallach: The First Organizer of the Terpenes." *Journal of Chemical Education* 24 (1947): 106–8.

Paul, Harry W. "Die Entwicklung der Forschungsförderung im modernen Frankreich." In *Forschung im Spannungsfeld von Politik und Gesellschaft: Aus Anlass des 75jährigen Bestehens der Kaiser-Wilhelm/Max-Planck Gesellschaft (1911–1986),* edited by Rudolf Vierhaus and Bernhard vom Brocke. Stuttgart, 1989.

Pauly, Philip J. *Controlling Life: Jacques Loeb and the Engineering Ideal in Biology.* New York, 1987.

Perkins, J. A. "The Agricultural Revolution in Germany, 1850–1914." *Journal of European Economic History* 10 (1981): 71–144.

Pfetsch, Frank R. "Scientific Organisation and Science Policy in Imperial Germany, 1871–1914: The Foundation of the Imperial Institute for Physics and Technology." *Minerva* 8 (1970): 557–80.

_____. *Zur Entwicklung der Wissenschaftspolitik in Deutschland, 1750–1914.* Berlin, 1974.

Pinner, A. "Bericht über die am 20. Oktober erfolgte Einweihung des Hofmann-Hauses." *Berichte der Deutschen Chemischen Gesellschaft* 33 (1900), *Sonderheft*: iii–xvi.

Pinson, Koppel S. *Modern Germany: Its History and Civilization.* 2d ed. New York, 1966.

Prandtl, Wilhelm. "Das chemische Laboratorium der bayerischen Akademie der Wissenschaften in München." *Chymia* 2 (1949): 81–97.

Price, Derek J. de Solla. *Little Science, Big Science.* New York and London, 1963.

"Protokoll der 29. Hauptversammlung des Vereins zur Wahrung des Interessen der chemischen Industrie Deutschlands e. V." *Die chemische Industrie* 29 (1906): 523–47.

"Protokoll der 34. Hauptversammlung des Vereins Deutscher Ingenieure: Gewerblich-technische Reichsbehörde." *Zeitschriftdes Vereins Deutscher Ingenieure* 37 (1893): 1436–38.

Prussia. Landtag. Haus der Abgeordneten. *Stenographische Berichte über die Verhandlungen.* Berlin, 1848/49–1916/18.

―――. Statistisches Landesamt. *Preussische Statistik.* Vols. 150, 167, 193, 204, 223, 236. *Statistik der Preussischen Landesuniversitäten.* Berlin, 1898–1914.

Pyenson, Lewis. *Cultural Imperialism and Exact Sciences: German Expansion Overseas, 1900–1930.* New York, 1985.

―――. *Neohumanism and the Persistence of Pure Mathematics in Wilhelmian Germany.* Philadelphia, 1983.

Rasch, Manfred. "Coal Liquefaction—Caught between Economic and Political Interests: The Example of Germany (1900–1945)." Paper presented at the Eighteenth International Congress of History of Science, Berkeley, Calif., 31 July–8 Aug. 1985.

―――. *Vorgeschichte und Gründung des Kaiser-Wilhelm-Institut für Kohlenforschung in Mülheim a. d. Ruhr.* Hagen, 1987.

Rassow, Berthold. *Geschichte des Vereins deutscher Chemiker in den ersten fünfundzwanzig Jahren seines Bestehens.* Leipzig, 1912.

Rathenau, Walther. *Zur Kritik der Zeit.* Berlin, 1912.

Reingold, Nathan. "National Science Policy in a Private Foundation: The Carnegie Institution of Washington, 1903–1920." In *The Organization of Knowledge in Modern America, 1860–1920,* edited by Alexandra Oleson and John Voss, pp. 313–41. Baltimore, Md., 1979.

Rejewski, Harro-Jürgen. *Die Pflicht zur politischen Treue im Preussischen Beamtenrecht (1850–1918): Eine rechtshistorische Untersuchung anhand von Ministerialiakten aus den Geheimen Staatsarchiv der Stiftung Preussischer Kulturbesitz.* Berlin, 1973.

Remak, Joachim, and Jack Dukes, eds. *Another Germany: A Reconsideration of the Imperial Era.* Boulder, Colo., 1987.

Ress, Franz Michael. *Geschichte der Kokereitechnik.* Essen, 1957.

Rhodes, Richard. *The Making of the Atomic Bomb.* New York, 1986.

Richards, Theodore W. "Minority Report of Advisory Committee on Chemistry." *Carnegie Institution of Washington Year Book* 1 (1902): 85–86.

Richter, M. M. *Lexikon der Kohlenstoffverbindungen.* 1st ed., 1882. 2d ed., 1899. 3d ed., Leipzig and Hamburg, 1912.

Riesser, Jacob. *The German Great Banks and Their Concentration in Connection with the Economic Development of Germany.* 3d ed. Washington, D.C., 1911.

Rife, Patricia E. "Lise Meitner: The Life and Times of a Jewish Woman Physicist." Ph.D. diss. Union for Experimenting Colleges and Universities, 1983. Forthcoming (in German) as *Lise Meitner.* Düsseldorf, 1990.

Ringer, Fritz K. *The Decline of the German Mandarins: The German Academic Community, 1890–1933.* Cambridge, Mass., 1969.

———. *Education and Society in Modern Europe.* Bloomington, Ind., 1979.

Ritter, Gerhard. *The Schlieffen Plan: Critique of a Myth.* London, 1958.

———. *The Sword and the Scepter: The Problem of Militarism in Germany.* Vol. 2, *The European Powers and the Wilhelminia Empire, 1890–1914.* Coral Gables, Fla., 1970. Translated by Heinz Norden from *Staatskunst und Kriegshandwerk,* 2d ed. Munich, 1965.

Root-Bernstein, Robert S. "The Ionists: Founding Physical Chemistry, 1872–1890." Ph.D. diss., Princeton University, 1980.

Roth, Guenther. *The Social Democrats in Imperial Germany: A Study in Working-Class Isolation and National Integration.* Totowa, N.J., 1963.

Ruske, Walter. *100 Jahre Deutsche Chemische Gesellschaft.* Weinheim/Bergstr., 1967.

———. *100 Jahre Materialprüfung in Berlin: Ein Beitrag zur Technikgeschichte.* Berlin, 1971.

———. "Reichs- und preussische Landesanstalten in Berlin: Ihre Entstehung und Entwicklung als ausseruniversitäre Forschungs- und Beratungsorgane der politischen Instanzen." *BAM Berichte* 23 (Nov. 1973): 1–40 [entire volume].

Sachse, Arnold. *Friedrich Althoff und sein Werk.* Berlin, 1928.

Schmidt-Ott, Friedrich. *Erlebtes und Erstrebtes, 1860–1950.* Wiesbaden, 1952.

Scholz, Hartmut. "Zu einigen Wechselbeziehungen zwischen chemischer Wissenschaft, chemischer Industrie und staatlicher Administration . . . in Deutschland in der Zeit des Übergangs zum Monopolkapitalismus." Dissertation B, Humboldt-Universität zu Berlin, 1989.

Schorsch, Ismar. *Jewish Reactions to German Anti-Semitism, 1870–1914.* New York and London, 1972.

Schroeder-Gudehus, Brigitte. "Caracteristiques des relations scientifiques internationales, 1870–1914." *Cahiers d'histoire mondiale* 13 (1966): 161–77.

———. "Division of Labor and the Common Good: The International Association of Academies, 1899–1914." In *Science, Technology and Society in the Time of Alfred Nobel,* edited by Carl Gustaf Bernhard, Elisabeth Crawford, and Per Sorbom, pp. 3–20. Oxford, 1982.

Schröter, Alfred. *Krieg-Staat-Monopol, 1914–1918: Die Zusammenhänge von imperialistischer Kriegswirtschaft, Militarisierung der Volkswirtschaft und staatsmonopolistischem Kapitalismus in Deutschland während des ersten Weltkrieges.* Berlin, 1965.

Schumpeter, Joseph A. *Imperialism and Social Classes,* edited by Paul M. Sweezy. London, 1951. Translated by Heinz Norden from *Zur Soziologie der Imperialismen.* Tübingen, 1919.

Servos, John W. "Physical Chemistry in America, 1890–1933: Origins, Growth, and Definition." Ph.D. diss., Johns Hopkins University, 1979.

Siemens, Wilhelm von. "Zur Frage der Gründung neuer wissenschaftlicher Forschungsinstitute." *Elektrotechnische Zeitschrift* 22 (1911): 229–31.

Sitzungsberichte der Königlich preussischen Akademie der Wissenschaften zu Berlin, Jahrgang 1890.

Simson, Dr. von. "Die Kaiser-Wilhelm-Gesellschaft zur Förderung der Wissenschaften. *Soziale Kultur und Volkswohlfahrt während der ersten 25 Regierungs-Jahre Kaiser Wilhelm II,* pp. 79–84. Berlin, 1913.

Stranges, Anthony. "Friedrich Bergius and the Rise of the German Synthetic Fuel Industry." *Isis* 75 (1984): 643–67.

Strauss, Herbert A., and Kurt R. Grossman, eds. *Gegenwart im Rückblick: Festgabe für die Jüdische Gemeinde zu Berlin 25 Jahre nach dem Neubeginn.* Heidelberg, 1970.

Stutzer, A. "Zur Begründung einer chemischen Reichsanstalt." *Zeitschrift für angewandte Chemie* 19 (1906): 419–20.

Suhling, Lothar. "Walther Nernst und der 3. Hauptsatz der Thermodynamik." *Rete* 1 (1972): 331–46.

Szabadvary, Ferenc. *History of Analytical Chemistry.* Translated by Gyula Svehla. Oxford and New York, 1966.

"Technische Tagesordnung, 1. Die Begründung einer chemischen Reichsanstalt." *Verhandlungen des Vereins zur Beförderung des Gewerbefleisses,* Jahrgang 1906, 113–23.

Thackray, Arnold, Jeffrey L. Sturchio, P. Thomas Carroll, and Robert Bud. *Chemistry in America, 1876–1976: Historical Indicators.* Boston, 1985.

Tietze, E. "Bemerkungen zur Frage der freien Forschungsinstitute." *Verhandlungen der K. K. Geologischen Reichsanstalt,* 1912, no. 1:60–74.

Tilden, William A. *Chemical Discovery and Invention in the Twentieth Century.* London, 1916.

Tipton, Frank B., Jr. *Regional Variations in the Economic Development of Germany during the Nineteenth Century.* Middletown, Conn., 1976.

Trumpener, Ulrich. "The Road to Ypres: The Beginnings of Gas Warfare in World War I." *Journal of Modern History* 47 (1975): 460–80.

Turner, L. C. F. *Origins of the First World War.* New York, 1970.

Turner, R. Steven. "The Growth of Professional Research in Prussia, 1818 to 1848—Causes and Context." *Historical Studies in the Physical Sciences* 3 (1971): 137–82.

———. "The Prussian Universities and the Research Imperative, 1806–1848." Ph.D. diss., Princeton University, 1973.

Ungewitter, C. See: Verein zur Wahrung der Interessen der chemischen Industrie Deutschlands.

Veblen, Thorstein. *The Theory of the Leisure Class.* 2d ed. New York, 1915.

Verein zur Wahrung der Interessen der chemischen Industrie Deutschlands e. V. (C. Ungewitter). *Ausgewählte Kapitel aus der chemisch-industriellen Wirtschaftspolitik, 1877–1927.* Berlin, 1927.

Verhandlungen über Fragen des höheren Unterrichts, Berlin, 6. bis 8. Juni 1900.

Halle, 1902. Reprinted as *Deutsche Schulkonferenzen*, vol. 2. Glashötten im Taunus, 1972.

Vierhaus, Rudolf, and Bernhard vom Brocke, eds. *Forschung im Spannungsfeld von Politik und Gesellschaft: Aus Anlass des 75jährigen Bestehens der Kaiser-Wilhelm/Max-Planck Gesellschaft (1911–1986)*. Stuttgart, forthcoming.

Vorläufiger Entwurf einer Denkschrift über die Begründung einer chemischen Reichsanstalt. Privately printed. Berlin, 1905.

Vorschläge betreffend die Bergründung einer chemischen Reichsanstalt. 1st ed. Privately printed. Berlin, [1905]. 2d ed. 2 vols. Privately printed. Berlin, [1906].

Warburg, Emil. "Die Physikalisch-Technische Reichsanstalt in Charlottenburg: Vortrag gehalten in der Vollversammlung des Osterreichschen Ingenieur- und Architekten-Vereins am 28. März 1908." Vienna, 1908. Reprint from *Zeitschrift des Österreichschen Ingenieure- & Architekten-Vereins*, Jahrgang 1908, Nrs. 32–33, 28 pp.

Weber, Max. "Capitalism and Rural Society in Germany" (1904–6). In *From Max Weber: Essays in Sociology*, edited by Hans H. Gerth and C. Wright Mills, pp. 363–85. New York, 1946.

Wehler, Hans-Ulrich. *Das deutsche Kaiserreich, 1871–1918*. Göttingen, 1973.

Weinberg, Alvin M. *Reflections on Big Science*. Cambridge, Mass., 1967.

Weinberg, Arthur von. "Emil Fischers Tätigkeit während des Krieges." *Die Naturwissenschaften* 7 (1919): 868–73.

Welsch, Fritz. "Bemerkungen über die Zusammenarbeit der chemischen Fabrik Griesheim-Elektron mit Wilhelm Ostwald und Walther Nernst nach 1900." *NTM—Schriftenreihe zur Geschichte der Naturwissenschaften, der Technik und der Medizin* 22 (1985): 77–82.

Wendel, Günter. *Die Kaiser-Wilhelm-Gesellschaft, 1911–1914: Zur Anatomie einer imperialistischer Forschungsgesellschaft*. Berlin-DDR, 1975.

Wer Ist's. 10th ed. Berlin, 1935.

Wertheimer, Jack. *Unwelcome Strangers: East European Jews in Imperial Germany*. Oxford, 1987.

Wichelhaus, C. H. "Carl Alexander von Martius." *Berichte der Deutschen Chemischen Gesellschaft* 53 (1920): 72–75.

Wilamowitz-Moellendorf, Ulrich von. *My Recollections, 1848–1914*. London, 1930. Translation by G. C. Richards of *Erinnerungen, 1848–1914*. 2d ed., Leipzig, 1928.

Wilhelm II, Emperor. *Ereignisse und Gestalten aus den Jahren 1878–1918*. Leipzig and Berlin, 1922.

Willstätter, Richard. "Carl Dietrich Harries Lebensbeschreibung." *Berichte der Deutschen Chemischen Gesellschaft* 59 (1926): 123–57.

————. "Franz Oppenheim zum Gedächtnis." *Berichte der Deutschen Chemischen Gesellschaft* 64 (1931): 133–49.

————. *From My Life: The Memoirs of Richard Willstätter*. New York, 1965. Translated by Lilli S. Hornig from *Aus meinem Leben*, edited by Arthur Stoll. Weinheim, 1949.

Winkler, Heinrich A., ed. *Organisierter Kapitalismus*. Göttingen, 1974.

Witt, Otto N. *Das neue technisch-chemische Institut der Königlichen Technischen Hochschule zu Berlin* . . . Berlin, 1906.

———. "Wechselwirkungen zwischen der chemischen Forschung und der chemischen Technik." In *Chemie*, edited by E. v. Meyer, pp. 475–527. Leipzig and Berlin, 1913.

Witt, Peter-Christian. *Die Finanzpolitik des Deutschen Reichs von 1903 bis 1913: Eine Studie zur Innenpolitik des Wilhelminischen Deutschland.* Lübeck and Hamburg, 1970.

Wohlgemuth, L. Max. "Zur Begründung einer chemischen Reichsanstalt." *Zeitschrift für angewandte Chemie* 29 (1906): 275.

Zahn-Harnack, Agnes von. *Adolf von Harnack.* 1st ed., Berlin, 1936. 2d ed., Berlin, 1951.

Zur Begründung einer chemischen Reichsanstalt. Privately printed without author's name (Ernst Beckmann), place (Berlin), or date (1908).

Zur Errichtung biologischer Forschungsinstitute durch die Kaiser-Wilhelm-Gesellschaft zur Förderung der Wissenschaften. Privately printed. [Berlin, 1912?]

Index

Abderhalden, Emil, 132
Academic system, German, 22, 27, 40, 49, 65; elites, 13; chemical laboratories, 42; resistance to modernization, 106; relations between institutions, 161–67; role of Kaiser Wilhelm Institutes in, 179; reforms in, 207. *See also* Academy of Sciences, Berlin; Colleges of technology; Kaiser Wilhelm Institutes; Kaiser Wilhelm Society for the Advancement of the Sciences; Universities, German; individual colleges of technology; individual Kaiser Wilhelm Institutes; individual universities
Academy of Sciences, Berlin, 16, 23, 43, 44, 102, 106, 109, 110, 124, 159, 166, 181; relations with Kaiser Wilhelm Society, 161–62
Agfa dye firm, 25, 34, 54, 70, 91
AG für Theer- und Erdölindustrie, 130
Agriculture, 10, 13, 14, 16, 17, 20, 25, 49, 54, 58, 60–62, 68, 71, 79, 82, 83, 85, 98, 104–6, 108, 118, 125, 126, 188, 195, 204; and opposition to Imperial Institute, 62, 73–74
Alcohol industry, 14, 62, 73, 104
Algeciras conference, 49
Althoff, Friedrich, 114, 160; and centralization of scientific institutions, 17, 66; role in Imperial Institute proposal, 19–20, 49, 51, 59, 61, 62, 65, 66, 67, 77, 79, 83, 85, 86; and lack of funds for academic laboratory, 43–44; promotes private support for research, 45; plans for scientific center in Dahlem, 107–9
"Americanization": opposition to, in Germany, 160
Ammonia. *See* Resources, strategic

Anti-Semitism, 11, 89, 182, 198
Arenberg, Duke Engelbert von, 117
Aristocracy, Prussian, 10, 11, 14, 74, 160, 204; limited gifts to Kaiser Wilhelm Society, 116–17
Armaments and munitions, 2, 16, 39, 49, 58, 80, 87, 102, 113, 126, 131, 178, 186–95, 209
Army League, 114
Arnhold, Eduard, 113, 124
Arons, Leo, 16, 196
Arrhenius, Svante, 29, 44, 124
Association for the Advancement of Chemical Research, 147
Association of German Chemists, 26, 36, 54, 58–59, 73, 76
Association of Laboratory Directors, 30
Auergesellschaft, 113, 119

Bacon, Francis: on knowledge and power, 5, 201, 202
Baeyer, Adolf von, 22, 37, 52, 105, 109, 112, 183, 192; as leader, 23; on changes in chemistry in 1905, 33
Ballin, Albert, 161
BASF, 25, 26, 34, 39, 54, 78, 80, 91, 105, 123, 126, 130, 137, 138, 147, 157, 187, 189, 193; reluctantly joins Institute Association, 97
Bayer Dye Factories, 1, 25, 30, 31, 34, 59, 70, 79, 91, 118, 124, 130, 131, 138, 187, 188, 190, 193
Beckmann, Ernst, 51, 87, 96–97, 128, 135, 155, 157, 160, 162, 164, 165, 184, 185, 188, 192; on big industry in Institute Association, 98; appeals for government support for Imperial Institute, 101–2; appointed president of Imperial Institute, 104–5;